AF529036

Indigenous Knowledge in Traditional Folk Panorama

Genesis, Development & Applications

Indigenous Knowledge in Traditional Folk Panorama

Genesis, Development & Applications

R.M. Sarkar

SERIALS PUBLICATIONS
NEW DELHI (INDIA)

First Published – 2011

ISBN: 978-81-8387-470-0

Published by

SERIALS PUBLICATIONS
4830/24, Prahlad Street, Ansari Road
Darya Ganj, New Delhi-110002 (India)
Phone : 23245225 Fax : 91-11-23272135
E-mail: serials@satyam.net.in

Dedicated to

The Traditional Folk of India whose innate propensity for learning from the Nature as well as their inartificial benevolence to Her have made the environs meaningful.

Contents

Preface

People in the indigenous cultural state gather knowledge not from books or from any other written sources but directly from the eventuality of their natural milieu. The phenomenon of comprehension is activated by direct observations on multifarious circumstances of life-situation subsequently processed by deep-based feelings and sentimental orientations. Indigenous knowledge covers the tradition-based cultural expressions. The very term indigenous suggests that it is generated by the local people who have been trying their level best to foster that knowledge through time and space. Right from the primeval period the humans could acquire some basic learning from their immediate environmental sphere which they had to exploit in the course of their continuous struggle for existence. The learning pattern ultimately developed into a tacit knowledge system which ultimately took shelter in the psycho-philosophical setting of the people concerned. It then started disseminating through generations. As a necessary consequence this sort of knowledge is not only generated by the local people but also it is extensively expressed through the diversified media of the concerned social system. This tradition-oriented cultural expressions are reflected in the form of stories, folklore, belief-pattern, art and architecture, song and dance including other recurring revelation.

There is a close-set linkage between indigenous knowledge and folklore. Folkloric materials work as the efficacious media to transmit age-old conceptual understandings to the succeeding generations. As because folklore and indigenous knowledge are the tradition-bound resources of the common people, so these are seen to be integrated in a unique fashion. The reciprocal obligations unifying these two ends are needed to be highlighted properly for better understanding of the situation. Of late, there has developed a global awakening with respect to the indigenous knowledge which is evidenced by the concensus of the scholars and political personalities in evaluating the indigenous knowledge system for utilising this in the sustainable development of the region concerned.

The present compendium is, no doubt, the outcome of close cooperation of some distinguished researchers who have been working on this significant sphere of understanding. The vast amount as well as the diversified conceptual features of the invaluable native expertise can never be recorded properly until and unless the direct expressions gained by the enthusiastic workers are added to the total programme of exposition of such endeavour. It is obviously invigorating to note that some of the scholars working on the subject-matter concerned has taken special care to come forward to respond properly and effectually to my invitation to contribute their valuable observations and analytical proceedings to make this venture a success. I take this opportunity to express my heart-felt gratitude for their close cooperation despite their varied pre-occupations. I am well aware of the fact that this anthology has seen the light of the day by the effective intervention with profound interest by Sri S.K. Jha, Director, Serials Publications, New Delhi, and obviously by his working team. I owe deep debt of gratitude for this sort of collaboration. I shall, no doubt, consider myself fortunate enough if this anthology, comprised by the labour and love of the different authors from multifarious dimensions, proves itself helpful to mobilise the prospective workers in the domain of exploring and appraising of the indigenous knowledge pattern and perspective.

R.M. Sarkar

List of Contributors

Mihin Dolo– Senior Research Fellow, G.B. Pant Institute of Himalayan Environment and Development, North East Unit, Itanagar, Arunachal Pradesh.

Prasanna K. Samal– Scientist Incharge, G.B. Pant Institute of Himalayan Environment and Development, North East Unit, Itanagar, Arunachal Pradesh.

Vanlalruali– Dept. of Agricultural Extension, Bidhan Chandra Krishi Viswavidyalaya, Kalyani, West Bengal.

Sagar Mondal– Reader in Agricultural Extension, Bidhan Chandra Krishi Viswavidyalaya, Kalyani, West Bengal.

Debabrata Basu–

Rupak Goswami–

Hari Charan Behera– Assistant Professor, Centre for Rural Studies, LBSNAA, Mussoorie, Uttarakhand.

R.M. Sarkar– Anthropologist, Editor, Man In India, and Journal of Social Anthropology, Mayurakshi, Kolkata.

Atul Chandra Bhowmick– Retd. Professor, University of Calcutta, Uttarayan, Palta, West Bengal.

Kalyan Chakraborty– Director of Research, Bidhan Chandra Krishi Viswavidyalaya, Kalyani, West Bengal.

Tuhinsri Sen– Department of Botany, University of Kalyani, West Bengal.

Monanjali Bandyopadhyay– Department of Bengali, Vidyasagar University, Midnapur, West Bengal.

K. Sasicoumar Brumot– Research Scholar, Dept. of Anthropology, Pondicherry Central University, Pondicherry.

T. Subramanyam Naidu– Dean, School of Social Sciences, Pondicherry Central University, Pondicherry.

Samares Kumar Das– Assistant Professor, Department of Veterinary and Animal Husbandry, Central Agricultural University, Mizoram.

Babul Roy– Research Officer, S.S. Division, Office of the Registrar General of India, New Delhi.

Bulu Imam– Convenor, INTACH, Hazaribagh Chapter, Sacred Grove, Dipugarah, Hazaribagh.

Amitabha Sarkar– Anthropological Survey of India, Govt. of India, 27, Jawaharlal Nehru Road, Kolkata.

Samira Dasgupta– Anthropological Survey of India, Govt. of India, 27, Jawaharlal Nehru Road, Kolkata.

Sumit Mukherjee– Anthropological Survey of India, Govt. of India, 27, Jawaharlal Nehru Road, Kolkata.

S.K. Pramanik– Sociologist, H/4, Parui Govt. Housing Estate, 169 Biren Roy Road, Kolkata.

N.C. Nandi– Zoological Survey of India, Govt. of India, M-Block, New Alipore, Kolkata.

D.C. Nanjunda– Centre for Advanced Development Research and Policy Management, Kushal Nagar, Karnataka.

K. Basu– Anthropological Survey of India, Govt. of India, 27, Jawaharlal Nehru Road, Kolkata.

Bhubaneswar Sabar– Ph.D. Scholar, Tata Institute of Social Sciences.

K.M. Sinha Roy– Anthropological Survey of India, EN/79, Sector IV, Salt Lake City, Kolkata.

Arnab Karar– Senior Research Fellow, Anthropological Survey of India, Govt. of India, 27, Jawaharlal Nehru Road, Kolkata.

Suvendu Kundu– Junior Research Fellow, Anthropological Survey of India, Govt. of India, 27, Jawaharlal Nehru Road, Kolkata.

Nilanjan Khatua– Anthropological Survey of India, Southern Regional Centre, Bogadi, Mysore.

George T. Haskip– Research Scholar, Manipur University, Imphal.

Ganesh Chandra Mallick– Department of Anthropology, North Bengal University, Darjeeling, West Bengal.

R.M. Sarkar– Anthropologist, Editor, Man In India and Journal of Social Anthropology, Mayurakshi, Kolkata.

1 Introduction

R.M. Sarkar

I

In consequence of their time-long and hospitable as well as close set interactions with the bountiful nature and substantial milieu the people in the traditional contextual domain could develop an intrinsic thought-pottern and integrated comprehension about the worldly affairs around them. That specific development gave vent to explore the mysteries of nature through the application of their prolonged observations as well as perpetual comprehension though times and spaces which ultimately made the concerned people to throw discernible light on the different facets of the world around them to interpret the situational context relating to the different happenings. The knowledge base related to these attempts and generated by the local people form the essence of what is called *Indigenous Knowledge* or native consciousness. It is, so to speak, rooted to the very soil of the native inhabitants whose life and activities are specifically governed by customs and traditions. The experiences gained and in course of time activated to fit into the way of life are subject to transmission undoubtedly through the oral traditional materials. This knowledge pattern is regarded a unique to a particular society and culture. It is this uniqueness that provides the requisite foundation and disseminates the motivating force in organizing the decision making programmes and their implementation in the utilization of the local resources as well as their conservations. The indigenous communities living and drawing their sustenance from neighbouring eco-environmental settings are, no doubt, well-acquainted with the every nook and cranny of their surroundings and thereby to utilize the diversified elements in their locale with the help of their tradition-oriented technological devices. It is to be noted with great concern that the working procedures and patterns of supervision in the indigenous perspective are always oriented in the close set understanding of sustainability and it has been accentuated by the direct influence of customs, beliefs, taboos and other related social legislations. The primitive and rural technology that has been devised and is being governed by the tribal and rural folk specially in the spheres of production of food, fodder, fuel and fertilizer without the spoiling and damaging the environment pin-point the interrelationship between indigenous knowledge and sustainable development we are really surprised to feel the depth-orientation and sagacity of the indigenous scientific philosophy contrived by the indigenous and local communities in the folk-tribal panorama.

Indigenous knowledge conditioned by tradition-bound cultural demonstration is subject to flow down through generations by means of oral as well as written folkloric materials which gradually became more and more substantial with the addition of further experience and understanding about the surroundings. The implication of this specific knowledge related findings is that the observations and cognizances drawn out of these are the outcome of centuries of trial and error, as well as thinking and rethinking effectuations. In the background of this mode of happening the present day scholars, researchers and programme formulators are at liberty to examine these basic principles contained in the indigenous knowledge domain with respect to the concerned locality or localities. It has now become unanimously accepted that the peoples' knowledge in relation to their respective locales is of more value-oriented and efficacious in comparison to those persons who have not such direct experience about the minor details of the surroundings as well as who lack that skill in observation. Of late, there has developed a global awakening with respect to the indigenous knowledge which is evidenced by the consensus of the scholars and political personalities in evaluating the indigenous knowledge system for utilizing these for the viable development of the country and the people.

As a unique land of tradition-bound villages having variegated conventional tribal communities following chequerd way of life India holds no less dominant position in the world perspective so far as the vastness as well as profundity of the indigenous knowledge system is concerned. It is needless to say that the rural-tribal folk throughout the country has not yet been brought into focus in a broad perspective though there are some stray attempts. The data relating to the indigenous knowledge system must be collected following the distinct methodological procedures of social sciences which would minimize the danger of exaggeration as well as understatement. Special care should be taken to see that the haphazard collections by the amateur persons may not be conducted as it never presents the real picture of the situation, and, if it is done, there is every possibility of getting the total context impaired. It is always to be kept in mind that the indigenous knowledge base is characteristically seen to be mingled in the psychocultural, religio-philosophical and socio-economic settings of the people concerned. Until and unless peoples' holistic life centering round the above consequences is thoroughly unfolded the integrated pattern of indigenous knowledge base can never be brought to light with due seriousness. As because this knowledge base is the upshot of the multiple interactions of diversified domains of life, so the effective nature of investigation into this knowledge pattern demands the depth-oriented enquiries covering the total life-situation in the background of the concerned locales.

Knowledge is characteristically indigenous. It developed at the very earliest phase of human differentiation from the animal ancestors. Biological evolution as a continuous and time-long procedure of change and adaptation brought multifarious alterations in the human life and thought. In the remote past some man-like animals put a specific mark in their life by the fashioning of tools out of crude stones and in so doing they raised themselves to the level of man. The process through which animals became man was, no doubt, the direct result of the application of knowledge which was lacking in .other animals. The knowledge is the direct outcome of the fundamental perspective of the brain. During primate evolution the cerebral cortex of the brain increased in size which contributed to the effective development and elaboration of special senses. In this cortex some specific centres faced expansion which were concerned with conscious control over complex behaviour and voluntary control over the muscles. These two specific biological phenomena jointly gave vent to the formation of a pattern of sensitivity leading to the understanding of the situations. It was through that sensitivity the prehistoric man could develop certain thinking which gave him the idea of making stone tools. These stone tools were the resultant forces of various necessities in the line of struggle for existence of the early men and certainly the effort was associated with the conspicuous biological change so far as the body formations are concerned. By becoming bipedal through a very complicated and time-long process the man-like animals of those days could release their hands from the activities of locomotion. There was a sharp differentiation between hands and feet - the formers were for grasping and lifting the things and the latters were meant only for supporting the body and helping in movement. Side by side with these neuroanatomical changing situations aggravated his ability to develop perception on the various happenings on the earth. Tool making was the direct and immediate response to these situational contexts.

It is commonly supposed that tool-making forms the beginning of culture and it is termed as the 'backbone' of cultural evolution. Somewhere in the distant past, in some earliest humanoid groups, an individual in course of his interaction with the surroundings learned, by accident or intelligent planning, to make a stone tool. If he was intelligent enough to comprehend the method by which the tool was made, he was able to promulgate the technique of making the tool to other individuals. But how? Was there any communicable language to express the technical procedures to others? Certainly, there were certain media, if not vocal language, to take essential roles in the transmission of ideas contained in tool-making.

Culture is such a phenomenon of human being that is based on ability to symbol. A symbol is a thing with physical form which gives meaning to those who use it. The physical form may be of various types that are associated with the movement of the bodily parts, making of sound with certain frequencies. The physical sensation thus formed of these activities is transmitted to the brain when a meaning is attached to the physical sensation by dint of its organized neurological tissues. Symbols are understood arbitrarily. Whatever may be the fact, the symbolism took a dominant role in the early man's communication system. There is no denying of the fact that the symbols of diversified types helped man in the diffusion of cultural traits. After the successful attempts for making of stone tools by a few persons those were found useful in the day to day activities and subsequently the method was circulated. Soon all the people in the groups were making and using similar stone tools. Individuals of superior ability then improved the patterns of the tools and communicated their methods to other individuals, and thus the tools of superior patterns were diffused throughout the groups. This process was continued through the ages, leading to the accumulation of knowledge of methods and the general development of the stone tools, it was followed by the production of simple metal tools, and ultimately to the most complex of modern machines.

Man could not have produced, sustained and augmented culture without the ability to transit his knowledge and experience to his offsprings other than by example. This means speech. Man's articulation of speech is directly related to his possession of a brain far advanced over those of other primates flourished much earlier. The origin of human symbolic vocal communication i.e. language is centred round the unique mode of development in both the spheres of biological and cultural processes. Man's whole-hearted effort to imitate the sounds heard in his surroundings as well as from other animals is taken as one of the roots of origin. The area of the brain meant for speech and language is located in the left hemisphere. It is the area which is characterized by having the cortical centres for auditory perceptions, motor control of face, mouth as well as larynx for the production of speech. The origin of the language has a very remote happening and many authorities believe that language started in the hominid groups in the distant past and it was associated with the appearance of tools and beginning of enlargement of brain.

Cultural evolution takes place through the invention and use by groups of what we generally call "pattern ideas". These become embedded in the group tradition and objectified in language, tools and institutions. They thus become cultural patterns. Any given culture or civilization is really a great complex of pattern ideas or cultural patterns which dominate the behaviour of the members of that cultural group in order to accumulate experience, groups must possess verbal language or articulate speech. It is generally taken for granted that human history in the strict sense of the term did not begin until man acquired his power of speech. Speech, from the very inception, acted as the highly powerful medium of the transmission of ideas from generations to generations. In societies which lack writing, their accumulated knowledge is enormously valuable to the community. In this case the older people take the responsibilities of transmitting the lore of the past to the future generations. In this way the ideas and values as well as the acquired knowledge of the groups are maintained. With the passage of time the indigenous knowledge based on close-set observations and integrated feelings runs down through the series of generations which are characteristically processed and refined with the addition of further knowledge and related interpretations.

Indigenous knowledge is the end product of the thinking of the people as a whole where group mentality always prevails. Knowledge based contemplation of the illiterate people very naturally takes in media like folklore and traditions for its diffusion amongst the population groups. The indigenous knowledge based conceptual ideas adopted by the primitive groups of people to maintain the economic and environmental perspective with which they have been in close-set association must, as they think, be continued for their survival. It is to be noted that the indigenous knowledge always tries to promote sustainable development. It is surprising to note that what, in the specific modern scientific age, we are thinking regarding the conservation of natural vegetational surroundings, the primitive people thought it long ago. The tribal people have got totemic relationship with different varieties of plants and animals, and through it they want to create amicable relationship with the plants as well as animals by assigning these respectable position in the ancestral domain. Mention may be made that this association between man and the natural objects is universal amongst the tribal and/or indigenous communities throughout the world. It is the oldest tradition in the history of man and still it is functioning without any pause during the present period. Totemism is the strongest socio-religious institution amongst the tribal people and especially among the Australian aborigines this phenomenon is seen to develop in a very complex pattern. The Australian aborigines are still in a very primitive stage but their complicated socio-religious institutions are highly discernible. The belief-patterns and attitude behind all these institutions influenced by diversified cults run down through their richest folkloric traditions impregnated with various folk narratives which act as the activated repositories of such oral expressions. These communities are still exclusively devoid of any written language but their meaningful thinking patterns processed by indigenous knowledge are compactly functionable in the society concerned because of the fact that the various customary laws and social regulations have their uninterrupted flow through the different folk sayings and folk beliefs with which the people have got profound regard.

The hunter-gatherer people of the world even today specifically depend on nature and they collect the different essential elements of life from the natural surroundings directly. They hunt different animals in the forests and collect various roots, tubers, fruits from there when they feel their requirements. The forest is regarded to them as their store house. But they do not cut down the trees indiscriminately for making their houses and for such other purposes or they do not engage themselves in hunting the animals haphazardly. There are lots of social legislations that are seen to be flourished in their folktales, folk proverbs and folk taboos which put restrictions in the indiscriminate use of forest and forest products so that no injurious effect would be caused to the natural balance. As for example, the Birhors of Chotanagpur, a noted forest-based tribe in the world context, have got various instructions to protect the forest from wanton destruction in the form of popular sayings constituting the oral traditions which are out and out respected by these preliterate primitive tribal group facing various socio-economic and ecological problems during the present period. Their traditional tales depict the fact that they are the kings of the forest and have got traditional rights on the forested regions. Thus they consider it is their duty to nurture it and save it from unjustified demolition. Birhor folk narratives depict that the forests are the sacred places where the gods and goddesses dwell in peaceful atmosphere. Therefore, it is desired that the forest should be kept free from all sorts of hazards and anxieties. Among the Birhors there is a traditional custom of implanting the saplings at the advent of rainy seasons. This practice conditioned by traditional norms is also seen amongst the Bushmen of Africa - a forest-oriented indigenous community. It is through the application of their indigenous knowledge they have readily understood that the human existence is specifically conditioned by forested atmosphere constituted by different plants and animals. They have made it a great concern and despite their various adversities they have managed to communicate that understandings through the help of traditional lore with which these illiterate primitive people are closely associated in various walks of their life.

Clan exogamy is a very rigid social legislation to be followed at the time of marriage negotiations. Clan, as we know, is the unilateral division of mankind who are tied together by a belief in common descent. The members of the clan are believed to have a common blood relation as they have been descended from a common ancestor. Thus they are all regarded as brothers and sisters, and very naturally the establishment of marital relation amongst them is tabooed. The tribal people till today maintain the taboo strictly because of the fact that marriage within them would be an incestuous alliance. People are afraid of this and thus they keep themselves far away from that phenomenon. On analysis it is seen that the clan is, no doubt, a fictitious organization - it is far from reality but the concept of clan exogamy has been developed from the indigenous knowledge and there is specific truth behind the situation. It may be explained like the following.

During the hunting-gathering stage of existence there developed a trend amongst the people to form groups to facilitate hunting expeditions with meagre tool kits. There were numerous such groups and probably they were identified with the name of different plants and animals. Amongst each group there were common endeavours; cooperations and coordinations amongst the group members were present and the sexual relations were indiscriminate amongst them. It went unabated through the ages. But in course of time some people by dint of their close-set observations could understand that in-group sex relations resulted weakest progeny and their numbers faced diminution. Moreover, the children became affected with various abnormalities. In order to get rid of those misfortunes a specific need was felt to put prohibitions on in-group sex relation. It was through that effort the rule of clan exogamy was resulted. For the purpose of introducing effective out-group mating the imposition of the fictitious idea of common ancestral linkage had to be made on the thinking patterns of the people which found a dominant position in the folklore of the different communities that ran down without any interruption through the ages.

If we look into the science of genetics we clearly understand that inbreeding in the human groups causes various abnormalities amongst the progeny. In the phenomenon of sex-relations amongst the close relations the chance of meeting the different recessive genes carrying abnormal traits is greater. Therefore, the geneticists advise to broaden the marriage circle. It is no doubt a matter of surprise that knowledge of the indigenous people could explore, according to their understandings, that mating within the small group was harmful for human existence and on the basis of which the in-group mating was abandoned. It found a suitable place in the rich traditional heritage of the primitive communities. It is universal in nature, and thus it indicates the authenticity of indigenous knowledge set to resist the unfortunate situation in human societies.

Conservation and sustainable use of biodiversity has been the fundamental philosophy of the life of the primitive/indigenous communities everywhere which is reflected in their cultural traditions. The very plans and procedures of organizing *Sacred Grove* in the folk/tribal world set a concrete example of an outstanding instance for traditional conservation practices. The marvelous system of resource management by the traditional societies through the effectual application of indigenous knowledge pattern is not only comparable to the modern scientific ecosystem approach but also in some cases the indigenous knowledge oriented strategy proves itself far reaching human conscience because of its sentimental appeal. Sacred Groves are universal among the traditional communities in many ancient countries of the world. The societies practicing and nurturing this sacred grove culture are intimately interconnected with the environment and there is no denying of the fact that their development through the ages has been allied with the different environmental situations. But the tradition-bound sacred grove culture had to face victimization by the onset of the system of exploitative management which goes by the name of modern scientific process. The thoroughly different vision in comparison to the folk-ecological standpoint in later years has done a great deal in exerting the tremendous blow to the eco-religio-cultural matrix of the traditional system devised in an indigenous understanding. The *Sarnas/Jaherthans* of the tribal villages in central India were designed to protect and conserve the significant diversities of plants and animals of the local origin. All the tribal villages in that region had the traditional custom of maintaining the primeval forest after the clearance of the dense forest-infested land for habitational purposes. Still today inspite of tremendous unfavourable situation, the tribal villages in this region maintain the *Sarnas* with due devotion and sincerity. To the Mundas and the Oraons the *Sarnas* stand for the temples where their village gods and goddesses are believed to reside. These are to be always kept clean and peaceful. No leaves, flowers and fruits can be plucked from the plants and tress of the *Sarnas*. During festive occasions the villagers are allowed to make an entry here and thereby to feel the gravity of the situation. The assembled persons irrespective of ages and sexes develop a reverential attitude as well as *Joyous* feeling due to the organization of the large scale worship of the deities concerned and the observance of festivities. The *Jaherthans* of the Santal villages are planned in the same way and their intentions are similar to those of the *Sarnas*. The *Jaherthan* is a cluster of *Sal* (Shorea robusta) tress under the shade of which gods and goddesses are believed to live peacefully. All the religious ceremonies are performed here. Though during the recent time the density of forest has been dwindled dangerously yet the Santals' *Jaherthan* must be represented by a cluster of tall trees which indicates the primeval forest. Alongwith different important deities here lives the Lady of the Grove. All the tribal communities in India which possess the sacred grove culture maintain the same principles and procedures without any deviation.

In the different ecological zones where some local communities are in the habit of practicing shifting cultivation there is the characteristic presence of *Sacred Groves* which indicate a concrete example of indigenous attempt for conservation of biological diversities. The climatic condition of humid tropics is such that there is *exuberent* growth of vegetation but soil is not prosperous. This situation instigated the native people in the humid tropical area to take the means of slash and burn type of cultivation. It is true to mention that this type of cultivation is the root cause of the loss of splendid forest resources and thereby the people become the victim of such unwanted consequences. But it is to be noted that in the areas where the practice of shifting cultivation is in vogue, there are sincere attempts to protect the significant forest cover in the indigenous way i.e. by the development of sacred groves. It has been seen that the traditional practice of keeping some forest regions as sacred in the shifting cultivation oriented areas help, to some extent, in keeping the balance of biodiversity. The very practice of shifting cultivation has now been out and out discouraged today due to its multifarious injurious effect on the green vegetation. Production of crops at the cost of such exuberant forest resources has totally been discouraged. But side by side with these there are attempts to connect various integrated factors of socio-cultural beliefs and practices as well as some sorts of local securities with this pattern of native economic network which plays the crucial role in the process of continuity of this type of cultivation. It has been noted by some scholars in this sphere that the agro-eco system in a traditional society, i.e. human manipulated eco-technology, is finely coordinated with the concerned ecological, socio-economic and psycho-cultural perspectives which give vent to the co-evolution of culture and environment. On specific issue it is to be noted that the proper comprehension of the linkages between social and ecological factors relating to the agro-eco system function would be resulted in the formation of base line concept to facilitate both the work of management and conservation of biological diversity. After studying the nature and extent of native way of looking at the process of conservation it has been remarked by the scholastic personalities that the different conventional methods nurtured by the aboriginal inhabitants of a locality pin-points various remarkable potentialities. For the promotion of the process of innate conservation in the traditional societies the impact of the religion and culture is undoubtedly effectual as it traverses into the very root of the peoples' cognizance and sentimental appeal. During the present turmoil a universal suggestion has been put forward for the revival of the traditional beliefs as because these are in the process of rapid dwindling in the name of modernization.

The richest tradition of our rural/tribal folk shows diversified ways in the preservation of the flora and fauna in a balanced form. These are no doubt needed for human consumption and also for using these as the means of subsistence through trading or exchanging these as per circumstances. But there are restrictions in extravagant consumption of these elements of nature. The observance of different food taboos specially which are time and season oriented have got value oriented approach in the conservation of species. The rural folk in India keep a constant vigil in the maintenance of strict taboos regarding the taking of fishes during their breeding seasons. Taking of some types of fruits and vegetables are tabooed for the specific time period (generally month-wise restriction) to let the fruits mature and to allow the vegetative plants requisite time to flower and thereby to produce seeds. These are all meant for preservation of the species, and there are concrete evidences that the imposition of the socio-religious restrictions have been accentuated by the application of the indigenous knowledge gained through time-long experience and trial and error related situations.

Folklore reflects the creativity of human mind and various innovative efforts result in the genesis of customs, beliefs, manner, usage, norms and formality which are owned by the folk society concerned through traditions running down generations after generations. There are usages for various technological devices in the building of houses, making tools and implements as well as different architectural designs. Then there are artistic activities as well as crafts having various designs and mechanisms of presentations. These many a time transmit through verbal traditions and a few find non-verbal ways to come down the generations. Different inventions and innovations as well as the knowledge gained through time-long observations and native experimentations become the heritage of the folk society. This particular phenomenon has been influencing the folk categories of population generations after generations through a continuous process of spontaneous transmission since remote past periods. It is high time to look into the richest traditional matters and thinking patters contained in the numerous folkloric materials of diversified trends and concepts and thereby to devise broad-based methodological principles for the collection of folkloric treasures of the country which are impregnated with invaluable thoughts and ideological principles and close set perceptions about various worldly affairs. In each and every step of folk performances and in their allied indications the nature and extent of wealth of indigenous knowledge is beyond description. It is our sacred duty to protect this knowledge from rapid deterioration and not only so this knowledge base should be evaluated in the background of the situation of events and thereby these are to be cultivated to empower the existing modern knowledge patterns.

The tribal people of India are the custodians of indigenous medicines of diversified nature. Tribal/primitive medicine is governed by traditions and, so to speak, it reflects the integrated perspectives of man, magic, religion as well as native science. In addition to various supernatural procedures applied for detecting out the causes and for adopting the means for their care these people extensively use various herbal preparations. It is needless to mention that they have got a broad-based knowledge on the different plant species growing wildly in their surroundings which is conditioned by the close set understandings of congeniality as well as respectability. Their cognizance on the intrinsic quality of diseases and various bodily abnormalities is very naturally based on thousands of years of watchful behaviour and native scientific experimentation. The results of these surveillances have ultimately found place in the folklore of the people. The folkloristic traditions thus developed in consequence of the impact of the indigenous comprehensions of these tribal folk started running down through generations. It is to be noted that in the tribal realm a specific philosophy has been emerged which highlights the primitive sentiments relating to the medicinal herbs and human gratitude to the vegetative world. Thus the primitive medicine pin-points an indigenous system which has woven into the socio-cultural, ritualistic as well as philosophical settings of the holistic life salutation.

Indian traditional societies are very rich in the observance of diversified folk cults in the background of which there are numerous folk narratives signifying the importance and inevitability of these folk festivals. In the traditional peasant societies centering round agricultural economy in India there are concrete examples of observance of various cults which are meant for the protection of crops. During the days when categorical science and technology were not in existence the farming communities adopted various indigenous means to solve the problems of their day to day life and activities. What is significant in this connection is that the implication of the cults attached to these are interpreted in the rich folkloric traditions in the forms of folktales and ballads to get whole-hearted public opinion and support in the strict observance of these cults. The Dipanwita or the Festival of Light is an all-India celebration, the central idea of which is to kindle fire and to light up innumerable oil lamps. This specific custom of lighting the dark night has been illustrated in the popular folk sayings amongst the illiterate peasants of rural India in different ways. Peoples in association with the particular territories conform to the regional sentiments and consider it as their sacred duty to perform the ceremonies accordingly. Whatever may be the general implications of this Festival of Light it is nothing but an agro-based thinking pattern evolved through the indigenous knowledge on environmental hazards causing serious injuries to the immature crops. In this case, the hazards are created by the pests-the multitudes of these pests are spread over the paddy fields with the growing crops. These pests suck out the milky fluid from the immature grains in a rapid pace to make these abortive. During the period when there was no broad-based chemical pesticides to check those pests, peoples adopted a specific way to demolish those injurious elements. It was through the application of indigenous knowledge people observed the behaviour-patterns of the pests and discovered the fact that they had a congenital attraction towards the burning fire. Their inherent characteristic of life was utilized by the rural peasants in their destruction which was inevitable.

The Festival of Light is time-specific - it is held during the time when the paddy grains are at the point of maturity. Thus by burning fire in the various village spots they allure the pests in the field who rush to the glowing fire in the villages in lacks and crores like a flood stream and ultimately jump into the fire as if with a self-sacrificing mood. The situation underneath this biological behaviour of insects has been and are being utilized in a traditional perspective as a specific measure to control the hazardous effect caused by the pests. In this way a large number of factual illustrations can be highlighted after looking into and analyzing the traditional practices of the rural and tribal communities throughout India to evaluate the patterns and perspectives of the indigenous knowledge formation and its application through the folkloric appeal.

The indigenous knowledge is recently being viewed in a different way which departs from the path followed earlier. During the present situational context when we are thinking deliberately about the sustainable development for the activated effort towards the maintenance of amicable man-nature relation and also to put resistance to natural hazards without causing injurious effect to the surroundings we specifically need the assistance of indigenous knowledge. It is to be noted with great concern that indigenous knowledge is exclusively the contribution of the people as a whole from all walks of life. It is based on their practical experience and finds expressions in their own understandings. Thus it is explicitly people-oriented and highly suitable for the activities for the development of the people. It creates no cultural constraints since the methods for development are designed by the people themselves having close linkage with their value-attitude system. It has been acknowledged by the anthropologists that large mass of modern scientific processes are embedded in the indigenous knowledge. On this specific issue it has become a conspicuous trend in the world's scientific arena not to neglect and throw away the indigenous knowledge put forward by the tradition-oriented people whatever may be their educational standard and status of life, but to put special stress on the actual nature and extent of the locality-based knowledge system. The appeal has become, so to speak, universal.

India is unquestionably a fertile field for the development, spread and application of indigenous knowledge. India's traditional societies especially characterized by rural and tribal communities have developed this knowledge system which is centralized on the items like agricultural activities, forestry, health and hygiene, traditional medicine, traditional education, population control, food and nutrition, soil conservation and many others. In addition to these Indian indigenous knowledge is highly discernible in the sphere of social and administrative control, local and self-government, art and architecture, music and dance and even in habitational planning, The richest traditional know-how and allied technicalities, are found to be embedded in the folkloric materials of diversified nature which are still pulsating in the folk tradition of India. The Father of Indian Anthropology, Sarat Chandra Roy, once (1932) remarked that "the people of India live in an atmosphere of folklore from cradle to the grave." So, to understand the people of India we specifically need to make a meaningful entry into the vast ocean of Indian folklore and to analyze systematically through the application of scientific methodology for exploring the inner significance of these workings in the background of Indian native science, traditional life and psycho-philosophical settings.

Of late, it has been taken for granted that in the vast domain of modern scientific field various new conceptual ideas can be tapped in a conspicuously profitable way if the barriers to the feasibility in the past knowledge traditions are triumphed over. The field of this traditional knowledge, which is extensively influenced by the shamans, aboriginal medicine men, farmers and other like rural personalities, is being brought under the specific, perceptional standpoint of the modern scientific realm with a view to link this traditional knowledge base to the biotechnology oriented modern scientific domain before the former is wipped out. The imaginative efforts have sometimes instigated various biotechnological organizations in having partnership deals with the local knowledge groups for identifying and taking creative measures in using this knowledge system based on indigenous appeal. Recently, there are lots of examples in the world perspectives where ethnoecology, which is rooted to the very ingenious ways of discerning, governing and utilizing recourses, has been brought to the limelight for the purpose of thwarting the social and ecological destructions. Various researches in this line has proved the fact that the development programmes centred round the tradition-oriented indigenous knowledge system would explore the active dimension of ecologically sound production leading commercially viable consequences. Various researches in African countries have highlighted the fact that the local ingenious knowledge and cultural traditions have been proved extensively fruitful in environment education and development efforts among the African aboriginals.

The trend of success in the implementation of such programmes for human uplift has caused a great deal in putting requisite respect for the local knowledge patterns. This situation has led to the taking of the efforts for reappraisal of agriculture. Here top-down expertise given by the external specialists has cut a sorry figure and thus a recommendation has been adopted to go back to the indigenous knowledge system. Thus there has developed an explicit indication on this issue that at the time of inflicting any innovation the existing indigenous knowledge should be given special attention. Various sources of indigenous knowledge system feed modern scientific methods and technological principles which ultimately creates a potential for the inflow of diversified conceptual ideas from the indigenous philosophical settings to the modern scientific specialty. This process, no doubt, provides ample opportunities to the latter to enrich its contextual setting by the contribution of multiplex direct experience-oriented sagacity.

II

The present treatise has been moulded as per specific strategy with the stringing together in a requisite pattern the valued contributions put forward by the different erudite scholars and devoted researchers which ultimately has bestowed the compendium a befiting perspective.

Indigenous knowledge is not only a time honoured human quality but also it traverses through all the spheres of life amongst the diversified human communities in the different levels of culture. But the tribal and rural folk in India are the distinctive custodians of the traditional knowledge bases which they have been utilising through the times and spaces in the maintenance of their day to day life and in the performance of their multifarious activities. Rightly speaking, Indigenous knowledge is like a vast ocean and thus it is practically difficult, if not impossible, to get an overall view of the situation. Therefore, the state of affairs demands that the attempt for understanding the perspective of social heritage must be made in the different dimensions of the variegated human communities by the team of researchers having close set interactions with the way of life of the people. When all the stray works are properly fastened in an integrated whole, there would develop a picturesque extent of the field of indigenous knowledge. In the present anthology, twenty seven papers have been presented which are centred round the nature and consequences of the age-old indigenous knowledge system among the different communities at various geo-physical habitational contexts in their array of activities.

In the first paper, Mr. Mihin Dollo and Dr. Prasanna K. Samal highlights the fact that the traditional ecological knowledge has a pivotal role in the sustaining of soil and human health. In the background of their study in Arunachal Pradesh specially characterized by eco-cultural diversity under the impact of multifarious tribal groups in the background of the ecological setting of the Eastern Himalayas, they have understood that the ethnic groups here possess specific types of traditional ecological knowledge (TEK) that are finely adapted with the local environmental situation which is subject to refinement as well as evolution through time. This traditional ecological knowledge is perfectly utilised by the native people here in the conduction of agriculture. This particular knowledge provides the people the activated way for utilising the natural resources in order to get nutrient rich organic crop farming. In the landscape the authors' study on the Monpas practicing agro-forestry type of land utilization focuses the different angles of the working patterns of the traditional wisdom on crop-soil interaction, soil-water conservation, nutrient management as well as ethno-pedology effected into the evolution of sustainable production system through the decades. But at the same time the authors have noted that owing to the eroding of traditional knowledge pattern agro-ecosystem and human health are losing their sustainability.

The shifting cultivation, otherwise known as Jhum and the process is called jhuming, is not only an archaic type of crop-raising method but also it has penetrated into the agro-economic and socio-psychological settings of the people. What is more important is that this sort of economic pursuit has direct linkage with the eco- environmental perspective and that has put forward a great concern to the working philosophy of the ethnic group. In their field work based research in Mizoram Ms. Vanlalrulai and Dr. Sagar Mondal have highlighted the integrated patterns of working and understanding of jhuming here with the three principal objectives - (1) Delineation of major activities in the process and the associated festivals, (2) Perception of the Jhum Cultivators about the impact of environment and (3) Influences of the factors like agro-economic, socio- psychological in the jhuming procedures. Jhum cultivation has been examined here in the realistic view-points after putting forward its adverse effects and advantages. Both the negative and positive features of jhuming have been evaluated in the background of the total situational contexts constituted by the topography of the region, basic ecology and environment, eventualities of deforestation as well as food security backed by mixed cropping, low cost procedure, ritualistic integration and the generation oriented inheritance pattern of the jhum fields. The study investigates that though the jhumias are well aware of the adversities of jhum cultivation yet it cannot be totally discarded by them due to certain sentimental issues. As because jhum cannot be fully replaced by terrace cultivation in Mizoram, so certain recommendations have been put forward by the authors to bring certain modernistic approaches to make the jhuming less detrimental.

Sri Debabrata Basu and Rupak Goswami have taken a concrete attempt, in their paper, to discuss the technicality of the word knowledge and its nature and extent of utilisation at different spheres. They have started their thematic discussions with the existing issue of dichotomy in the sphere of two dimensional view-points like traditional and scientific/modern knowledge system. They are of opinion that the craziness with the Indigenous knowledge system which prevailed earlier, have become obliterated. But the interface of the knowledge system, it is to be noted, provides such an atmosphere which gives rise to the specific implication for developing certain types of vital insights for the future generation of intellectuals in gaining productive thinking procedures. The authors have keenly analysed the basic distinction between the scientific and traditional knowledge as have been generally accepted in the broader perspective of previous discussions. As because the indigenous knowledge lacks any positive evidences and/or recorded criteria to prove its actuality, so its contributions fail to find the credibility. Thus there must be an urgent attempt for documentation and sharing of the findings though there are conspicuous problems in the way of doing these. Agricultural sciences are regarded as the ideal sphere where traditional and scientific knowledge present themselves as an effective confluence. By means of presenting a lot of practical issues this paper puts forward the particulars of mutual validation in the perspective of the two domains of knowledge.

The phenomenon of different indispositions is the root cause of various adversities in the social arena and the people especially in the rural/tribal settings try to resist these misfortunes with the help of their indigenous knowledge system. It is to be noted that in the background of the limited understandings on the world phenomena the primitive people are not in a position to assess the particular cause of the different ailments as well as various other bodily disasters. In lieu of highlighting the basic biological reasons their comprehensions, most of the times, have been and are being evaluated in the perspective of various cultural traditions and psycho-philosophic practices and mode of beliefs. This situation very often gives rise to a network of supernaturalism which delves deep into the social matrix of the society or societies concerned. Side by side with these the native communities have long been in the regular habit of utilizing multifarious herbal medicines which grow wild in and around their habitat. These have very naturally been accentuated by the continuous process of trial and error as well as close-set observations. In order to get an overall picture of the sphere of understanding on the belief-patterns as well as treatment perspectives in relation to various ailments of any traditional community there is undoubtedly a specific need to explore the concerted belief-attitude system revolving round the very efforts for combating diseases. Dr. R.M. Sarkar, in his paper, has tried to highlight this situational context by putting a concrete illustration from a primitive tribal community as a case in point. These forest-oriented tribal people – the Birhors – show a specific panoramic view on the multidimensional indigenous therapeutic system. The paper also puts forward the patterns of interactions, during the recent period, between the tribal herbalists and the people of the advanced societies through the selling of medicines and forwarding suggestions for cure of ailments.

Sri Haricharan Behera, in his paper, deals with the nature and pattern of the traditional agricultural activities as are prevalent among the Kandha tribal community in Orissa. These people are accustomed to the raising of crops by both shifting and settled types of cultivation. The specific feature of their cultivational process is that from the selection and preparation of land upto the threshing and storing of crops they still cling to their traditional knowledge and for this they are intimately connected with the nature and the different natural phenomena. The methodology for organising shifting cultivation reflects their native knowledge system on the issue of maintaining the biodiversity. They are highly conversant in the selection of soil for the cultivation and growth of different varieties of seeds. Their knowledge regarding pest control, of course traditional, is highly effective. The storing process of seeds is subject to checking and cross-checking in different climatic situations. The production of multiple varieties of crops is the output of their traditional wisdom. Utilisation of the spring water in the settled cultivation is done in a very careful way. The traditional knowledge in agricultural activities of these people is intertwined with the social system which is processed by different ritualistic performances, taboos and norms. The production strategy of turmeric and the different stages of the work culture prove the depth of their traditional wisdom.

Prof. Atul Chandra Bhowmick speaks on the traditional textile of Bengal which once won the world-wide fame because of its elegant workmanship and finest execution. At the very outset he has tried to put forward the nature and extent of the muslin of Dhaka (the then Bengal) starting from the detail discussions on the different raw materials. The specific category of cotton – the basic material – has been brought to light and the detailed process of spinning of cotton rolls into fine yarn has been analysed together with the discussions on the different material objects that were used for spinning and related work. The muslins were of various qualities and those were developed through the diversified indigenous methods adopted by the weavers. In addition to his supplying of different informations on this issue the author has put forward the references from some historical records having authentic sources. In discussing the popularity of Dhakai Muslin he has traversed through some basic accounts given by the scholars of those days, who most of the time referred the luxurious delicate translucent woven-air muslins of Bengal. Besides muslin, jamdani was also considered as a classic work in the sphere of spinning which reached a climax and considered by all concerned as a proud production. The different design and motifs that were employed to make those highly attractive textile materials which were the result of long traditional experience of the weavers for centuries. The other worth noting textile elegance is included in the production of baluchari, chikan, nakshi-kantha and a lot of others. The different colouring materials used in these works were all from the different vegetative specimens. The paper discusses in details the extraction of dyes from the vegetative sources and utilization pattern to serve the work of ornamentation. In the conclusion the impact of the British weaving industry has been pointed out which exerted a severe blow from the different angles.

Mango is not only a palatable fruit of highest elegance but also it has specific linkage with the folk tradition. Mango plant, its leaves, flowers and fruits are all worshipped with due devotion and it is an India feature. Dr. Kalyan Chakrabarti and others efficiently have put forward the different perspectives of Mangolore, belief, taboo, totemic idea and wisdom related to this fruit. After describing the historicity of Mangolore in the traditional literature the authors have given a conspicuous observation on the ten specific folk varieties of mango from the Gangetic West Bengal. The folk wisdom that has developed centering round mango is highly practicable in using it at the micro level in a given agro-ecosystem. The conceptual ideas relating to folk wisdom and folk knowledge have been examined here in the background of their approaches in mango cropping patterns. Folk varieties of mangoes which are produced at the referred site have been put forward as related to the culture and heritage of the rural folk and on this particular attempt lies the specific significance of this paper.

K. Sasicoumar Brumot and Subramanyarn Naidu's paper deals with ethnomedicine - its traditional pattern of activities in the therapeutic strategies as well as its survival in the present day changing circumstances. The authors are of opinion that despite the challenges of medical pluralism on ethnomedicine the system in question is still surviving. The study is based on the direct survey on the health culture of the Kadar tribe living in Indira Gandhi wild life Sanctuary where four other tribes also are seen to live. After conducting the detailed study on the ideas and behaviour-pattems about the health and disease of the Kadar people the authors have found out that this tribal group has got an age-old ethnomedicinal system in which the people concerned find conspicuous relief. But the situation has faced some changes. The authors have noted that after the introduction of modem medicine the former popularity and reliability of ethnomedicine have considerably been eroded. There has developed a tendency among these people to come under the fold of modern medicine though ethnomedicine is still viable, the pros and cons of which have been explored here with explanation.

Forest is not merely the assemblage of trees, shrubs and other vegetative bodies but an embodiment of cultural traditions amongst folk and tribal communities. The tribal people live on forest produce and in turn they care for the forest. It is like a two-way process. They have got an innate propensity to conserve the greenery of the forest which is centred round their indigenous knowledge enriched by reasonable and practical thinking patterns. In his study Sri Samares Kumar Das tries to pin-point the nature and extent of indigenous knowledge of the tribal people on the forest and its multidimensional effects on the total life-situation of the people concerned. The study is based on the Kora tribe of a village in West Bengal. The author feels that the indigenous knowledge system as possessed and utilised by the tribal people is needed to be collected with due seriousness which would, no doubt, contribute effectually towards the effort for sustainable conservation and management of the forest resources considerably. The study has been conducted through the adoption of methodology of Participatory Appraisal of Natural Resources.

Babul Roy's study on Zeme Naga ethnomedicine presents a separate dimension in the traditional belief system as regards folk medicine of a distinctive tribal group inhabited in a region that is relatively cut off from mainstream India. Zeme Naga traditional medicines are centred round the different varieties of plants and their products. In addition to these, some species of animals are regarded as the constituent ingredients of Zeme pharmacopoeia. Some non-biological components are also used in the preparation of medicine. The author here has shown that the species of plants and animals used by these people are deeply interwined with their magico-religious sphere of life. Living very close to nature since long time past the Zeme Nagas could have been able to make an intimate relation with their ecological surroundings and through a process of age-old searching these people ultimately explored the mysteries contained in the elements of nature, principally plant and animal species. It is a kind of native perception. The considerable perspective of Zeme traditional medical knowledge could not yet been explored. The author heartily feels that this traditional wisdom must be documented for the purpose of conservation of this valued treasure of centuries oriented native medicinal system.

In his paper, Bulu Imam presents the indigenous knowledge centering round herbal medicines as has been adopted by the Birhors - a hunting-gathering tribe living very close to the forest ecology and having the forest dominated life-philosophy. The Birhors have got the special intuition in recognising the different varieties of plants surrounding them. Mati or the traditional medicine man of the Birhors is considered as experts in the healing practices. During the recent period Birhor traditional medicines has come to the market and the selling of these herbal medicine has become the source of income of some of them. The author of this paper has presented the nature and extent of expertise of a Birhor woman in the sphere of traditional healing practices. It categorically discusses the multifarious experience of Kamli-the Birhor medicine women-which she has gained in course of her becoming the healer. Her acquaintances with diversified medicinal herbs and their individual identities in relation to the treatment of different diseases and abnormalities deserve serious attention.

Dr. Amitabha Sarkar and Dr. Samira Dasgupta believe that the indigenous knowledge, which is the product of interaction between a community with its instanteous environmental conditions, helps categorically in the concerned peoples' subsistence contrivance in a sustainable way. The life and activities of the people living in the variegated ecological settings are everywhere supported by the indigenous knowledge base which provides them the strategy for survival. The specific potentiality of indigenous knowledge makes it possible to persist in the face of abrupt modernization and the impact of cultural pluralism in India. While depicting the life-situation of the people and the close intimacy with the nature and natural objects in Sundarban region the authors have been able to highlight the implication of traditional knowledge in the overall adjustment of the inhabitants with the ecology and economy. In course of their dealing with such modes of approach they have examined the trends and endeavour of the ethnic groups like the Abujh Maria of Bastar, the Birjia and the Mal Paharia of Jharkhand and the Toto of West Bengal in fashioning their modes of life by the application of traditional knowledge.

In his paper, Sri Sumit Mukherjee has presented a very fascinating study in respect of a tribal community like the War Khasis of Meghalaya regarding their indigenous technology which has helped them to devise a unique natural resource management through generations. These horticulturists have faced the challenges of high slopes. The War Khasis from the time immemorial have been depending solely on the indigenous knowledge system to raise the crops in the various unfavourable circumstances like difficult slopes in the lands with less fertility. But their environmental wisdom and deep base perception provide them to fight against the adversities and thereby win over the way out. The orchards of orange as constituted by them are provided with different varieties of orange which are cultivated and nurtured according to their traditional knowledge that are transmitting through generations from long time past. After making a thorough investigation into the peoples' traditional wisdom centred initiative the author considers it essential to look into the mystery of their success for the benefit of the modern developmental methods.

Sundarban coast waters have now been facing an alarming decrease of the different varieties of marine fish species due to the unregulated expansion of fishing fleet throughout the year. Dr. S.K. Pramanik and Dr. N.C. Nandi have shown from their extensive field study and close set observation that indiscriminate fishing in the Sundarban waters has been the root cause of ruination of the deep-based possibilities centering round fishing. There was a time when the traditional wisdom of the native fisher folk made positive attempts to develop the indigenous management practices and allied regulation to protect the fish crops from wanton destruction. The authors have put forward the concrete cases of various constraints in marine fisheries in Sundarban and then side by side with these they have discussed the nature and extent of some indigenous regulation and management practices having various socio-cultural traditions of the community and the locality concerned. Of late, Fishermen's Association takes certain positive measures to check various unsystematic and unethical fishing as well as behavioural activities in the fishing zones. The authors observe that the problems of Sundarban fisheries have been aggravated and have become complicated in such a fashion that the existing indigenous management practices and regulations have lost their appeal. Here some suggestions have been made on this issue to help solve the problems to a considerable extent.

Dr. D.C. Nanjunda, in his paper, has made an intensive observation on the traditional medicinal system and its multifarious impact on the people specially belonging to the indigenous communities. At the very outset he tries to present the readers specific characteristic features of the traditional healing practices. The trends and patterns of plant based medicines have been discussed here categorically and the plants have been regarded as an excellent reservoir of bioactive compounds having the hidden qualities for treating the ailments. The phenomenon of bioprospecting has been focused here as a potential and significant source of new therapeutic leading to drug research and allied investigations. It has been noted with great concern that the indigenous knowledge system centering round traditional medicines is being plundered by the sophisticated drug houses. The question of biopiracy has become a basic problem in the interest of the indigenous medicines. The author has pin-pointed it as the steeling of intellectual wisdom nurtured through the ages by the native communities. It is a very painful affair. In spite of all hazards the author feels that collaboration between the modem drug houses and the organisors of indigenous medicine could establish a sustainable and mutual profitable relationship.

Boat making technology has a great antiquity. In ancient times the boat making was specifically characterized by indigenous knowledge and its spread was extensive throughout the different parts of the world. In a paper Dr. K. Basu engages himself in the indigenous boat making practices of the people of Sundarban. As the only means of transport in the major part of Sundarban criss-crossed by rivers having severe tidal waves the boats of different types play the essential role in the life of the people here. As a necessary consequence the boat or dingi, in the local term, became the symbol of the people of Sundarban. The traditional boat makers have requisite expertise which is typified by the native comprehensions that have been running through generations. The author has taken here a deep concern in presenting the details of the boat making techniques. This folk technology is the concrete example of the application of traditional knowledge on the river system, different tidal features and the wave orientation together with the climatic conditions. The shape, size and technology of the boats are always conditioned by these factors. The author has very distinctively studied the technology of boats, boat making processes and the different taboos and restrictions that are observed in this regard.

In all the human societies health is regarded as the most essential factor for survival. But it must be devoid of diseased condition. Thus care must be taken to see that the ailing situation is to be tackled with properly. Among the native communities the system of combating diseases is centred round various traditional procedures. While focusing light on the traditional system of medicare among the Chuktia Bhunja tribe of Orissa Sri Bhubaneswar Sabar, first of all, puts forward the concept of health among them and it has been shown that the impact of different belief system is influenced extensively the total therapeutic behaviour of the people concerned. The two traditional health practitioners – the Gunia and the Baiga – exert various integrated influences on the patterns and perspectives of the diseases among the Chuktia Bhunja. In addition to these four types of disease specialialists are seen who are bone setters, snake bite curers, general disease curers and child birth attendants. The roles played by all these traditional medical personnel have been put forward here with the presentation of examples. The relationship patterns amongst the different specialists has been brought out and the impact of supernatural powers on the very assumption for causation and cure of diseases has also been evaluated in the background of traditional knowledge patterns on this primitive tribal group.

Sri K.M. Sinha Roy examines, in his paper, the reflection of traditional, wisdom in wood crafts as are found among the Nicobarese - a primitive tribal group living not only very close to forest ecology but their life has been intermingled with the forest resources. While discussing the manufacturing of the wooden crafts by the Nicobarese of Katchal island the author has pointed out that these people show marked efficiency in making the dugout outrigger canoe. The canoe among the Nicobarese is not merely a transport but a symbolic representation of them. While studying the canoe making method among the Nicobarese in Katchal island it has been recorded by the author that this tradition bound methodological procedure runs down through generations. There are lots of ritualistic practices that are observed at the different stages of canoe making. During the course of canoe carpentry the people are to follow strictly certain taboos for maintaining the sanctity of the canoes. The author has successfully presented the indigenous calendar of the Nicobarese which is wholly tallied with the ecology and environment of their island home.

Sri Umesh Kumar and Samir Biswas have discussed, in their paper on the Nicobarese of Katchal island in the Bay of Bengal, the mode of adaptation to the natural surroundings in an island ecological setting. The interface between land and sea creates a lot of adverse situation to cope with until and unless these adversities are challenged by various inventive genius. Utilisation of resources in a befitting manner also needs some technicalities. The authors have traversed through the daily mode of life activities of the indigenous people of Katchal island through a methodical field investigation and they have found that these peoples have devised various ways to adjust themselves with the island ecology. Various technicalities in the adaptation process have been developed in the domain of economy, society, religion as well as environmental factors through which these people maintain their survival strategy in that strange island setting. The authors observe that the social organization of the Nicobarese is an outgrowth of the practical systems for making a living, rather than their cause. On this issue a close interlinkage is to be felt between the ownership and management of resources and social organization in this island society.

Arunachal Pradesh is specifically enriched with the vast and green covering of nature making it highly attractive to the eyes as well as providing mental pleasure to each and everybody. In this greeny environment the basic economic pursuit of paddy and fish cultivation highly utilize the bamboo and cane growing lavishly in their surrounding environment for making different types of baskets, containers, haversacs, plates, chairs and toys. The canes are also used in other types of handicrafts. The Apatanis apply their traditional knowledge in the making of different types of handiwork from long time past. The paper written by Arnab Karar and Suvendra Kundu highlights, in a brief perspective, the various types of utilization of bamboo and cane handiworks in their socio-economic and religious life. Practically speaking the ziro valley of Arunachal Pradesh – the ideal habitat of this picturesque community – is symbolized by the delicacy of bamboo-cane handicrafts which is exclusively governed and dominated by the traditional knowledge system of the Apatanis living in the midst of lustrous eco-environmental setting.

Dr. Nilanjan Khatua puts forward the nature and circumstances of the traditional knowledge among the Kamar tribe - the shifting cultivators of Chhattishgarh - in respect of utilization of the ethnomedicinal plants. The study is based on direct field investigation and in course of this the author has tried to make a record of their food and drinking habits. The nature of dependence of the patients on the traditional healers or Vaidhs has been examined. The Vaidh is believed by these people to have an all rounded expertise in giving relief to the ailing persons. His depth of understanding about the numerous medicinal plants and their individual qualities of disease curing activities is acknowledged by the people and they exclusively rely solely on his expertise. Owing to ecological destruction the medicinal plants are on the wane which raises some constraints during the present period to depend exclusively on their own health care system. As a natural consequence, specific inclination is now being developed towards modern medicines.

As a native and time-long process the shifting cultivation is not only to be regarded as a special method for the raising of crops but the culture-linked feature of activities devoted to the cultivation of crops. In spite of different objections put against the practice of this type of cultivation and its continuance it is still being practiced unabated by many of the tribal groups in India as their mainstay in the economic domain because of the fact that they are pledged to the tradition-bound social system which is endorsed by the customs and usages. In a paper on the Kuki tradition and shifting cultivation, George T. Haokip, has shown the pattern of investigation of the people and the specific process of cultivation. The different stages of the Jhum Cultivation have been brought forward here along with their specific features. Various customary entitlements of the payments of tributaries to the chief as the centralised authority have been brought into focus for easy understanding of the traditional working patterns. This pattern of cultivation is deeply rooted to Kuki psyche and has been processed by various customary beliefs and folkways.

Revealing of the ideas implicit in the Tamang Shamanistic healing procedures is the principal intention of the paper presented by Sri Ganesh Chandra Mallick. Owing to the influence of Tibetan Culture the Tamang ethnic group of Darjeeling Himalayas depend more on the psychological aspect of disease recovery than the physiological side. The traditional medicine man or the Jhakri plays the main role in the context of etiology of diseases and their treatments through magico-religious as well as ethnomedicinal ways. In the later type of treatment multifarious herbal preparations are used. The Jhakri has good command over the medicinal herbs in the mountainous ecological setting. Unquestionably it is based on age-old traditional knowledge enriched by the life-long observations of these traditional medical practitioners. The author observes on the basis of direct field investigation the overall Tamang way of life with special emphasis on their health and disease and understands that psychotherapeutically the Tamang shamanic healing procedure is of special significance in the context of health culture.

Dr. R.M. Sarkar highlights the folk tradition underlying the conceptual ideas on the varied ailments and the various strategic devices for their mendicants. Folklore is governed by tradition and naturally the therapeutic mechanism in this domain is principally, if not wholly, controlled by the traditional elements characterized by age-old thinking patterns, socio-religious perspectives, psychological orientation as well as moral values. As because the diversified nature of healing practices of the rural-tribal folk are interwoven with the cultural matrix of the people, so the attempt for integrated study into the medico-socio-ritualistic sphere is expected to explore the broad horizon of the traditional wisdom which has bestowed on the requisite competence to frame a native scientific principle for coping with the bodily hazards and anxieties. While exploring the cases of the Deyashis–the traditional priest-cum-medicine men of the folk deities–he has gone to the inner recess of their technicalities that are exclusively governed by native beliefs and practices in which supernaturalism plays a major role. Looking into the tribal group of people having primitive way of life it has been seen that their traditional knowledge works very perspicaciously in the broad domain of their herbal medicine as well as various psychotherapic devices that are categorically oriented with the cultural traditions.

REFERENCES

Atran, S. (1990), Cognitive Foundations of Natural History– Towards on Anthropology of Science, Cambridge. Cambridge University Press.

Babu, S.C. & B. Rajsekharan (1991),"Agroforestry, Attitude Towards Risk and Nutritional Availability – A Case study of South Indian Farming System", in *Agroforestry Systems,* Vol. 15, No. 1.

Bell, M. (1974), "The Exploitation of Indigenous Knowledge or the Indigenous Exploitation of Knowledge – Whose use for What?" in *Institute of Development Studies,* Vol. 10, No. 2.

Berline, B. (1992), Ethnobilogical Classifications – Principles of Categorization of Plants and Animals in Traditional Societies, Princeton, New Jersey, Princeton University Press.

Bhasin, M.K. & S.L. Malik (Eds) (1998), Contemporary Studies in Human Ecology, Delhi, Kamala Raj Enterprises.

Dasgupta, Samira & Amitabha Sarkar (2005), Reflection of Ethno-Science–Study on the Abujh Maria, New Delhi, Mittal Publication.

Dubos, Rene (1968), Man, Medicine and Environment, Harmandsworth, Penguin Book.

Goonatilake, Susantha (1999), Towards a Global Science, Mining Civilizational Knowledge, New Delhi, Vistaar Publications.

Grenier, L. (1998), Working with Indigenous Knowledge – A Guide for Researchers.

Henson, Robert (2006), The Rough Guide to Climate Change, London, Rough Guides Ltd.

Landy, David (Ed) (1977), Culture, Disease and Healing – Studies in Medical Anthropology, New Delhi, Macmillan.

Mundy, P. & L. Crompton (1991), "Indigenous Communication and Indigenous Knowledge" *Development Communication Report*, Vol. 74, No. 3.

Posey, D.A. (1984), "Ethnoecology as Applied Anthropology in Amazonian Development", *Human Organisation* Vol. 43, No. 2.

Ramkrishnan, P. & Suprava Patnaik (1992), "Jhum – Slash and Burn Cultivation in India", in *Indigenous Vision*, ed. By Geeti Sen, New Delhi, Sage Publications & India International Centre.

Roy, S.C. (1995), The Mundas and their Country, Ranchi Catholic Press, 2nd Reprint Edition.

Roy. S.C. (1937), Oraon Religion and Custom, Ranchi, Man In India Office.

Sachchidananda (1989), Shifting Cultivation in India, New Delhi, Concept Publishing House.

Sarkar, R.M. (2001), "Hunger and Struggle in a Primitive Tribe", *Journal of rural Development*, Vol. 20, No. 1.

Sarkar R.M. (2004), Human Communities and Cultural Traditions – An Interactional Pattern of Development Strategies, in Social Security in a Developing World Context, ed. By Vijay Kumar & Scott Fritzen, New Delhi, Serials Publications.

Sarkar, R.M. (2008) , "Indigenous Knowledge and Folk Traditions – As Vehicles for Communication" in *Folklore Research Journal*, Vol. 15, Special Number.

Savita, S. (2006), "Protection of Traditional Knowledge – A Case for Concern", in *Intellectual Property Rights* ed. By C.B. Raju, New Delhi, Serials Publications.

Sen, Geeti (1992), Indigenous Vision–People of India, New Delhi, Sage Publications & India International Centre.

Sengupta, Sarthak (Ed.) (1999), Health, Healers and Healing–Studies in Medical Anthropology, Gwahati, National Publishers.

Vaijayanthi & V.Z. Ubaidullah (2006), Indian Folklore–Protect Me! Protect Me! In 'Role of University in Promotion of Intellectual Property' ed. By K. Rajamohan Rao, New Delhi, Serials Publications.

Warren, D.M., L.J. Slikkerveer & D. Brokensha (Eds.) (2002), The Cultural Dimension of Development–Indigenous Knowledge System, London, Intermediate Technology Publications.

William N. & G. Baines (Eds.) (2001), Traditional Ecological Knowledge, Wisdom for Sustainable Development, Canberra, Centre for Research and Environment Studies, Australian National University.

2 Traditional Ecological Farming Sustaining Soil and Human Health in Arunachal Pradesh, North East India

Mihin Dollo and Prasanna K. Samal

INTRODUCTION

In the modern global milieu, with colossal industrial revolution, cultural imperialism, and quantum bound in technology, human beings have increasingly become estranged from innovative traditional knowledge, species preservation (Cunningham, 1991), environmental conservation and human health management (Lipton, *et.al.* 2006). A fundamental concern of the world today is better ecosystem services and sustainable development. The indigenous tradition, custom and cultures are intricately linked with the natural environment and its sustainable management system (Gadgil and Berkes 1991, Nabhan 1997, Sundriyal and Dollo 2004). Disquiet for sustainable development, scientific communities are leaning back on traditional ecological knowledge (TEK) as a possible option (Warren and Rajasekaran 1993) that has evolved through decades of informal experimentation with an intimate understanding of the environment in a given cultural landscape (Nabhan 1997). The development of TEK is a dynamic process that changes with the availability of resources and the demands of traditional communities (Dollo and Choudhury, 2006). Most of the time, TEK is transferred orally, and is vanishing over the years, urgently necessitating revitalization and documentation of such knowledge. This has been accepted as a challenge by the scientific community.

In recent past, there has been increasing thought engaged on TEK by academics, natural resource managers, and commercial concerns. The emerging ethno-scientific approach to TEK blended the methodologies of anthropology and biology to accentuate the past and current linkages between nature and culture (Farooquee, *et. al.*, 2007). As agriculture is an important economic activity for livelihood sustenance and is closely linked with human health, the innovative TEK may help the scientific world to evolve sustainable agricultural production system to meet the present needs by keeping the system (soil quality and micro-environment) intact for future generation (Dollo *et. al.*, 2006). TEK offers a diverse set of institutional solutions for ecological sustainability where a substantial number of traditional communities maintain a high level of ecology and human health, while sustaining natural resources in good condition (Cunningham, 1991).

Agriculture and human health are intricately linked together, where traditional ecological farming can have a pivotal role to play. Policy interventions in agriculture and human health are often pursued in a parallel and independent approach (Klein-Schwartz, *et. al.* 1997). Yet coherent, joint action in agriculture and health could have greater potential benefits and substantially reduce the health risk of traditional farming comminutes (Coitinho, 2005). In recent past, there is growing recognition that agriculture influences health, and health influences agriculture, and that both in turn have profound implications for poverty reduction (WHO, 1992). This recognition suggests that opportunities exist for agriculture to contribute to better health, and for health to contribute to higher agronomic yields (Lang, 2006). It is imperative to understand the precise linkages between the two sectors for sustainable crop production and better health (Johns, *et al.*, 2006).

UN Millennium Development Goals report clearly indicated that four of the eight goals are targeting health related issues, which included environmental sustainability (MDGR,

2007). Inspite of clear and close connection between human health and production system of agricultural crop, the thoughts and practices on the ground at different levels, including policy, programme and schemes have not well reflected the fundamental relationship between the two components, particularly in Eastern Himalayan context. The primitive concept of enhancing agronomic yields through the application of inorganic fertilizers, insecticides and pesticides are well entrenched with the policy planners and implementing agencies (Dollo, 2007). As in recent past, these are given emphasis by the implementing agencies across the Arunachal Himalaya. Health risks linked to the applied chemicals through food chain are well recognized since long back. However, application of chemicals is not reducing over the year in most of the developing countries and is rather encouraged in Arunachal Himalaya. Dilemma is being created on mostly illiterate tribal farmers whether to continue their traditional ecological farming practices or to adopt the modern methods of high external inputs (Dollo *et. al.*, 2006[a]).

The paper is based on the research effort made during the year form 2002 to 2006, covering two districts (Tawang and West Kameng) of Arunachal Pradesh, India inhabited by Monpa tribe, highlights some of the agricultural linked issues with human health and soil fertlity.

GEO-ECOSYSTEM SETTINGS OF STUDY AREAS

The present study covers the two districts in the western Arunachal Pradesh, which are totally dominated by Monpa tribal community in Tawang district while Monpa with Sherdukpen, Miji, Bugun and Aka tribes in West Kameng district. However, only the Monpa tribal community of Tawang and West Kameng districts was taken into considerations for detail investigation.

Geographically, the Tawang district is situated in between 27°45′ N and 90°15′ E at the northwest extremity of Arunachal Pradesh. The altitudes of the district ranges between 1850 and 6800 m msl. It was carved out of the West Kameng district that adjoins it to the south and east. It is also bounded by

Bhutan in the west and Tibet in the north. The mountainous terrain of Tawang comprises of the snow capped higher Himalayan ranges and sparsely populated plateaus and valleys, which are drained by the Tawangchu and Nyamyanchu rivers. The geographical area of the district is 2085 km^2 with its headquarters located in Tawang. It is divided into three subdivisions Tawang, Lumla and Jang, and eight circles, i.e. Tawang, Lumla, Jang, Mukto, Zemithang, Thingbu, Dudunghar and Kitpi.

The total population of the district is 38,924 and a literacy rate of 47.30% with a sex ratio of 782 females for 1000 males (Table 1). Most of the inhabitants are found in lower altitude, where they enjoy a cool temperate climate. Their houses are built with stones and timbers. The economy is primarily agrarian where they raise potato, maize, millets, etc. in lower belt while practice transhumance pastoralism in higher belts particularly of yaks, sheep, ponies and goats. Besides, handicrafts are the forte of the local women folk who practice weaving and make incense sticks.

Table 1
Population Profile and Workforces of Tawang and West Kameng Districts

Parameter	*Tawang*	*West Kameng*
No. of Household	8294	15637
Household size	4.7	4.8
Population		
Total	38924	74599
Rural	30548 (78.48)	67906 (91.03)
Urban	8376 (21.52)	6693 (8.97)
Sex ratio	782	754
Population 0-6 year(s)	6515 (16.74)	12569 (16.85)
Literate	15337 (47.30)	37687 (60.80)
Total worker	21727 (55.80)	34362 (46.10)
Main worker	18134 (46.60)	28850 (38.70)
Marginal worker	3593 (9.20)	5512 (7.40)
Non worker	17197 (44.20)	40237 (53.90)
Work participation rate	55.8	46.1

Note: Value in parentheses is in percentage in each category.

West Kameng district of the state Arunachal Pradesh is situated between 91° 30' and 92°40' E and, 26° 54' and 28° 01'

N. The district is surrounded by Tibet in the North, Bhutan in the West, Tawang district and East Kameng districts of Arunachal Pradesh are in the Northwest and East, respectively. The name of the district is derived from the Kameng river, a tributary of the mighty Brahamputra, that flows through the district. It is a mountainous tract in Western Arunachal Pradesh, which covers an area of approximately 7422 km^2. Bomdila is the district headquarter, which is situated at an altitudes of nearly 2600 m msl. Administratively, the district has been divided into three subdivisions (Bomdila, Rupa and Thrizino, and 12 circles namely Dirang, Bomdila, Kalaktang, Balemu, Bhalukpong, Jameri, Sinchung, Nafra, Thrizino, Rupa, Thembang and Shergaon.

The total population of the district is 74,599 and a literacy rate of 60.80%, which is significantly higher compared to Tawang district. The sex ratio of the district is marginally lower than Tawang district with 754 females for 1000 males. The population density of West Kameng district is 10 persons per km^2 while that of Tawang is 16 persons per km^2. As in Tawang district, agriculture is the main livelihood sustenance of the community while transhumance pastoralism prevails in higher altitudes. The agriculture is slightly diversified as compared to Tawang district with the evolution of wet rice cultivation, which is not evident in the Tawang district. The main crops are maize, millet, rice, soyabean, etc.

However, in recent years, horticultural crops such as kiwi, apple, orange and geranium are gaining importance in the selected region of Dirang and Kalaktang circles. The mean annual minimum temperature is -0.5°C and maximum mean value is 16.87°C, and the annual average rainfall recorded is 1433.3 mm.

PEOPLE AND CULTURE

The Monpas are an ethnic group of Tibetan descent inhabiting the western Arunachal Pradesh, with a population of 45,000, centered in the districts of Tawang and West Kameng. Of that nearly 20,000 of them live in Tawang district, where they constitute about 97% of the total district's population, while almost all of the remainders are found in the West Kameng district, where they form about 77% of the total district's population. They settled in eco-culturally and strategically important part of western Arunachal Himalaya bordering Tibet (China) in north and Bhutan in south and west. Their language belongs to the Tibeto-Burman family and has the Tibetan script. Generally, Monpas have patriarchal society and practice monogamy, though the polygamy may not be ruled out. Due to slight variations in dialects Monpas can be divided into six linguistic groups, namely Tawang Monpa, Dirang Monpa, Lish Monpa, Boot Monpa, Kalaktang Monpa and Panchen Monpa, which may be due to geographical barriers. Monpas are Mahayana Buddhist by religion with close cultural and religious affinities with Bhutanese and Tibetans. All houses have the small altars and chapels with statues of Buddha. Offering water in little cups and burning butter lamps are the daily rituals. They believe in transmigration of the soul and reincarnation. Although, some members of the Boot Monpa practice Bon and Animism.

The Monpas perform many pantomime dances of which the 'Ajilamu' dance is the most popular. Losar and Choskar are the major religious festivals of Monpas. Losar is celebrated to commemorate the entry of New Year. There is great marry making and dancing during Losar festival. In Choskar festival, the Lamas read religious scriptures in the Gompa (Buddhists temple) for a number of days. Thereafter, the villagers carry the religious books on their back in the procession under the guidance of the senior Lama and procession goes around the cultivation fields. The significance of this performance is to assure better cultivation and protect the grains from insects and wild animals and also for the prosperity of the villagers in general.

Due to the cold climate of the Himalayas, the Monpa, like most of the other Buddhist tribes, construct their house with stone and wood with plank floors, often accompanied with beautifully carved doors and window frames. The roof is made with bamboo matting, keeping their house warm during the winter season. Sitting platforms and hearths in the living rooms are also found in their houses. Nearly 80% of the community is depending on agriculture while rest is either on transhumance pastoralism or serving government agencies. Agriculture, the livelihood sustenance for large group of the population is confined upto 2600 m msl while pastoral economy is common upto 4500 m msl.

DEVELOPMENTAL INTERVENTIONS FOR HIGHER YIELDS

Arunachal Himalaya is the eastern part of the fragile Himalaya ranges, which need location specific pre-tested technologies and developmental interventions. This only will cater the necessity of inaccessible, illiterate and poor faming community thriving in the rough topographic and climatic conditions. Arising from different developmental initiatives, policies and programs in India, Government of Arunachal Pradesh has initiated interventions in agriculture sector since fifth five year plan (1974-1979). Some of the important initiatives of the Department of Agriculture are Food Crop Production Programme (1974-75), Commercial Crop Development (1985-86), Watershed Development Project (1992-93), Vegetable Mini-kit Programme (1992-93), Accelerated Maize Development Programme (1992-93), Micro-management for Development of Agriculture (2000-01), etc., by using high yielding varieties, inorganic fertilizers and plant protectants.

These initiatives were implemented without considering the local community aspiration and undermining the environmental and human health risk of the region. The schemes were vigorously promoted by the government agencies with limited success or total failure. The main constrain in these approach as narrated by the farmers were the high cost of inputs as most of the inputs were of external sources, which need more cash for acquiring the materials. Besides, they expressed that, it also deteriorated the soil health and some farmers viewed that commercial cropping leads to declining crop diversity most of which have traditional values for rituals and health.

REJUVENATED TRADITIONAL PRACTICES

Monpa tribe of the Arunachal Pradesh is leaning back on their traditional farming practices. It is based on local resources available with limited or no external input at all, which is a very kind of human modified ecological process. However, without considering and incorporating the traditional ecological knowledge evolved through century old experimentations, policy planners and developmental agencies are enforcing modern methods of crop production with high external input. For nearly three decades government agencies, particularly department of agriculture has been emphasizing the use of chemical fertilizers and plant protectants to improve agronomic yields. In fact, the use of chemicals adversely affected the soil vigour and human health, where the former is well understood by the farmers in relation to yield, soil texture and earth worm population while later is unseen infestation to the illiterate farming community. The WHO and many more scientific communities revealed that, besides socio-environmental factors human health is affected by diet quality. Therefore, it is utmost important to rethink on nature based traditional crop farming with limited or no external input.

Over the years, viewing the gravity of soil deterioration and gaining awareness on health risk of chemical application, Monpas are leaning back on their traditional practices. Though, dilemma still exists among some section of farmers who are trying to generate more cash in sort period without considering the sustainability of fragile land resources, majority of the villages practice traditional farming systems.

SUSTAINABLE SOIL HEALTH MANAGEMENT

Soil nutrient optimization is the crucial for the sustainable agro-ecosystem in fragile Arunachal Himalaya. Interestingly, Monpa tribe managed it through a type of agro-forestry by maintaining oak (*Baisnang Sing; Baisnang*- mean oak, *Sing* mean tree) forest in the periphery of agricultural land. The oak (*Quercus* sp.) tree generally shed their leaves during January-February month, which are collected and kept in one corner of the agricultural field. The collection and mulching is basically done by the females in group called *Mila*. After, the emergence of seedling and attending a height of nearly 12-18 cm, mulching of oak leaves are done with some care. The mulched leaves have ecological and economic value by protecting soil erosion and runoff, maintaining soil moisture and soil health, which in turn enhance economic yield per unit area.

Besides ecological and economic benefits, it helps to maintain as organic crop production system by limiting the use of chemicals, which ultimately benefits the health of the community. By observing the importance of oak forest and gaining awareness about the health risk of chemicals, Monpas are leaning back on their traditional practices. Now, in this modern period, traditional institution *Chhopa* has also reestablish its value by developing some local norms and rules to sustain its population and avoid conflict to access the forest. The private and community oak forest lands are demarcated separately using stones or some other traditional symbols. This helps to avoid any conflict between the owners while accessing the leaves. If someone is collecting leaves beyond the demarcated areas assigned or overexploiting the oak tree, a fine of a sum of Rupees 2,000 to 20,000 is imposed by *Chhopa* headed by *Gaon Burah* (village head). However, in olden days the fine was imposed in terms of yaks, cows, pigs and sheep. The size and age of animals given as fine are decided according to the nature, productivity and age of the oak tree and amount of leaves collected. Meanwhile, the *Chhopa* reserves the right to reduce the fine depending on economic status of the guilty person. The collected money from the imposed fine is used by the community in social welfare activity, managing natural resources like plantation in community land. Traditional community honours the decisions made by the *Chhopa*, but with the passage of time transitions have taken place where the resourceful persons became more influential on discussion making.

MIXED CROPPING TO SUPPORT NUTRIENT NEEDS

The Monpa classified their agricultural land into 7 broad categories (Table 2). However, of that shifting cultivation is found in few pockets of Kalaktang circle only. As many as 53 species of vegetable, grain and tuber crops and 7 species of fruit crops are grown in different crop combinations in traditional agro-ecosystem. Besides, giving food security during environmental stress periods, these crops provide nutrient requirements of the human body. Maize, a protein rich grain is the staple crop and firmament food (*Çhurpi*) of soyabean is also extensively used by the community. It has been observed that traditional diets are combination of different vegetables, grains, tubers and fruits produced without use of chemicals to maintain the farmers' health.

Table 2
Traditional Agricultural Land Use Classification of Monpas

System	*Local Name*	*Importance*
Home garden	*Chur-ung*	Varieties of vegetables, pulses, chillies etc.
Rain-fed farming	*Penang-ung*	Maize as main crop in summer and wheat in winter, however variety of vegetables, pulses are grown along sides
Millet farming	*Khompu-ung*	Millet as main crop sometime maize is integrated.
Wet rice cultivation	*Re-ung*	Varieties of paddy land races is cultivated
Paddy nursery	*Re-ung*	Raising of paddy, particularly in rain-fed plot near forest.
Fruit garden	*Seshing-ung*	Varieties of crops such as apple, orange, kiwi, walnut, etc.
Shifting agriculture	*Ya-ung*	Maize and millet as main crop, variety of vegetables, pulses, chilly etc are also grown.

In developmental interventions, government agencies emphasized the cultivation of mono-cropping that in reality exhausted the soil fertility in short time period (Box 1). Initially the farmers enthusiastically adopted the interventions,

Box 1
Strengths, Weaknesses, Opportunities and Threats (SWOT) of Monpa Agro-ecosystem

Strength

- Highly evolved traditional agro-ecosystem with maximum utilization of natural resources.
- Indigenous technology of oak leaves mulching, which enhance soil fertility, check soil erosion and control weeds.
- Indigenous soil and water conservation by mulching, terracing and stonewall.
- Management of oak forest, a keystone species for indigenous agro-ecosystem.
- Recycling of household and animal excreta in agricultural field- an organic farming.
- Very limited/no uses of inorganic chemical and fertilizer

Opportunity

- Complete rejuvenation of efficient traditional practices to achieve the synthetic chemical free farming.
- Strengthening traditional soil and water conservation measure by integrating appropriate scientific innovation.
- Agro-forestry and horticulture farming, and terraces cultivation in gentle slope and valley
- Presence of value traditional crops well adopted with local environment for future.

Weakness

- Low cropping intensity and long fallow period
- Marginalization of land due to population growth and acquisition of maximum land area by well-of farmers, which may chance of landless farmers.
- Lack of promotion of organic products.

Threat

- Forestland is reducing by extension for agriculture and large scale harvesting for commercial purpose and other household requirements.
- Slow take over of oak by pinus vegetation, which will reduce the efficient mulching management by traditional communities.
- Eroding of social setting and community organization due to urbanization and modernization.
- Declining crop diversity and chance of losing better genetic resources.

however in present condition they leaned back on the traditional practices. In this, they mainly grow the crop combinations of cereals, vegetables and nitrogen enriching plant pulses. It helps in maintaining soil health and supply nutrient needs of the farming community.

There are a large number of crops grown either singly or mixed type in the upland and valley agro-ecosystems. To understand the complexity of input and output in the agro-ecosystem, individual and mixed croppings are taken into consideration. The crop analysed included rice, maize, finger millet, wheat etc. The agronomic yield was calculated by using harvesting techniques for different crops or crop combinations within the agro-ecosystem. It was observed that almost all the crops grown in study sites are local varieties with exception of wheat, cabbage and potato, which are either local or improved varieties. Major inputs are human and bullock labour, and seeds. Maximum labour input was observed during maize/ buckwheat/ wheat (529 ±6.87 mandays and 59 ±2.08 bullock days) cultivation and minimum in dry rice with 207 ±1.96 mandays and 31±0.58 bullock days (Table 3). The agronomic yields of vegetables, tuber and pulses are fairly good with exception of millet cultivation. Monetary output/ input analysis is suggestive of the economic efficiency of the agro-ecosystem. It has been recorded that the mono-cropping of maize and double cropping of maize and wheat showed the most efficiency with 2.44±0.14 and 2.02 ±0.26 respectively. While, rest of the crops and crop combinations are almost similar in terms of economic efficiencies that range between 1.22 ±0.02 and 1.88 ±0.06 (Table 3). Almost all the productions of cereal crops are used either for household consumption or for barter with the pastoral community. However, vegetables and pulses are usually sold in the local or nearby markets to meet daily cash needs.

CONCLUSION

Traditional agricultural systems may need to be integrated with appropriate technologies developed based on TEK, rather than quantum change, as anything drastic change may not be

Table 3
Crop, Cropping Patterns and, their Input and Output in Monpa's Agro-Ecosystem

Crops	*Botanical Name*	*Input (ha^{-1} y^{-1})*			
		Mandays (Nos.)	*Bullock (Nos.)*	*Seed (Rs.)*	*Total (Rs.)*
Mono-cropping					
Wet rice	*Oryza sativa* L.	286 ±2.72	–	719.97±8.42	13847.97±125.80
Dry rice	*Oryza sativa* L.	207 ±1.96	31 ±0.58	819.1±5.14	12954.1±104.12
Maize	*Zea mays* L.	239 ±7.36	30 ±1.50	1281.6±12.68	14906.6±412.89
Finger millet	*Eleusine coracana* (L) Gaertn.	195 ±2.18	32 ±0.50	144.52±2.64	10621.52±110.05
Mixed cropping					
Maize/wheat	*Z. mays/ Triticum aestivum* L.	386 ±5.30	59 ±2.08	3148.42±168.14	26758.42 ±376.94
Finger millet/ wheat	*E. coracana/ T. aestivum*	342 ±3.33	61 ±1.29	1789.91±112.03	22251.91±111.99
Maize/ buckwheat/ wheat	*Z. mays/ Fagopyrum esculentum* L./*T. aestivum*	529 ±6.87	59 ±2.08	3251.68±192.63	33819.68±443.93
Maize/ spices/pulses/vegetables	–	255±1.78	18±1.41	3467.92±193.2	16758.92±77.34

Contd.

Output (ha^{-1} y^{-1})		
Yield (q)	*Total (Rs.)*	*Output/inputratio*
25.13 ±1.12	25125 ±1119.90	1.81±0.07
15.89 ±0.287	15888 ±286.57	1.22±0.02
19.01 ±0.12	36435 ±1772.93	2.44±0.14
11.46 ±0.14	13752 ±172.30	1.30±0.03
35.85 ±0.64	54108 ±1474.04	2.02±0.26
29.09 ±0.26	31380 ±262.15	1.41±0.01
47.64 ±0.64	63499 ±1485.76	1.88±0.06
13.59±0.31	22360±189.48	1.33±0.02

Note: Values are mean ± std error.

accepted by the traditional communities. Most of the TEK are eroding over the years because of high cash demand, lack of community labour etc. Therefore, it is important to document and revitalize the TEK given the urgency of preserving biological and cultural diversity, which is quickly disappearing in indigenous communities. These efforts, however, will only succeed if the contributions of traditional communities are valued and they are considered as rightful partners in the conservation of biological and cultural diversity, which in turn will help to preserve TEK. Monpas being conservative in nature and having highly evolved traditional agro-ecosystem integrated with TEK can be easily influenced for the revitalization of TEK and may be developed as a model for such activities. Most of the TEK of Monpas still exist either in the hand of elderly people or is practiced in the field, which will be easier for documentation and revitalization.

Extensive developmental interventions without considering location specific socio-ecological problems may have drastic impact on the ecological process and socio-cultural setting of the farming community. Before any intervention, peoples' perceptions have to be understood, and undermining of which may result in the failure of programme and policy initiatives. Land use change for horticulture crop by wealthy families, and slow and steady take over of pinus over the oak forest are real causes of concerns for future survival of traditional ecological farming.

Government agencies have to value the traditional ecological knowledge on agriculture and any developmental intervention shall be a coherent and multifaceted approach. Considering linkages between agriculture, forest and human health rather than single approach in agriculture development will strengthen the socio-ecological and economic status of the traditional farming community.

REFERENCE

Cunningham, A.B. (1991), Indigenous Knowledge and Biodiversity: Global Commons or Regional Heritage? *Cultural Survival Quarterly* (Summer):4–8.

Coitinho, D.C. (2005), Health Perspective: How Does Agriculture Influence Human Health? In: *Symposium on the Occasion of World Food Day: Poor Health, Food Insecurity and Poverty – How to break a vicious circle?*. Berne, Switzerland.

Dollo Mihin (2007), Back to Traditional Farming Systems –A Case of Monpa Tribes. *LEISA*. 9(3):12.

Dollo Mihin and Choudhury, D. (2006), Eco-cultural Heritage of Arunachal Pradesh. In: *Interpreting the heritage of North-East,* (ed. Rajeshwari Tondon). Lodhi Estate, New Delhi: INTACH, India. 12-59.

Dollo Mihin, Chaudhury Shivaji and Sundriyal, R.C. (2006), Traditional farming and land tenure systems in West Kameng district, Arunachal Pradesh. In: *Shifting agriculture and sustainable development of North-Eastern India,* (eds. P.S, Ramakrishnan, K.G Sexena and K.S. Rao). UNESCO-MAB series, Oxford & IBH, New Delhi, India. 293-315.

Dollo Mihin, Samal, P.K. and Kumar, K. (2006[a]), Traditional Ecological Knowledge in Sustainable Agricultural Practices of the Apatanis in Arunachal Pradesh. *Hima-Paryavaran*. 18(2): 18-20.

Farooquee, Nehal A., Dollo Mihin and Kala, C.P. (2007), Traditional Wisdom of Apatani Community in the Management and Sharing of Natural Resources in North Eastern India. In: *Traditional Knowledge in Contemporary Societies: Challenges and Opportunities* (eds. Kamal K. Misra). Pratibha Prakashan, Shakti Nagar, Delhi, India. 362 p.

Gadgil, M., and F. Berkes (1991), Traditional Resources Management Systems. *Resource management and Optimization* 8(3-4):127–141.

Johns, Timothy; Smith, Ifeyironwa Francisca; Eyzaguirre, Pablo B. (2006), *Agrobiodiversity, Nutrition, and Health: Understanding the links between Agriculture and Health*. International Food Policy Research Institute (IFPRI), Washington, D.C.

Klein-Schwartz, W., Smith, E., & Gordon, S. (1997), Agricultural and Horticultural Chemical Poisonings: Mortality and Morbidity in the United States. *Annals of Emergency Medicine*, 29:232-38.

Lang, Tim. (2006). *Agriculture, Food, and Health- Perspectives on a Long Relationship: Understanding the links between Agriculture and Health.* International Food Policy Research Institute (IFPRI), Washington, D.C.

Lipton, Michael; Sinha, Saurabh; Blackman, Rachel (2006), *Agricultural Technology and Health: Understanding the Links between Agriculture and Health.* International Food Policy Research Institute (IFPRI), Washington, D.C.

MDGR (2007), *The Millennium Development Goals Report*. UNITED NATIONS, New York.

Nabhan, G. P. (1997), *Cultures of Habitat: On Nature, Culture, and Story.* Counterpoint, Washington, D.C., USA.

Singh, K.I., S. Chaudhry, D. Saha, M. Dollo and R.C. Sundriyal (2004), Natural Resource Utilization and Management by the Monpas in Arunachal Pradesh, India. In: *International Symposium on Recent Trends in Plant Ecology and Biodiversity Research*, 20-22nd May, 2004, NEHU, Shillong, India. p. 16-17.

Sundriyal, R.C. and M. Dollo (2004), Apatani Cultural Landscape: Integrated Natural Resource Management and Community Development-towards Local Assets Building and Transformations. In: *Ninth International Congress on "Ethnobiology, Social Change and Displacement"*, 13-17th June, 2004, University of Kent, Canterbury, UK.

Warren, D. M., and B. Rajasekaran (1993), Putting Local Knowledge to Good Use. *International Agricultural Development* 13(4):8–10.

WHO (1992), Basic Documents, 39 ed. Geneva: World Health Organisation.

Plate 1. Agricultural Landscape

Plate 2. Oak Forest and Agricultural Landscape

Plate 3. Mulched Oak Leaves in Mixed Crop Field

Plate 4. Drying of Maize in Agriculture Field

3 A Study on Jhumias and Factors Associated with Jhuming in Mizoram

Vanlalruali and Sagar Mondal

INTRODUCTION

The shifting cultivation portrays its remote amiquity and the existence of which can be traced back to 9000 years ago on the basis of archeological data. In the history of cultivation it is regarded as the first transitional step towards agriculture from food gathering and hunting to domestication and cultivation of useful cultivars for human survival.

The system has been variously termed as primitive agriculture, nomadic agriculture, slash-and –burn agriculture, migratory agriculture, primitive horticulture, band tillage, hoe and burn, bush-fallow cultivation, swidden agriculture and shifting cultivation or jhum cultivation etc.

About 2 million people cultivate nearly 11 million hectares of land following these practices in India. It is known in different areas by a variety of local names. In India, it is known as "jhuming" in north-east; "khallu" or "kurwa" in Bihar; "dahiya" in Madhya Pradesh.; "podu" in Andhra Pradesh and Orissa and as "kumri" or "kumari" in Western Ghats. There are differences in their mode of operations, cropping pattern and duration of cultivation on the same land from place to place.

SHIFTING CULTIVATION IN THE NORTH- EAST REGION

Shifting cultivation, locally named as "Jhum" as a system of land use and agriculture is widespread in the mountainous areas of the north eastern region of India. The ideal conditions for shifting cultivation prevail in the region because of extensive forest resources and sparse population. The region which constitutes less than 8% of the country's geographical area comprises little more than 25% of the country's forest cover of 63.34 million ha.

Thus, mountain topography, hot humid climate, deep and fertile soils, scanty indigenous population and communal ownership of land constitute the ideal conditions for the rise and continuation of shifting cultivation in north-east India. These estimates, however, make one thing clear that shifting cultivation is widespread in all the states of north-east India where it constitutes a way of life.

Table 1
Shifting Cultivation in North-East Region

States	*Annual Area Under Shifting Cultivation (Sq. Kms.)*	*Fallow Period (in years)*	*No. of Families Practising Shifting Cultivation*
Manipur	900	4 – 7	70,000
Arunachal Pradesh	700	3- 10	54,000
Assam	696	2- 10	58,000
Meghalaya	530	5 – 7	52,290
Mizoram	630	3 – 4	50,000
Nagaland	190	5- 8	116046
Tripura	223	5- 9	43,000
Total	3869	–	4,43,336

Source: Basic Statistics of NER, 2002, Govt. of India, North Eastern Secretariat, Shillong, p. 42

SHIFTING CULTIVATION IN MIZORAM

Mizoram is a small state located between 21° 58′ N and 24° 35′N latitude parallel and 92°15′ E and 93°29′ E meridians longitude. It encompasses about 21087 sq.km. and population of 888573 persons (2001 census, Statistical Handbook, Mizoram, 2006).

As per the statistics of North-Eastern Hill Region the average annual area under shifting cultivation in Mizoram was 530 Sq.km. involving as many as 50,000 families operate minimum 63,000 ha. under this method of cultivation. However, the area under this system of agriculture as well as the number of families have come down drastically every year as it is no longer a paying proposition..

JHUM CYCLE

Jhum is a method of cultivation in the hilly areas of Mizoram. Because of the rapid loss of fertility, the jhum land is abandoned after one or two years of cultivation and a new plot is selected for fresh cultivation. In the process a plot once used is left fallow for a number of years to regain fertility. This is known as **jhum cycle**. The farmers in the Mizoram who are cultivating through the methods of jhum are called **jhumias**.

The jhumias cultivate patches of land on the hill slopes for one year only and shift to a new patch to return to the same land after some years. The jhum area lies around the village, rotating the cultivation which makes the jhum cycle. The cycle of cultivation varies from village to village depending on the availability of jhum land within the village jurisdiction and the number of families dependent on it in the village. Logically villages with high population density should have short jhum cycles. The important parameters of jhum cycles are: i) rural population density (ii) number of villages per 100 sq. km and (iii) number of cultivators per sq. km.

SYSTEM OF JHUM

A brief resume of the practice of jhuming existing now-a-days will not be relevant. Earlier the village chief and the village council headed by him had much power and control over the villages, which is lost to a large extent now. Instead, lately formed Mizo Hills District Council has made a number of Acts, regulations and rules pertaining to various economic practices including jhuming, collection of forest produces and other agricultural uses of land, which are executable through the Village Council of the region. According to these rules, each village council has to present a written report by September regarding allotments of jhum lands, number of families and amount of land to be allotted, etc, to the Executive Committee of the District Council.

On receiving such reports instructions are issued for distribution of land which rests to the power of village council, and usually accomplished by early January. Mode of distribution of jhum land now is either i)by draw of lots to distribute previously demarcated jhum lands, or ii) by draw of lots to divide the order of preference by which selection of jhum shall be done

Though shifting cultivation has long been viewed as a problem, in the absence of any workable alternative, people continued "jhuming" on the slopes much as they have been doing for generations. At the same time, farmers have started feeling pressure of growing population and thereby shortening shifting cultivation cycle. As a result, shifting cultivation is widely practiced in the whole state.

ADVERSE EFFECT OF JHUMING

Although the system of jhuming was good for a time when it emerged, yet, it is considered to be wasteful for the present time. The various adverse effects of jhuming are summarized below:-

- Some experts are of the opinion that this system of cultivation as a means for economy is very harmful as it destroys the forest cover and lowers the fertility of the soil.
  - In areas of extensive exploitation by shifting cultivation, it has been noted that the soil is rapidly washed away and trees can no longer grow there.
  - There has been large scale deforestation resulting denudation of hill tops and slopes.
  - Further, since the hill tops are the sources of water, deforestation of hill tops leads to elimination of these sources.

- There is large scale soil erosion due to deforestation and cultivation on hill slopes without effective soil conservation practices. This in turn leads to several effects.
  - Erosion of soil in catchment areas resulting in shifting of reservoir and streams leading to floods in plains (Goswami, 1968);
  - Removal of top soil leads to loss of fertility which cannot be easily restored or replenished. This leads to low productivity and subsequent pressure on land.
  - Productivity from the point of view of land use is low under shifting cultivation. (Barkakoti 1990)
- Continuance of primitive form of agriculture offers very little scope for introduction of modern technology. This along with loss of fertility leads to such a low level of productivity that the farmers live in near famine condition. (bear subsistence level) (Saha, 1973 and 1976).
- The system is labour-intensive with low technology resulting in low productivity (Roy Burman and Sharma 1970). Further, there is no scope for development of sources of subsidiary income for the farmers. Besides these, which are directly related to agriculture, there are other aspects which adversely affect social welfare. The public health, education, communication and such other basic facilities are difficult to be developed when there is no permanent settlement.

ADVANTAGES OF JHUMING

Inspite of all these problems or adverse effects of jhuming, there are a number of advantages of shifting cultivation as envisaged by the jhumias. These are presented below:

- Low labour cost, as no labour from outside the family is employed. The amount of the land allotted to each family essentially depends upon the size of it, i.e., number of able bodied members.

- Inputs required for cultivation are much less which include nothing but seeds and a few simple agricultural implements.
- The problems of attacks from insects are almost nil if the firing is done effectively.
- The jhum double cropping or multiple cropping is also possible with the application of some local improved variety of seeds. e.g.,"Phulbun" which, if sown 6 feet apart, can produce much more yield. These seeds can also be sown in terraced field of dry condition with good result.
- Damage of crops by birds is more when small area is under cultivation. This argument of the farmers justifies for larger area under jhum.
- Combination of different crops not only helps in optimizing the use of natural processes but it also contributes in a significant way to soil and water conservation and enrichment and also in disease and pest control.

OBJECTIVES OF THE STUDY

- To delineate the major activities undertaken during jhum cultivation and festivals associated with jhuming in Mizoram
- To study the perception of the jhumias relating to environmental impact of jhuming.
- To delve into some agro- economic, socio- psychological factors contributing to jhuming in Mizoram.

METHODOLOGY

Pilot Study

A pilot study is a preliminary study pattern conducted on a limited scale before the actual studies are carried out in order to gather some primary informations, on the basis of which the main project would be planned and formulated.

Pilot study enables the researcher to acquire some systematic knowledge of universe and its population. It plays a vital role in identifying the variables involved in research, the nature of the problem, the nature of the respondents, kind of responses that are likely to be available etc. On the basis of the information gathered or experience gained during such a study, the schedule/ questionnaire is then framed.

A pilot study was undertaken in Chhingchhip village under Serchhip district in order to access the feasibility of the research study. For this purpose, the researchers stayed with her relatives in Chhingchhip. A Pilot study was conducted in the month of January 2007.

Informal discussions were made with a few villagers and village council personnel during the period. Exhaustive list of information was collected from different sources. The information collected was used for preparation of the schedule for data collection.

Selection of District

As per Statistical Handbook Mizoram 2006, this state Mizoram has 24 Rural Development blocks under 8 Districts. The study was conducted in the village Chhingchhip under Serchhip district of Mizoram which is about 80 km away from Aizawl, the capital of Mizoram. The Tlangnuam Rural Development block in the district of Aizawl was also selected purposively for conducting the study.

Selection of Villages

The village Chhingchhip under Serchhip district and the village Airfield area under Aizawl District were selected purposively. The village Chhingchhip was consisted with three paras (wards) which is called '**veng** 'in local language. The name of this veng was **Venghlun, Mualpui, and Venglai,**. The study was conducted in venghlun veng (para). According to the book', **chhingchhip khaw chanchin'** (About the Village

Chhingchhip) by Upa. Haukhama published in 2008, the total number of houses at the village Chhingchhip were 709, total number of families were 708, total no. of population were 4148; out of which total no. of male persons **(mipa)** were 2018 and that of female persons **(hmeichhia)** were 2130. The study was conducted in **Venghlun Veng** of the village Chhingchhip.

Selection of Respondents (Jhumias)

For selection of respondents Non- probability sampling method was followed. Since, the total number of jhumias families in Venghlun para of village Chhingchhip could not be ascertained, and also due to limitation of time and other constraints, instead of adopting random sampling method, non- probability sampling method was followed. In this type of sampling, the items (respondents) for the sample are selected deliberately instead of using the techniques of random sampling.

For the present investigation total 40 (forty) respondents (jhumia) have been selected. Thirty Jhum cultivators (Jhumias) were identified in the village Chhingchhip and were selected and interviewed. Only 10 Jhumias have been selected deliberately by the researchers from Airfield area under Aizawl District.

EMPIRICAL MEASURES OF VARIABLES

A variable is something which varies. More specifically variables are those attribute of objects, events, things and beings which vary and can be measured (Ray and Mondal, 2004)

For selection of appropriate variable, the experts in the Department of Agriculture, Government of Mizoram were consulted by the researchers and available literature on jhum cultivation in the North East in general and particularly in Mizoram were collected and gone through. By following specific objectives of the study, the theoretical basis for selection of variables and their empirical measures are presented.

Major Activities Undertaken during Jhum Cultivation: Jhuming as practiced by Mizo's involves some specific activities which are to be performed within one full cycle. The activities are as follows:-

- Selection of land
- Cutting of forest
- Natural drying
- Burning of dried forest
- Cleaning
- Sowing of seeds
- Weed control
- Construction of watching house (Thlam)
- Harvesting
- Threshing/winnowing/drying
- Storing of crop, and
- Marketing

In the present investigation it was intended to find out the calendar year (month of operation), time required (in no. of days), whether it is performed by male or female and some festivals associated with these activities.

Perception of Jhumias Relating to Environmental Impact of Jhuming: The system of jhum cultivation involves cultivation of crop on hill slopes after clearing the land by cutting down the jungle and burning the dry debris on which seeds of different crops are sown by dibbling or broadcasting before the onset of rain. Though shifting cultivation has long been viewed as a problem, in the absence of any workable alternative, people are in the habit of continuting "jhuming" on the slopes much as they have been doing for generation. At the same time, farmers have started feeling pressure of growing population and shortening shifting cultivation cycle. As a result, shifting cultivation is widely practiced in the whole state.

Although the system of jhuming was good for a time when it emerged, yet it is considered to be wasteful for the present time. Some experts are of the opinion that this system of economy is very harmful as it destroys the forest cover and lowers the fertility of the soil. There has been large scale deforestation resulting in denudation of hill tops and slopes. Removal of top soil leads to loss in fertility which cannot be easily restored or replenished. This leads to low productivity and subsequent pressure on land. Further, since the hill tops are the sources of water, deforestation of hill tops lead to elimination of the sources of water.

The present investigation was intended to study the perception of the jhumias relating to environmental impact of jhuming. According to Cambridge Advance Learners Dictionary (2005), perception is an awareness of things through the physical senses especially sight. It is the belief or opinion often held by many people and based on appearance.

To study the perception of the jhumias relating to environmental impact of jhuming, the following steps were taken into consideration.

COLLECTION AND INITIAL SELECTION OF ITEMS

The items (statement) relating to the environmental impact of jhuming were collected from different sources such as books, literature, Mizo Farmers Union, Cooperative Society, scientist of Agricultural University, expert in the Department of Agriculture, Govt. of Mizoram and the researchers own experience.

Initially 18 items relevant to the study were collected. These were edited as per criteria set up by Edwards (1969). The general guidelines for editing the statements following Edwards are presented below:-

- The statements should be short, simple, clear, direct and easily understandable.
- Each statement should contain only one idea. There should be no insignificant idea or repetition of idea
- Statements that are irrelevant or may be interpreted in more than one way should be avoided.
- The use of double negatives should be avoided

FINAL SELECTION AND SCORING OF ITEMS

The items were pre tested with the jhumias to judge their relevance in field situation. After discussion with expert in the Department of Agriculture, Govt. of Mizoram, Village Council of Mizoram, 11(eleven) items were finally selected for the administration of the respondents (jhumias).

The responses were obtained through nominal level of measurement (Yes/No) which means numbers are assigned to objects or events that can be placed into mutually exclusive and exhaustive category.

Agro-Economic, Socio-Psychological Factors Contributing to Jhuming in Mizoram: The present investigation was aimed to identify some important factors which are responsible for jhum cultivation in Mizoram. The different factors of jhum cultivation are as follows:

- Socio- psychological factors of juming
- Agronomic factors of juming
- Economic factors of juming

Apart from agronomic factors for jhum cultivation there are also some sociological and psychological factors that are contributing for jhuming since time immemorial. Some socio-psychological aspects like inheritance of jhuming from their fore fathers, maintenance of harmonious relationship among the community, involvement of women in jhuming and some important festivals in Mizo community namely **Chapchar-kut, Mimkut** etc have been associated with jhum cultivation and these factors cannot be ignored or obliterated

Collection and Initial Selection of Items

The items relating to the agro- economic, socio-psychological factors contributing to jhuming were collected from different sources, such as books, literature, jhumias, village council members, experts in the Department of Agriculture, Govt. of Mizoram and the researchers own experience. Initially 17(seventeen) items relating to socio-psychological aspect, 11(eleven) items relating to agronomic aspect and 10(ten) items relating to economic aspect were collected. These were edited as per criteria set up by Edwards. The general guidelines for editing the statement have been mentioned earlier.

Final Selection and Scoring of Items

The items were pre tested with the jhumias to judge their relevance in field situation. After discussion with the expert of the Department of Agriculture, Govt. of Mizoram the items (activities) were divided into three categories viz. socio-psychological aspect where 10(ten) items out of 17(seventeen) were finally selected for the administration to the respondents. Under Agronomic aspect 6(six) items were selected out of 11(eleven) items and for economic aspect 6(six) items out of 10(ten) items were selected finally for administration to the respondents (jhumias).

Each item was provided with a two point scale, agree or disagree and the jhumias were asked to indicate their agreement or disagreement in respect of each statement under agronomic, socio-psychological and economic aspect.

Statistical Methods Used

In the present study all the data are nominal and there have been measured by nominal level of measurement which means the numbers are assign to objects or events which can be placed into mutually exclusive and exhaustive categories. The statistical tools frequency and percentage has been used for the present study.

Field Data Collection

Relevant data from the jhumias were collected on the basis of personal Interview method with the help of Interview Schedule. Field data were collected in 2 phases viz.(1) In summer season i.e, May 2007 and in winter season, December 2007. The researchers went to the village Chhingchhip, 80 km away from Aizawl city and stayed there for a number of days.

Responses from 30 jhumias were obtained at village Chhingchhip under Serchhip district. During data collection the researchers visited the houses of the jhumias either in the evening or in the morning as because during day time they used to go to their jhum field. Responses from ten jhumias were obtained from Airfield area adjacent to Aizawl. The data were collected in the end of December 2007 to 1st week of January 2008.

Plate 1: Researchers in the Jhum Field with Jhumia

Plate 2: Researchers Interviewing the Jhumias During Data Collection

RESULTS AND DISCUSSION

The results of the investigation are presented and discussed herein after statistical analysis. These are presented according to specific objectives of the study:-

Major Activities undertaken during Jhum Cultivation and Festival Associated with Jhuming: Shifting cultivation that is known as jhuming in the state of Mizoram and the rest of the North-East India is an agricultural practice evolved as a reflex to certain inherent difficult physiological characteristics of land that renders hoeing or ploughing undesirable on hilly and slopy land. Jhuming is more than an occupation in Mizoram. It is a life style of the mizo people in rural area. It is also an integral part of the socio-cultural life of Mizo's. In the present investigation it was intended to find out the major activities of the jhum cultivation along with the important festivals associated with jhuming in Mizoram. This is presented in Table 2.

The Village Council allots the forest land for cultivation. The individual has no ownership over the land. Cutting of forest was done in the month of November and December. Small trees and bamboos are cut using indigenous implements. And the fallen vegetations are left in the field to dry for one to two months.

Plate 3: Chapchar Kut Festival in Mizoram

Plate 4: Jhum Implements

Table 2
Major Activities Undertaken During Jhum Cultivation and Festival Associated with Jhuming

N= 40

Activities	*Calendar Year*	*Time Required (In Days)*	*Performed by (Male/ Female)*	*Festivals*
Selection of land	October-November	10 days	Male	-
Cutting of forest	November-December	24 days	Male	- Pawlkut
Natural drying	January-February	50- 60 days	-	-
Burning of dried forest	20 February-15 March	1 day	Male	Chapchar kut
Cleaning	March	7 days	Male & Female	-
Sowing	April- June	20- 25 days	Male & Female	-
Weeding	i) May- Aug	30- 50 days	Male & Female	-
	ii) Sept- Oct	121 days		
Construction of watching house(Thlam)	March	7 days	Male & Female	-
Harvesting	October- November	60 days	Male & Female	Mimkut
Threshing/ Winnowing	November	30 days	Male & Female	-
Storing	November- December	30 days	Male & Female	-
Marketing	August- October	100 days	Male & Female	-

Table 3
Perception of Jhumias Relating to Environmental Impact of Jhuming

N = 40

Items	*Response Category*	*Frequency*	*Percentage*
Ecology PerceptionDo you know that-			
Jhum cultivation (due to deforestation) helps to endangered wild animals and birds	Yes	40	100
	No	0	0
Jhum cultivation destroy the flora and fauna	Yes	39	97.5
	No	1	2.5
Jhum cultivation causes in loss of soil fertility	Yes	38	95
	No	2	5
Jhum cultivation reduces the water holding capacity of the soil	Yes	38	95
	No	2	5
Jhum cultivation indirectly causes to increase the temperature in your locality	Yes	38	95
	No	2	5
Jhum cultivation causes in soil erosion	Yes	37	92.5
	No	3	7.5
Jhum cultivation causes destruction of forest	Yes	37	92.5
	No	3	7.5
Jhum cultivation increases the occurrences of drought/ flood	Yes	37	92.5
	No	3	7.5

Contd.

			N= 40
Economy Perception Do you know that:			
Jhum cultivation reduces the yield of crops	Yes	20	50
	No	20	50
Indiscriminate cutting and burning of timber, forest trees, bamboo etc., means loss of money of the Govt	Yes	23	57.5
	No	17	42.5
Jhum cultivation gradually reduces the quality of seed.	Yes	18	45
	No	16	40
	could not reply	6	15

The Village Council declares a suitable day for burning on each of the selected slopes where a consolidated block of plots is located. All jhum lands of a village are burned on a single day. Cleaning is done after burning; they collect the unburned material for re-burning. Jhum shelter (**Thlam**) is constructed on the field where members of the family stay during long periods of work. Sowing is done after burning where different crop seeds like vegetables, paddy, maize, cotton, chillies etc. are sown together. All the activities are performed by both male and female.

The calendar of operations of shifting cultivation controls their social life, festivities and religious observances. Almost all operations are connected with socio-religious functions. There are many dances, songs, folk tales associated with this type of cultivation in the study area. Some of the festivals are **Chapchar kut**, **Mimkut** and **Pawlkut** which are associated with jhuming but after the advent of Christianity most of these festivals disappeared.

Perception of Jhumias Relating to Environmental Impact of Jhumming: In this chapter it was intended to study the perception of jhumias relating to environmental impact of jhuming. For this purpose 11 items or statements relating to environmental impact of jhuming were presented to the respondents in order to ascertain whether the jhumias are well aware of the adverse effects of jhuming. The perception includes both ecology and economy oriented perception and the results have been presented in Table3.

ECOLOGICAL PERCEPTION

The study reveals that the jhumias are well aware of the harmful ecological impact of jhuming. Most of the jhumias agreed with all these items relating to harmful ecological aspects of jhuming. When forest areas were large and the population was small, the practice of shifting cultivation created no adverse effects on forest and the environment and worked in perfect harmony with nature. But with the increase of population in the last centuries and reduced forest area shortened the cultivation cycle, which has adversely affected forests and the environment. Shifting cultivation causes large-scale damage to the forests and has resulted in deforestation and denudation of hill slopes.

Shifting cultivation reduces the diversity of species in the environment. Several species of trees have already been disappeared due to continuous cutting and burning. Birds and animals are more difficult to sight and sing today than was the case several decades ago. The jhum is also liable to soil erosion caused by the direct impact of raindrops and are cited as causes of flood in the plain areas. Burning and high temperatures reduces the organic matter and leads to rapid mineralization and volatilization of inorganic nutrients.

ECONOMICAL PERCEPTION

The jhumia in the study area also perceived that jhuming also causes loss of property and money for the Government of Mizoram. The production of agricultural crops under shifting cultivation areas is usually low. Their resistance to modern inputs and their reluctance to produce for the market labels them as primitive farmers. The system of shifting cultivation provides no opportunity for infrastructural development which could be helpful in increasing agricultural production and providing basic amenities, such as public health, roads, education, communication, etc. since there is no permanency of settlements and agriculture. Valuable trees are gradually replaced by useless shrubs and more resistant tree species. Already trees of larger size are almost absent. Cutting and burning of such valuable timber species is a national waste.

Agro-Economic, Socio-Psychological Factors Contributing to Jhuming in Mizoram: In the previous discussions it was found that jhumias in study area are well aware of the harmful consequences of jhuming on ecology and environment. Still they are practicing jhum generation after generation. The present investigation was aimed to identify the important factors which are contributing the jhum cultivation in the state, Mizoram. The important factors of jhuming have been identified as follows:

- Socio-psychological factors of jhuming
- Agronomic factors of jhuming
- Economic factors of jhuming

The findings have been presented in Table 4.

SOCIO-PSYCHOLOGICAL FACTORS

Community Integration

Jhuming has been equated to the way of life of the jhumias because it was considered to be so important in their lives that all other activities of the group as well as their values, attitude and beliefs were supposed to revolve around it. It was claimed that their society, polity and culture were all based on this form of agricultural practices.

From Table 4, it is found that 85 percent jhumias agreed with the statement that jhuming can help to maintain a harmonious relationship among the community. The community life of the mizo's (jhumias) is deeply embedded in agricultural activity which invites the whole community to share both pleasure and pain. The community life is comprehensive and free from any rank or status consciousness. They participate in all social or religions functions without any consideration of social hierarchy.

The community festivals associated with jhuming have promoted community feeling and helped in influencing the attitude of the jhumias. Every festival is accompanied with dance and music which is the symbol of their love and fellow feeling. Among the community festivals called **Kut** in mizo. **Pawlkut, chapchar kut** and **mimkut** are most important. These are celebrated on specific occasions of the agricultural cycle. **So community integration is an important aspect of jhum cultivation.**

Inheritance of Jhum

Jhuming is a socially learned behavior which affects social organizations, and on the higher level upon the organization of the entire community and subsequently the populations.

Table 4
Important Factors of Jhuming in Mizoram

N= 40

A. Socio-Psychological Factors of Jhuming			
Items/ Statements	*Response Category*	*Frequency*	*Percentage*
Community Integration			
I practice jhum because jhum can help to maintain a harmonious relationship among the communityAgreeDisagree	Agree	34	85
	Disagree	6	15
I practice jhum because our community is habituated with jhuming	Agree	31	77.5
I practice jhum because I want to save my identity from the non- jhumias	Disagree	9	22.5
I practice jhum because some important festivals in our community viz., (chapchar kut, mimkut etc.) are performed with jhuming	Agree	26	65
	Disagree	14	35
If I do not practice jhum I may be isolated or detached from my community	Agree	23	575
	Disagree	17	425
Inheritance of Jhum			
I practice jhum because I have learnt it since childhood	Agree	34	85
	Disagree	6	15
I practice jhum because my father/ forefather use to practice it	Agree	33	82.5
	Disagree	7	17.5
I practice jhum because our women are also efficient in jhum agricultural operation	Agree	31	77.5
	Disagree	9	22.5

Contd.

Tlawmngaihna			
I practice jhum because I get mental satisfaction through jhuming	Agree Disagree	35 5	87.5 12.5
I practice jhum for promoting the spirit of selfness service to needy person (Tlawmngaihna)	Agree Disagree	32 8	80 20

N= 40

B. Agronomic Factors of Jhuming

Items/ Statements	*Response Category*	*Frequency*	*Percentage*
Mixed Cropping and Food Habits			
I practice jhum because from jhum I can get variety of crops which cannot be raised by settled cultivation/terrain cultivation	Agree Disagree	40 0	100 0
I practice jhum due to non- availability of irrigation water	Agree Disagree	39 1	97.5 2.5
I practice jhum because the taste and flavour of jhum rice is better than other crop	Agree Disagree	28 12	70 30
I cultivate jhum because burning of forest helps in control of pest and diseases	Agree Disagree	14 26	35 65
Topography			
I practice jhum because limited flat land is available	Agree Disagree	30 10	75 25
I practice jhum because enough jhum land is available in Mizoram	Agree Disagree	22 18	55 45

Contd.

C. Economic Factors of jhuming

Items	*Response Category*	*Frequency*	*Percentage*
I practice jhum because by jhumming I can store foodgrains which are under my control	Agree	40	100
	Disagree	0	0
I practice jhum because other wage income is uncertain and only jhum can give me food security	Agree	39	97.5
	Disagree	1	2.5
I practice jhum because mixed cropping in jhum helps to increase food production	Agree	38	95
	Disagree	2	5
Low Cost Practice			
I practice jhum because jhum is performed by my family members	Agree	39	97.5
	Disagree	1	2.5
I practice jhum because agricultural inputs viz., chemical fertilizers, pesticides are not required which are costly inputs	Agree	38	95
	Disagree	2	5
I practice jhum because jhum cultivation requires only indigenous agricultural implements	Agree	35	87.5
	Disagree	5	12.5

It was found that about 85 percent of the jhumias agreed that they practice jhum because they have learnt it since childhood. About 82 percent respondents agreed with the statement that they practice jhum because their father/ forefather used to practice it.

Women labour force can be fruitfully utilized, if shifting cultivation were to be practiced side by side with settled agriculture. Jhum operations can be performed by women also. Sowing, weeding and harvesting are done by both men and women, assisted by children. About 77 percent of the jhumias agreed with this statement that women are also efficient in jhum agricultural operation.

Tlawmngaihna

In Mizoram the term **tlawmngaihna** means helping a needy person who is unable to perform his job due to sickness, or any other reason. According to the principles of tlawmngaihna, it is a well- established convention for people, to assist families lacking male members in the task of jhuming. Opportunities for such service were frequently found in the event of sickness, death or other misfortune.

Eighty seven percent of the jhumias responded that they get mental satisfaction from shifting cultivation and it is more of a convenience and compulsion rather than a choice to fulfill the basic needs of food. The stock of grain by jhuming which is under the control of the farmer can provide one type of psychological security.

Their code of morals and good form '**Tlawmngaihna**' (prescribing courtesy, consideration, selflessness, courage, and industry) was manifest in a high degree of mutual support and cooperation. According to this principle, the group of people jhuming on a particular slope carried out a number of activities jointly such as construction of jhum road, clearing vegetation to a height of about five feet. A group of ceremony was performed halfway through operation and a feast was held on completion.

AGRONOMIC FACTORS

Apart from socio- psychological factors of jhum cultivation there are also other factors for which the Mizo people are practicing jhum cultivation generation after generation. The agronomic factors such as advantages of mixed cropping in the jhum field and topography also play an important role for continuance of jhum cultivation in the North- East States.

Mixed Cropping and Food Habits

The main interest of the cultivators of Mizoram is to produce almost everything that he needs. Therefore he grows not only a variety of cereals but also vegetables, oilseeds, fruits, spices, cotton etc. The requirements of timber and fuel are easily met and therefore, no importance is usually attached to trees.

It was found that most of the shifting cultivation plots were being used for growing vegetables, fruits and other cash crops. For jhum cultivation the forest in the hill slope is cleared and burnt. The land is then roughly prepared with crude implements such as wooden digging stick and hoe and the crops are raised in mixed types. These include paddy, maize, and vegetables of various kinds. Only a few crops are grown as single crop by the tribal people.

Climatic factors such as the timing and quantum of rainfall, and the incidence of storms, site factors like aspect, attitude, and slope, decisions on crops, varieties, mixtures and placement, and the application of human effort and skills all add up to influence the productivity of a jhum.

In settled/ terrain cultivation, irrigation is not available, so only a single crop can be grown. Ninety seven percent of the jhumias responded that they practice jhum due to non-availability of irrigation water. They also responded that settled cultivation incurred high costs which require not only high investment but also high recurring expenses. Thus, the mixed cropping which is the characteristic feature of shifting cultivation regime once considered primitive is now being propped up as a way of increased food production in Mizoram.

Seventy percent of the jhumias agreed with the statement that the taste of the flavour of jhum rice is better than other crop; it is purchased by non-jhuming families who can afford to do so. There are numerous indigenous varieties of each crop jhumias favoured. In maize, there is '**sticky mimban**' and '**non sticky mimpui**' varieties which are locally grown. In chillies, varieties like large '**hmarchapui**' the bird eye **hmarchate**; and in paddy 23 varieties are grown eg., **Buhbial** (early medium duration, roundish grain), **Buhpui** etc.

Thirty five percent of the jhumias agreed with the statement that burning of forest helps in control of pest and diseases. Burning must take place at a stage when the felled bamboos or trees are completely dried so that they burn well. The role of fire and mixed cropping together make jhuming one of the few surviving methods of organic farming. **This has enabled jhumias to reach the brink of twenty first century without feeling the need for chemical fertilizer, weedicides, pesticides or insecticides.**

Topography

Shifting cultivation occurs generally in areas where extensive hilly habitat with steep slopes and no flat areas or valleys, plenty of forest around the hills, low population density, humid climate and with little development of communication facilities are available.

Though shifting cultivation has long been viewed as a problem in the absence of any workable alternative people continued 'jhuming' on the slopes much as they have been doing for generations. Seventy five percent of jhumias agreed with the statement that they practice jhum because limited flat land is available. So they prepare proper seed beds in steep slopes where any disturbance of the surface by hoeing and ploughing will result in washing away the fertile top soil.

Each year the Village Council select consolidated blocks of land to be jhumed, which may be located on one or more slopes. The jhuming regulations laid down the process by which the council was to distribute plots among the village families. It is not always that the same household would cultivate the same plot of land. Very frequently individual household do not have absolute ownership right over the lands cultivated by them. They can hold the land so long as they make effective use of the same. As soon as they stop their operations, their right ceases. Fifty five percent respondents agreed with the statement that due to long fallow period, the jhum lands are far from the village. The jhum lands are being increased from 1 tin area to 5 tin areas in the present situation(1 tin Area= 3 Bighas).

By and large the permanent fields (homestead, irrigated fields, orchards etc.) are owned individually while the bulk of the land under shifting cultivation is communally owned. There are two distinct sections of population in each village. One who claim ownership on large chunks of land and therefore, own some permanent fields besides claiming rights over the jhum land. The second category made of subsequent settlers have access to land for only shifting cultivation whatever is allotted by the village council. In such cases also only right of use is enjoyed by members undisturbed and continuously but they can not sell the land at their will though it is heritable.

An exceptional feature of shifting cultivation in Mizoram, which has survived generations of cultivators, is the freedom of each family to jhum as much land as it wants. This can only be feasible in a situation where land is perceived as plentiful.

ECONOMIC FACTORS

The present finding also reveals that not only socio-psychological and agronomic factors are responsible for jhuming, the economic condition of the Mizo people in particular and the people of North- East in general are also responsible for jhum cultivation in the region. The two parameters food security and low cost practice have been identified which are discussed below:-

Food Security

According to FAO (2002), food security implies, "a situation that exists when all people, at all times, have physical, social and economic access to dietary needs and food preferences for an active and healthy life".

According to United Nations, a household secure when it has access to food need for a healthy life for all its members (adequate in terms of quality, safety and culturally acceptable) and when it is not at undue risk of losing such access. Food security should have three specific aims: namely, ensuring production of adequate food supplies; maximizing stability in the flow of supplies; and securing access to available supplies on the part of those who need them.

A perusal of table 4 reveals that most of the jhumias agreed with the statement that they are used to practice jhum because by jhuming they can store food grains which are under their control. The stock of grain a jhumias maintain provides him a psychological security. Ninety eight percent respondents agreed with the statement that other wage income is uncertain and only jhum can give them food security. Experiences show that money income cannot be fully trusted for physical subsistence in the far flung mountain areas. Therefore the jhumias is driven to shifting cultivation so that he may replenish his stock of food grains which is visible, within his reach and under his control. He is therefore psychologically not prepared to opt for an uncertain wage income however attractive it may be in lieu of shifting cultivation.

Combination of different crops not only helps in optimizing the use of natural processes but it also contributes in a significant way to soil and water conservation and enrichment and also helps in pest and disease control. The multiple choice principle also helps in the management of agriculture because harvesting of crops is not one time operation which is generally followed in settled cultivation. The choice of crops is so considered that the gestation period of the crops is any where between two and eight months. Thus, harvesting of products under shifting cultivation is continued for a longer period of the year and it generally starts from July to January which is not available in settled cultivation system.

The wide stretch of sowing and harvesting season and the variety of crops grown are an insurance against the uncertainties of rain both in terms of quantity and timing. Thus, the mixed cropping which is the characteristic feature of shifting cultivation regime once considered primitive is now being propped up as a way of increased food production.

Low Cost Practice

The labour requirement for sowing, rearing and harvesting for the variety of crops is evenly spread over a long period of time and not peaked seasonally. It helps in intensive use of manpower in the sparsely populated mountain areas. The labour is manual and tools are of indigenous agricultural implements.

Land being abundant for jhum cultivation in Mizoram, the jhumias having more working hands in command can produce more crops. Under the jhum economy the size of a family farm is directly related to the number of working members in a family.

Jhum operations like clearing of the jungles, burning, and construction of jhum hut **(thlam)** are performed by man. Men, women as well as children performed in various operation like sowing, weeding, harvesting and marketing.

The act of burning has many benefits other than building up soil fertility. The destruction of weeds and improvement of tilth necessary for a proper seed bed are achieved with the help of fire which jhuming alone made to improve the fertility of the jhum land. Ninety five percent of the jhumias do not use agricultural inputs viz., chemical fertilizers, pesticides which are costly in nature.

Plate 5: Thlam (Jhum Shelter) Constructed by the Jhumia

The desire to invest in agriculture is greatly hampered due to lack of opportunities. The jhumias generally do not prefer high yielding varieties of seeds for different reasons. They are afraid of losing soil fertility and production in the second cropping if they use high yielding varieties (HYV's), Use of indigenous seeds and implements is, therefore, a measure of self reliance and food security in a non-intensive system of land use in the interior hill areas. The application of chemical fertilizers in hilly slopes is considered useless as these will be washed away with heavy rain.

CONCLUSION AND RECOMMENDATIONS

The whole issue of "sustainable development" of jhum-centered land- use system has to be viewed from a variety of different perspectives viz. population pressure on land, social organization and function as part of a given cultural landscape, conservation and management of biodiversity linked natural resources, and land degradation issues.

Since jhum is a way of social life in Mizoram where many factors like food security by way of mixed cropping practices, taste and flavour of the jhum food, culture and festivals associated with jhuming, community integration and inheritance of jhuming from forefathers and even the topography of the North-East in general and Mizoram in particular— all have been intermingled with jhuming over the last few centuries which is very difficult to dissociate these from the Mizo community.

Whereas the nature and extent of cultivation of the village concerned would surely persist in jhuming, cultivation of low-volume high- value crops in the jhum lands rather than cereals (paddy) may be encouraged as an immediate measure, to start with keeping the topography and landscape of the village in view, plantation of horticulture crops may be taken up as long-term measure which has caught the imagination of a great majority of jhumias. As the system is multidisciplinary in nature, separate education and training for development, management and extension of agro forestry system at different levels are required. Whilst access to markets is difficult for a large number of communities in view of the lack of infrastructure, alternative solutions to the remoteness of communities should be considered.

Processing and small manufacturing facilities such as cottage industries, notably, cane- works may also be a viable proposition. There is an abundant reserve of this natural resource in the nearby forests for the cane- works industry which remains to be tapped and exploited fully. To start with, provisions may be made for financial assistance and incentives for undertaking such ventures. Promoting value addition through processing of farm and homestead products particularly, fruits, vegetables, ginger, tea etc. through the indigenous entrepreneurs, in order to increase returns and to retain wealth within the region. Inputs such as fertilizers, seeds and plant protection chemicals and equipment etc. may be made available within the easy reach of the farmers to encourage cultivation of vegetables on commercial scale.

Jhumia's Co-operative Society can play a pivotal role in accelerating the tempo of rehabilitation of the jhum land. The Co- operative Society will create awareness among the farmers and motivate them to implement rehabilitation programmes of jhum land. They should arrange timely disbursement of short, medium and long term credit. The jhumias will get technical guidance from the experts through the Society. Processing and marketing of the produce of the members by the Society will also facilitate the timely recovery of loans and hence the problem of overdues will be automatically solved. Thus, it is apparent that Co-operative Society can solve the problems of the jhumias and help in improving the overall quality of life of jhum cultivation, leading to the formation of egalitarian social order.

RECOMMENDATIONS

In order to improve the socio-economic condition of the jhumias in the study area, the following recommendations are made which may be examined for adoption by the concerned leaders and planners of Village Councils and by the

Department of Agriculture and Horticulture, Govt. of Mizoram.

Jhuming with Plantation Crops and Orchards

Since jhuming is a way of life and ensures **food security** by way of mixed cropping for the Mizo people, total replacement of jhuming in Mizoram is undesirable and impossible also.

In order to enhance their economic condition, a portion of the jhum field allotted by the Village Council to the jhumia may be utilized for orchards or plantation crops which is a profitable enterprise and can harvest good return. Appropriate rules and regulation may be framed up by the Village Councils who has the responsibility to distribute the jhum land and provision of high yielding varieties (HYV) of planting materials of orchards should be ensured for the jhumias by the Department of Agriculture and Horticulture, Govt. of Mizoram.

Organic Jhum Farming

It is evident from the study that continuous jhuming with reducing the jhum cycle accelerates the environment degradation and extinction of flora and fauna to a great extent.

In each and every household of Mizoram, particularly among the jhumia family, rearing of poultry and piggery is a common practice. Although the excreta of the animals are used in the kitchen garden in a limited scale, there is an immense scope of application of these animal excreta in the jhum field as an organic manure which not only enhance the production and productivity of crops but also improve the soil health.

The Department of Horticulture and the representatives of Village Council should take necessary steps for changing the knowledge and arousing the interest regarding the application of organic manure through the use of mass media.

Value Addition and Marketing Facilities of Horticultural Crops

Horticultural crops like ginger, passion fruits, banana, lemon, pineapple etc. are abundantly growimg in Mizoram. A food processing unit (**MIFCO, food processing and training center**) near Chhingchhip has been established and different vegetables and fruits are processed in this plant. There is an immense scope of marketing facilities of this bottled juice specially the passion fruits, bamboo shoots pickles etc, in other states in India.

Development of Cottage Industries

The forest areas of Mizoram are blessed with plenty of Bamboos and trees, herbs and shrubs. Different cottage industries, notably, cane- works may also be a proposition, provided that marketing facilities are given top priority by the State Govt., there is abundant reserves of this natural resources in the nearby forest which remains to be tapped and exploited fully.

REFERENCES

Barkakoti, S. (1990), 'Alternatives Plan for Jhum Area Development' in D. N. Majumdar (ed.), shifting cultivation in NE India, Om Sons Publications, New Delhi.

Basic Statistics of NER (2002), Govt. of India, North Eastern Secretariat, Shillong p. 42.

Edwards A.L. (1969), Techniques of Attitude Scale Construction, Vakils, Feffer and Simonds Pvt. Ltd. Mumbai

Goswami (1968), Shifting Cultivation in the Hills of North- East India. *Indian farming* XXI (4) pp. 10-13.

Nunthara, C. (1981), Social Dimension of Rural Development in Mizoram. North-Eastern Hill Regions of India-Problems and Prospects of Development, Agricole Publishing Academy, New Delhi pp. 105-111.

Ray, G.L. and Mondal Sagar (2004), Research Methods in Social Sciences and Extension Education: Second Edition, Kalyani Publishers Ludhiana.

Roy Burman, B.K. and Sharma, B.D. (1970), Quoted from Tripathy, R.N. Agricultural Problems in Tribal Areas. Perspective on Tribal Development and Administration, National Institute of Community Development, Hyderabad.

Saha, N. (1973), Economics of Shifting Cultivation in North- East India. Agro- Economic Research Centre, Jorhat.

Saha, N. (1976), Levels of Production and Income under Shifting Cultivation in North-East India. Proceedings of the Seminar on Shifting Cultivation in North-East India. North-East India Council for Social Science Research, Shillong.

Statistical Handbook of Mizoram (2006), Mizoram at a Glance: (2006), Directorate of Economics and Statistics Government of Mizoram.

Upa Haukhama (2008), Chhingchhip Khaw Chanchin, Mizoram Publication Board, Aizawl.

4 Scientific and Traditional Knowledge: The Agenda for 'Mutual Validation'

Debabrata Basu and Rupak Goswami

Writing on such an issue of historically uncompromised dichotomy often renders the narration drifted away from the core. Dominant paradigm giving rise to such dichotomy stands in the way of reconciliation (often raising questions at the epistemological level) and until we reach the conclusion we use terms like 'our/their knowledge'. That is why we mention it at the outset; more to give hint to the historical baggage of the issue rather than taking it for granted.

When the word 'knowledge' is used, neither the user uses it with sufficient technical meaning, nor is it taken with enough technicality by its receiver. However, during the apprehension of traditional/indigenous knowledge (TK/IK) the technicality of the word becomes central[1]. Our present article starts from this point and compares the system of knowledge production from two extreme points of a continuum–scientific and traditional. In doing so, the article stands at the centre of a long standing discourse and tries to address it with definite directionality. We move from the 'generation' aspect to the 'validation' concern of knowledge production and then address the issues related to the ongoing efforts of 'documentation' and 'dissemination' of such knowledge. While dealing with the uniqueness, strength and limitations of knowledge, beyond the continuation of the comparison, the importance of agricultural sciences as the ambit of such reconciliation gets highlighted with the underlying rationale. The policy implications with the latent fear of its romanticisation are dealt with briefly. We then take a distinct turn towards the discourse of 'knowledge' and 'power', a step ahead to understand knowledge system with more critical and radical vision.

SCIENTIFIC AND TRADITIONAL KNOWLEDGE: BASIC DISTINCTIONS REVISITED

In fact the system of scientific production of knowledge (methodologies) has itself gone through certain paradigmatic transformations. Still some of these paradigms go parallel to or counter each other; even paradigmatic overlapping is not unnatural to notice. However, to be scientific, at the first place, the system of **knowledge production** has to resort to systematic investigation. Second, and perhaps the most important aspect of such knowledge is the **validation** it requires. It does not restrict itself within the objective drive for approximating truth and is associated with the politics of (or dilemma of Kuhnian 'paradigm') recognition and acceptance. Needless to say, these two are two facets of a single truth. This is the crux of the issue where the present discourse gets the theoretical as well as actionable base and asks for critical understanding.

Scientific knowledge, rather institutionally produced knowledge, as its archetypal representative, envisages 'ideas' like–generalisability, value freedom/value neutrality, testability and power of prediction. In course of comparing the two systems of knowledge production the above mentioned 'ideas' act as critical checks and need adequate attention. For sake of a theoretical understanding, we start from the comparison of the (origin of) traditional and scientific knowledge production system with special reference to the above stated 'ideas'.

Without entangling ourselves into any epistemological dilemma, we can observe that any scientific study/research starts either from observation of fact or from a theory. It then proceeds to contribute to theory construction or test the tenability of the theory in question, respectively. For convenience we can conceptualise it as a **cycle of inductive and deductive methods**. Then, what happens to the traditional knowledge production system as far as such inductive-deductive process of enquiry is concerned? It is obvious that most of the cases here start with observing real life situations or solving day-to-day problems. In academic scientific research, the criteria for selecting a problem and defining it often streams out of the interest of the researcher, although researching to accomplish organisational objectives is also common. In case of IK production system, problems are real situations which are alien, and for which there is no ready response available by instinct or by previous experience; although farmers conducting research in real life situations is common and has received due attention much later[2]. In this sense, both these systems share an empirical basis. But if one thinks that the production of TK is only inductive in nature, he would probably undermine common people's cognitive potential/deductive logic. Just like the researcher deduces lower order propositions (hypothesis) from the theory, the producer of the TK also bear some alternative explanations/ solutions in mind. They then go for the elimination process based on their common sense and years of experience[3]. Had they not had such hypotheses in mind, the astonishingly rich pool of rational knowledge at their disposal would not have been possible with blind trial-and error method[4].

At one point, of course, the scientific method of knowledge production will stand distinctly away–the positivistic approach it often banks on. The belief of an objectively operating/lying reality often takes the form of supernatural/god in traditional knowledge system (which is never derogative in sense, but reflects the holistic nature of the indigenous cosmology). However, as far as the **'truth' concern** is concerned-first of all-TK, rather the user of TK, never claims itself to be absolutely true; they are rather interested in judging whether the produced knowledge is useful or not, and that too within a given context. This will be dealt with at length while we will be discussing the validity and power of prediction of knowledge.

One of the major criteria of being a scientific knowledge is that it has to be **capable of being tested**. Whether one goes with verificationist stand or Popperian view of falsifiability, TK do not, in any way, detours this challenge of testability. Unlike the so-called scientific theories it is not ritualistic regarding the testing of propositions. On the contrary, the producer of TK with his every new observation tests his previous standing, supports it or changes it (adapt/readapt) if required. Every new situation is a scope of TK's testing. In fact, the domestication and adaptation of many plants and animals is the result of testing and retesting of numerous concepts and technologies.

Let now have a look into the issue of **value freedom** of knowledge production. The production of scientific knowledge often believes in value neutrality/value freedom (of course if the research does not have an intrinsic paradigmatic outlook of not having such stance); the researcher remains independent of self reflection and personal subjectivity. The dualism of fact and value is the idea central. In true sense, no question of value freedom arises regarding the TK production (elimination of value is relevant only when the producer of the knowledge believes in an objectively existing truth). TK generally address practical problems and hence are bound to the very social context from where it gets generated. The concern of value freedom, like paradigm-mentored knowledge production system, is not independent and of little importance here. Moreover, the production of scientific knowledge is itself divided over the issue and even the supporter of such stand can hardly claim to select and carry out research on the basis of neutrally determined research problem/agenda.

The **validation** of a newly emerged scientific knowledge does not end in the successful testing of its hypotheses. It rather goes further to get fitted into a particular coherent tradition of scientific research. Though this later part has itself been at the crux of epistemological debate, to be general, one can view the validation aspect as the embodiment of parallel/

conflicting/overlapping dynamics of changing paradigms at the academic level[5]. Much has been said about the scientific element present in the TK and the validation of TK. However, the issue is perhaps more important, functional and direct at the phase of the application of the produced knowledge. The validity of an IK/TK is very much context bound; its validation depends on the user of the knowledge in the society. Whether scientifically justified or not, these knowledge do have validation at the very context where it gets its origin (though many IK/TK have been found to be extremely rational/logical/scientifically justified). When an objective finding of natural science claims its **generalisability** beyond the spatio-temporal context of its origin, in a society it may not be accepted. Whereas, a TK in that society may have significant validity. This acceptance should also be considered as a dimension of validity and argued as a basis of positive discrimination[6], if not an alternative paradigm. Still, speaking strictly, we can not go with the 'anything goes' methodological approach, which in other sense could be thought as an interface of these two types of knowledge production system. It then seems much related with the emancipatory commitment of knowledge rather than the truth concern, though in no sense it is of less importance.

At the time of application of knowledge (**predictability**), the degree of precision is crucial; and undoubtedly, as far as the precision of produced knowledge is concerned, scientific knowledge would have a definite edge over TK. This becomes obvious when the TKS breaks down in the face of environmental crisis. But – forget not - behind this observation flows a counter logic which is often overlooked, if not suppressed politically. Richards (1979) raised the basic question against it. "… if African peasant farmers were capable of managing their environmental resource base and responding to environmental changes in the past why are they increasingly incapable of doing so now?" The break down of the TKS is, in most of the cases, result of outsiders' intervention. The overemphasis of agricultural science and the key role assigned to the 'expert' were the way to establish technocratic hegemony in furtherance of the interests of 'agri-business' or 'state capitalism' in the developmental process. The issue of 'predictability' is thus a subject far from easy resolution.

This far we have compared the traditional and scientific knowledge system from the Western point of view. But, IKS has its own way of knowing. Yunkaporta (2007) mentions eight broad categories of indigenous knowledge in contrast with Western ways of knowing. These are Holistic knowledge, Communal knowledge, Ancestral knowingness, Intellectual biomimicry, Circular logic, Indigenous pluralism, Synergistic knowledge and Deep narrative. However, the details of these indigenous cosmologies are beyond the scope of the present article (see http://aboriginalrights.suite101.com/article.cfm/indigenous_knowledge_systems for details).

Agarwal (2004) observes that the attempt to create two categories of knowledge – indigenous/traditional vs. Western/scientific—ultimately rests on the possibility that a small and finite number of characteristics can define the elements contained within the categories. He shows that the attempt fails on each of the three counts: substantive, methodological and contextual. Agarwal posits that "in examining specific forms of investigation and knowledge creation in different countries and different groups of people, we can allow for the existence of diversity within what is commonly seen as Western or as indigenous. Hence, instead of trying to conflate all non-Western knowledge into a category termed 'indigenous', and all Western knowledge into another category, it may be more sensible to accept differences within these categories and perhaps find similarities across them.

FROM DICHOTOMY TO 'MUTUAL VALIDATION'

One has to be conscious about the fact that much of today's debates related to TK are embedded on a long standing dominant paradigm, which has often been taken for granted. Last few decades has seen a valiant upraise of alternative approaches both at the academic and practical level. But, often the origin of the dichotomy is less targeted than the paradigm itself. TK/IK had/have often been visualised as a negative challenge to the scientific knowledge as far as the epistemology (rather the supporters of modernisation project) is concerned[7]. However, the question should have been coughed in a different term[8]. The pluralistic approach (of multiple and co-existing system of knowledge production) with a truce for the time being is not going to do any good to the system of knowledge production. The question is of approximating the truth without sacrificing the emancipatory power of knowledge.

The TK/IK approaches the truth/reality in a holistic manner with an all pervasive system approach[9]. That is why we would like to emphasise the concept of 'mutual validation'. With the explicit recognition of context boundedness of TK (weak external validity, while TK never strives to achieve so) and scientific knowledge (many of them are true within the research station conditions and tries to impose external validity through blanket recommendations) the essence lies of course in eliciting science from TK and ensuring 'meaningful' validity of scientific knowledge. Formalisation of TK through documentation and sharing with subsequent rationalization by formal science has been thought of as an obvious strategy of validation. This certainly is one facet of our 'mutual validation' agenda. The second one is the incorporation of traditional knowledge (traditional populace) into formal research and development endeavour. Gupta (2007) asks for incentives to grassroot innovation and its wider recognition apart from the networking strategy where formal science will be working together with informal innovators to produce economically viable technologies for world market. We will be addressing some of the above said issues in later part of this article. The issue of power and knowledge will follow in due course.

The researchers have not seen hard evidences to prove or disprove the existence and value of TK (farmers' knowledge in particular). This is partly because farmers seldom record their accomplishment, write papers and attach names and patents to their innovations. The result is that the history of agriculture is written without reference to the main innovators in the long-term process of technological change. The disciplines like anthropology and economics, which could have documented it, have not delved into the matter (Chambers *et al.*, 1989). This is helpful to understand two interrelated issues– documentation and validation of produced knowledge.

DOCUMENTATION AND SHARING

Now we have, perhaps, gained an understanding to appreciate the importance of IT/TK documentation. Unlike scientific knowledge, IK have never been documented, nor have it been disseminated through formal or informal communication channels. As a result, where scientific knowledge has got a definite edge due to its cumulative precision, while TK could not, in most of the cases, transcend its locality. Following lines are extremely helpful to discern the heart of this fact–

> "Research is an institution composed of people who act together and communicate with one another; as such it determines, through the communication of researches, that which can theoretically lay claim to validity." (Habermas, cited in Delanty, 1997: 84)

Since indigenous knowledge is essential to development, it is often suggested that it must be gathered and documented in a coherent and systematic fashion (Brokensha *et al.*, 1980; Warren *et al.*, 1993). As more studies of indigenous knowledge become available, its relevance to development will become self-obvious. Such studies should be archived in national and international centres in the form of databases, the information in which could be systematically classified. The collection and storage of indigenous knowledge should be supplemented with adequate dissemination and exchange among interested parties, using newsletters, journals and other media (Warren *et al.*, 1993).

In fact regional and national IK knowledge resource centers have embarked on systematic recording of IK systems for use in development. Three global centers CIKARD (USA), LEAD (The Netherlands), and CIRAN (The Netherlands) facilitate the establishment of these centers. The functions of national IK systems resource centers include: a) providing a national data management function where published and unpublished information on IK are systematically documented for use by development practitioners; b) designing training materials on the methodologies for recording IK systems for use in national training institutes and universities; c) establishing a link between the citizens of a country who are the originators of IK and the development community.

Once IK systems are systematically recorded, the next step is to compare and contrast them with comparable global knowledge systems. Such a process strengthens the capacities of regional and national agricultural research and extension organizations by generating sustainable agricultural technological options rather than standard technical packages of practices. The incorporation of IK systems into agricultural development consists of three essential components–conducting participatory on-station agricultural research (research scientists and farmers); secondly, conducting on-farm farmer-oriented research (research scientists, extensionists, and farmers); and, thirdly, validating farmer experiments (farmers and extensionists). The first two components are successive stages of the interactive technology development process, whereas component three is a separate entity (Warren and Rajasekaran. 1993).

THE PROBLEM OF *EX-SITU* CONSERVATION OF IK

Agarwal (1994) pointed out that the prime strategy for conserving indigenous knowledge by *ex situ* conservation, i.e., isolation, documentation and storage in international, regional and national archives is technically the easiest and politically the most convenient strategy, but it is unconsciously yet fatally at odds with the desire to maintain distinctions between scientific and indigenous knowledge.

First, if indigenous knowledge is inherently scattered and local in character, and gains its vitality from being deeply implicated in people's lives, then the attempt to essentialize, isolate, archive and transfer such knowledge can only seem contradictory. If Western science is to be condemned for being non-responsive to local demands, and divorced from people's lives, then centralized storage and management of indigenous knowledge lays itself open to the same criticism.

Second, because of the dynamic nature of indigenous knowledge and its changing character against the background of the changing needs of peoples, the strategy of *ex situ* conservation seems particularly ill-suited to preserving indigenous knowledge. In spite of the inadequacy of such strategies in the context of combating the erosion of biodiversity and save genetic germplasm (Altieri, 1989; Wilson, 1992), the advocacy of the same problematic strategies to preserve knowledge, which is integrally linked with the lives of people and is constantly changing, seems ironic. Moreover, many theorists accept the utility of indigenous knowledge in itself, and most writings first propose the validation of indigenous knowledge by means of scientific criteria (Rajan and Sethuraman, 1993; Richards, 1980). If Western science is the ultimate arbiter of knowledge, then there seems little point in advocating the distinction between scientific and indigenous knowledge.

Agarwal warns *ex situ* preservation of indigenous knowledge is likely to fail–creating only a mausoleum for knowledge; and even if it is successful in unearthing useful information, is likely to benefit the richer, more powerful constituencies–those who have access to international centres of knowledge preservation–thus undermining the major stated objective of conserving such knowledge: to benefit the poor, the oppressed and the disadvantaged.

AGRICULTURAL SCIENCES AND TRADITIONAL KNOWLEDGE

The importance of agricultural sciences as an ideal sphere where TK and scientific knowledge can have a meaningful confluence/conciliation has almost historically been demonstrated[10]. As a discipline, agricultural science gets enriched by judicially drawing from useful research outcomes of theoretical as well as applied natural sciences. Most of the researches in agricultural sciences are experimental in nature and do not go on to construct theories. At the same time, TK/IK associated with agriculture and allied subjects are the result of experimentation of thousands of years and most of them have been selected, maintained and adapted for solving practical problems (like the selection, maintenance and adaptation of plant for higher productivity, pest and disease resistance; plant protection measures; soil management; storage etc.). Hence it is more likely to have so called scientifically justified or refinable TKs in the field of agriculture and allied subjects. This is an endowment of this very discipline which can contribute to, as we have mentioned earlier, the 'mutual validation' of knowledge systems. Moreover, as the research outcomes are meant to be used by the large farming community, the policy makers at the regional, national and international level often takes its account for rational reasons. In fact, the revolutionary zeal regarding people's knowledge of last few decades, both at the academic (the famous rise of participatory research) and practical/functional level, has been more political rather than theoretical in nature. The extension system (agriculture undoubtedly remains central to most of the extension activities), both private and public, operating in between, has, as a response, undergone substantial transformation in its approach by this time. The bottom-up approach of most of today's developmental and research endeavours have created the scope for a promising interface between TK and scientific knowledge.

THE RIGHT TO PARTICIPATE IN AGRICULTURAL RESEARCH

The issue does not, of course, end in the validation and documentation of (agricultural) knowledge[11], but the 'right' to do so. It is now the question of partnership in research[12], facilitating people's research and paying dividend for the research outcome along with its recognition and documentation. Participatory Technology Development is nothing new a concept now and practiced by many NGOs and international donor agencies. On-farm research and farmer's conducting research at the research stations are both widely practiced. Although, the magnitude and degree of such endeavours are not beyond question and mainstreaming has been elusive at the institutional level[13].

At the root of the problem lies the fact that officials–agricultural extension staff, planners, research workers, 'experts' and others–depend on scientific knowledge to legitimise their superior status. They thus have a vested interest in devaluing ITK and in imposing a sense of dependence on the part of their rural clients. This suggests that change may only be brought about through an assault at the level of ideology, and through a reorientation of reward systems (Chambers and Howes, 1979).

They continued to observe that the problem is not just one of stocks of ITK, but of undermining the foundations for indigenous participation in the process of generating new technical knowledge. In principle, there is no reason why the process of increasing dependence of rural people on external knowledge should not be made to operate in reverse–with people gaining confidence and acquiring knowledge as a result of being drawn into the processes of generating technology–but in practice, there is little evidence that this happens[14].

TK ARE UNIQUE: ARE WE READY TO GO BEYOND MERE EXTRACTION?

There is some uniqueness of TK/IK in agriculture and related areas which transcends the approach of comparison and deserves separate mentioning. Unlike any other knowledge system, its potential varies within and across the communities, according not only to the aptitudes of individuals, but also their economic status and function. Previously we mentioned the power of generalisability of knowledge system and observed that TK often do not claim so outside the spatio-temporal context of its origin. But, at the same time, one has to remember that it is much more difficult to generalise about the circumstances conducive for TK production and its potential, although the wealth of case study information is considerably large. Now, many of the scientists' comments about TK/IK concerns rural people's classification system (of plants and soils). Unlike institutional sciences, it is based on functional criteria and reflects the local realities more exhaustively. But, the question to be posited again is that, whether this recognition is functional from the scientist's point of view only (that means, is it only to extract valuable information and does not return proportionate recognition and dividend). Anyhow, in the interest of cost-effective research, IKS should be strengthened so that their capacity to clarify, evaluate, and to some extent predict the outcome of innovations in the local environment can complement science based development of technology. Astonishingly, this point has been overlooked and ignored by the researchers and the state planning[15].

MERGING THE DUAL RATIONALE: NATURAL RESOURCE MANAGEMENT, PEOPLE'S PARTICIPATION AND INCORPORATING IK IN AGRICULTURAL DEVELOPMENT PROGRAMMES

Traditional knowledge, at the end of its users, can claim importance on the basis of at least two merits–first, it is understood, used and altered by the users in a totality and acted upon the locally available resources. Hence, it is a key to the **sustainable maintenance of local resources** as was the case of much of African communities before they came in contact with the Western people. Secondly, from the material point of view (though it is not easy to identify and isolate IK/TK as there might have been some sort of diffused scientific knowledge present already), the issue of patenting people's long preserved knowledge through Intellectual Property Right not only provide dividend to people's/community's knowledge, but also recognise and empower them. This, as a consequence, stimulates and motivates **people's participation** in development activities/endeavours, especially the **natural resource management** projects. Brokensha *et al.* (1980) rightly observe that "to ignore people's knowledge is almost to ensure failure in development.

Theories of development, if we look seriously into, have themselves been formulated and improvised at the academic level, or at places which certainly is not near the soil. The recognition and application of IK in different development projects can do justice and offset the discrepancy. Howes and

Chambers (1979) while pointing out the implications of IK proposed six points for successful integration of IK into the agricultural development programmes.

- *Rural Exposure for Extension and Research Staff:* Extension and research staff could be confronted more directly than is usual with the realities to which their work relates.
- *Checklists:* Checklists could be used to draw attention to factors which might otherwise not be considered in determining research priorities or extension advice. Some examples of factors that may be overlooked with an innovation are implications for women, profitability, effectiveness and efficiency, availability and access to inputs and complementary items, whether a farmer can afford an innovation, risk, social significance and acceptability, lightness for carrying and 'mendability', labour requirements, and effects on diet and on the variety and timeliness of food supply.
- *Local-level Influence on Research Priorities:* To improve the criteria chosen in research and then to see they are acted on. Further, priorities could be set by national research committees which consulted at the local level.
- *A Cafeteria System:* Farmers could be offered different packages and left to decide for themselves which they would adopt.
- *Starting with Indigenous Practice:* A more radical proposal is that research should take existing indigenous practice as its starting point, seeking to refine this in various ways and then to feed results back into the system.
- *Experimental Work in Rural Conditions:* The process might be taken a stage further, perhaps through full-blown experimental work on farmers' fields and with farmers' collaboration. In general, people are more likely to operate and exploit a new technology

successfully if they have themselves taken part in its creation.

OVER-ROMANTICISATION: PROMISES NOT KEPT

In recent times, the danger of IKS being too popular too soon and romanticizing the phenomenon of indigenous belief system has been noticed among the development practitioners[16]. This may even be detrimental to sustainable development. But the allegation of 'romanticism' often tagged with the Indigenous Knowledge System approach is more important than is usually thought to be[17]. This is not only confined to the academics and its trajectory opens to a new way of exploitation, which was previously associated/alleged to be associated with 'modernity-traditionalism' or 'top-down'-'bottom-up' discourse. Intellectually, this new danger related to 'romanticism' is far from letting go with mild derision, but more challenging at this point of time than ever before. Frenzied endeavour with almost a revolutionary zeal, in part of the researchers and practitioners (often drawing on huge funds of international agencies), in the last few decades has not given the producers of indigenous knowledge due recognition (outside papers) and more importantly material dividend that could at least match the magnitude of seriousness shown at the academic level (or epistemological level, if you want to say). This vacancy, ironically, has perhaps filled up with the sort of reactionary efforts both at the academic and political level.

BEYOND 'MUTUAL VALIDATION': KNOWLEDGE AND POWER

The attempts in part of the scientists and practitioners to validate TK is also not beyond question and been objected by scholars. The essence is whether the effort of legitimising TK is in the eyes of the scientific community, by picking out the practical information, or whether to strengthen and preserve its cultural integrity. Juma (1987) feared that IK could be 'delegitimised' in the eyes of local people if isolated from its cultural aspects and forced into the frame work of western epistemology. "Legitimising local knowledge may be important in maintaining a people's sense of values and in opposing cultural threats from outside, but to achieve that necessary recognition by discarding aspects of knowledge which refer, through symbolism, to social values, is self-defeating and contradictory" (Chambers *et al.*,1989). Unfortunately, this has often been the case. That is why we would like to remind the concept of 'mutual validation'.

However, the debate regarding knowledge systems can never be elaborated unless we see it as a social construct, a product of power structure in society and beyond society. In analysing so, we will find most of our previous deliberations at odd with this shifted discourse. This has in fact been the central theme when the scientists moved towards a 'beyond farmer first approach'. The assumption that recognition of and emphasis on the rational nature and sophistication of rural people's knowledge, and that it could be blended with or incorporated into the formal scientific knowledge system are not and/or may not be enough to result in greater attention to the priorities of rural people, and as a consequence, render more effective and lasting result. Scoones and Thompson (1994) while comparing the 'farmer first' with the 'beyond farmer first' viewed knowledge as multi-layered, fragmentary, diffuse knowledge with complex, inequitable, discontinuous interactions between (local and external) actors and networks.

Foucault (1971) observe that the 'criteria of what constitutes knowledge, what is to be excluded and who is designated as qualified to know involves act of power'. Long and Villareal (1994) point out that power differences and struggle over social meaning are central to an understanding of knowledge processes. Power and knowledge are both 'ever-present conditions' and 'continuously reproduced outcomes' of human agency (Roy Bhaskar, 1979). It is, therefore, the 'battlefields of knowledge' (Long and Long, 1992), through a dynamic process of contestation and assimilation that innovation and knowledge creation operate. And it is in this dynamic social setting that research and extension is practised (Scoones and Thompson, 1994). Therefore, thinking of knowledge or TK has to take place within the context of farmer's/local people's interface where power has much to do in creation, validation and dissemination of knowledge[18].

This leads us to the rethinking of knowledge systems rather than comparing and/or finding ways of reconciliation. It raises basic questions against western epistemologies and finds the way of empowerment through negotiation and convergence of 'epistemic communities' (Long and Villareal, 1994).

THE VISION AHEAD

Many people often talk about 'Western science' and most often assume science to be Western. Both these are fallacies, but more especially the latter. While the institutionalization of the pursuit of knowledge is Western in origin, science must be regarded as the potential of the human mind to strive for universal principles in a certain field...This is not a proposition of a political compromise with regard to issues of intellectual property, nor is it a relativist projection of knowledge in the way of a postmodernist tradition. It is a deconstruction of intellectual inequality that was historically constituted in a way that emphasises a common human capacity towards intellectual streamlining in the context of varied socio-cultural expertise.

The objectivity of science is often exaggerated. When it comes to objectivity there is a continuum, the extreme edges of which are quite dangerous to reach...science is the universality of operative principles that we often aspire to reach but can never reach absolutely and completely. Perhaps the lack of objectivity that is often levied hurriedly towards the religious realms of cultures must be reconsidered (Sithole, 2004).

Then where does this discourse lead our 'mutual validation' agenda? The answer probably transcends the epistemic battle and emphasizes agency factor of knowledge production and validation. Speaking honestly, it should be purely between traditional and scientific knowledge and not between the producers of those knowledge (that is, modern and indigenous populace) as is usually mistaken for. It is like a process where modernity and traditionalism tends to merge together in an organic manner and we do not need to write 'our knowledge' and 'their knowledge'. The moment power imbalance of 'core' and 'periphery' (outsider-insider, have-have nots or other analogous dichotomies) dissolves–leading to 'mutual validation' of knowledge producers'–our agenda gets its true meaning. And we end up our article with the following lines (which keeps the truth concern of knowledge along with a space for dialogue, negotiation and emancipation) putting a definite vision ahead:

> The truth which can be formulated by any individual or by mankind at any particular time is always approximate, incomplete and subject to correction. But individuals learn from each other, both from each other's achievements and from each other's mistakes; and the same applies to the succeeding generations of society. Therefore the sum of incomplete, particular, provisional and approximate truths is always approaching nearer to but never reaching the goal of complete comprehensive, final and absolute truth (Cornforth, 1952).

It is thus the 'mutual validation' of knowledge producers that paves the way for 'mutual validation' of different knowledge systems. An old truth that never ages.

REFERENCES

Agarwal, A. (2004), Indigenous and Scientific Knowledge: Some Critical Comments, *IK Monitor* 3(3).

Altieri, M. (1989), Rethinking Crop Genetic Resource Conservation: A View from the South, *Conservation Biology* 3(1):77-79.

Behl, V. (2003), What Went Wrong with 'History from Below', *Economic and Political Weekly*, 38(2).

Biggs, S.D. (1989), Resource-Poor Farmer Participation in Research: A Synthesis of Experiences from Nine Agricultural Research Systems, OFCOR Comparative Study Paper No. 3, ISNAR.

Biggs, S.D. (1989), *Resource-Poor Farmer Participation in Research: A Synthesis of Experiences from Nine National Agricultural Research Systems*, ISNAR, The Hague, Netherlands.

Borlaug, N. (1992), Small-Scale Agriculture in Africa: The Myths and Realities, Feeding the Future. *Newsletter of the Sasakawa Africa Association*, 4:2.

Brokensha, D., Warren, D.M. and Werner, O. (eds) (1980), *Indigenous Knowledge System and Development*, University of America Press: Lanham, New York and London.

Chambers, R. (1983), *Rural Development: Putting the Last First*, Longman Scientific and Technical: England.

Chambers, R. and Howes, M. (1979), Rural Development: Whose Knowledge Counts? *IDS Bulletin*, 10 (2).

Chambers, R., Pacey, A. and Thrupp, L.A. (eds) (1989), *Farmers First: Farmer Innovation and Agricultural Research*, Intermediate Technology Publications: UK.

Cornforth, M. (1952), *Dialectical Materialism, Vol. 1: Materialism and the Dialectical Method*, Lawrence & Wishart Ltd.: London.

Delanty, G. (1997), *Social Science: Beyond Consturctivism and Realism*, Open University Press: Buckingham.

Fals-Borda, O. and Rahman, M.A. (1991), *Action and Knowledge: Breaking the Monopoly with Participatory Action-Research*, Intermediate Technology Publications, The Apex Press: London.

Farrington, J. and Martin, A. (1988), Farmer Participation in Agricultural Research: A Review of Concepts and Practices, Agricultural Administration Unit, Occasional Paper 9, Overseas Development Institute: UK.

Foucault, M. (1980), *Power/Knowledge: Selected Interviews and Other Writings 1972-1977*, Colin Gordon (ed), Harvester: London.

Gupta, A. (2007), How Local Knowledge Can Boost Scientific Studies, http://www.scidev.net/en/agriculture-and-environment/opinions/how-local-knowledge-can-boost-scientific-studies.html.

ICSU and UNESCO (2002), Science, Traditional Knowledge and Sustainable Development, *Series on Science for Sustainable Development*, No. 4.

Juma, C. (1987), Ecological Complexity and Agricultural Innovation: the use of indigenous genetic resources in Bungoma, Kenya, IDS Workshop.

Levi-Strauss, C. (1966), *The Savage Mind*, Weidenfeld and Nicholson: London.

Long, N. and Long, A. (1992), *Battlefields of Knowledge: The Interlocking of Theory and Practice: in Social Research and Development*. London: Routledge.

Long, N. and Villareal, M. (1994), The Interweaving of Knowledge and Power in Development Interfaces, In: Scoones, I. and Thompson, J., (eds), *Beyond Farmer First: Rural People's Knowledge, Agricultural Research and Extension Practice*, Intermediate Technology Publications: London.

Nakashima, D. and Roué, M. (2002), Indigenous Knowledge, Peoples and Sustainable Practice, In: Timmerman, P. (Ed.). *Encyclopedia of Global Environmental Change*, John Wiley & Sons: Chichester.

Rajan, S. and Sethuraman, M. (1993), Indigenous Folk Practices Among Indigenous Irulas, *Indigenous Knowledge Development Monitor* 1(3):19-20.

Richards, P. (1979), Community Environment Knowledge in African Rural Development, *IDS Bulletin*, 10 (2):28-36.

Richards, P. (1980), Community Environmental Knowledge in African Rural Development, In: Brokensha, D., Warren, D.M. and Werner, O. (eds) *Indigenous knowledge systems and development*, University Press of America: Lanham. pp. 183-95.

Rogers, E.M. and Shoemaker, F.F. (1971), *Communication of Innovations*. The Free Press: New York.

Scoones, I. and Thompson, J. (eds) (1994), *Beyond Farmer First: Rural People's Knowledge, Agricultural Research and Extension Practice*. Intermediate Technology Publications: UK.

Sithole, M.P. (2004), Science Versus Indigenous Knowledge: A Conceptual Accident, Ingede: *Journal of African Scholarship*, 1(1): 1-5.

Warren, D.M., and Rajasekaran, B. (1993), Putting Local Knowledge to Good Use. *International Agricultural Development* 13(4):8-10.

Warren, D.M., Liebenstein, G.W. Von and Slikkerveer, L. (1993), Networking for Indigenous Knowledge, *Indigenous Knowledge and Development Monitor* 1(1):2-4.

Wilson, E.O. (1992), *The Diversity of Life*. W.W. Norton: New York.

Yunkaporta, T. (2007), Indigenous Knowledge Systems: Comparing Aboriginal and Western Ways of Knowing. http://aboriginal rights.suite101.com/article.cfm/indigenous_knowledge_ sys tems.

NOTES

1. There has been use of several closely related terms (people's science, ethnoscience, local knowledge, rural people's knowledge) which have mostly been interchangeably used rather than for discriminatory purposes. However, there are problems with all these terms (Chambers, 1983). Nakashima and Roué (2002) find shortcomings in all these terms. The terms 'traditional knowledge' and 'traditional ecological knowledge' (TEK), for example, may be misleading as they underscore knowledge accumulation and transmission through past generations, but obscure their dynamism and capacity to adapt and change. Another widely used term, 'indigenous knowledge' (IK), emphasizes attachment to place and establishes a link with indigenous peoples. For some, however, this connection is problematic because it narrows the term's application and excludes certain populations who may not be officially recognized as 'indigenous people by their respective governments, but who never the less possess sophisticated sets of knowledge about their natural environments. In contrast, terms such as 'local knowledge' are easily applied to a variety of contexts, but suffer from a lack of specificity. Other terms that are encountered in the literature include 'indigenous science', 'farmers' knowledge', 'fishers' knowledge' and 'folk knowledge'.
2. Booth, as mentioned by Chambers (1983), gets the pulse of the issue succinctly: "... a vast majority of research workers prefer to do research about a problem rather than research to solve a problem. Thus biological scientists keep busy, and happy, breeding new varieties, developing disease control system, or new storage designs..."
3. As the scientific methods are more structured and predetermined the serendipity/chance factor will perhaps be more prominent in the sphere of TK production system; but it is only a relative concept and should not be denominated in any sense.
4. Levi-Strauss (1966) argued forcefully against such a distinction on the grounds that human societies could not, for example, possibly have acquired the skills to make water- light pots without a genuinely scientific attitude and a desire for knowledge for its own sake. ITK, like scientific knowledge should, therefore, be regarded in the first instance as something which became possible as a result of a more general intellectual process of creating order out of disorder, and not simply as a response to 'practical' human needs such as sustenance and health. Chambers (1983) observes that those who have to survive in extreme conditions cannot afford inaccurate observations or misleading inferences. For other rural people in less extreme conditions, and more so for those with secure or affluent livelihoods, there is more leeway and their knowledge may be correspondingly less sharp and exact.
5. "Systems of knowledge are many. Among these, modern science is only one, though the most powerful and universal. Rural people's knowledge is...differing...in its modes of experimenting and learning...These differences are reflected in and reinforce power and weakness. Scientific

establishments and local elites...link together and monopolise some types of knowledge...knowledge (is not) just a stock, but a process...the questions (however) are how those who are variously poor, weak, vulnerable, female and excluded can be strengthened in their own observations, experiments and analysis to generate and enhance their own knowledge..."[parenthesis added] (Robert Chambers forwarding *Beyond Farmer First: Rural people's knowledge, agricultural research and extension practice*).

6. "... (P)ositive biases may be no bad thing. The colonising force of outsiders' knowledge is programmed to override and burry other paradigms and to impose its own. It needs to be offset by countervailing power. To balance it not only requires an independent and open mind; it also requires positive discrimination." (Chambers, 1983)
7. Here we would remind the observation of Everett M. Rogers (1971) while lamenting about the detraction against his **diffusion theory** and defending his stance by making 'modern' and 'traditional' norms explicit only to provide a framework of analysis. We quote him in a selective but dialectic manner - "These two kinds of norms are ideal types, conceptualisations based on observations of reality and designed to facilitate comparisons...(it has been) developed purely for methodological reasons, ideal types provide a framework for analysis...Our conception of traditional and modern norms is a synthesis..." [parenthesis added]
8. Juma (1987) demonstratively deals with this issue. He asks not to employ a reductionist methodology and treat TK (genetic resources) separately from their socio-ecological concept. While speaking about plant breeding conducted by the farmers he asserts that this research can not be regarded simply as a case of farmers doing basic scientific research. Nor is it sufficient to regard local knowledge of botany and ecology as 'technical' knowledge only, which implies that it is based on a western epistemology. Rather it is based on a distinctive epistemology which is unique to these popular cultures.
9. Remind Engels, although in a slightly different context: "(T)ruth and error, like all concepts which are expressed in polar opposites, have absolute validity only in an extremely limited field... As soon as we apply the antithesis between truth and error outside that narrow field... both poles of the antithesis change into their opposites, truth becomes error and error truth."[Engels, *Anti-Duhring*, Part I, ch.9, quoted by Maurice Cornforth in '*Dialectical Materialism*']

10 "... (I)t is in agriculture that rural people's knowledge has its most marked local advantages, and that of outsiders has been at its weakest. It is also in agriculture that the strongest reversals have taken place, and where there has been most learning from rural people – through interviews, observing farmers' practices, surveys, on-farm trials, and on-farm experiments with farmers as colleagues. Professional outsiders' knowledge of agriculture has already gained much by trying to fit together what small farmers want and know and what scientific agricultural research can do" (Chambers, 1983).

11. The African Department of the World Bank launched the Indigenous Knowledge for Development Program in 1998. The IK Program has developed a number of instruments and services for the capture, dissemination, and application of these practices. These include: the creation of an IK database of over 200 indigenous practices; a monthly publication, "IK Notes," appearing in two international languages (English, French) and two local languages (Wolof, Swahili), with over 20,000 readers; and a multilingual website. The program has also helped IK Resource Centers in eight countries to improve their national and regional networking capacity. Honey-Bee Knowledge Network of the Indian Institute of Management, Ahmedabad has been used to augment grassroot inventors and overcome language, literacy and localism. A large number of grassroot inventions have been identified and documented as short multimedia presentations with a vision of creating a database of such innovations and making them accessible via a Wide Area Network.
12. See Biggs' (1989) classification of mode of farmers' participation in agricultural research, from 'consultative' to 'collegial'.
13. The thesis that farmers have an important role in agricultural research logically leads to two questions. First, what is the empirical, as opposed to romantic or emotional, basis for elevating farmers to an equal partnership in research development? Second, how do we match up the comparative advantages of each class of specialists (scientists and farmers) in a truly meaningful way? (Chambers *et al.*, 1989) This has been a bar to the rationalization and mainstreaming of FPR at national and international agricultural research and extension system.
14. Howes and Chambers (1979), however, remind that certain aspects of knowledge-generation will always have to be centralised and formally organised. "Opinions differ, however, about the extent to which this is desirable". Much formal R and D has three phases: problems; a period of development and testing removed from that environment – on a research station or in a laboratory; and a period of re-entry and testing, during which the innovation is brought into the rural environment. For any technology, the question is what balance is optimal between these three. For mechanical and engineering technology, the case appears strong for much more work in the rural environment and with rural people. With seed-breeding programmes, in contrast, a phase in the controlled conditions of a research station is desirable for efficiency. Similarly, in developing a vaccine for cattle, some work in a well-equipped laboratory may be essential. Although opinions differ, it may be generally more efficient, in terms of ultimate benefits to rural people, for much more R and D to be conducted in rural environments and with rural people than is current practice. Before any radical proposals are put forward, the authors reminded, attention should be paid to the experience gained by the International Agricultural Research Centres and by national research institutions. At the same time, there is scope for making these formal systems more responsive to the views and needs

of those whom they are supposed to serve. Formal R and D is still struggling to get to grips with the variability of tropical environments, and with the accordant need to decentralise research to involve local people more actively in it.

15. Brokensha, Warren and Werner (1980) consider that indigenous knowledge systems should be regarded as part of national resources, 'although so far nearly all nations have virtually ignored this national asset'.
16. While writing on the state of agriculture in Africa, Borlaug (1992) declared: "Development specialists...must stop 'romanticising' the virtues of traditional agriculture in the third world". Though he added that "leaders in developing countries must not be duped into believing that future food requirements can be met through continuing reliance on...the new, complicated and sophisticated...technologies".
17. See What Went Wrong with History from Below by Vinay Bahl in *Economic and Political Weekly*, Vol. 38(2), Jan 11-17, 2003 for a detailed understanding of the discourse.
18. Foucault (1980) points that nearly all of the knowledge of the oppressed and the marginalized has been disqualified as inadequate and unscientific by the dominant forces.

    Fals-Borda and Rahman's (1991) observation is also basic to understand the marginalisation of people (or knowledge system). They mention three ways of domination: (i) control over the means of material production, (ii) control over the means of knowledge production, and (iii) control over power that legitimises the relative worth and utility of different epistemologies/knowledge.

5 Disparate Indigenous Dimensions of Thwarting Ailments in a Tribal Community

R.M. Sarkar

The scenario of evolvement of the concept of ailments and the attempts for their successive treatment has a long and continuous history which is crowded with diversified thought-patterns and behavioural activities. The phenomenon of indispositions not only causes a biological mishap but also this adverse situation delves deep into the very matrix of the social setting. The event of indisposition has been causing tremendous mental disruptions through time and space, and the people during different times and in all levels of culture have been seen to take sincere efforts to cope with the various adversities in their own line of thinking as well as within the boundary of the specific socio-cultural setting. On looking back into the history of mankind it would be readily understood with the help of different eventualities that the people in the remote past period even in the prehistoric stages of life-situation were highly motivated by the emotions of sympathy and generosity; and as a result of which they were always under the impression to make all possible efforts to provide relief to their kinsfolk and neighbours from the grip of various types of diseases. It is to be noted that the medicine is the provider of relief to the ailing persons. It, no doubt, originated out of sympathy and processed by necessity. But in the background of very limited dimension of knowledge on the world phenomena the primitive man was not in a position to reach the exact causes of ailment and related unfortunates. As a natural consequence his observations became centralised round the traditional perspectives of the allied community– it was patterned on their own philosophical principles. In that state of affair there was hardly any attempt to locate the causation of the ailment in the background of biological contemplation rather the mode of thinking undertook a specific way categorically processed by the basic cultural traditions and psycho-philosophical settings of the people concerned. That particular situational context persuaded them to think in terms of the mysterious phenomenal activities which worked beyond the conventional human perception.

Supernaturalism is such a belief pattern in which the people in all levels of cultural development try to find expressions of all or most of their day to day problems. It is a world full of mysterious beliefs and happenings. It seems to be governed not by the natural laws but by some non-human agents. But this pattern of thinkings is characterized by conspicuous differences when this is evaluated in the background of various human communities. Supernatural and natural conditions-their concerned beliefs and attitudes vary from society to society. It depends greatly on the socio-economic level, psychological perspective and philosophical setting of the people concerned. Thus it is seen that what is supernatural to one community is simply a natural happening to another. Thus an attempt cannot be made to draw a concrete line of demarcation between these two stages of thinking patterns-supernatural and natural. Supernaturalism is principally centred round various supernatural forces which have been developed in the social settings of mankind through a long course of interactions amongst diversified thoughts and ideas. The multitude of deities and spirits are the basic substratum of supernatural beliefs and ideas. Various thought-patterns that are central themes of the origin, development and processing of various deities and spirits are specifically characterized by supernaturalism. In order to solve the diversified crisis in day to day human life these supernatural powers are extensively propitiated and the people concerned are seen to be totally dependent on these powers and entities. The concepts of different diseases, especially in preliterate societies are found to be interlinked directly in this sphere of belief. Various diseases are caused by the wrath of the supernatural powers whose influence on man and society is multidimensional, and nobody can remain outside the influence of these powers. Supernatural Powers are believed to interact with man and it is due to these interacting patterns a large number of misfortunes in the form of disease and related abnormalities result. This particular belief, so to speak, is universal in character. Thus we see that amongst the different preliterate and rural societies in the world there is a full-fledged development of diversified deities and spirits, spiritual medicine men, diviners and indigenous healers with the supernaturally oriented healing art who are in the continuous struggle with the demons of disease by the adoption of the occult way.

Occultism is a specific development in the line of thinking. These practices are based upon hidden and mysterious ways of functioning. The occult practices are everywhere associated with rigid secretness - herein the secret powers are approached through a specific class of specialists who are dedicated to the realm of hidden and mysterious powers. Most of the human misfortunes result through occult ways and thus these must be resisted through the occult practices. Occultism, it is to be noted, is not a haphazard phenomenon based on some unrealistic thought patterns of the primitive mind but it is based on age-old experience and belief-attitude system in the context of human and superhuman ideas. In order to attain the desired end the people belonging to these societies cling to the "beyond the knowledge" factors and through these they try to come out of the problems of life which are the common happenings in human existence. In the age-old tradition of healing art amongst the primitive people there is seen a great development of various occult practices and these exclusively hidden procedures open up a particular psycho-cultural perspective that is highly effective in understanding the social psychology of the community concerned. The very attempt for assessing the different puzzling situations and their subsequent effort for immediate emotional response gave the concerned specialists an opportunity to develop some notions and concepts about the occult powers and thereby to control their malpractices that are resulted in the form of disease.

The fact that the diseases are assessed in the background of their causation in the primitive societies in terms of natural, supernatural and human agencies their treatments are always centralized on their understandings of the causal relations. All the factors responsible for the causes of disease are specifically evaluated in terms of mysterious powers and it is for this reason there develops diversified complicated procedures of combating diseases which very naturally are influenced by their own comprehension of the world at large. Primitive medicine is characterized by a system of trial and error and the therapeutic devices always fit with the cultural settings of the people concerned (Majumdar, 1958). The primitive healers are tradition bound people and their life-philosophy is always governed by a network of spiritualistic performance. They look at the world in a way which is highly patterned through the beliefs and dependence on the supernatural powers hovering around them. It is to be noted that there is no universal methodology of recipe. The manner of treatment in any society is dependent on the world view of the concerned people. The concept and treatment of diseases are attuned to the core of human sentiments (Sarkar, 1993). Medicine is regarded as a craft as well as a philosophy (Grossinger, 1982). Therefore it is very natural that the studying pattern of the medicine and its related aspects requires an overall knowledge and understanding of the life philosophy and cultural traditions of the people concerned. In the primitive sentiment the total etiology of disease revolves round the integrated perspective of the varied knowledge and experience that have been acquired through time and space.

Primitive medicine is thus governed by traditions-it reflects the integrated perspective of man, magic, religion as well as native science. The whole system is highly influenced by various ritualistic, procedures, charms, amulets, exorcism, and in addition to these there are some herbal preparations. Most of the primitive people live, work and think in two separate environs – one is the Supernatural and the other includes the Vegetative world. These people have got a broad-based knowledge on the different plant species with which they have got age-long physical as well as spiritual connections. They understand these plants as their friends and protectors. At the one hand they collect fruits, flowers, roots and tubers to earn their livelihood and, on the other hand, they utilise most of the plants as the readymade medicines to cope with the problems arising out of ailments. The tribal experts in this line have got a close intimacy with these medicinal plants – they not only recognize these perfectly but also they know the intrinsic qualities contained in these. Most of the time these plants have found their conspicuous places in the folklore of the community. These folkloristic traditions run down through generations and surrounding these a specific philosophy has been resulted which reflects the primitive sentiments in relation to these medicinal herbs and human gratitude to the vegetative world. In this way it is seen that the primitive medicine pin-points an indigenous system which has woven into the socio-cultural as well as ritualistic web of their totalistic life situation and this is why the primitive system of medicine needs to be properly evaluated to understand the practical value underlying these age old procedural activities. The primitive tribes have been living in isolation for a long time and they have devised their own methodological principles in the treatment of various diseases, of course, according to their specific knowledge and perception which deviate from the thinking pattern of the modern society. As this particular approach to the medicinal system differs from society to society and from culture to culture, so there is a need for the interest of the social science to conduct micro study amongst the different human communities for highlighting the therapeutic tradition in the perspective of the cultural patterns of the concerned communities. Medicine has been understood as an institution in human society and in this domain there develops an integrated phenomenon of variegated thoughts, ideas, beliefs, values including biopsychical and physiological factors depicting the total life-philosophy of the people. In the primitive society the healing art complex is characteristically influenced by the activities of the native practitioners popularly known as priest-cum-medicine men, whose activities are always governed by the age-old cultural traditions of the society. These cultural traditions have got deep root into the social concern and in no circumstances these can be avoided or neglected.

The socio-cultural matrix of health and disease in relation to a particular society must be understood for inflicting any change of concepts for the purpose of the implementation of any developmental programme. During recent period tribal health and hygiene are being looked into with the putting of much emphasis. In the matter of implementation of the Public Health Programmes the tribal people at the various levels of culture are being brought into specific consideration. In this specific attempt an interaction between indigenous patterns and modem scientific principles is highly conspicuous. If the two traditions work as conflicting factors and throw out one from the other, then no effective change can be conducted despite requisite sincerity and seriousness. Therefore, there is a specific necessity to explore the well-knit system of relationship between man and medicine in the primitive tribal communities and it is to be done in an unbiased manner as well as putting of due honour to the thought patterns and evaluation perspectives conditioned according to their ethics, ideologies and world views.

II

In the study of the nature and extent of medicine and its multifarious roles in the social settings of the primitive tribal community the cases of the Birhor tribe have been taken into consideration here. This tribe still represents a conspicuous example of hunting-gathering group of humanity whose life situation revolves round the forest ecology. They are principally seen to inhabit in the Chotonagpur region of Jharkhand with their main concentrations in Hazaribagh,

Palamou, Ranchi, and Singhbhum districts. They are also seen to live in the Mayurbhanj district of Orissa. The very name of the Birhors implies their close and intimate connection with the forests because *bir* means forest and *hor* indicates man. Thus the Birhors are nothing but the men of the forest. Their complete dependence on forest has been resulted in the development of a specific well integrated man-nature relation (Sarkar, 1994). The forest ecology is highly effective in the life and activities of the Birhors and it is in a process of continuous functioning in diversified nature. This specific ecology is rather indispensable in their life which has seen its fullest development in consequence of constant interactions with the forest. To them the forest is not simply an agglomeration of plants and creepers but a living embodiment the pulse of which is felt by them all through the time. Within the forest they are in search of the requisite materials of living – they seek not only the provisions for food but also the spirit for survival. Mention may be made that the forest economy has made the Birhors nomadic. In order to get a more or less regular supply of food and other necessities of life they are to move from one place to another. When the materials at one spot is exhausted through continuous collection they are to change their place. This change of place is associated with the movement of the whole population, and hence there develops a migratory character. This movement through the forest is not haphazard; rather it follows a planned procedure. The Birhor band consisting of 10-15 families move in a more or less circular path throughout the season. They have got full understanding and cooperation at the time of coping with the natural surroundings (Williams, 1968). The very patterns of their food quest is the root cause of their nomadism. This nomadism has become the controlling factor of the totalistic life-situation (Raghaviah, 1958). As nomads the Birhors are always in the search of unfettered freedom and in no circumstances they like to give it up. The nomadic philosophy of the Birhors is rooted to their fullest understanding of life which is assessed according to their own line of thinking – their specific value-attitude system (Vidyarthi, 1960).

Birhor Culture is the end product of diversified interactions between man and forest. It is the forest which has shaped their life and understanding. On the overall survey and analysis of the whole perspective of Birhor life it would be readily understood that the forest plays an indispensable role in the personality formation of the nomadic community (Sinha, 1958). The Birhors utilise the forest as the store house of their food materials which are constituted by different small game animals, numerous roots and tubers. The Birhors are expert hunters – they can move through the forest in an efficient way, they can perceive the presence of animals by studying the natural situation. At one time they were skilful monkey hunters. Chotanagpur forest was famous for monkey. The Birhors used to catch all these monkeys with the help of specially prepared nets. Those nets were so large and heavy that those required the joint enterprise and coordinated activities of a large number of persons. Monkey hunt, known as, *Gari Sendra* among the Birhors, was the specific economic as well as cultural trait of these people and, according to Roy, it distinguished the Birhor food groups from other neighbouring communities in Chotanagpur (Roy, 1978). The practice of monkey hunt demands intellectual capacity together with quality of swift action and "the selective intelligence of man can here be seen dealing with the environment in its own way even in such a rude community as that of the Birhors" (Roy, 1978 : 33). Now this practice has been totally stopped due to the total disappearance of monkeys from this region. The present generation of the Birhors is not, therefore, connected to this specific hunting procedure - it has become their past event.

In addition to their regular gathering of roots and tubers, fruits and leaves from the jungle the Birhors are in the habit of collecting chop fibres. These are the essential vegetative materials for the preparation of their traditional ropes. The chop is a kind of creeper (Bauhinia scandens), a very common flora in the Chotanagpur forest. Through a continuous process of trial and error the Birhors have been able to find out the technique of processing these fibres to prepare strong ropes which they sell in the market or exchange these with the neighbouring agricultural communities for various items of food. These ropes have been proved as tremendous helpful in tying up various objects relating to agricultural operations and other like purposes. Birhor life is based on *tanda* organisation. It is a small village unit, more or less temporary. The Birhor *tanda* is characterized by specific features and it is exclusively a socio-religio-economic unit in which the individual and collective life of the Birhors flourish in all dimensions. Each tanda is comprised by a few leaf-made water proof huts - locally known as *Kumba*. The *Kumba* represents an excellent workmanship. The small branches of the trees, leaves and creepers are so beautifully knit together and so neatly prepared that go beyond our expectation. The *Kumbas* are conical huts, circular in ground plan. The technique of construction of the *Kumbas* runs down through generations. The technology and adaptive skill travel through the tribal tradition. The *Kumbas* have got leafy covering; the leaves are arranged and tied together in such a beautiful way that during heavy rains not a drop of water percolates through the leaf-made roof, if it does, it not only brings discredit to the builder but also the situation will be the cause of social calamity as this particular happening is considered as inauspicious (Sarkar, 1990). The *Kumba* is provided with a small doorway which is so small that one needs to crawl through it. These are proved as comfortable throughout the year–these are designed as weather conditioned. During hot summer in the Chotanagpur region the inside part of the *Kumba* becomes cool as no hot air can get a free entry into it. When the winter season of the region brings down the temperature as a whole the inside atmosphere of the *Kumba* remains comfortable and the Birhors *with minimum clothings* and without any beddings can easily keep themselves in the normal condition. When the son of a Birhor marries, he must build his separate *Kumba*. If a death occurs *within the Kumba*, it is to be deserted and ultimately it will be burnt down. On the birth of a child inside the *Kumba* some changes must be effected. The child should be brought out by cutting a new doorway at the backside of the *Kumba* and in no circumstances it can be taken out through the original doorway. Therefore,

Kumba in Birhor life represents not only a mere hut for living – it is oriented with diverse socio-cultural and religious beliefs and practice as well as sentimental issues.

The social organisation of the Birhor tanda is categorically *influenced* by different principles centred round their socioeconomic patterns linked up with forest ecology. The life in the *tanda* is influenced by close cooperation during the time of stay within the *tanda* as well as while they are on the move through the forested regions. The family life is seen to function through an orderly principle and amongst the family members there is always a wave of tolerance and compromise in the working out of the economic perspective (Sarkar, 1992). Amongst the tanda members there is always a communicating mood and if a person faces any problematic situation the other peoples stand by his side. So far as the internal structure of the society is concerned, it is seen that the Birhor tribe is divided into a number of clans. The clans are totemic in nature. The totemic names of the clans have been derived from the diverse plants and animals that are commonly found in the forest. This particular pattern of behaviour reflects their close association and friendly relation with the various natural objects as well as phenomena. The clans are strictly exogamous – each of the totemic clans is provided with a definite mythological origin which the Birhors sometimes recollect especially during any worship relating to clan deity. Killing, destroying and eating of the clan totem is regarded by the Birhors as equivalent to the killing of clan members. The Birhors inspite of their rude economy, forest based nomadic life with full of uncertainties do not live in isolation. They are always in the effort of making direct contact with the other communities. It is one of their techniques of adaptation. Their very economy based on forest ecology requires regular connection with the neighbouring peasant communities for selling or exchanging their principal items of handicraft i.e. the rope made of chop. They also sell various forest products including chased animals to the people of the locality. It is for this reason the Birhors are in the necessity of maintaining regular social contact with other peoples.

The Birhor tanda is now in the process of changing situations effected by the planned resettlement programme launched by the government. Owing to the gradual deforestation of Chotonagpur region the life and activities of the people, dependent on forest, received a set back. Forest wealth was spontaneous and the tribals living in association with the forests used to utilise it according to their requirements (Blackburn, 1982). But everything disappeared with the destruction of the forests. In consequence of the large scale industrialisation in Chotanagpur belt the problem became more acute and this situation is still in a continuous process. All these factors are enough to exert a tremendous blow to the traditional life of the Birhors oriented with forest ecology. Moreover, the imposition of National Forest Policy has forced the Birhors alongwith other forest tribes in India to stop regular chasing in the forest and cutting of forest trees and creepers to eke out their existence. This sort of dissociation, caused by deforestation as well as legislation, with the forest had resulted a disequilibrium condition in the smooth and free life of the tribal people. As because they have got no practical idea about any secondary education save and except the hunting and gathering the economic organisation of the people has been disorganised bringing effective influence on the other related aspects of life also. Now the Birhors are under the programme of resettlement that has been framed and implemented by the government. The Birhors are now provided with resettlement camps where there are brick-built houses, tube wells, masonry wells and community buildings. Almost all the families have been allotted agricultural lands in the vicinity of the resettlement colonies together with requisite agricultural implements and bullocks. They are not allowed to construct the traditional Kumba with the help of jungle trees and creepers. They have been and are being trained up to cultivate the crops like other agriculturist tribes in order to keep themselves off from the forest based economy. Owing to these induced changes in the traditional tanda based life the total socio-economic perspective of the tribe has met conspicuous alterations and have been unsuccessful to bring any effective result in the positive side. The Birhors have failed to love the changes that have been effected through the newly constructed colonies trying to guarantee some certainties in the maintenance of day to day life. The interaction between the traditional and changed way of life is so acute that even after the spending of large amount of money, sufficient time and inartificial energy the resettlement colonies of these people cannot be made successful in the proper sense of the term.

III

The life of the Birhors are full of uncertainties. The food quest is influenced by day long struggle and in spite of this there is every possibility of getting nothing. Thus they are on the move – they move with all their belongings as well as their fate. They are destiny oriented people and they believe in multiple spiritual powers who, according to them, orient the line of life and activities of the Birhors. The spiritual world around the Birhors is very effective and influences, in an integrated manner, all the behaviour patterns of the people concerned. Supernaturalism is the prime factor of Birhor life. In each and every aspect of life this supernaturalism acts as the indispensable trait and in the sphere of health and disease this has given rise to a trait complex which is to be understood to focus the manner of combating diseases amongst them. The Birhor finds everything around him are pulsated with life and to him "everything above, below or around him is animated either by a spirit or by a spiritual energy or power, as every living being is animated by a soul or souls (Roy, 1978 : 45). These spiritual bodies are always revered by the Birhors and to make contact with these powers there is a specialised person who is known as Mati. The Mati is the person who keeps spiritual connection of the tanda with the supernatural world. He is believed to have the power of sacred sight through which he can perceive the activities of the spiritual powers and their interactions. Generally a *tanda* has its own Mati. Mati is to undergo a long course of training from a senior *Mati* before he takes the office. Also he is to observe some restrictions in diet and he must have got proper courage in the performance of occult practices. Mati is to consult with the *Naya,* the official priest of the tanda - during all types of problematic situations arising out of the influence of the occult forces. *Mati's* recognition as medicine man of the community is not only universal but also it is indispensable in the day to day life of the inmates of the tanda. Birhor concepts of diseases are specially related to their belief in supernatural environment within which all the features relating to the health, disease and medicine are controlled. Mati knows all the spirits residing within the *tanda,* on the mountain tops, in the inner recess of the forests as well as in the vast open fields. He has got well acquaintance with them individually and also he has the capacity to understand, through occult practices, what kind of disease results from what type of spirit or evil force. His specialization in this respect is not only acknowledged whole heartedly but also the people concerned think that it is due to *Mati's* control over the hunting spirits their life becomes out of danger. When a person becomes ill or feels any abnormal situation in relation to the body and mind the Mati is promptly consulted. Through the help of his occult power the Mati tries to find out the particular spirit by the evil influence of which the ailment has been resulted. The diseases are more often caused by the wrath of the bongas - the formless spiritual powers who are found everywhere in the environment where the Birhors live and work. The concept of deities and spirits is as old as human existence and this concept is inextricably interwoven within the social fabric where a well-knit tying of the individual within the society is specifically seen. Within the social system the ritualistic belief patterns are very much effective and these are mostly practiced for the maintenance of the good health of the individual as well as the society and to treat and /or avert the different diseases caused by diversified agencies. The following deities and spirits are held responsible for causing various diseases amongst the Birhors and they have got specific powers in punishing the people. These include Devimai, Buri Mai, Bonga Ora, Mahali, Chaati, Larankia Bhut, Manita Bhut, Hepram or ancestor spirits, Sangi Bhut, Sakti Bhut and Ningchha Bhut etc. The Mati knows all these deities and spirits individually and he can identify and specify the evil act of the particular spiritual force owing to the cause of which the disease has been resulted. Through his broad-based training the Mati approaches the deity or spirit concerned by occult way and after his actual understanding of the facts he prescribes for the treatment. Amongst the Birhors, it is seen, that when a man becomes ill and if it creates troubles, then the patient concerned goes to the *Mati* or in special cases the *Mati* is called in. After coming to the patient *Mati* examines the mode of behaviour of the patient. Sometimes he performs some magical rites or simply tries to think over the situation and then suddenly finds out the cause of the disease. Sometimes the diseases may be caused by witchcraft. It is regarded as a kind of secret art, and it can be acquired through a long course of rigid training. The witches have got many powerful qualities to inflict harm and to make serious injury to the body and mind of the persons. The Birhors have got full belief on the evil eye and evil mouth as the causes of different diseases. These persons who have got this sort of evil activities are looked down upon by the people. The medicine man fights with the witches through his spiritual powers and compels the witches concerned to vacate the body of the patient. When the diseases are caused by the influence of the malevolent spirits the exorcism is conducted by the Mati in a complicated procedure. The following table will provide an idea regarding the symptoms of the disease, their causes and manner of treatment in relation to a particular tanda at Churchu Block in Hazaribagh District.

The belief that the diseases are caused by the action of some mysterious agencies is very much dominant amongst the Birhors and this is why their faith and dependence on the *Mati* is conspicuous in all the spheres of their life. *Mati,* the medicine man is thus the progenitor of the professions. This medicine man of outstanding qualities comes down to the patients at the time of combating with the demons of disease. Mention may be made that there is a very close cultural linkage between the doctor and the patient amongst these primitive people. It is so integrated that there develops a bond of love and respect

Table 1
Symptoms, Causes and Treatment of Diseases Among Birhor

Symptoms of Diseases	*Causes of Diseases*	*Treatment Patterns*
Feeling of tremendous weakness and breaking up of the health	Wrath of ancestor spirits due to negligence of them	Ancestor spirits are to be called through invocation and then they are propitiated properly
High fever and blood vomiting	Witchcraft	Adoption of supernatural method to avert the influence of witch.
Failure in keeping contact with the daily activities.	Evil influence of Bonga ora	Through the worshipping of the particular spirit
Tremendous pain in the abdomen and shivering of the whole body	Activities of Manita bhuts	Through exorcism and then propitiation of the deity
Irregular menses of the women and other acute female diseases	Wrath of Ningchha bhuts or *Durha bhuts*	Through special propitiation to the concerned deities.
Frequent fainting associated with fever	Negligence to the spirit of the chase like Chandi	Organising special worship in the forest.
Group sickness causing troubles to the tanda mates	Anger of *Buru Bonga*	Long term worship to be made to *Buru Bonga*.
Small pox / cholera epidemic	Dissatisfaction of the Devi Mai	Worship and sacrifices to the deity, Devi Mai.
Mental derailment and allied abnormality	Evil influence of Sangi bhut / Sakti bhut	Conducting a process of exorcism.
Snake bite causing gradual collapse of body	Punishment given to the man concerned by the God for his sinful acts.	Through magical procedures.
Sudden illness started outside	Evil action of *Kundra bhut* due to some sort of negligence to him	Field propitiation where *Kundra bhut* is believed to live.

amongst these two personalities. The patients have got full regard with the Mati and they consider the medicine man as the mediator between the divine world and the human being on the earth. In spite of having specific supernatural qualities the *Mati* never thinks himself a distant personality from the general mass of population. *Mati* presents himself as their friend, philosopher and guide during the crises in life. The payment to the *Mati* is nominal and it is always made in the traditional ways and thus the economic stringency of a person does not debar him from getting the treatment of *Mati*. In this treatment pattern of *Mati* the medicine and philosophy run hand in hand. The total medicinal system is found to be well-knit in the cultural matrix of the tribe and, therefore, the medicine and related instructions are accepted whole-heartedly. In this primitive concept and treatment of diseases it is not the medicine and the related procedures which function in the process but the total psychotherapeutic action made by the traditional medicine men over the native patients bring success in the total perspective. In Birhor society magic and medicine are interrelated. A large number of magical practices are performed all the time to keep the people and the society out of dangerous situation as regards health and mind. The Birhors have got a very powerful and effective supernatural perspective which is imagined to be spread over the forests, hills, mountains, open fields, riversides as well as within the tanda. This particular world can be brought under control through magical procedures which assume occult causes and work in an atmosphere of mystical unreality. The Birhors have got a large number of taboos and each and every person is pledged to follow these as rigidly as can. These are negative type of magic and it is universally believed that the violation of taboos brings disaster to human life. These have got supernatural sanctions and the persons who break the taboos are subject to be afflicted with different diseases that are caused by the wrath of supernatural forces. If the medicine man perceives that the disease of a particular person is the direct or indirect cause of violation of taboos, then he sends message, through magical way, to the supernatural force concerned the appeal of the taboo breaker to forgive him and thereby grant relief from the disease.

The taboo breakers always suffer from mental agony as they have committed sin through intentional or unintentional violation of the unwritten laws having supernatural sanction. Therefore, when the traditional medicine man having full control over the supernatural forces acts as the medium between the taboo breakers and the supernatural forces, the mental disturbance of the persons concerned comes to an end, and naturally they start feeling easy. Beside this Birhor aetiology pin-points complicated psychological perspective of these simple folk. They specifically indicate various significance of the dreams that are dreamt by them. Dreams may bring calamity to human life; dreams with bad signs are the bearers of misfortune. So these must be restrained through the adoption of occult methods, as, they think, the dreams are nothing but the indication sent by the spiritual forces. It is for this reason the Birhors have got a dream tradition in which various dreams are interpreted according to their nature and composition. These have got practical value in understanding the mysterious horizon of ailments of the human beings.

IV

The Birhors have got a treasure house in the forest so far as their medical herbs, roots and tubers are concerned. From time immemorial they have been living very close to the nature and the very development of their integrated intimacy with the natural environment has been the root cause of an age-old tradition of herbal medicine. The Birhors know the medicinal values of many of the plants in the forest which have been understood by them through a long process of trial and error. It is true that they have got no systematic pattern of herbal medicines as is found among the neighbouring agriculturist tribes like the Santhals, the Mundas, the Oraons etc., but they are provided with the first hand knowledge on the specific qualities of many plants which abound in the forests with which the Birhors are in friendly association. Though most of the people in the *tanda* have got some knowledge on the plants yet it is the specific spheres of some experts in this line to properly identify and categorically apply these according to the nature and extent of diseases.

The elder members of the Birhor family know, to a greater or lesser extent, the modes of application of these herbal medicines. All the minor ailments are treated through the traditional knowledge on these plants, roots, and tubers but in critical cases the matters are referred to the herbalists, generally the medicine men, who by dint of their personal experience together with the power of occultism can easily prescribe the actual herb and its mode of application, according to the disease. The herbal preparations sometimes go along with occult practices. The creative value of the plants are recognised by the Birhors and they have seen the specific qualities of the plants in their day to day life. The tribal people with conspicuous spiritualism in all spheres of life very naturally assess these medicinal plants as the blessings from the heaven. Forest is regarded by them as the abode of gods and goddesses and the forest plants and trees which give the Birhors food, shelter, happiness as well as remedy for diseases are thought to be the part and parcel of the divine world.

Birhors' dependence on the herbal medicines is based on traditions. They prepare various medicinal doses from the extracts of many indigenous plants, roots, tubers and leaves. Many a time various bodily remains and excretions of animals are also used for the cure of the diseases. It will be evident from the different Birhor *tandas* at the time of enquiring into their life-activities and behaviour patterns in relation to their spiritual contexts. The *Barkijari* or the large root is extensively used as a curative for coughs and colds. This light coloured root is well known to these people. Then there is *Chotkajari* or small root. If a stone is detected in the stomach, the *Chotkajari* is ground and mixed with water together with five types of roots like *Simar-Kunda, Bhojraj, Hem Raj, Satwa,* and *Tej Raj* which are also ground in equal proportion and then mixed with ten grains of black pepper, and some sugar and water. The solution is very effective if it is taken in an empty stomach for consecutive nine days. *Kulu Kanda* tuber is used to cure the severe types of *eczema* and other *skin ailments*. It is, first of all, thoroughly ground into a paste like material and then it is mixed up with *Karaonj oil*. After that it is applied on the affected parts of the body. *Lahir Jari* relieves the women from pain after child bearing. *Rajgurumba* root is used for the relief of severe pain. There are combinations of diversified extracts from various roots. For the treatment of gastric troubles as many as 18 roots are ground up to make a paste like formation which is mixed up with water. This medicine is to be taken daily in an empty stomach for at least a week. *Ooth* is a kind of parasitic tree mushroom with obnoxious smell. It is ground and mixed with mustard oil and then is applied to cure filaria. A slight massage to the affected parts is necessary. For the treatment of hydrocele nothing is to be taken orally but a particular seed pod of *Eksira* plant is to be worn on a black thread around the waist. The wood and bark of *Bhengraj* is boiled with water and then strained to get the juice. It is regarded as a curative for dysentery. The root of *Bum Champa* is ground and mixed up to treat the patients of blood dysentery. The root of *Ralli* is cut into small pieces and are given to the patients with whooping cough to suck like lozenges. This process gives substantial relief to these patients. Worms are extracted from the body of the worm affected patients by the application of *Kirmi* root extract. The *Haser* root is believed to have an immediate effect in the addition of required strength to the sexually weak men. The root is first of all ground to powder and it is mixed up with *Karaonj oil* to form a paste. Then it is to be applied, on the external genital organs, for at least a week. To rectify menstruation irregularity of the women the *Barkijari* root is extensively used. The root is carefully dried up and then a fine powder is prepared by grinding it. The powder is mixed with cold water and the patient is asked to drink for seven consecutive days in the early morning. The *Bowad* is a kind of wild ginger. It is ground with ten grains of black pepper and mixed up with water and used as a curative to asthma. *Anatmul* is used to give relief to the patients having acute constipation and the root of *Oponom* is boiled in coconut oil and applied to the sculp for preventing the falling of hair.

For acute blood dysentery especially amoebic dysentery the root of *Karijari* is ground and mixed with water. It is then taken early in the morning in an empty stomach. In order to get relief from gastric trouble the leaves and small tender branches of *maradraj* are ground to get juice in which some grains of black pepper alongwith a small quantity of sugar are mixed. It is to be taken for consecutive five days. In order to cure the urinary troubles the root of *Kamraj* is smashed with water and it is taken in an empty stomach in the early morning. It is to be taken for five days. In the treatment of snake bite a kind of bark known as *talibaha* (brown coloured) is ground and mixed with water and it is given to the patient to drink. It is to be taken for three consecutive days. In addition to this the patient is advised to smell *isamulgurmi* (a kind of herb) immediately after the snake bite. The pain in the knee-joints especially during the advanced ages is a problematic issue. The Birhors try to cope with this situation by grinding the *gaithiajari* which is to be taken with water or with the milk of a black cow preferably. It is to be taken once in a day and the process is continued for nine days at a stretch. Three types of roots like *Kewakanda, Chiriakanda* and *Kamraj* are used jointly for the treatment of diabetes or blood sugar which is known as *Chini-peshab* to the Birhors. These are all ground finely and after the extraction of the juice it is put in a bottle with water. The mixture is given to the affected person once in each morning in an empty stomach. The process is to be continued regularly for at least a month or more if needed. When a woman lacks milk for breast-feeding her infant, the root of *dudhraj* is prescribed to bring an end to this mishap. After grinding of the root it is mixed with cow milk which is then given to the concerned woman for drinking. A little quantity of candy or sugar may be added to the solution. Five doses of this medicine are prescribed and it is needed to be taken in the early morning. For the treatment of fileria, the seeds of *bon-sarso* (wild mastered) are ground together finely and after boiling it in a small quantity of mastered oil, it is applied to the affected parts.

The Birhors have got the specific powers for identifying these medicinal plants, roots and tubers. Their skill in identifying medicines and applying these as per diseases is highly recognised by the neighbouring tribal communities as well as the other caste and community groups. As people of the forests their speciality in the line of detecting medicinal herbs is beyond any question and most of the local people do visit Birhor tandas for getting these herbal medicines to cope with their different ailments. People belonging to other communities have deep faith in these medicines as the Birhors are believed to possess requisite magical powers which bring immediate effect when the medicinal herbs are processed through these spiritual qualities. For the detecting of diseases and thereby prescribing the requisite medicines the Birhor experts receive customary payments in cash or kinds. Sometimes they demand a small amount of money to meet the expenditures for conducting worship to the connected deities.

The tradition-bound herbal medicines of the Birhors are now severely threatened by large scale deforestation, climatic change and grazing of the cattle population. The Birhor medicinal herbs are the thousands of the very small forest floor plants which are, of late, in an imminent danger of being wiped out in consequence of diversified factors including the present day open cast coal mining in the region where the Birhors live (Imam, 1994). Throughout the Damodar valley the destruction to natural environment is in a rapid pace owing to large scale mining activities. The Birhors who have been living for centuries in the lap of nature in this picturesque valley region are being driven out, thus dissociating them from the natural wealth like the virgin forests which ultimately brings calamity to their tradition-bound knowledge and perception on herbal medicines. It is in a dying out condition as many of the medicinal herbs are being lost for ever due to wanton destruction. Formerly the Birhors used to implant various herbs inside the deep forested regions to maintain their continuity; they were also in the regular habit of looking after many medicinal herbs while roaming through the forest when they were completely dependent on the forests for the food and shelter. Now the total situation has been changed. Being dissociated from the forests due to the implementation of the National Forest Policy the Birhors cannot think forests as the Earth Mother and Provider as they did formerly. It is in this juncture of time and space the rich tradition of Birhor herbal medicines is to be broadly documented and properly evaluate and these are to be done now or never. If this particular tradition fails to come down through generations supplemented by the practical perceptions on the medicinal herbs, it will be lost in the way bringing an immediate end to the thousands of years of efforts and experience on the herbal medicines.

Birhors' herbal medicines have now come to the regular market. From *tanda* oriented *jaributi* of the tribal folk these medicines have been developed into a regular practice in the urban setting. A number of Birhor men and women who are the collectors and givers of herbal medicine regularly visit the Law Court compound at Hazaribagh town which is populated by the diversified people coming from different places. Birhor medicine sellers display the medicinal herbs in the open ground and discuss the importance and functional patterns of the different medicinal roots, tubers and leaves before the curious clients coming to get their diseases treated. Through the instant selling of medicines the Birhors medicine sellers earn ready money. In addition to this, a direct interaction takes palace in between the Birhors and the general public which goes a long way in the effectual exchange of thoughts and ideas between these two groups of humanity. These medicines need immediate recording through proper investigations, the native science that has been developed round these medicinal traditions through generations is specifically required to be analysed in its proper perspective. These simple medicines of these very simple folk have enabled the people concerned to flourish in a lively manner without taking any outside help to keep their bodies fit and make these out of danger. Here lies the strength and authenticity of their native medicines.

Thus, it is to be noted with great concern that the indigenous medicinal system and its utilization pattern is characterized by time-long close observations on the different herbal species and products which grow and develop around the people even at their door steps. The very nature and circumstances of the ailments of their kins and companions in the face to face society are specially taken notice of with habitual sincerity and seriousness. All these observations and understandings have particularly been put together in the attempt for thwarting different types of diseased conditions. It takes very naturally a long process of trial and error. The results are distinctly noted within the background of successes and failures. Repeated attempts were necessarily made in the process of devising of various medicines alongwith their methods of applications to get their proper perspectives of relevance to the causes and cure of different indispositions. The continuous venture became practical when it received the positive response. Indigenous procedural activities based medical system, which in other words is called folk medicine tradition, is neither to be neglected as a farce strategy nor it can be laughed at while going to appraise its nature and extent in human domain. Rather these demand a thorough, sympathetic and scientifically oriented search not only in the interest of the indigenous patterns of medicine but also for the cause of exploring further research territory in the sphere of modern scientific medicine. Of late, special stress has been laid throughout the world on the realistic and effectual evaluation of the authenticity of the indigenous patterns of medicine that have been practised by the numerous so-called primitive communities living in the different parts of the globe. It has already been pointed out elsewhere in this paper that there exists a close-set linkage of concept and philosophy between the primitive indigenous tradition of medicine and the modern scientific convention focusing the identical intention relating to the whole-hearted effort for combating the diseases. On the basis of this thinking pattern if proper steps are taken to evaluate in the strict sense of the term the trends and abstractions underlying indigenous therapeutic system it would, on the one hand, explore the realistic picture of the primitive traditional medicine in the midst of various queer customs and practices and, on the other, this endeavour would be beneficial for the modern scientific medicine in the integrated appraisal of various primitive healing practices conditioned by age-long experience which may add new perspective to the modern scientific enquiries in this particular domain.

REFERENCES

Ackerknecht, E.H. (1971), Medicine and Ethnology: Selected Essays, Ed. By W.H. Walser and H.M. Koelbing, John Hopkins, Baltimore.

Blackburn, R.H. (1982), In the Land of Milk and Honey: Okieu Adaptation to their Forest and Neighbour. In E. Leacock and R. Lee (Eds): *Politics and History in Band Societies*. Cambridge: Cambridge University Press.

Grossinger, R. (1982), Plant Medicine: *From Stone Age Shamanism to Post Industrial Healing*. London: Shambhala Publications.

Imam, B. (1993), The Story of Kamli: A Birhor Medicine Woman, *Man in India*, 73, 4.

Joggi, O.P. (1973), *Folk Medicine*, Atma Ram & Sons, Delhi.

Landy, David (Ed.) (1977), *Culture, Disease and Healing*–Studies in Medical Anthropology, New Delhi, Macmillan.

Majumdar, D.N. (1961), *Races and Cultures of India*, Bombay: Asia Publishing Hosue.

Raghavia, V. (1958), *Nomads ... New Delhi* : Bharatiya Adimjati Sevak Sangha.

Roy, S.C. (1978), *The Birhors–A Little Known Jungle Tribe of Chotonagpur*, Ranchi : Catholic Mission Press.

Sarkar, R.M. (1986), *Regional Cults and Rural Traditions*. New Delhi: Inter India Publications.

Sarkar, R.M. (1990), Eco-cultural Perspective of Sedentarization of Nomadic Birhors. *Man in India*. 70, 3.

Sarkar, R.M. (1992), From Nomadism to Sedentism: Adaptation and Response as Exemplified by the Birhors of Chotanagpur, *Man in India*, 72, 3.

Sinha, D.P. (1958), Cultural Ecology of the Birhors. *Journal of Social Research*. 1, I: 86-96.

Vidyarthi, L.P. (1960), The Birhors : A Study in Ecology, Economy and Wandering. *Selected Paper of the Fifth International Congress of Anthropological and Ethnological Sciences*. Philadelphia.

William, B.J. (1968), The Birhors of India and Some Comments on Band Organisation. In R. Lee and I. Devore (Eds) : *Man The Hunter*. Chicago: Aldine Publishing House.

6 Traditional Agriculture: A Case of Tribal Community in Orissa

Hari Charan Behera

INTRODUCTION

Traditional agriculture pin-points a discussion that encompasses local knowledge, beliefs, technology adoption and other customary practices in agriculture of the Kandhas, a tribal community in south-central part of Orissa. The Kandhas are considered to be one of the well-known traditional agriculturists in Indian tribal history (Padel, 1995, Boal, 1997). Like other indigenous communities, the Kandha community in Orissa possess some uniqueness in its beliefs, perceptions, rationality, knowledge, and technology adoption. The Kandhas are also well known turmeric cultivators. Both shifting and settled cultivation are practised by them. Traditional cereals, pulses, millets and cash crops of the region attract a special attention of the outsiders.

TRADITIONAL BELIEFS OF KANDHAS AND PRACTICES OF CULTIVATION

The Kandhas are nature lovers. They believe their origin to be from *dangar* (hill) along with other plants and animals. They respect soil, hill, forest and other natural objects as their deity. They believe hill as their mother locally called, *Saru Penu* because both plants and animals originated from the hill soil. According to them, it is the Mother Earth that decides the existence and development of crops on her surface. It provides nutrition for the growth of crops and controls both rain and weather, which are pre-requisites for the growth of crops.

The Kandhas believe man alone cannot predict the climate. There are some animals and plants sent by the mother for them to predict the climate before the onset of a season. The Kandhas have identified several birds that alert the farmers to be ready for cultivation in the next season. According to them, if a bird sounds like *matatapu* it is the time to store the seeds for the next season. In the earlier days when the Kandhas, most of their time, remained intoxicated in consumption of liquor prepared out of date palm, sago palm, or *mahua* flower the bird only enabled them to know about the onset of seasons. It was being believed that if the same bird sounds *"birinpiyadi"* it is the onset of monsoon. Traditionally, *rajabani* (a bird) enabled them to know the time and the auspicious days. However, in due course, this has become a story of the past. People are now more aware of the modern technologies with the mode of electronic media such as radio, television and other form of communication systems.

Origin of Agriculture

The Kandhas believed that agriculture was introduced by "Saru Penu", the hill deity. Mother Earth taught them how to produce crops. However, many writings depict that the Kandhas mainly knew about settled agriculture from the non-Kandhas (Baily, 1957; Thurston, 1902; Boal, 1997; and Pathy, 1984). But still many myths exist in the Kandha society. Kandhas belief that '*Dand Penu / Saru Penu* (hill mother)' had enabled them to know about ploughing, sowing, weeding, harvesting, etc. They know about the agricultural practices since time immemorial. It is believed that 'Dand Penu' had demonstrated the Kandhas about ploughing through an agent. The deity came in dream of the agent and demonstrated about ploughing. This was the initiation of ploughing among the Kandhas. Thereafter, this became a general practice. The Kandhas believe that the *Saru Penu* has her own animal called Sambar (a deer like animal) for ploughing purpose. This agricultural practise was inherited from the mother through some spiritual agents and finally reached to the community.

HILL CULTIVATION (*PODU CHAS*)

The first of any agricultural practices among the tribals is the hill cultivation. According to them, the hill cultivation or *Bagad Chas* did not arise spontaneously. They believe that it was the handiwork of *Saru Penu*. Sometimes, the Kandha call it as *Podu Chas*, as the cultivation was done by slash and burn method. The crops that were produced from the podu cultivation included large varieties of millets, some cereals and pulses.

Process of Cultivation: Local Practices

Slash and Burn Method (Podu)

Before the onset of rainy season, the Kandhas cut the bushes and trees. They collect and accumulate them at a place to let them dry in the sunny days during February and March. These dried plants are set on fire after performing a ritual, called *Bagad puja*. All the villagers along with the ritual leaders assemble at the place of *bagad*. The ritual process is observed with the sacrifice of fowl or by offering eggs. Rice and turmeric are offered along with the fowl. The fowl is sacrificed on the spot and a few drops of blood are dropped on the wood gathered on the field. After the ritual, the ritual leader set on fire to the dried woods. After which, all the people assembled there take some pieces of charcoal or burnt end of the wood to add in the podu soil of their respective lands. This ritual is observed with the faith that the plants that grow on the podu land would never be destroyed by the natural and man-made events. Forest mother (*Gassa penu*) is worshipped to bring happiness for the seasons ahead with all her graces.

The Kandhas prepare the podu land in a particular direction and with perfect angle. The ploughing of land is made in a criss-cross manner in order to make the soil more porous and lighter. The ploughing of the lands is done both horizontally and longitudinally and it is based on the crops selected. The ploughing that is made in a longitudinal shape is called *'ekasiuhasu'* and the ploughing with horizontal shape is *'rasilakuhasu'*.

There is no ridge prepared on podu land. Water is allowed to flow down smoothly on the soil. The seeds are transplanted with caution so that it won't be washed away by the water flow. Soil erosion was less in this type as the field is surrounded by the forest. Each patch of land is separated and divided with the presence of the forest. Therefore, the land is otherwise called as forest land *(gassa ketanga)* or bagad.

Soil Type

The podu land contains *kala bira and balu bira* (black and sandy soil). The soil type is porous, and the moisture content is normal throughout the year. According to some Kandhas, even thirty years back the podu land was so fertile that a single plant of *kanga* (a pea variety plant) could even produce 5 kgs of seeds. There was no harm to the soil either by irregular rainfall or sunlight. As the soil was porous and light, the water holding capacity of the soil was better. The soil could receive air. As a result the crops grew well on the podu land.

In order to maintain fertility of the soil, the Kandhas leave the land fallow for a period of 4 to 5 years. During the time of cultivation, the crop rotation mechanism is followed by the Kandhas. Mixed cropping was also another mechanism to protect the soil- fertility on the podu land.

Crops Cultivated

Traditionally, the Kandhas used to cultivate varieties of cereals, millets, pulses and cash crops on the podu land. Cereals such as paddy, *jower* and maize, millets such as *kuiri, ragi and klingiraka* and spices like turmeric and ginger were being grown on the land. Podu land is suitable for growing up of above crops.

These millets were the main staple crops till 1970's. Millets and pulse varieties used to be cultivated on a rotation basis in the same land. If this year they cultivated kanga (a pulses variety) on the portion of podu land, the same land is used for millets in the next season. This rotation mechanism in cropping pattern formed main feature in traditional agriculture.

The traditional cropping pattern among the Kandha is mainly mixed cropping. No millet is cultivated in isolation. However, the seed of different millet varieties are sown with a limited interval of time in the following order.

Kuiri → Ragi → arca → Kangu.
(In a limited interval)

The selection of these crops is done in such a way that the plants could be identified and differentiated from each other after they grown up.

The land is usually ploughed with the help of bullock. In March and April, people sow seeds. They wait nearly for two months until the heights of the plants reach at least seven to eight inches. Weeding is done in *Asadh* (June-July) and *Sravan* (July-Aug). Mainly, women do the weeding activity. The people watch the crop field to protect them from the threats of the animal and this continues till *Aswin* (October-November) until the crops start maturing. The crops need six to seven months for a total cycle of production. First, a woman broadcasts *kuiri* seed. The broadcasting is done with the skill so that the seeds spread across equally all over the soil. Sometimes, it is replaced by *ragi*. *Arca* is broadcasted just after the *kuiri* but in a definite row or column to differentiate it from each other. However, all the millets are grown on the same field. The purpose to broadcast a variety of seeds in the same land is to maintain the fertility of the soil and for producing multiple millets from a specific cultivation procedure at a single time. They say that it was also done in order to protect the land from wild animals and birds. The limited cultivable land located at a particular place was easy to watch by a few people. Therefore, broadcasting the seeds in different lands at different location was not suitable from the security reasons as well as because of shortage of human forces.

Kanga or Kangul (Pulse/Dal Variety)

Kanga seed is broadcasted on the soil in March and April. Seeds start germinating in May and June. The first weeding takes place in June. In a period of one and half months the plants grow to a particular size, which needs a second weeding. The plants start bearing flower in September and October. In November, generally the tender pods come out. The pods get matured in a period of three to four months time. Harvesting of Kanga is done after the observation of a ritual called, *kanganenju*. In this ritual, both men and women take part. Celebration of ritual is done with great fervour. The first fruit after harvesting is offered to the goddess earth. Like other rituals in the region, the ritual leader, *Dehuri*, offers flower, rruits, newly harvested kanga seeds and sacrifice fowl to the mother earth. After that, men celebrate by consuming liquor. This ritual symbolises the respect and obligation to the mother earth. Good production brings happiness among the Kandhas.

Table 1
Types of Crops Grown on Podu Field

Cereals	*Millets*	*Pulses*	*Cash Crops*	*Vegetables*	*Oil Seeds*
Kudinga (Paddy)	*Arca*	*Masanga* (biri)	Sidiganga (Turmeric)	Sainga (*jhata*)	*Sorasa* (Mustard)
Maize	*Rende*	*Munguka* (mung)	Ginger	*Jadeka* (Banana)	*Rasi* (*Til*)
Jower	*Kuiri*	*Kanga* (kangul)		*Sejeka* (brinjal)	
	Dedi	*Kaltaka*			
	Klingiraka	*Kadkanga/jhudunga*			

Source: Primary data collected from field)

Turmeric Cultivation

Turmeric is the most significant cash crop in the region. This is locally called as *sidiganga*. Kandhas have been cultivating it since time immemorial. There is no evidence about the exact beginning of the turmeric cultivation in the region. It is believed that the origin of turmeric dates back to Mouryan period in the 9th century. "The growth of turmeric is almost a religious rite with the Kandhas and it was to improve its culture and output that human sacrifices used to be performed since mid nineteenth century. It is their chief source of income, as they export it in large qualities, bartering it for grain and salt to drivers of pack bullocks, who come from Ganjam, Sambalpur, Cuttack, Puri and Tributary States (Dist.Gazetter, 1908)".

Turmeric thrives well in a sandy or clay loam soil. Such type of soil is available in an area of 1.43 lakh hectares of upland in the district out of which turmeric is grown only in 10,000 hectares.

Production Strategy

The Kandhas prefer podu field or hilly areas to cultivate turmeric. For turmeric production, *balubira* (sandy soil) is preferred because the tuber can grow well in the sand. As the podu land contains sandy and black soil types, the Kandhas generally prefer it for the cultivation. In cultivation of turmeric no fertilisers, pesticides and insecticides are used because the podu field supplies adequate nutritional requirement for the growing plant. As the turmeric has also the quality of germicide, the pests and insects do not affect it.

The entire turmeric production cycle is around one year. After mulching, the burden of work comes down. In turmeric production, maximum labour requirement is called for during the time of twigs collection. Both men and women collect twigs of *sal* trees from the nearby forest. Using a serrated knife they cut down the branches hanging around the trees. The same day or in following days, the Kandhas carry all the branches and cover the turmeric field like a sheath. The land is then left untouched for nine to ten months till the time of harvesting. During harvesting time, both men and women contribute equal labour. While the men dig the soil and collect the tubers carefully, a woman picks up the tubers out of soil and cleans them properly. After the collection of turmeric, women carry it to their home. They use bamboo baskets to carry the turmeric.

Processing

Within a few days all the harvested turmeric are processed. The turmeric is kept in the open field and allowed to dry up. After some days, the Kandhas boil the turmeric in a high temperature. The boiling process is done carefully by the women members. A big hearth is made on the ground. The women plaster around the hearth with mud or sometimes with cow-dung. After two to three days of readying the hearth, the fuel woods are used to provide enough heat for turmeric boiling. The turmeric is kept in a big pot and boiled at high temperature. While boiling, the container is covered with a plate. It is done to retain the steam inside the container. After boiling for three-four hours, turmeric is collected from the pot and brought in the open air. They are allowed to dry completely for a few days. After complete drying, the turmeric size is reduced to one-third of its original size. The cortex of the turmeric becomes deep yellow while the sheaths become greyish brown.

Use of Turmeric

Turmeric is not only used as a spice ingredient to prepare curry but as an important medicine. The Kandhas know that the turmeric has antibiotic and antiseptic properties. It is used as a medicine to cure stomach infection, skin disease, heat effect of the body, etc. After all, the Kandhas use it as a panacea for all diseases. Apart from the medicinal importance, turmeric has ritual importance too. In each and every ritual, turmeric is used as a symbol of purity. The girls after puberty and the women after menstruation consume turmeric. They use the turmeric paste in order to avoid any sorts of bacterial or fungal infection.

Traditional Knowledge of Crop Rotation

In the past, a farmer regenerated the fertility of the farmland by changing or rotating crops, intercropping or multiple cropping, and leaving fields fallow. The production practices of traditional crops show their traditional wisdom. Knowledge about soil fertility was well known. As already highlighted, there was practice of intercropping and crop rotation in traditional agricultural practice. Although the practice is very old, yet scientifically it is considered as an advanced technique to improve the soil fertility and facilitate soil conservation. Intercropping constitutes a better use of the land and available rainfall, when the plants compliment each another.

Cultivation of short duration varieties of crops avoids drought situation and ensures safe yielding as compared to long duration varieties. Crops like millets, pulses require less water as compared to paddy. Kandha lands being mainly hilly terrain and upland the kind of millets preferred to be cultivated. For various needs such as fruits, fodder, timber and fuel, trees have to be planted on sloppy uplands as these are not susceptible to drought. The Kandhas grow turmeric and ginger on sloppy lands in order to avoid excessive water that affects the tubers.

Choice of Cropping Pattern

Practice of inter-cropping or mixed cropping is better than mono-cropping in the rain-fed areas, which ensures some yield during the aberrant weather conditions or pest problem in stead of complete crop failure apart from providing higher yield during the good years.

The practice of sowing another crop in the standing crop before harvesting reduces the cost of land preparation and water requirement for second crop and thereby avoids drought.

SETTLED CULTIVATION

In traditional agriculture, settled cultivation has also a significant position. But settled cultivation is not as old as the podu cultivation. Before India's independence the settled cultivation did not hold the significant position among the tribals. Podu cultivation provided the basic food requirement and was suitable for them to produce the needed cereals and pulses, the people didn't bother for an alternative immediately. In addition, there was no legal restriction in podu cultivation. The use of simple tools and techniques did not affect their production. Whatever the yielding they had was sufficient for their limited population's requirement. The climate too favoured the practice. The surrounding dense forest was congenial to maintain balanced moisture and temperature of the soil. Based on these, the podu cultivation was prevalent in the region. As the podu cultivation was common in the region, the Kandhas gave less importance to their plain agricultural land. The customary behaviour of the village ritual leader to continue the *'Saru Penu puja'* and uphold the practice was another reason. There was traditional norm to cultivate the podu land as a symbol to respect the mountain mother. As a result, the tribals were guided to continue the practice of mountain cultivation without any hesitation.

The consumption pattern during that time was mainly associated with the crops cultivated on podu land rather than plain land. As the crops grown were easily adaptable to *podu* land rather than plain land, the tribals preferred to continue with podu cultivation. In this way, the consumption habits and climatic adaptability were some of the important factors to adopt podu cultivation as customary practice.

Traditional Landholding

Traditionally, the land situated on the mountains was communal property. Private ownership of land could not probably be possible in that period when the shifting cultivation was not easy to carry out alone. The united actions in defence and offence as well as to protect the crops from the raiders and the wild animal did not allow them to go for private ownership (Pathy, 1984). The Kandhas had no permanent rights except to a piece of land around the site of the village. The evolution of ownership rights among the Kandhas of Kandhaland broadly reflects the predominant land character in the Mahals during the nineteenth century (ibid). Since the tenth century the states surrounding the Ghumsar region periodically tried to assert their sway over Kandhaland. The Kandhas resisted outside political dominion till the seventeenth century. This was when the Oriyas began to settle in fortified villages within Kandhaland and cultivated on irrigated land around the settlements. To facilitate administration, the area was divided into *Muthas* (10-15 villages) under the control of the headmen who were supposed to pay a tribute to the raja (ibid). However, in due course of time, more particularly, after the independence the village tribal council distributed the podu land to the concerned villages. In 1960s, the village councils again distributed the podu land to the individual households. The lands were distributed to the households based on the family size. In the same way the distribution of plain lands was done with the help of tribal council and village council members. Each household was distributed with the lands of different types. Many landholders still do not have record of rights to their landholdings. Community responsibility and Kui Samaj in the region have managed to avoid any land related conflicts.

The traditional landholding pattern of the Kandhas shows that the pattern of land inheritance follows according to patrilineal rule. The land is directly inherited from father to son. A daughter never demands her share on father's property. In feudal system, some households from among the Kandhas were selected in a particular territory to collect the taxes from the landholders. These selected groups were surnamed as Mallick. The Mallick Kandha families were given extra land as reward for their effort to collect taxes from other families and deposited to the *mutha* heads who are mainly the non-tribals from the plain regions. In that way, traditionally, the mallick families in the same community possessed more landholding than their counterparts. The Mallik families after collecting tax from the respective households deposited the same with the *muthadar*.

Production of Traditional Crops in the Settled Cultivation

Over the centuries, the Kandhas have also been growing traditional crops on the settled lands. In *saiki siati,* the kitchen garden, the Kandhas grow vegetable plants like papaya, *jadeka* (plantains), pea varieties like *Sainga* (pea variety plant), etc

Sainga is a common crop variety in the region. The crop is preferred due to drought resistance nature. As the crop is of creeper type, the Kandhas use large thorny branches of bamboos and sal branches to support the creeper. The production strategy of the *sainga* is not very complex. The Kandhas simply make furrow on the soil with the help of wooden spade or *pikash* and prepare the soil bed for sowing the seed. The women continue watering plant until the plants grow to a medium size. After a particular growth the creeper is supported by the *ranja* (creeper supporter). It allows the creeper for growing on it. They are also planted near, but inside the fences to support the creeper in order to protect the plant from the cattle.

There are different species of *sainga* being grown in the region. The species are identified based on the pod and seed shapes and also colour. The colour of the pod and the seed varies across species. The Kandhas, at present use seven *sainga* varieties that are of different species but belong to same genus.

The common variety of *sainga* is the medium size pod with both ends curve like U-shape. Each pod varies in size from two to three inches. The seed after getting dry turns black in colour and round in shape. The round seed is usually considered as of good quality. There are also some varieties with flat pods. While the former one is used for perched rice, the latter is used for curry. The colour of the pod varies from a little greyish green to dark green. Some are a little dark in colour.

The Kandhas select the crop based on the taste too. According to the Kandhas the *sainga* with round shape and green colour pod is often preferred due to its taste. The round-shape *sainga* is the most preferred one because of its yielding and disease resistance qualities. This produces more seeds and less prone to disease.

Jadeka (Plantain)

The plantain, locally called *jadeka*, is one of the oldest vegetable types among the Kandhas in the region. As the region is rich in natural vegetation and the springs flow down across the land, the Kandhas produce the plantain on the banks of the spring. However, there was no importance of *jadeka* cultivation in those days due to less preference among the Kandhas for its consumption. The local varieties of plantain are usually bigger in size and possess rich nutritional content. For a longer time, the *jadeka* attracted a number of traders to the regions because of its size and taste quality. However, *jadeka* could not be a popular crop due to less market opportunity and consumption demand in the region.

Jowar

Jowar is a cereal variety mainly cultivated on the *dhipa jamin* (uplands) during rainy season. The Kandhas prefer sowing of seed on a specific direction of the land position before the onset of rainy season. Mostly, the sowing of seed is done with a gap of 5-6 inches in a longitudinal direction. The logic of leaving the gap in seeding is to allow the growing seedlings to receive enough air and water. The emerging seedlings grow better than the plants having no gap. The old varieties of jowar are healthy and each *kenda* (bunch of pods) produce almost half kilogram of jower. The jowar is too preferred because of its healthy nutritional value. Both the Kandhas and Panas prepare *halwa* and other items out of jowar. The Kandhas boil the seed and produce gruel. They add kanga or other boiled cereals with the jowar gruel to make a little solid type for their consumption. In fact, jower cultivation continues in some part of the district, but gradually losing its ground due to restriction on podu cultivation and domination of paddy cultivation on the settled land. After the introduction of new varieties of paddy and chemical pesticides the soil too was no longer suitable for the production of jower.

Ginger Cultivation

The Kandhas started ginger cultivation way back in the twentieth century. This cultivation began with the interaction of the non-tribal traders with the tribals in the region. The ginger cultivation, in a limited period of time, took an important place in the form of major cash crop production along with the turmeric. Both turmeric and ginger cultivation was done on the hilly land and on the plain land where the soil was usually sandy type. This sandy soil is called as *balubira*. The ginger quality from the region was very good. It produced good aroma. The size was usually bigger and produced good stems. In traditional ginger growing, there was no application of fertiliser as the soil was more fertile. The traditional way of seed treatment was done by allowing the seeds be dried in the sunlight. The seeds are stored on a dry and cool place for the next season's cropping. While the branches of the main tubers were sold, the main cortex was stored for the cultivation purpose. In due course, the ginger cultivation has been stopped in the region. There was frequent use of new varieties of seeds imported from the state, Kerala. As a result, there was complete mixture of both traditional seeds and imported seeds in the region. This mixture resulted the loss of original quality of traditional local seeds. The local seed which is better adapted to the local climate was not available easily to the farmers. Again, the imported seeds didn't suit to the regional climate. May be because of these reasons the ginger cultivation stopped in the region.

Mung and Mustard

Mung and mustard seeds are used for mixed cropping. The Kandhas sow the mung seeds, a little before paddy harvesting, i.e, towards the end of rainy season. The same land is used for mustard cultivation a few days after the mung is sown. In Kandha villages women play a major role in sowing seeds. The Kandhas think that the use of both the types in the same field produces a better result.

Paddy Production

Paddy is the most preferred crop among the traditional crops cultivated on the plain land. Traditionally, the Kandhas cultivated more than fifteen varieties of paddy. Some of which, they inherited from their fore fathers and some from the outsiders such as itinerant traders coming from Ganjam, Nayagarh and other regions.

Till 1970 the people used to cultivate only these local varieties in their field. They cultivated those varieties that are suitable for their land, their consumption pattern, ritual behaviour, profitability, etc. The adoption of multiple varieties was done since the time of inception. Over the years, it is said that the farmers developed most of the varieties by frequent experimentation and observation.

Selection of Crop and Crop Variety

There was time when a large variety of crops were grown in the region. However, these crops are restricted to millets, cereals and a limited variety of pulses. Among the varieties, millets were preferred by the Kandha as they were suitable for preparing the gruel. So the consumption behaviour was the major factor for the selection of crops in traditional agriculture. The other factor was the climate of the region. In

Table 2
Local Paddy Varieties

Name of the Variety	*Characteristic of the Variety*	*Use Pattern*
Mata Saka	Dwarf and fat, white colour, produce better gruel	Daily
Nadia satanga	White, thin and medium size, scent normal, yield medium, plain land can be used for the cultivation. More grain	Daily
Kalitolashaka	Medium, thin, black colour scented, yield capacity-less.Low land will be preferable	Occasional, during festival and rituals. Used as *khiri* item
Bukuranga	Very thin, smaller size, white colour, strongly scented, can be grown on uplands. Yield-mediumEarly variety	Occasionally used during rituals and festivals
Ajalanga	Big size, white, yield medium, upland variety	Daily
Brihadlanga	Very fat, long and big size. Red colour. Lowland is better. Resistant to pest and insect infection	Daily
Kundadhan	Big size with big crown, red colour, better husk production, upland is suitable. Early production	Daily
Tureka	Medium size. In any type of landEarly variety	Occasional, mainly for preparing *lia* (a food item)
Nagar dhan	Medium, red, low land, need much water, late variety	Daily
Daspalianga	Red colour, big size, low land is preferable	On special occasion for preparing *lia* and *mudhi* (puffed rice)
Putkudianga	Small, scented, low land variety	Occasional use

podu cultivation the crops grow well. According to the Kandhas respondents, they abide by the rules of the nature. They would prefer to continue with that which is well adapted to the local climate and culture. People preferred the millets such as arca, klingiraka, dedi, etc as these crops are well adapted to the climate of that time.

Rationale in Selecting a Variety

The better yielding of paddy is not always preferred. Their consumption pattern determines the preference. For example, traditionally, the Kandhas prefer the varieties, which produced better gruel. There are many other factors, which also determine the selection of the variety. For example, the Kandhas also consider the resistance qualities of the crop, the water and temperature requirement of the varieties of the paddy, etc. Some varieties are preferred for having ritual importance. For example, *kalitolashaka* and *Bukuranga* are preferred because they are strongly scented and better for *khiri* preparation. The Kandhas choose certain varieties even when the yielding of these varieties is less. *Tureka* and *daspalianga* are preferred for preparation of puffed rice and *lia*.

Similarly, the selection of *sainga* is based on the criteria like suitable climatic condition, more yield and easy production and consumption preference. *Sainga* is also preferred for its taste and nutritional qualities. Apart from the *kanga, sainga* is suitable to be used as an ingredient for the preparation of gruel by adding it with rice.

Traditional Knowledge of Crop Diversification and Others

The cultivation of multiple varieties of paddy depicts the nature of diversification in agriculture. The adoption of multiple varieties, which is there since centuries, is the result of their experience. Historically, their ancestors have developed these varieties through their knowledge and experiences. Today their products are the result of multiple experiments already done by their predecessors. The Kandhas have superior knowledge to select the varieties through frequent scrutinising.

The scientists in agricultural research centres develop hybrid seeds, produce genetically modified crops by selecting the pollen of new and superior plant species through the process of transfusion, and develop new mechanisms for better yielding. In tribal communities, the knowledge in cross-pollination or genetic modification may not be there. But the tribals do it differently. The Kandha farmers scrutinise and select the best seeds out of the existing varieties. They store them and cross check them in different soil and different climatic condition. They observe which varieties grow well in which type of soil and under what condition as in the case of paddy selection. In entire Katingia panchayat, the Kandhas have generated improved varieties of turmeric, beans, and *sim* (another pea variety). More particularly, they strongly claim that the improved local bean varieties are their local property. Some people are aware of patents and patent rights. They claim that they need to get patent for this local variety. They have developed this variety by their cumulative effort. Regarding this Harekrishna Pradhan of Sudhipara village said that the selection of pure seeds for further cropping needs an experienced person who is already in this field for over the years. We select some pure seeds based on its size, shape, colour, smell and others. We protect it from heat and store in a normal temperature. The dry seed is stored in dry places only. All farmers do this. But a few get only good seeds and yielding as well. So the seed out of selected pods is again kept safely and people observe and experiment as to what possible extent they can collect good seed for further sowing. So, people after experiments in different climatic condition reach the conclusion as to which one would yield more under the particular circumstances.

The better yielding varieties are used for the daily consumption and less yielding varieties for occasional and auspicious events. The Kandhas say that the varieties, which yield more, are more prone to diseases than the less yielding varieties. The less yielding varieties usually possess some better qualities like odour, taste, appearance and disease resistance.

Though the belief system among the Kandha was so strong and it influenced agricultural practices, innovation was never lacking. According to Choudhury Pradhan, a 107 years old man,

> 'The people had strong belief on nature and supernatural objects. Frequent experimentation on agricultural practices continued to get better production out of the podu land. However, any loss to crop was often considered as the cause of the wrath of these supernatural powers. The production of multiple varieties of millets is the output of their traditional wisdom. He claims that the millets have never been borrowed from other communities. In due course the people developed these varieties along with some of the crops that already existed. People developed and adopted technologies based on the needs of the individuals and the community. Unnecessary exploitation of nature was against the norm of the community'.

Indigenous Knowledge about Crop Prtection

The pest control mechanisms among the farmers included the using of traditional herbs and other ingredients. In paddy fields the Kandha farmers have been using sal sticks or *salap* leaves (sago palm leaves) to check out the pests and insects. They fix these leaves and keep these in the centre of the paddy field for not allowing the insects or pest to grow over there. The farmers say that the salap and sal leaves have some scents and this keep the insects at distance from it. This also has some chemicals for which the insect never attack this plant. Therefore, the use of the stick and leaves of these plants becomes helpful in preventing the insect and pest infection to the growing crops. Sometimes, they collect spiders from the old houses and leave these in the paddy field. This shows the indigenous technical knowledge of the Kandha farmers.

Water Management

The water management mechanism in traditional agricultural system in tribal areas is the result of interlink between social organisation and availability of resources. Natural flow of water in the form of small spring and springs is common as the area is deeply surrounded by the mountains and dense forest. In Katingia the water flows down to the plain areas from the fringes of the hills. Traditionally, the Kandhas utilised this for drinking as well as for the agriculture purpose. The spring water never goes waste, ever since the Kandhas started practising settled agriculture.

TOOLS USING IN TRADITIONAL AGRICULTURE

The Kandhas had specific social beliefs in using traditional tools for the *podu* cultivation. Many Centuries back, the Kandhas never cut the crops with a sickle having serrated edge, such as used by the plain Oriyas. They used straight-edged knives for the above purpose. Cattle were not used to thresh crops after they were harvested. The Kandha used to do all the works starting from threshing to harvesting crops with the help of simple and traditional tools made up of wood and iron. The serrated sickle was not used, which produces a sound like that a cattle grazing, which would be unpropitious. If cattle were used in threshing the crop, it is believed that the Earth God would feel insulted by the dung and urine of the animal (Thurston, 1902). Thus *Podu* cultivation appeared to be not only an economic pursuit of Kandha community, but it accounted for their social life. Group cooperation in labour contribution was essential for shifting cultivation. This group activity with specific norms had cherished some values. As already discussed the podu land distribution was managed by the village committee and the sharing of labour was maintained by both men and women. There was no conflict over possession of land and sharing of produce. In this way their social structure, economy, political organisation and religion were all accountable to the practice of shifting cultivation.

The major characteristic of the traditional agriculture in the region is the use of only traditional tools and handmade local tools. The oldest form of ploughing land is by cow or bullock. In addition, traditional tools like *pikash*, *rampa*, etc were used for the purpose.

Other Traditional Tools

The cultivation of traditional crops was also associated with the use of traditional tools and techniques. The use of traditional tools and techniques varies from simple to complex ones. The following tools are used for the traditional crops in the *podu chas.*

Kodi	–	Preparation of land
Kata	–	For making siara and canals
Pikash	–	For ploughing hard soil.
Gadi	–	For digging soil
Langal	–	For ploughing
Kuradhi	–	For cutting trees
Korada	–	To prepare plain land in hilly area

Rationality in Adoption and Use of Technologies in Traditional Agriculture

Most of the technologies in the tribal areas are derived from nature. Their knowledge is based on making the maximum use of the forest. When the market opportunity was less followed by the inadequate support from the public and private agencies, the farmers had to depend on the traditional tools and technologies for the agricultural purpose. All the necessary implements were derived not only from the forest, and from the other available resources also. *Pikash* is the traditional implement developed to break the hard soil. This was developed based on the climatic condition of the region. *Korada* is the tool used for pushing the soil from the uneven land in order to make it plain. The tools developed were less energy consuming and easy to handle. Use of manual labour was enough to handle the tools. The techniques to handle these have been inherited from their forefathers. This process continues and transmitted to the next generation. Moreover, leaving tools and techniques adopted by the forefathers is against the morality, as the Kandhas said.

In traditional agriculture, the adoption and preferences among the Kandha is mainly on ecological base. The introduction of new technologies was not possible as the area was having little communication facilities. The market facility was beyond their expectation. Communication with the outside world was very limited. That did not allow them to access to new opportunities. They had little communication facilities, which made them to be restricted within.

SUM UP

The above study specifically presents some basic issues on the traditional beliefs, knowledge and practices in agriculture focusing the uniqueness of the community concerned. Their beliefs in origin of agriculture, prediction of climate through birds, beliefs in nature and supernatural entities are important part of the community culture. Shifting cultivation is the oldest and most traditional form of crop production. The process of shifting cultivation, crop production activities, crop rotation procedure, water management, and management of retention of soil moisture signifies the native knowledge of Kandha community. Millets like *kuiri, arca, klingiraka,* etc were most preferred food items while jower, maize and paddy are the main traditional cereals. The Kandhas have identified different varies of millets, pulses and cereals. Even they have identified multiple varieties of paddy. The selection of crop is based on the basic principles and rationalities. They have developed their own agricultural tools and implements, water management mechanism and crop protection techniques.

REFERENCES

Baily, F.G. (1957), Caste and Economic Frontier: A Village in Highland Orissa, Manchester University Press.

Boal, B.M. (1997), Human Sacrifice and Religious Change, New Delhi: Inter India Publications.

Malley L.S.S.O.' (1908), Bengal District Gazetteers, Anugul, cited in Orissa District Gazetteers, Boudh-Kandhamal, 1983, pp. 42.

Padel F. (1995), The Sacrifice of Human Being: British Rule ad the Konds of Orissa, New Delhi: Oxford University Press.

Pathy, J. (1984), Under Development and Destitution: Essays on Orissan Society, New Delhi: Inter-India Publications.

Thurston, E. (1902), reprinted (1909) Caste and Tribes of Southern India, Madras: Government Press.

7 Traditional Textiles of Bengal and the Indigenous Knowledge of the Weavers and Embroiderers

Atul Chandra Bhowmick

Bengal once earned a world-wide reputation for her filmy *muslin, jamdani, Baluchari,nakshi-kantha, kasida, chikan, namabali* traditional textiles which were characterized by age-long devotion to develop the textual artistry and nurturing hard-earned expertise through time and space.

The raw material of Dhaka *muslin* is *kapas* (white cotton–*Gossypium herbaccum* Linn.) separated out from its seeds by a ginning machine, a wooden box-like contrivance and then carded with jaw-bone of the *boili* fish(*Siluria boalis*) having small, curved and closely set teeth in it as fine comb to remove earth, vegetable and all other extraneous matters attached to it as foreign materials. The separated out cotton was thrashed with a *dhanuk* (hand-bow) to a state of light downy fleece and rolled into a quill(roll). The quills were enveloped in the soft skin of the *cuchia* fish(*Amphipnous cuchia*) protecting them from dust. The spinning of cotton rolls into in yarn was done by women, as stated by Dr. James Taylor in his book, *A Descriptive and Historical Account of the Cotton Manufactutre of Dacca* by widows of tender ages having good eye-right, delicate flexible finger, physical advantage and they could pay deep concentration as mentally they had no or less desire of further worldly belongings. He recorded, 'A *feti*(skein/reel) which a Native weaver measured to be of 250 miles to the pound(=about 454 gms.)(p.82 and Sir George Watt's book Indian Art at Delhi, pp.281-282). A skein cotains 840 yards of thread and twenty such *fetis* formed a *mora*(bundle). And the standard quality of the yarn used in the manufacture of *muslins* intended for Delhi court was 150 cubits(hath) of length per 1.75 grains(1 grain1/2 *rati*=I *kucha*=1/96 *tola*, 1 *tola*=16 annas=I rupee weight) and one spinner spinned 90 grains in a month devoting the whole morning till 10 O'clock. In summer season both in spinning and weaving water vessel was put in the hut for impart some amount of moisture from the water by evaporation. Otherwise the fine threads had chances to tear and this was an indigenous mathod of prevention. Ordinary horizontal pit loom wove the *muslin*, wooden spools bobbins(*nolis*) were immersed in starched water made of *khai*(parched paddy) so that the weft threads remained slippery and on shuttle(*maku*), *shana*(read) and lay mustard oil was occasionally applied to reduce the impact of friction between the threads and *shana*, etc. as weavers' indigenous practice. The *sabnam*(Morning dew), *abhyayan*(Running water), *baft-hawa*(Woven air) and *malmal-khas*(King's muslin) were very transparent fine *muslin* varieties and their fineness was testified from the story that once Princess Zeb-un-Nissa appeared publicly in the court dressed in 20 feet long and 20 ozs. In weight *sabnam*, wrapping her body seven times round. Emperor Aurangzeb, father of Zeb-un-Nissa rebuked her for desecrating the dignity of the royal court by being insufficiently clad or Persian ambasaor Mohammad Ali Beg presented his Sovereign Shah Safy a muslin turban measuring 30X1 yad in a coconut shell or deemed fit as animperial use if passed easily through a lady's finger ring. Such was its fineness woven in Dhaka in indigenous weaving technique. How fin a *muslin* piece manufactured with the simple and crude indigenous pit loom aided with ginning machine, bamboo *takua*(Spindle whorl), *latai/cheki/charka*(wheel), *shana* heddle(cotton bow), *noli*, *maku*–all simple gadgets was vouched from a statement of Forbes J. Watson in his book *The Textile Manufactures and the Costumes of the People of India*, with all our machinery and wonderous appliances, we have hitherto been unable to produce a fabric which for fineness or utility can equal the 'woven-air(*Baft-hawa*) of Dacca'?(Mookherjee: 1964 : 15). Of course, he mentioned here the machine made Manchester products. Raman ladies had a great of love for fine *muslins* and Roman historian Pliny in his Natural History, 77 A.D. wrote there was, "No year in which India did not drain the Roman Empire of a hundred million sesterces"(15 million Indian rupees). He bitterly complaint about the huge drainage of imperial gold coins to India for the purchase of luxurious delicate translucent woven-air *muslins* during the reign of Emperor Claudius Caesar Nero(37-68 A.D.). These fabrics were fashional in Rome under the names as *nebula* and *venti* textiles. The statement of Pliny is corroborated by the actual discovery of a large number of Roman coins in India, which must have been paid by Romans every year for the Indian such goods and others, and carried here by way of trade. The ruling class grudged nothing to pay for the superior excellence *muslins*. To achieve whitness, *Dhobee* bleachers boiled the *muslin* fabrics in water mixed with *saji-mati/multani-mati*(Fuller's earth–caustic earth–calcium carbonate, which acted as an alkaline detergent for presence of shell lime(Calcium carbonate), the *Dagh-dhobee* removed the spots with acid juice of the *amole* plant(*Oxalis cirniculata* Linn.) leaves and the displaced threads were rearranged by combing(*kata*) with the spines of the *nagphance* plant(*Emphorbia nerilifolia* Linn.)–all were indigenous processes.

Dhakai Jamdani(Fr. Chef-d' Oeuvre, a master piece, Per. *Jamdar*, flowered/figured/embossed) delicate fabrics were produced by the Dhaka weavers, who had a long traditional experience for centuries past. Different designs and motifs employed to embellish these are *pan-buti(*betel leaf-*piper betle* Linn.-heart-shaped), *kalka, toradar, kabutarkhop*(Pigeon hole), mayor-pankhi(Peacock-shaped, boat), *dora-kata/doria*(striped pattern, like river course). *Jhalar* with a network of floral motifs, *phulwaris/phulwar*(having running floral patterns), *chameli* (jasmine-*Jasminum officinale* Linn.). genda(marigold–Tagetes erecta Linn.), *gul dandi* (chrysanthemum–*Chrysanthemum coronarium* Linn.) flora paterns, *karala*(balsam apple/bitter-gourd-*Momordica charantia* Linn.) with its leaves and flowers together, covering the entire field. The best *jamdani* was the *panna-hazara, tara-buti*(*tara*=star, *buti*-dot of flower-star-shaped), a thousand emeralds of gold and silver zari threads reflecting the similar effect of hundreds of scientillating jewels, *nilambari/asmantara*(star studded sky covering the entire deep blue field.like the dark sky), *agni-phool*(flower of fire-flame colour), *meghadambar*(dark rain cloud), etc. *The karala* is somewhat elongated and tapering to a point at each and with spikes all through its surface. Cut threads of different colours were inserted by hand as weft threads to suit the colour pattern between as many warp threads equal to the width of the pattern intended to produce, previously drawn on paper, with a small fine pointed bamboo(*Bambusa bambos* Druce) needle by a helper-weaver and whereby an effect of embroidery is effected. The most remarkable thing in *jamdani* fabrics had unquestionably been their rich variety of designs, some being Persian origin, e.g., *kalka*, core, locally called *turanji, toradar/ tora*(bouquet of flowers). Their perfect finish, balance and flowing rhythm of the composition – all combined to give the *jamdanis* a proud position. Such flimist cotton *jamdani* weaving was possible only in riverine Bengal, where the air contains an amount of moisture so as to prevent the fine delicate threads from breaking during weaving. Sir George Birdwood calls the fabric a fine *tanzab*(wonderous). Often calls it a dream fabric or *parir deser kapar*(cloth of the fairy country).

Silk *Baluchari sari*, gown piece, ladies scarf, ornamental *chaddar* handkerchief of Murshidabad drawn the attention of all for their magnificent designs. The best and finest variety of silk was produced from mulberry silk worms(*Bombyx mori*), while *tasar/tussar* was produced from other variety of caterpillar(*Artheroea mylibta*). Of all the products the *Baluchari* weavers lavished most of their skill in decorating the *anchala/ pallav*(end-piece) of the *sari* with a panel framing usually a row of five *kalkas* with a flora border and its entire field with *butis*, (sprays of flowers), arranged either in vertical or in *tercha*(oblique) rows, peacock, shown singly or in pairs, flowering twigs, either singly or twin, lady with a flower in her hand, man and woman smoking *hookah*(hubble-bubble), European seated on cushion and smoking *hookah* or dressed in hat, coat, trousers and bayonet or wine cup in hand and the steam engine. The weavers accepted the foreign objects as their now designs and recorded the change of the earlier conventional designs. These foreign designs were introduced by the Europeans when the land was under the British rule. Weavers were imbibed with new patterns and accepted these designs, particularly the last one, which had shown also the advancement of science in folk pattern. *Baluchari saris* with complicated designs were produced in *naksha* loom with harness cards, i.e., punch cards for design, which was undoubtedly a great achievement in weaving technique. And for such a design usually seven *ankshas* were employed, two for borders, two for figures, two for *anchala*, of these one each to weaver and draw-boy and one for beginning and finishingit up, and occasionally fourteen *nakshas* attached to two sets of harness cards, suspended from ceiling for most intricate designs. Pre-drawn *nakshas* in colour on paper were followed. The draw-boy manipulated the harness cards and the weaver put in the required coloured woof thread corresponding to the colour design. At Bishnupur, Bankura jackard machine has been employed to loom *Baluchari saris,* but the products are not so excellent in colour, design and quality than those produced manuallyoperated earlier pit-looms in Murshidabad, so also the *jamdanis* produced now at Fulia, Nabadwip, Santipur in Nadia district, because of their traditional pragmatic experience and skill what Dhaka *jamdani* weavers possessed. In delicacy of texture and grace, in design, in purity and in fastness of colour the earlier traditional such products held their place of pride against the massive enslaught of the machine made products.

The *nakshi-kantha* (embroidered rag) is famous for its rich folk embroidery executed by the rural women of all classes of Bengal. This is produced by the use of old and worn out discorded *dhotis* and coloured threads taken out of *sari* borders. The indigenous detergent used for cleaning filthy *dhotis* is, locally known as *khar* or *bashna,* made of burned ash of plantain(*Musa sapientum* Linn.) or *shim*(broad bean creeper-*polichas lablab* Linn.) or mustard(*Brassica napus* Linn.) or sesame(*Sesamum indica* Linn.) herbs or *panimarich/bishmantali* (*Polygonum hydropiper* Linn.) or small *panas/kanthal*(jackfruit, called *muchi*(*Artocarpus integrifolia* Linn. f.). The uncleaned *dhois* are boiled in wateer with the balls, prepared out of ash with gruel, which have an alkaline action to make them white.

Various raised embroidered designs are eight-petalled outstretched full blossomed lotus(*Nelumbium speciosum* Willd.), known as *visvapadma*(world lotus), centrally placed in the shape of a *mandala visvapadma*(world lotus). Centrally placed in the shape of a *mandala*(sphere) signifying the universe or *satadala padma*(hundred petalled lotus), known also as *hrid-padma*(lotus heart), a highly anspicious traditional motif in art and *kalka*, placed in four corners. The *kalka* is the stylized form of green mango or conch or earthen lamp or lotus petal or flickering fire flame. Besides these *kadamba* flower(*Anthocephalus indicus* A. Rich), *swastika*(auspicious cross emblem of the sun to avert calamity, good forture), *siva-linga*(phallus), car-chariot as outcome of their religious sentiment, bullock-cart, boat, palanquin, taditional media or rural transport, *kalmilata* (*Ipomoca aquatica* Forsk), *sankhalata*(conch chain), nut-cutter, *dhenki*(husking lever), box, tiger, elephant, snake, peacock, parrot, *ruhu* fish(*Labeo rohita*), prawn (*Palaeomo malcolmsoni*), etc. are embroidered illustrating how the woman embroideres of Bengal have been influenced by their daily household objects and physical environment around them. They did not search for designs from sources apart, but whatever they have seen in their daily life in the locality have inspired them to embroider. A repetitive design, wavy in appearance, embroidered in darn stitch at borders and twisted circular design suggest river waves and whirls produced due to high current in river courses, which they have observed in reverine Bengal. The animal figures are not anatomically perfectly articulated and the conventional floral and vegetal designs are quite attractive to look at all are free-hand work. Whatsoever intricate the designs are, the weaver and embroiderers of

Bengal broke the design in its simples form without any unnecessary details in their own right, yet the patterns are vigorous revealing the makers' depth of imagination and perception of beauty. This is possible only when they have observed the bio-diversity around them very closely and minutely. Different species of trees, shrubs, birds, reptiles and animals show the fleeting glimpse of the life and vegetation unraveled the wonders of Bengal. *Nakshi-kathas* are indeed significant documents of rural craft, telling the tale of the unsophisticated women, self-inspired and self-tutored and their patience and hard-work.

Kasida is an embroidered *muslin* product of Dhaka and this textile art was once a corollary to woven *jamdani.* The term *kasida* is a Persian word, which connotes embroidery of floral design with needle and thread. As early as 1851 James Taylor in his book *A Descriptive and Historical Account of the Cotton Manufacture of Dacca* describes that pieces of cloth were embroidered in the cotton portion of the warp with the needle and these are called *kasida.* Anand K. Coomaraswamy said, "fine darn and satin stitch work is done in gold and wheat coloured silk on *muslin*"(Coomaraswamy: 1964 : 140). Scarf, *rumal*(handkerchief and *pagri*(turban) *kasida* embroidery was done with wheat coloured *muga*(*Artheoea assamensis*) silk on *muslin* in darn stitch in Dhaka and this art of embroidery was probably originated and lived among the peasant class and had been handed down generation to generation as folk tradition. A special type of *rumal* is prepared heavily with untwisted *muga* thread on plain cloth. These *rumals* are exported by Arab merchants in large quantities to the Middle East, Persia, Mecca, Turkey, Morocco, Malta, Tunis, even to Egypt. Even the Bengali Muslim pilgrims to Mecca used to buy at a higher price *kasida* handkerchief without knowing that those were the products of Bengal. This excellent art object fell into decay since the wide introduction of fez(fur) caps.

Kasida folk embroidery is considered essentially a feminine art of Bengal. But the two main varicties of *kasida* production are *rumal* and *pagri* with circular, locally known as *bobby buti, pata*(leaf) *buti,* known as *jhumka phul*(passiflora) and small leaves arranged in a single file, but the leaf in each square is placed alternate to each other, thereby forms a flowing line on the ground of the cloth. *Pagri* is used as a headgear to protect the head from the scorching rays of the sun in the torrid zones. *Rumal* is square, 36" each way and a four petalled big size flower is embroidered at its centre, while the corners are covered with *kalka* motif. The central flower is full blossomed with outstretching petals, which look like a *padma*. But the squares disposed in the ground are filled up with trifoliate leaf pattern.

Chikan was originated in Dhaka. A.K. Coomaraswamy. Abbe de Guyon and J. Dhamija hold the idea. But Sir George Watt holds a contrary opinion and said that *chikan* was a distinct and indigenous work of Lucknow. So, it is a debeatable unsolved problem. *Chikan* embroidery had most probably been brought from Dhaka to the Muslim courts of Lucknow, Rampur and Delhi during the later Mughal period.(Dhamija : 1925 : 25). *Chikan* embroidery was done on white cotton base cloth, usually of *malmal* variety of *muslin* with white threads of cotton. The finer grade of *muslin* lend itself suitable to produce such a product lend itself suitable to produce such a product. The open meshes of the cloth allow the humid air to soothe the body in the tropical climate of Bengal. The *jali*(net pattern), *muri*(fried rice-shaped pattern) and *phanda*(spherical millet-shaped pattern) are coped from things they used in their daily life. The embroiderers were not in need of patterns. They invented their own patterns from sources of domestic objects and nature, and gave expression to their innate aesthetic urge through the designs thus formulated by themselves.

Orange or yellow coloured *namabali* is the traditional hand block-printed textile worn in several ways to suit the comforts of the wearers. During religious festivals and *sangkirthan* (chanting of the names of the god) *vaishnavas* of Nabadwip and Brindaban and priests of all places worn across the shoulders or it could even be worn loosely across the back and supported by elbows and wrist or very elegantly diagonally across the chest and casually knotted at the waist. *Namabali* is inscribed line by line with *Hare Krishna, Hara Krishna,* etc.

sixteen words, either in *Devanagari*(Sanskrit), or Hindi or largely in Bengali scripts on one surface of the cloth, arranged in rectangular panels boardered with *tulsi*(*Ocimum sanctum Linn.*) leaves or floral creeper motif *kadamba* flower, *mandala*, *om*(praise to god), word often within a circular *mandala*, *trisula*(trident), foot prints of *Visnu* under the biparted *tulsi* twig, stylized conch, etc. at two end pieces. After printing the cloth is placed in a solution of cowdung, called dunning for fixing the colours and to make the cloth shining.

The Bengal weavers used to prepare dyes mostly from vegetal sources in indigenous process. Different natural dyes of sober tone were extracted from flowers, fruits, fruit rinds, leaves, roots, stems, seeds, barks, wood and insects. Lac is the only insect dye and *gochana*(urine of cow) is the animal dye.

PREPARATION OF DYE

Red

1. *Kusuma* flowers(safflower–*Carthamus tinctorius* Linn.) were dried under shade in basket. Exposure to the sun would weaken the dye. After the florests were sufficiently dried, they were kept in an earthen jar. To get rid of the yellow colouring matter from the dried florests these were pounded well and about ½ 1b(1.1b=about ½ seer,(1 seer=about a kilogramme=about a litre) of these flowers were mixed with two seers of cold water. It was agitated briskly for about fifteen minutes. The water, which was of a dirty yellow colour, was decanted. Fresh cold water was again added and the whole mixture was put into a cloth hanging to filter down gradually. This process might be repeated several times until the yellow tint was removed. Then *saji-mati* was added to the solution in cold water to dissolved the red colouring matter. The mixture was then well thrushed by foot and then straind through a piece of cloth. Strained out solution is a best type of deep red colour. Ashes of burnt plantain peel or pods of palm(palmyra-*Borassus flabellifer* Linn.) flower was also added as substitute for *saji-mati* and lime(calcium carbonate), instead of it

tamarind(*Tamarindus indica* Linn.) or mango(*Mangifera indica* Linn.) or curd had to be added as acid for neutralizing the effect of *saji-mati* or lemon(*Citrus limon*(Linn.) Burm.f.) juice was added very often to give further brilliance to the colour. This solution made cotton red and silk rosy.

Kusuma yielded best flower dye and this dye was great demand in Bengal. It contains two pigments, viz., *kusuma* red and *kusuma* yellow which are considered as an emblem of holiness and for that orthodox Hindus used these dyes for colouring their wedding apparels.

Several other varieties of compound colours were obtained by mixing of separated out mixing of separated out yellow water of *kusum* with other ingredients, as under–

i) Orange(*narangi/kamlai*-orange yellow)– The infusion of *kusuma* mixed with *haldi*(turmeric-*Curcuma longa* Linn.)

ii) Deep orange(*chamai-badami*(almond colour)– same as *narangi*. Only a greater amount of turmeric is mixed.

iii) Rose(*golabi/piyaji*)(*Palendu*-onion-Allium sativum Linn.) colour)- By mixing the infusion of *kusuma* with a little more acid, such as tamarind or mango juice and lime as fixer.

iv) Purle(*baiguni*)– By mixing the infusion of *kusuma* with indigo(blue) and acid.

v) *Surmai*(blue black)– By mixing red dye of *kusuma* and indigo.

vi) *Masi*(deep black)– By mixing fresh yellowy water of kusuma and turmeric.

2. *Mandar*(*Erythrina indica* Lam.) tree grew wild in Bengal, which yields flowers of bright red colour. A little heating of the flowers in water would produce a red dye.

3. After fedding cows with mango leaves *gochana* was collected and mixed with lime and boiled for red colour. Its use was very limited and used only as a pigment in printing cloth.

4. Lac incrustation is a glutinous product of *Coccus lacca* insects, deposited on the branches of the *aswatha/ peepul*(*Ficus religiosa* Linn.), th *palas*(parrot tree-*Butea frondosa* Roxb.) and the *kusuma* trees and was taken off during the period from March to October in Birbhum, Bankura, Midnapore and Murshidabad districts. This stick lac is grounded into a fine power with a mortar and pestle. Then water and *sagi-mati* were added to it and the liquid was strained. The strained liquid was allowed to settle to form a thick sediment. Lime water was added to it in order to help a quick sediment. The clear tap watery part was poured out and the bottom sediment thus got was pressed into cakes. The lac cakes were boiled in water and thus a flaming red colour was obtained,
5. *Mehudi*(*Lawsonia alba* Lam.) leaves were pasted in whet stone and mixed with khadira(katachu-Akacia ketachu) in water. The mixture was strained through a piece of cloth and the filtered solution was a deep red dye. *Mahudi* was used for tinting the borders of *saris*, worn mainly on spring festival.
6. The thin roots of atleast three years old cultival *nil/ al*(*Indigofere tinctoria* Linn.) plant were cut into small pieces and pounded well until these were converted into powder. The pulverized substance was steeped in water a red dye was obtained with a variety of shades from yellow, pink to dark brownish shed. The dye contained the bark of roots of this plant happens to be the best of reds, whereas that contained in the woody part of the roots is redish yellow than red.
7. The roots of *aich* (*Morind citrifolia* Linn.) were cut into small pieces and steeped or boiled in water. A little of *saji-mati* was mixed to the liquid so obtained and it gave a reddish yellow dye. Juice of small green jackfruit and lime were added to the solution to make the colour permanent.
8. The pulp of the seeds of *latkan*(annatto-*Bixa orellana* Linn.) fruits grown wild were dried, pounded and boiled in three seers of water and half *tola* of alum to produce two seers of red colour.

If *saji-mati* is mixed instead of alum gives a yellow colour for dyeing silk fabrics.

9. The bark of *bakam*(*Caesalpinia sappan Linn.*) as well as the old big tree was cutinto small pieces and sun dried, and then pounded into powder. The powder was boiled in water for five to eight hours in a proportion of four *chattacks* the avoirdupols is I *chattack*=about two ounces, I OZ=1/16 of a pound=28 4 ml.) of powder to four seers of water to produce a madder dye. Alum was added as a mardant.

Orange

10. White petals of the *sephali/sephalika/sioli*(*Nyetanthes arbortristis* Linn.) were cast off and the orange *coloured* corolla tubes were made to dry under the sun, sometimes for two to three days. The plants is found growing wild in homestead and it is an autumn flower that blossoms in the evening and drops in the morning. The corolla tubes were boiled until two or three parts of the water remained and strained. The infusion thus obtained gives an orange colour of very fleeting nature and easily washable. By intermixing alum, an oxidized aluminum salt as mordant and lemon juice as fixer, the colour was made less transitory and bright yellow.
    1. Brilliant red petals of *palas* were simply boiled or steeped in hot water and yellowish dye extracted. The colour thus produced was a fugitive yellow inclined to red. Sometimes lime or alum as fixer was used to darken the colour. Silk, previously soaked in alum water was dyed brown by that yellow water. *Palas* does not rendered a fast colour, it is easily washable. However, by using alum as mordant the dye colour be fixed and made fairly fast.
    2. *Kusuma* flowers were dried under shade in basket. After the florests were sufficiently dried, they were kept in an earthen jar. These were pounded well and about ¼ 1b. of these flowers were mixed with two seers of cold water. It was agitated briskly for about fifteen minutes. A dirty yellow colour was obtained.

3. *Kumkum*(*Crocus sativus* Linn.) flower's stigma and stamen, an autumnal flower gave a bright yellow(saffron) colour after boiling in water.

4. The epidermal rind of *kamala*(orange-*Citrus reticulate* Blanco) was dried under the sun and powdered. *Sajimati* dissolved in water was boiled and as the boiling was going on, *Kamala* powder was thrown into the liquid and afterwards alum was added to produce reddish yellow colour. The cloth soaked in the dye stuff became yellowish colour.

5. The modified underground rhizome stem of *haldi* was soaked in water and then pounded. The pounded *haldi* was placed in a pot with water and strained, the resulted solution gave a yellow dye of fleeting nature.

In *gajan*(festival held in honour of the Lord *Siva* in the month of *Chaitra*(March-April) festival sannyasis(ascetics) coloured their robes in this colour

The other ingredients were mixed with the turmeric water to produce different shades of brilliant yellow colour, as under–

(i) *Basanti* (yellow)– Turmeric solution, *sephali* decoction and a little of alum when mixed together would produce a deep *basanti* colour.

(ii) *Sherbati*(pinkish yellow)– Turmeric solution, lime and dried mango powder when mixed together would produce pinkesh yellow colour.

(iii) *Dhani*(Yellowish Green)– A little turmeric solution and indigo(*nil*/blue) when mixed together produced *dhani* colour.

6. Sawdust of jackfruit tree and *bakosh* (*Adhotodia vasica* Nees) plant leaves were boiled in water. The decoction was then strained and gave a yellow colour. Often bark of jackfruit tree, instead of its sawdust with a little of lime produced a deep yellow colour, which was fast in nature.

Green

1. *Sabuz*(green)– An equal proportion of each turmeric and indigo solutions would give a *sabuz* colour.

Blue

1. Blue– Cultivated *nil* plant leaves were cut into pieces and allowed to rot in water. Shell lime was added to it and the solution was allowed to stand for about twelve hours. The deposit was dried and kept in the form of cakes. The cakes were dissolved in water for blue colour, but it was not a permanent dye. To achieve permanence *saji-mati* or pounded roots of *nil* tree, lime and molasses(*gur*) were added and the solution was stirred for three to four days at intervals for preparing blue colour.

Grey

1. Grey – A series of shades of grey were produced from the dry black *hurra/haritake*(myrobalan-*Terminalia chebula* Retz.) fruit. The rind of myrobalan contains a kind of colourless tannic acid and gives a white gelatinous precipitation with ferrous salt. It turns dark blue when exposed to air.

The indigenous process of dyeing the warp and weft threads of silk *Baluchari* textiles with colours thus extracted was not so simple. These were dyed usually in red deep purple, pink, deep blue, chocolate, green and yellow colours. There was no use of black, as black is not considered as an auspicious colour by Hindu and *Baluchari saris* are wedding apparels. But what has been traced as black in *Balucharis* is simply the deep chocolate.

Process of dyeing in different colours are as follows– Flaming red – The silk threads dipped in alum solution were first dyed with lac dye and subsequently dyed with turmeric.

Deep purple – The threads soaked in alum solution were put in lac dye and afterwards in an indigo solution.

Pink–Pink was simply light red. The process of dyeing was the same as in case of imparting purple colour.

Deep blue–Rarely employed as it was an expensive dye. The threads required three or more successive baths in indigo vat.

Chocolate– The threads soaked in alum solution put in lac dye and afterwards in a weak solution of indigo. Chocolate colour was locally called *banesh*.

Green– The threads soaked in alum solution were boiled in a decoction of *bakosh* mixed quantity of sawdust of jackfruit wood. After drying dyed threads, these were again put in a light indigo solution for green colour. This colour was not a so fast.

Yellow– There were two processes. (i) The threads soaked in alum solution were put in a solution of orange peel dust and sawdust of *bakam*. (ii) The alternative process of dyeing yellow the threads were put in a solution of *lodh* wood(*Symplocos racemosa* Roxb.) and boiled with alittle of *latkan*.

The threads dyed yellow in these two processes had two distinct shade of yellow, but none of these were pure yellow.

Cotton textiles were dyed red with *kusuma* and madder, yellow with *kusuma* and blue with indigo leaves.

Before dyeing the threads were soaked invariably in alum solution, then dipped in the desired dye vat(s). Alum acted as bleaching agant for taking colours in their true tints and far brightness as well. These all showed traditional tantis(weavers) ethno-science indigenous knowledge, their age-long practice, pragmatic experience and skill. It may not be unreasonable to think that in purity and fastness of colours, in delicacy of texture and in grace and designs the traditional textiles of Bengal may still hold their own place of pride against the massive onslaught of the machine-made textiles.

DIVISION OF LABOUR

Weaving was a caste based specific family profession. All members of the family-man, women and children lent their hands. The women spinned the yarn, prepared *tana*((warp), childred reeled the bobbins while males engaged in shana(reeding) and final weaving. Thus all the members of a family worked together for a common purpose and it thus formed a family enterprise. For pursuing this caste based occupation for generations together made them experienced and skill, and that talent was transmitted from generation to generation. They carried out their profession on a guild system. The weavers individual talent was transmitted to his progenies– its root reaching deep into the soil.

SOCIO-ECONOMIC POSITION OF THE WEAVERS

The *Yogi* weavers were considered low in the social scale and regarded as being of impure caste as they prepared starch by boiling rice and for starching the threads they used rice gruel. And therefore their touch was contributed to pollution. The Brahmin and other higher caste Hindus would not drink or even touch water drawn by person of the *Yogi* community.

The craft of weaving on a domestic scale had been one of the pivotal occupation in the economic structure of the weavers. Weaving was, however, not the sole means of their livelihood in case of most of the textile weavers, many of them also had lands, which they used to cultivate. Thus, weavers had double economic dependence, weaving, the primary and agriculture, the secondary source. As a family occupation the out-turn of production was generally quite considerable and hence, they had higher income. In the hey days of the *muslin, jamdani* and *Baluchari* weavers of such fine fabrics were in a good financial position. But in the British era the weaving industry was doomed due to imposition of high tax on sale of their products, levied high taxes even on spinning wheels, introduction of agent(brokers, acted as middlemen), mahajan(money-lenders) and duty-free Machester clothes. It was obvious that the money-lenders took the lion's share of profit. The Manchester clothes were forced the dealers to be sold in the market. So the sound economic condition of the weavers of the of the traditional textiles of Bengal ultimately broke down during the British rule and they had to struggle hard for their livelihood.

The fame of the Bengal traditional textiles was not attributed to the weavers alone. The skill and collective endeavour of spinners, indigenous bleaching method, colour preparation and nuances skill of weavers and the great care taken on every part of the different processes made these textiles famous and proved that the best and the most perfect instrument ever employed in the field of weaving technology were the human hands, though these were woven in traditional pit looms with simple gadgets, and this was due to the facts–

1. There was the force of tradition and devotion to work.
2. Hereditary experience and skill inherited though generations together
3. Climatic factor, i.e., the damp and most climate fesilitated weaving of such fine textiles.

   The *sabnam, baft-hawa, chikan* suit to feel the cool breeze in the hot breathless summer in tropical Bengal.
4. Leisure time offered scope to pursue embroidery work with love and patience.

REFERENCE

Alkzi, Roshen (2003), *Ancient India Costume,*(Second Reprint), National Book Trust, India, A-5, Green Park, New Delhi – 110016.

Banerjee, K.M. no date, *Cotton Dyeing and Printing,* Calcutta.

Banerjee, N.N. (1896), *Monograph on the Cotton Fabrics of Bengal,* Calcutta.

Banerjee, N.N. (1896), *Monograph on the Dyes and Dyeing in Bengal,* Calcutta.

Bhowmick, Atul Chandra (2000), *Traditional Textiles of Bengal, Indian Artisans–Social Institutional and Cultural values,* Edited by R.K. Bhattacharya And S.B. Chakrabarit, Anthropological Survey of Indian, Government of India, 27, Jawaharlal Nehru Road, Kolkata–700 016.

Birdwood, George C.M. (1880), *The Industrial Arts of India,* London.

Chattapadhyaya, Kamaldevi (1963), *Indian Handicrafts,* New Delhi.

Chattapadhyaya, Kamaladevi (1965), Origin and Development of Embroidery in our Land. In the *Textiles and Embroideries of India,* Bombay.

Coomarasamy, A.K., 1964, *The Arts and Crafts of India and Ceylon,* New York.

Dongerkery, Mamala S. (1951), *The Pomance of Indian Embroidery,* Bombay.

Dongerkery, Kamala S., no date, *The Indian Sari,* New Delhi.

Febri, Charles (1960), *A History of Indian Dress,* Calcutta.

Ganguli, Kalyn Kr. (1963), *Designs in Traditional Arts of Bengal,* Calcutta.

Geoghegan, J. (1872), *Soma Accounts of Silk in India,* Calcutta.

Ghosh, H.H. (1906), *Handloom Weaving,* Calcutta.

Havell, E.B. (1905), *Hand-Loom Weaving in India,* Calcutta.

Irwin, John (1951), *Indian Embroidery,* London.

Irwin, John (1965), Indian Textiles in Historical Perspective, in the *Textiles* and Embroideries of India, Bombay.

Jayakar, Pupul (1956), Indian Fabrics in Indian Life, in the *Textiles and Ornaments of India,* New York.

Jayakar, Pupul (1965), Textiles *and Embroideries of India,* Bombay.

Kangle, R.P. (1958), *The Costumes and Textiles of India,* Bombay.

Mehta, Rustam J. (1970), *Masterpieces of Indian Textiles,* Bombay.

Mitra, Debendra Bijoy (1978), The Cotton Weavers of Bengal 1757-1933, Calcutta.

Mookherjee, Ajit (1951), Indian Textiles, in the *Art in Industry,* Vol.11.No.2, Calcutta.

Mookherjee, Ajit (1964), *Folk Art of Bengal,* Calcutta.

Mookheerjee, Ajit, no date, Designs in India Textiles, in the *Art in Industry,* Calcutta.

Mookheerjee, Ajit, no date, Kanths, in the Indian Folk Lore, Calcutta.

Mookherji, N.G. (1894), The Silk Industries of Moorshidabad, in the Journal of *Indian Art and Industry,* Vol. V. No.38, Calcutta.

Mookherji, N.G. (1905), *A Monograph on the Silk Fabrics of Bengal,* Calcutta.

Taylor, James (1851), *A Descriptive and Historical Account of Cotton Manufacture of Dacca,* London.

Watson, Forbes J. (1864), *The Textile Manufacturers and the Costumes of the People of India,* London.

Watt. Sir Geore, *Indian Art at Delhi.*

Weston, A.T. (1929), *Report on the Survey of Cotton Industries in Bengal,* Calcutta.

8 Evaluation and Selection of Folk Varieties of Mango in Gangetic West Bengal by Participatory Rural Folk Appraisal

Kalyan Chakraborti, Tuhinsri Sen and Monanjali Bandyopadhyay

INTRODUCTION

Mango (*Mangifera indica* L.) is the most pre-eminent among the sub-tropical fruits of India in view of the acreage, production and admiration among the people. It is one of the oldest cultivated fruit crops, having been grown in India for at least 4000 years. This fruit is intimately associated with the Hindu religious beliefs and there are numerous ancient Sanskrit poems praising the blossoms and fruit. It is now widely spread all through the tropics and subtropics. Mango is attracted to all young or old and rich or poor. The colloquial name of mango is 'am' which implies 'the common'. It is not only typical throughout India, but is also the fruit of the ordinary folk people. From time immemorial Indians have a great fondness and attraction for this very fruit. They enjoy and adore the fruit more closely like that of date palm in Arabs and watermelon and grapes in Kandahar.

In West Bengal the mango is distributed throughout the length and breadth of the state except in hilly regions. The crop occupies about 67.763 thousand hectares in 2003-04 which is 42.12 per cent of the total area under fruit crops. The leading mango-growing districts in West Bengal are Malda (24.85 thousand ha), Murshidabad (13.45 thousand ha), North 24 Parganas (6.03 thousand ha), Hooghly (5.55 thousand ha) and

Burdwan (3.7 thousand ha). West Bengal contributes nearly 5.84 per cent of the total national mango production in 2001-2002. In the year 2003-2004 nearly 405.96 thousand metric tonnes of mango was produced in this state which is 20.27 per cent of total fruit production. Langra and Himsagar are the most significant commercial cultivars of this state.

From the scientific indication accessible, there is no doubt that mango originated in north eastern India and northern Myanmar region at the Himalayan foothills. (Gangolly *et al. 1957*; Singh, 1996). Truly wild mangoes are found in Chittagong Hills of Bangladesh and Assam (Nene, 2001). The latest paleobotanical study by Mehrotra *et al.* (1998) revealed presence of a 65-million-year-old fossil of a leaf pertaining to the genus *Mangifera* near Damalgiri (25°32´N; 90°07´E), about 16 km south-west of Tura in west Garo hills of the Indian state of Meghalaya in north-east India. This is, however, additional indication in advocacy of the origin of mango in India.

It is worth mentioning that decay of variability as an inevitable consequence of advancement in agriculture (Harlen, 1956). Decay may happen in two ways — either by replacing inefficient land races with improved crop varieties or by invading marginal areas where primitive cultivars are maintained under natural condition. Swaminathan (1978) also opined that progressive agriculture is characterized by many specialties in the field of adaptations resulting in their genetic base leading to blind alloy and concluding termination. It is true for mango improvement also. Success in plant breeding in mango is associated with loss of variability leading to genetic erosion. The gradual loss of variability in the cultivated forms and in their wild relatives is referred to as genetic erosion. The diminishing narrow genetic base of mango is due to commercial pure line or efficient mango varieties and recent hybrids which lend to displace not only the primitive cultivars but also local cultigens and folk varieties. The advanced propagation technique permits clonal multiplication of mango cultivars in place of seedling. Mango's wild relatives tend to disappear fast and their natural habitats are destroyed by agricultural extensions and other forces.

It is no doubt that variability is an endless source of evolution. It equips raw materials for biodiversity. The mango biodiversity, a complex understanding and valuable measure, is the total variety of mango in our planet. The variability may be escalated due to hybridization and migration. Natural selection, reproductive isolation act upon these variabilities to direct evolution. Variations resulted due to environmental impact are not inherited, but those take place through alteration in the genetic make up are permanence and hereditary. Genetic diversity ranges at the evolutionary level from indigenous progenitor to advanced cultivars, at the ecological level from components of pristine ecosystems to those of high input agriculture and horticulture, and at the genetic level from populations to genes.

Mango breeding has made tremendous contribution to increase crop productivity during the past four decades but loss of variability incurred due to this is also alarming as the primitive land races have been eliminated and the local folk cultivars are on the way of extinction. So it needs exploration, collection, and conservation of the diminishing land races and wild relatives. The advanced cultivars and residual breeding products should also be preserved for future use. The measures may be museum collection, gene bank or world collection of germplasm, compound mixture, mass reservoir of variability etc. (Simmonds, 1962). The sum total of hereditary material or genes present in a species is known as the germplasm of that species. The conservation of mango genetic diversities is most desired not only for plant breeding but also for environmental balance in mango based agro ecosystem.

In order to propel a successful varietal improvement programme, considerable efforts are to be made to collect a large number of important mango varieties from within the country and abroad. The real value of the different characteristics of leaf, flower and fruit is to be fully explored in preparing the descriptive blank. The pomological classification and a key for identification of folk varieties of mango are to be made. All the local varieties and the exotic germplasm are to be evaluated for tree vigour, regularity of bearing, fruit yield and quality and susceptibility to pests and diseases in a particular agro-ecosystem.

Last but not the least that human vitality in this planet is almost everywhere interlaced with and to a great extent depends upon flora. Similarly, importance of mango is deeply felt in the social and cultural life of the folk. 'Folk' means the populace of any akin social group, united by ethnic, semantic, theological and artistic affairs, Lore is spread in the life style and philosophy. The enormous wealth of folk culture is hidden under the umbrella of classic-lore which is compared to the submerged and invisible part of glacier sailing across the sea. Folklore, in fact, is the 'language of root' and the 'song of soil'. That is originated in the crop fields and meadows, in the trees and creepers and in the minds of human beings. This unknown, unlighted and undescribed life culture and mind culture is mostly agriculture based. The tremendous riches of folk knowledge on agriculture as well as horticulture is unrevealed under the cover of scientific wisdom. The culture allied to procurement of food is Farmlore. It is the base, and different super structures are created on it. Language, religion, superstition, ritual, dress, art, song, dance, festivals etc. are originated based on the ground production. Mangolore is an important part of Farmlore. It is the sum total of cultural heritage relating to mango.

In India mango plant has been used by different folk societies in religious rites, rituals and festivals in addition to its use as fruit. The recurrent need of this plant demanded its preservation and these ceremonies and religious veneration acted as germplasm conservation of today. Moreover, tribals are the followers of animism. They believe mango plants have souls like human beings and hence should be treated accordingly. The folk ancestors in ancient world did their duty pertaining to the problem of plant biodiversity in the form of the worship. Mango worship was in the vogue all over India vis-à-vis Bengal irrespective of caste, creed, religion and tribes. In the process of agricultural as well as horticultural development the eco-systems are modified gradually by the folk for the purpose of food, fibre and shelter. Consequently different plant lores are evolved in the agrarian folk societies in the form of oral tradition, magical believes and performing arts and crafts. Mangolore is not the exception. Just as mango grows in land and a smell of the soil sticks to it, similarly mangolore also has a smell of the soil and sap in it. The life philosophy of rural India vis-à-vis Bengal is to some extent reflected after the mangolore in the sphere of agro-ecosystems management.

Little effort was made to inspect closely the scientific principles and rationales involved in mangolore of the world. As a result, these age-old knowledge remain unexplored and are being gradually worn away after departure of elderly fruit growers from the stream of life. In the present work various categories of mangolore in literature, beliefs, totem and wisdom related to mango have also been described in brief.

AIMS AND OBJECTIVES

Keeping in view the above, it was considered worthwhile to undertake an investigation to explore the folk- diversities and lore in *Mangifera indica* L. in Gangetic West Bengal by travelling on the riches of mangolore in the perspective of agro-ecosystem management and to evaluate and select few of them based on physico–chemical traits.

REVIEW OF LITERATURE AND A FEW DEFINITIONS

Plantlore: Botany is a relatively modern invention. It is not surprising that before the scientific mode of looking at plant life there should go a more humble discipline, if this fairly pretentious name may safely be given to a set of beliefs or superstitions held by man on the subject of the vegetable kingdom (Krappe, 1964).

Mangolore : There is no recorded evidence of any study with Mangolore so far as the present author's knowledge goes. This study is one of the pioneering attempts to explore the mango based folklore of Bengal.

The present author is using the term 'mangolore' to denote the aggregate of cultural tradition delineating mango. This is a compound word by dividing it into 'Mango' and 'lore'. Lore means learning. It is a set of knowledge of folk. Lore created and possessed by the mango growers are called mangolore. Mangolore is the scientific study of folklore of mango by the experts.

Lack of studies in this area made it difficult to present a comprehensive review. However, relevant literature connecting both directly and indirectly supporting the objectives of the present study has been collected.

Abul Fazal (1590) in his great work *Ain-i-Akbori* mentioned a number of mango varieties cultivated in India during that period. The Mughals were never dubious about the superiority of mango fruits.

Europeans sometimes labeled mango the 'bathroom fruit' i.e. to be taken in a toilet as the juice could splatter on body while cutting the fruit with knife. (Gangolly *et al* . 1957).

Singh (1960) gave an idea how the mango spread from India to the different countries of all the continents. His treatise did not show countries such as Bangladesh, Nepal, Pakistan, Myanmar, Thailand and Sri Lanka. Nene (2001) discussed origin, spread, domestication and improvement of mango in a historical context. He told that people of India had preferred the 'sucking' type mangoes for millennia. They normally buried the seed of mango for further propagation. Trees producing good quality fruits were identified and retained whereas those producing inferior ones were cut down for timber. Mughals, Portuguese and the British who invaded and colonized India preferred 'table' varieties with firm pulp and thus varietal development was initiated. Bandyopadhyay and Chakraborti (2003) gave an account on mango in Bengali folk literature. They described some proverbs, rhymes, riddles on mango. Folk tales and rituals were also mentioned there in brief.

Geetha (1987) reported that leaves and flowers of mango were boiled with water and that liquid was used as folk medicine in Tamil Nadu for toothache and dysentery.

Sharangi(2000) described that the smoke of the burning leaves was supposed to cure hiccups and some throat troubles. The ripe fruit was diuretic and laxative. The gum and resinous substances exuded by the stem-end of the harvested fruit were used against scabies and cutaneous afflictions by mixing with lime juice. The mango pulp after baking and using sugar was given to the cholera and plague patients.

MATERIAL AND METHODS

Experimental Area

West Bengal is a part of the Eastern India, located between 21°31´ and 27°14´ N latitude and 85°51´ and 89°E longitude. The tropic of cancer passes through the middle of the state covering the districts of Nadia, Burdwan, Bankura and Purulia.

The experimental area is under the Gangetic Alluvial Zone. It includes Gangetic Flood plain Region. Climatically the region comes under tropical humid with rainfall of 1350 to 1650 mm, temperature maximum 35.0°C and minimum 15.6°C (Annual normal). The region is composed of alluvium carried by river Ganga and its tributaries and may be broadly classified into Ganga upland with relatively matured alluvial soil, Ganga flat land with matured soil and Ganga reverine receiving fresh alluvium recurrently.

Soils are very deep, medium, fine to medium in texture, neutral to mildly alkaline in pH. Calcareousness is significant in large section, base saturation moderately high, NP status medium to medium low and potash status is medium to high, external drainage medium to low and internal drainage is moderate.

Experimental Material

Survey or over viewing was conducted by setting up a sequence of sojourns to all the principal mango growing districts of Gangetic West Bengal during flowering, fruiting, harvesting withal.

These researchers also recollected the name of more than hundred folk mango varieties from the various places of Gangetic West Bengal by participatory folk data generation process. Out of these only ten folk mango varieties were selected at random from the list which were taken for further study. The sources of these folk varieties are presented in Table–1.

THE SELECTED FOLK VARIETIES

- Brindabani
- Kuha Pahara
- Michhrikon
- Lamba Bhadura
- Rakhal Bhog
- Dudhkumor
- Arajana
- Mohan Bhog
- Funia
- Surma Fazli

Table 1
The Provenance of Different Taxa Studied

Taxa	*Source*
Brindabani	Arhaidanga, Malda
Dudh Kumor	Ratua, Malda
Arajana	Kotoali, Malda
Kua Pahara	Arhaidanga, Malda
Michhrikon	Arhaidanga, Malda
Surma Fazli	Khaskhol, Malda
Mohan Bhog	Arhaidanga, Malda
Lamba Bhadura	Kotoali, Malda
Funia	Lalbathani, Malda
Rakhal Bhog	Ratua, Malda

OBSERVATIONS RECORDED FOR VARIETAL DIVERSITIES

The selected seedling germplasm, clonal selection, folk varieties and regional commercial varieties of mango were observed on the basis of the following characterization data. Certain modifications were also made based on minimal descriptors of Agri-Horticultural crops as compiled by National Bureau of Plant Genetic Resources, New Delhi (Mahajan *et al.*, 2002).

MANGOLORE SURVEY

Folk wisdom is knowledge that is unique to a given territory, culture and society. Folk wisdom is originated from the beliefs, culture and customs of folk people. This indigenous knowledge is used at the micro level in a given agro ecosystem. It is no doubt that for every folk technicality there was a primitive pathfinder or technician who actually innovates any idea or rule but with the passage of time that may be modified and amended by the folk people. Therefore, folk wisdom is the wealth of a folk, and the credit is not claimed by any individual. Wisdom may be of two types – technical and non technical. The folk technical wisdom is used as the basis for decision making pertaining to food security, human and animal health, natural resource management and other vital activities. There is a minor difference between folk wisdom and folk knowledge. Wisdom means the body of knowledge and experience that develops within a specified society or period. Knowledge means information and skills gained through experience or education. Folk wisdom means unique, elementary and inherent uninfluenced knowledge base of a particular folk group from time immemorial. That is obviously location and culture specific and transmitted orally generation after generation in simply words of mouth.

People's participation means getting people physically and mentally involved in certain activity. People's participation is a central feature of contemporary rural development and extension efforts throughout the developing countries across the world (Sen, 2002). Across the third world, examples are too many, sharing the extent of innovation and local level knowledge base possessed by the farmers. Such items of knowledge are strewn across the rural society in the form of practices, folklores, verses and words of mouth usually with the elderly persons, as it often happens in tribal societies. However, often the hardcore scientists are tempted to ridicule them and dismiss local knowledge as useless. But growing awareness on the value and potential of learning from such knowledge base are witnessed (Farrington and Martin, 1987)

There is astonishing facts that like other farmers, fruit growers as well as mango orchardists have valuable wisdom. They undertake their orchard experimentation in their own ways. A critical analysis of existing folk wisdom in the perspective of mangolore and integrating the same with scientific base for boosting productivity with a sustainable manner is of immense value. To achieve the objective of travelling on the riches of mangolore of Gangetic West Bengal, a brief methodology has been worked out and given here.

Participatory Rural Appraisal (PRA) was the methodology for interacting with the mango growers and traders as well as villagers, understanding them and learning from them. It provided an alternative framework for data collection and analysis. Because of its participatory nature, it is a useful methodology to focus attention on people, their relationships with socio-economic and ecological factors.

Participatory Rural Appraisal is the way of enabling communities to define, evaluate and influence their economic, environmental, health and educational status. It is an intensive and systematic learning experience carried out in a community.

For effective interaction between the mango growers and researcher, an ice-breaking session for building rapport was held with the help of village leaders and progressive farmers. Ice-breaking is an equalizing exercise where both the farmers or local people and the outsiders come closer mentally that lead to creation of an environment wherein Participatory Learning Exercises as a means of doing PRA may be accomplished more conveniently.

A transect walk and bio-diversity walk was undertaken by these researchers to observe and record details of diversity of mango based agro-ecosystems. The transect walk exercise is a systematic walk along with source mango growers with folk wisdom and experience profile to observe topography, water regime, soil type, vegetation, enterprises, problems, solutions etc. of a given agro-ecosystem. To gain an understanding of the complexities of a situation, to get in-depth information about community participatory data generation process was adopted.

PHYSICO-CHEMICAL ANALYSIS OF FRUITS

For recording fruit characters, three typical fruits of each germplasm and replication were sampled randomly at maturity from the exposed parts of each tree. Fruit length and breadth was determined by measuring the distance from the point of attachment to the extremity at the distal end of the fruit and the maximum distance between the two shoulders respectively with a slide calipers and their mean value was recorded. Individual fruit weight, peel weight and stone weight were taken with a physical balance, their average weight was determined and was expressed in g. Pulp weight of the fruits was determined by subtracting the sum total of peel weight and stone weight from the fruit weight and their mean value was recorded. Percentage of pulp, peel and stone were determined by dividing the pulp weight, peel weight and stone weight separately by the fruit weight and then multiplied by 100 and their mean value were recorded separately and expressed in per cent (%). After the physical examination, bio-chemical constituents of fully ripen fruits were made. For this purpose, fruit juice was extracted and passed through a fine cloth.

The total soluble solid of fruit was estimated with the help of a hand refractometer. A drop of squeezed out and strained juice was instilled on the plate to record the refractometer reading and calibrated in °Brix at 20 °C. The acidity percentage of fruit pulp was estimated by titrating the aqueous extract of known quantity of fruit juice against N/10 NaOH using phenolphthalein as an indicator (A.O.A.C., 1984). The total sugar and reducing sugar content of the fruits were determined by titrimetric procedures. Firstly the non-reducing sugar content of pulp sample was converted into reducing sugar by acid hydrolysis. After conversion, the sugar of the aqueous solution was determined by titrating against the freshly made mixture containing equal volume of Fehlings solution 'A' and 'B' and using methylene blue as an indicator (A.O.A.C., 1984). The reducing sugar content of the aqueous extract were determined by the titrating against the Fehling's solution as stated above. The non-reducing sugar content of fruit was determined by subtracting reducing sugar content from total sugar content of fruit and was expressed in per cent.

STATISTICAL ANALYSIS

The data collected from the studies were subjected to statistical analysis appropriate to the completely randomized design. The replicated mean data was calculated from three years of observation. The data obtained were analyzed by the analysis of variance method as suggested by Panse and Sukhatme (1989) and Gomez and Gomez (1983). The analysis of variance is the systematic algebraic procedure of decomposing the overall variation in the responses observed in a study into different components. Each component is attributed to an identifiable source of variation. The significance of different sources of variation was tested by error mean square by Snedecor's 'F' test of significance levels of 0.05. Critical differences (least significant differences) were calculated for comparison wherever the 'F' tests were significant. Treatments are declared significantly different at a specified level of significance if their difference exceeds the calculated CD value; otherwise they are not significantly different. In case of significant F or not, the Duncan's multiple range test (DMRT) was also used if pair comparisons among treatment means are required.

DMRT (at 5% level of significance) was used for group comparison of taxa of sampling for each direction where the sources of variations were year and taxon and the data structure under analysis was the replication wise mean data derived from three years study and the results were presented by using the alphabet notation to indicate which treatments are homogeneous and which are significantly different. Here similar alphabets in subscript beside treatment mean values denote homogenous treatment mean at 5 per cent level of significance.

Comparison of treatment means is also made easier by multiple or component bar diagram where taxa are represented on the X-axis and the volumes or frequencies are represented in the Y-axis. In multiple bar diagram data are classified by attributes and the taxa are to be compared within each attribute. In component bar diagram, instead of placing the bars for each component side by side, place these one on top of the other.

The principal component analysis (PCA) was followed based on correlation matrix. It is a data reduction technique where the primary good is to construct linear combinations of the original variables keeping total variation accounted for as much as possible. The successive linear combination were extracted in such a way, that they were uncorrected with each other and account for successively smaller amounts of the of the total variation. No transformation of character expression was required as the correlation matrix would be used to find out important factors and participating dominant parameters, which were loading each factor heavily. Depending upon those Eigen values which were more than one, the factors or principal components were extracted to diminish the dimension of the data matrix and these extracted factors all are orthogonal to each other. These factors would only help us to detect the performing treatments due to specific set of attributes or parameters under investigation. PCA helps us to identify the dominant characters important to diagnose class of similar treatments in two dimensional scales. Based upon the regression scores of treatments weighted by the loading of each character viz. factor-1 vs. factor-2, factor-1 vs. factor-3 etc. were displayed by scatter diagrams to show the clusters of treatments so produced. (Dillon & Goldstein, 1984)

Factor corresponding to Eigen values more than one and characters with loading between highest and allowed 20% reduction of highest one were only considered in this study.

Hierarchical cluster analysis has been utilized in classifying taxa. It identified cluster among taxa based on the given characters. It further indicated how similar each taxon is to each other, a procedure found very useful in distinguishing taxa.

Dendrogram using simple linkage (or nearest neighbour) methods of hierarchical cluster analysis based upon squared Euclidean matrix between taxa using characterization variables under study actually classifies the treatments into different homogenous clusters.

All the statistical analysis was performed using SPSS on a desktop P.C.

RESULT AND DISCUSSION

Folk Varieties

In Gangetic West Bengal hundred selected mono embryonic varieties have been evolved as chance seedlings as a result of open pollination, out of these only a few are commercially important and more than 95 per cent of the mango area is under those commercial varieties. The rest may be termed as folk varieties as those are closely related to culture and heritage of folk people in confined locations and are revealed in oral folk literature in those particular areas like Gombhira, Alkap folk dramas.

It is now common practices that orchardist-folk sells their orchards to the merchant-folk for a specific period of time. The

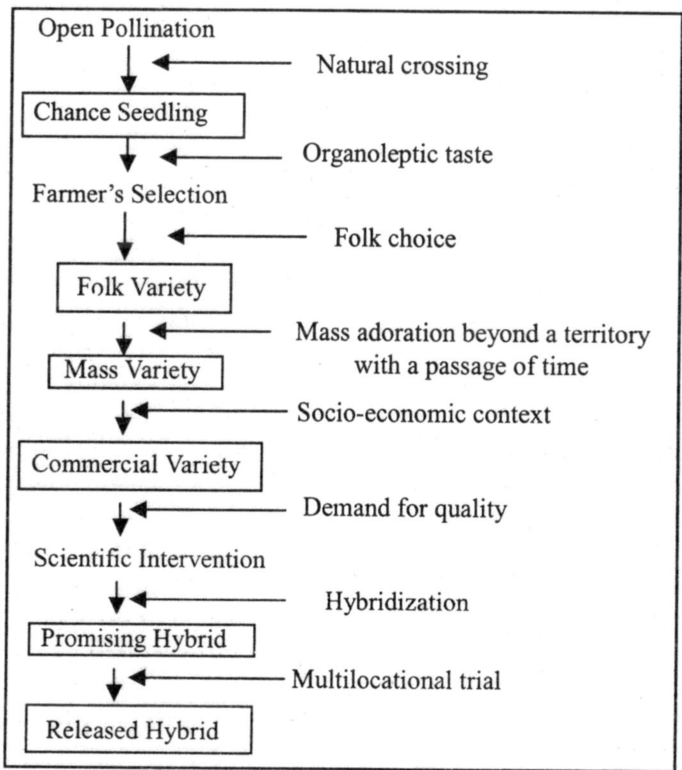

folk varieties as defined, are kept for their own consumption. The industrialists have developed recently new orchards with commercial varieties. They are engaged in large-scale production through scientific intervention. They have least interest in folk varieties and more frequently than not they avail the opportunity of felling those. So there is a transformation in the composition and character of folk in mango industry. The traditional orchardist-folk have their own traditional knowledge base and that agriculture is essentially a farming stage instead of industrial stage.

In this treatise it is proposed that folk varieties may be defined as the genotypes of an indigenous crop grown by a traditional farmer-folk in subsistence level of farming equipped with age old knowledge within a given territory over a period of time after natural evolution and selection. So, folk variety is closely related to culture and heritage of folk people. In this context a schematic diagram is given hereunder to depict the evolution of mango germplasm.

The plant, leaf and fruit characters of 10 selected folk varieties of Gangetic West Bengal are described in Table-1.1, 1.2 and 1.3 for easy identification. Table-1.1 shows that growth habit of Brindabani, Dudh Kumor, Kua Pahara, Michhri Kon, Surma Fazli and Lamba Bhadura are spreading but Arajana, Mohan Bhog, Funia and Rakhal Bhog are erect. Surma Fazli is vigorous to very vigorous; Kua Pahara and Michhri Kon are vigorous; Rakhal Bhog is semi-vigorous to vigorous; Brindabani, Dudh Kumor, Mohan Bhog and Funia are semi-vigorous and Arajana and Lamba Bhadura are dwarf to semi vigorous in nature. Moreover, Surma Fazli and Lamba Bhadura is dome shaped; Dudh Kumor and Arajana are oval and rests are round shaped.

Table-1.2 shows leaf characters in different folk varieties. The leaf shape of Brindabani and Surma Fazli are ovate lanceolate but rest are oval lanceolate. The leaf apex of Brindabani, Kua Pahara, Michhri Kon and Lamba Bhadura are sub-acuminate, Dudh Kumor and Arajana are acuminate and rests are acute. The margin of Funia is smooth; Surma Fazli is smooth to slightly wavy but rests are wavy.

Table 1.1
Plant Characters in Different Folk Varieties of Mango in Gangetic West Bengal

Folk Varieties	*Growth Habit*	*Vigour*	*Tree Shape*
Brindabani	Spreading	Semi-vigorous	Round
Dudh Kumor	Spreading	Semi-vigorous	Oval
Arajana	Erect	Dwarf to Semi vigorous	Oval
Kua Pahara	Spreading	Vigorous	Round
Michhri Kon	Spreading	Vigorous	Round
Surma Fazli	Spreading	Vigorous to very vigorous	Dome
Mohan Bhog	Erect	Semi-vigorous	Round
Lamba Bhadura	Spreading	Dwarf to semi-vigorous	Dome
Funia	Erect	Semi-vigorous	Round
Rakhal Bhog	Erect	Semi-vigorous to vigorous	Round

Table-1.3 shows fruit characters in different folk varieties. There is a variation in fruit shape and fruit beak. The most promising folk varieties, Surma Fazli and Dudh Kumor, are oblong-elliptic with slightly prominent beak and oblong-reniform with a point beak respectively. The fruit sinus is absent in Kua Pahara, Mohan Bhog and Funia. In Rakhal Bhog it is almost absent, in Dudh Kumor it is shallow in nature but in the rest varieties it is slightly present. The fruit apex of Brindabani, Dudh Kumor and Lamba Bhadura are broadly pointed; Arajana, Michhri Kon and Surma Fazli are rounded and Kua Pahara, Mohan Bhog, Funia and Rakhal Bhog are broadly rounded.

Table-1.4 represents the mean values of the physical parameters of fruits in different folk varieties. The results of Duncan's test for comparing mean values of these parameters are noted alphabetically where similar alphabets denote homogenous varietal means.

From Table-1.4 it is revealed that the mean fruit weight of Surma Fazli was significantly highest (635.08 g) than all other varieties and is denoted as 'a'. Significantly lowest fruit weight was recorded in Rakhal Bhog (138.58 g) and denoted as 'f'.

The mean value of fruit length was also significantly highest in Surma Fazli (16.64 cm) than all other varieties and is denoted as 'a'. Significantly least fruit length was recorded in Brindabani (7.80 cm) than all other varieties except Arajana,

Table 1.2
Leaf Characters in Different Folk Varieties of Mango in Gangetic West Bengal

Folk Varieties	*Leaf Shape*	*Leaf Nature*	*Leaf Apex*	*Margin*
Brindabani	Ovate-lanceolate	Crinkled to slightly folded	Sub Acuminate	Wavy
Dudh Kumor	Ovate-lanceolate	Crinkled	Acuminate	Wavy
Arajana	Ovate-lanceolate	Wavy	Acuminate	Wavy
Kua Pahara	Oval-lanceolate	Wavy	Sub Acuminate	Wavy
Michhri Kon	Oval-lanceolate	Slightly wavy to flat	Sub Acuminate	Wavy
Surma Fazli	Ovate-lanceolate	Flat	Acute	Smooth to slightly wavy
Mohan Bhog	Oval-lanceolate	Crinkled to slightly wavy	Acute	Wavy
Lamba Bhadura	Oval-lanceolate	Wavy	Sub Acute	Wavy
Funia	Oval-lanceolate	Flat	Acute	Smooth
Rakhal Bhog	Oval-lanceolate	Wavy	Acute	Wavy

Table-1.3
Fruit Characters in Different Folk Varieties of Mango in Gangetic West Bengal

Folk Varieties	*Fruit Shape*	*Fruit Beak*	*Fruit Sinus*	*Fruit Apex*
Brindabani	Oblong-Oval to Oblong-Reniform	Slight	Slight	Broadly Pointed
Dudh Kumor	Oblong-Elliptic	Slightly Prominent	Shallow	Broadly Pointed to Rounded
Arajana	Oblong-Oblique	Slight but Distinct	Slight	Rounded
Kua Pahara	Obliquely Oval	A-point	Absent	Broadly Rounded
Michhri Kon	Ovate Oblong	Slight but Distinct	Slight	Rounded
Surma Fazli	Oblong-Reniform	A-point	Slight	Rounded
Mohan Bhog	Ovate Roundish	Broadly Mammiform	Absent	Broadly Rounded
Lamba Bhadura	Oblong	A-point	Slight	Broadly Pointed
Funia	Oblong	Curved	Absent	Broadly Rounded
Rakhal Bhog	Ovate-Oblique	Almost Absent	Almost Absent	Broadly Rounded

Table 1.4

Physical Characters of Mango Fruits in Different Folk Varieties (Mean Values Along With The Duncan's Test Results)

Folk Varieties	*Fruit Weight (g)*		*Fruit Length (cm)*		*Fruit Breadth (cm)*		*Stone Weight (g)*	*Stone (%)*	*Peel Weight (g)*	*Peel (%)*	*Pulp weight (g)*	*Pulp (%)*
Brindabani	236.83	d	7.80	d	5.77	d	35.23	14.87	39.70	16.77	161.90	68.36
Dudh Kumor	192.67	dc	11.51	bc	6.37	bcd	21.81	11.32	25.10	13.03	145.76	75.65
Arajana	159.95	ef	8.25	d	5.99	d	20.35	12.72	30.10	18.82	109.50	68.46
Kua Pahara	234.18	d	9.39	d	6.70	bcd	25.51	10.89	44.87	19.17	163.80	69.94
Michhri Kon	150.33	ef	8.58	d	6.25	cd	23.20	15.43	30.54	20.32	96.59	64.25
Surma Fazli	635.08	a	16.64	a	9.40	a	54.07	8.51	96.00	15.12	485.01	76.37
Mohan Bhog	417.98	b	11.96	bc	9.35	a	68.09	16.29	74.06	17.72	275.83	65.99
Lamba Bhadura	357.95	c	12.96	b	6.95	bc	41.55	11.61	78.29	21.87	238.11	66.52
Funia	151.62	ef	11.08	c	6.22	cd	20.51	13.53	37.14	24.49	93.97	61.98
Rakhal Bhog	138.58	f	8.70	d	7.23	b	13.32	9.61	32.79	23.67	92.47	66.72
SE (m)	14.91		0.56		0.29							
CD (0.05)	31.11		1.18		0.60							

Michhri Kon, Rakhal Bhog and Kua Pahara and all are denoted as 'd'.

Significantly highest fruit breadth was noticed in Surma Fazli (9.40 cm) than all other varieties except Mohan Bhog (9.35 cm) and these are denoted as 'a'. Significantly least fruit breadth was recorded in Arajana (5.99 cm) than all other varieties except Brindabani (denoted as'd'), Funia (denoted as 'cd'), Dudh Kumor (denoted as 'bcd') and Kua Pahara (denoted as 'bcd').

The percentage of stone weight was the lowest in Surma Fazli (8.51%) and highest in Mohan Bhog (16.29%). That of peel weight was the lowest in Dudh Kumor (13.03%) and the highest in Funia (24.49%). Moreover, the percentage of pulp weight was the highest in Surma Fazli (76.37%) and the lowest in Funia (61.98%).

Table–1.5 represents the mean values of the bio-chemical qualitative parameters of fruits in different folk varieties. The results of Duncan's test for comparing mean values of these parameters are also noted alphabetically where similar alphabets denote homogenous varietal means.

From Table–1.5 it is revealed that the mean TSS value of variety Kua Pahara was significantly highest (18.93^0 Brix) than all other varieties. The least of that was recorded in Mohan Bhog (14.53^{0}Brix) than all other varieties except Dudh Kumor, Arajana, Michhri Kon and Lamba Bhadura. The mean value of total sugar was significantly highest in Surma Fazli (14.18%) than all other varieties except Rakhal Bhog. That of Michhri Kon was significantly lowest (9.09%) than all other varieties. The mean value of reducing sugar was significantly highest in Mohan Bhog (5.46%) than all other varieties except Brindabani and Arajana. Significantly least mean acidity was noticed in Arajana (0.20%) than all other varieties except Dudh Kumor, Surma Fazli, Rakhal Bhog, Kua Pahara and Brindabani. The mean value of TSS: acid ratio was significantly highest in Arajana (76.15) than all other varieties except Dudh Kumor, Surma Fazli and Rakhal Bhog.

Table-1.6 displays the PCA results where component matrix shows that factor-1 explains 40.17 per cent of total

Table 1.5

Fruit Quality of Different Folk Varieties of Mango (Mean Values Along With The Duncan's Test Results)

Folk Varieties	*TSS (°Brix)*		*Total Sugar (%)*		*Reducing Sugar (%)*		*Acidity (%)*		*TSS : Acid*	
Brindabani	12.27	b	12.80	b	5.31	a	0.39	cde	45.06	cd
Dudh Kumor	14.53	d	11.93	c	3.55	c	0.23	e	68.61	ab
Arajana	15.13	cd	11.02	d	4.91	ab	0.20	e	76.15	a
Kua Pahara	18.93	a	10.96	d	3.46	c	0.35	cde	53.72	bc
Michhri Kon	15.60	bcd	9.09	c	3.91	bc	0.65	a	27.32	d
Surma Fazli	16.40	bc	14.18	a	3.67	c	0.28	de	58.77	abc
Mohan Bhog	14.53	d	12.53	bc	5.46	a	0.45	bcd	33.34	c
Lamba Bhadura	15.73	bcd	10.67	d	3.05	c	0.57	ab	27.72	c
Funia	16.67	bc	10.36	d	3.06	c	0.52	abc	32.93	c
Rakhal Bhog	17.20	b	13.79	a	4.09	bc	0.30	de	58.84	abc
SE (m)	0.56		0.25		0.33		0.06		5.86	
CD (0.05)	1.16		0.53		0.69		0.12		12.22	

variance and traits like total sugar, fruit length, fruit breadth and pulp weight are highly positively loaded in this factor. Factor-2 explains another 21.52 per cent of total variance and highly positively loaded with traits like reducing sugar and stone weight.

Table 1.6
Component Matrix Due to Principal Component Analysis for Multi Trait Study of Folk Varieties

Variables	*Component* 1	2	3	4
TSS	-0.09	-0.57	-0.54	0.40
Total Sugar	0.79	0.10	-0.15	0.52
Reducing Sugar	0.04	0.90	-0.18	0.38
Fruit Acidity	-0.72	-0.16	0.57	0.05
Fruit Length	0.63	-0.31	0.68	-0.03
Fruit Breadth	0.60	0.05	0.61	0.47
Stone Weight	-0.65	0.68	0.24	0.01
Peel Weight	-0.69	-0.48	0.03	0.42
Pulp Weight	0.91	0.00	-0.16	-0.34
Eigen Values	*3.62*	*1.94*	*1.58*	*1.10*
% of Variance	40.17	21.52	17.54	12.17
Cumulative %	40.17	61.69	79.23	91.40

Regression factor scores are displayed at the scatter diagram (Fig. 1.1) and from such figure it is clear that Surma Fazli and Dudh Kumor are two distinct varieties where dominated traits of factor-1 are present with higher mean values. But Mohan Bhog followed by Brindabani and Arajana are only good for reducing sugar but with higher stone weight if only factor-2 is considered. From this figure it is clear that Dudh Kumor is only performing variety if all dominated traits of factor-1 and factor-2 are desired together with minimal stone weight. However, if total sugar is considered but not the reducing sugar then the best variety should be Surma Fazli.

From Table-1.6 it is also clear that factor-3 explains another 17.54% of total variance further and it is dominated by acidity, fruit length, fruit breadth and stone weight. Therefore, from Fig.1.2 it is clear that if stone weight and acidity are noted desired then Dudh Kumor is a better one than Surma Fazli.

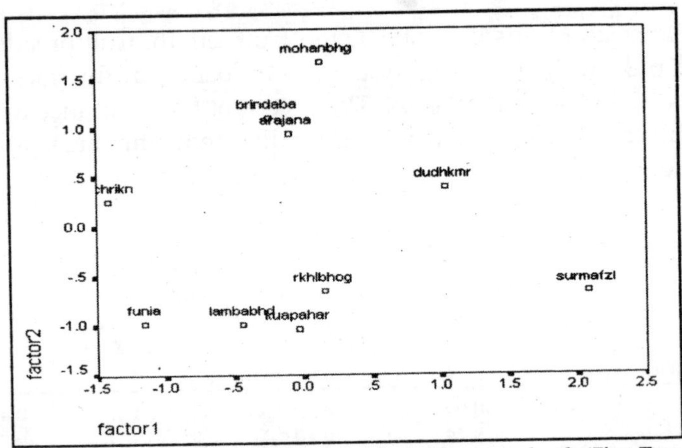

Fig. 1.1: Scatter Diagram of Regression Factor Scores under the First Two Principal Components to Show the Relative Positions of Folk Varieties

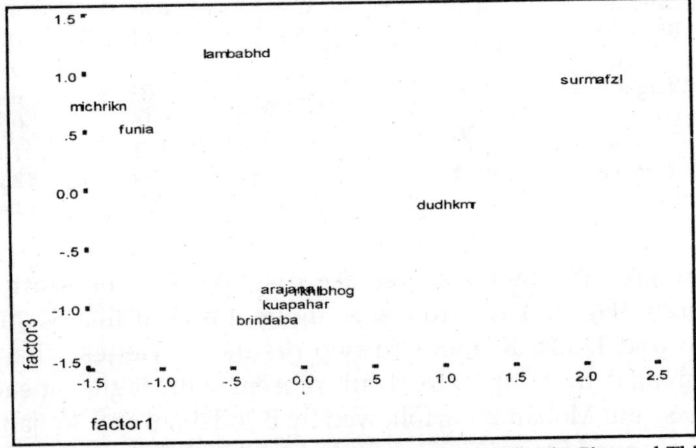

Fig. 1.2: Scatter Diagram of Regression Factor Scores under the First and Third Principal Components to Show the Relative Positions of Folk

From Table-1.6 it is further revealed that factor 4 explains another 12.17% of total variance and it is dominated by total soluble solid (TSS), total sugar, reducing sugar, fruit breadth and peel weight. From Fig. 1.3 it is clear that Surma Fazli is a better option than Dudh Kumor if TSS is asked to be higher. Though Rakhal Bhog followed by Mohan Bhog are only good for the dominated characters represented by factor-3 except for peel weight.

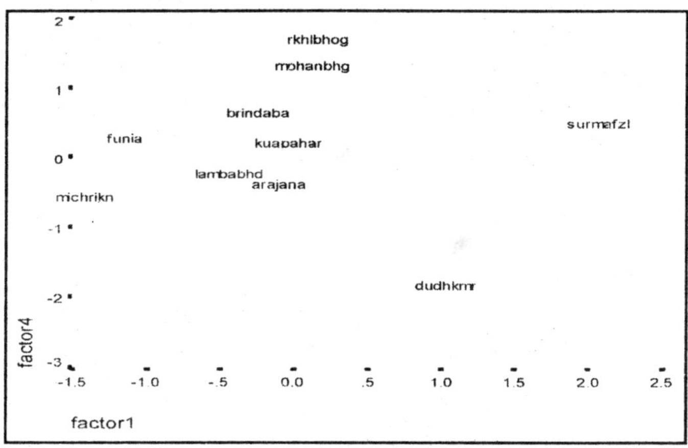

Fig. 1.3: Scatter Diagram of Regression Factor Scores under the First and Fourth Principal Components to Show the Relative Positions of Folk

Considering all factors, the promising folk varieties are Surma Fazli and Dudh Kumor for optimum presence of all physico-chemical traits under consideration.

Figure 1.4 represents the dendrogram due to cluster analysis to show the clusters of folk varieties on the basis of all the physical and bio-chemical parameters of folk varieties of mango in Gangetic West Bengal under study. Here, cluster analysis shows that if all the parameters are considered then Lamba Bhadura, Funia and Michhri Kon belong to same cluster but remaining varieties are distinct from each other.

CONCLUSION AND SUMMARY

The mango is distributed throughout the length and breadth of Gangetic West Bengal. In this zone a number of selected monoembryonic varieties have been evolved as chance seedlings as a result of open pollination. Out of these only a few are commercially important, and more than 95 per cent of the mango area is under the cultivation of those commercial varieties along with released hybrids. The rest may be termed as folk varieties as those are closely related to culture and heritage of folk people. These are confined in particular locations. It is now common practices that orchardist-folk sells their orchards to the merchant-folk for a specific period of time.

Fig. 1.4
Dendrogram following Single Linkage Hierarchical Cluster Analysis for Folk Varieties of Mango

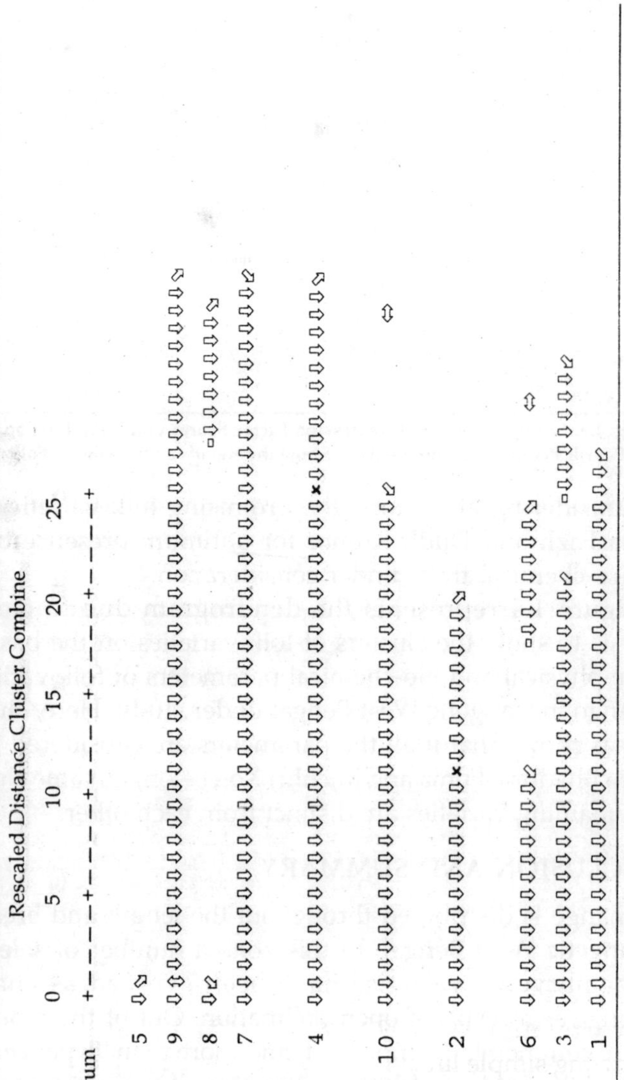

```
                        Rescaled Distance Cluster Combine

        C A S E         0         5         10        15        20        25
  Label           Num   +---------+---------+---------+---------+---------+

    Case 5          5
    Case 9          9
    Case 8          8
    Case 7          7
    Case 4          4
    Case 10        10
    Case 2          2
    Case 6          6
    Case 3          3
    Case 1          1
```

The folk varieties as defined, are kept for their own consumption. The industrialists have developed recently new orchards with commercial varieties and hybrids. They are engaged in large-scale production through scientific intervention. They have least interest in folk varieties and more frequently than not they avail the opportunity of felling those. So there is a transformation in the composition and character of folk in mango industry. The traditional orchardist-folk have their own traditional knowledge base and that agriculture is essentially a farming stage instead of industrial stage. In this treatise it is proposed that folk varieties may be defined as the genotypes of an indigenous crop grown by a traditional farmer-folk in subsistence level of farming equipped with age old knowledge within a given territory over a period of time after natural evolution and selection. An effort has also been made to evaluate and compare ten such varieties of Gangetic West Bengal in the perspective of mango-lore. It is proposed that the term mango-lore may be coined to denote the aggregate of cultural tradition delineating mango. Mango-lore is originated from the beliefs, culture and customs of folk people and it covers the tradition based cultural expressions exemplified by non-material folklore (viz. riddles, proverbs, sayings, folk tales, folk songs etc.) and material folklore (viz. folk foods, folk medicines, folk implements, folk varieties, etc.). The plant, leaf and fruit characters of those varieties are described for easy identification and future dissemination. These folk varieties are measured on the basis of different physical and biochemical characters during the year 2002 to 2004. Factor analysis like principal component analysis based on correlation matrix and hierarchical cluster analysis following simple linkage method based on Euclidean distance matrix are made to compare the performance of these varieties and to identify the homogenous varieties on the basis of multiple criterion measures. Considering all factors, the most promising folk varieties are Surma Fazli and Dudh Kumor for optimum presence of all physico-chemical traits under consideration.

REFERENCES

A.O.A.C. (1984), Official Methods of Analysis. Association of Official Analytical Chemists. Washington. D.C. USA.

Abul Fazal (1590), *Ain-i-Akbari* (Tr : H. Blochman. 1927). The Asiatic Society. Calcutta : 741 (2nd Edition reprinted in 1993).

Bandyopadhyay, M. and Chakraborti, K. (2003), Fruits in Bengali Proverbs. Paper presented in 10th West Bengal State Science and Technology Congress at Vidyasagar University (Midnapore, West Bengal, India) during Feb 28-March 2. Abstract Vol : 73.

Dillion, R.W. and Goldstein, M. (1984), Multivariate Analysis: Methods and Application. John Wiley and Sons. New York: 23-52.

Farrington, J. and Martin, A. (1987), Farmer Participation in Agricultural Research: A Review of Concepts and Practices, *Agricultural Administration*, Occasional Paper No. 9, ODI, London.

Gangolly, S.R., Singh, R., Katyal, S.L., and Singh, D. (1957), The Mango. Indian Council of Agricultural Research. New Delhi : 3-29.

Geetha, V. (1987), Folk Medicine With Special Reference to Tamil Nadu. *Folk India* : 16-28.

Gomez, K.A. and Gomez, A.A. (1983), Statistical Procedures for Agricultural Research. John Willey & Sons. New York : 20-29.

Harlan, J.R. (1956), Brookhaven Symposia in Biology 9 : 191-206.

Krappe, A.H. (1964), The Science of Folklore. The Norton Library. New York : 230-244.

Mahajan, R.K., Gangopadhyay, K.K., Kumar, G., Dobhal, V.K., Srivastava, U., Gupta, P.N. and Pareek, S.K. (2002), Minimal Descriptors of Agri-horticultural Crops. National Bureau of Plant Genetic Resources. New Delhi : 144-150.

Mehrotra, R.C., Dilcher, D.L., and Awasthi, N. (1998), A Palaeocene *Mangifera* like Leaf Fossil from India. *Phytomorphology* 48 : 91-100.

Nene, Y.L. (2001), Mango through Millennia. *Asian Agri-History.* 5 (1) : 39-67.

Panse, V.G. and Sukhatme, P.V. (1989), Statistical Methods for Agricultural Workers. ICAR. New Delhi : 97-128.

Sen, D. (2002), Changing Perspective of Participatory Extension in India. In: Readings of Winter School held in Bidhan Chandra Krishi Viswavidyalaya, West Bengal, India on Dec. 2-31, 2002 : 18.

Sharangi, A.B. (2000), Standardization of Stone Grafting of Mango (*Mangifera indica* L.) under West Bengal Condition. Ph.D. thesis submitted to the Bidhan Chandra Krishi Viswavidyalaya (West Bengal) : 3-4.

Simmods, N.W. (1962), *Biological Reviews.* 37 : 442-465.

Singh, L.B. (1960), The Mango-Botany, Cultivation and Utilization. Interscience Publishers. New York.

Singh, R.N. (1996), Mango. Indian Council of Agricultural Research. New Delhi : 134 (2nd Reprint).

Swaminathan, M.S. (1978), National Symposium on Plant and Animal Genetic Resources. IARI. New Delhi.

Photographs of Some Folk Varieties of Mango

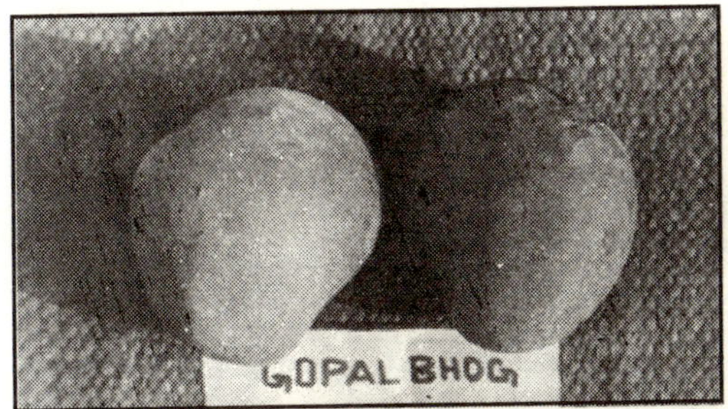

Gopal Bhog

Dudhkumar

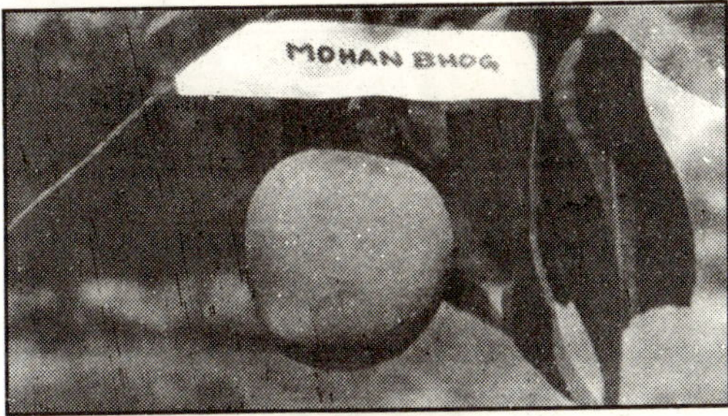

Mohan Bhog

Ashwina

Lakshman Bhog

Sita Bhog

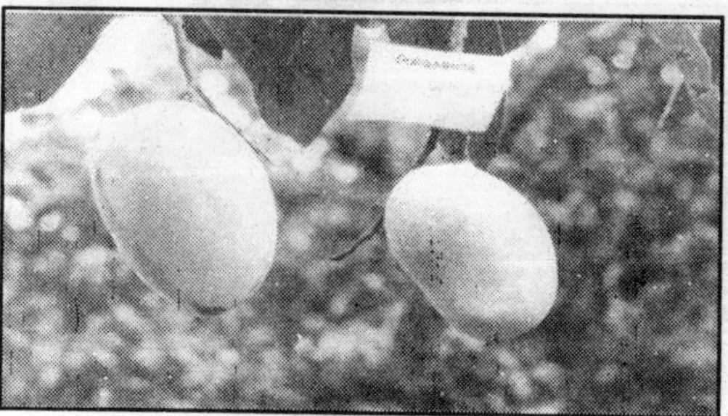

Durga Bhog

Lamba Bhadoria

Kamala Bhog

Kelua

Surma Fazli

9 Survival of Ethnomedicine in the Modern Medical World: A Study Among the Kadar Tribe of Indira Gandhi Wildlife Sanctuary in Tamil Nadu

K. Sasicoumar Brumot and T. Subramanyam Naidu

INTRODUCTION

Ethnomedicine refers to the study of traditional medical practice, which is concerned with the cultural interpretation of health, diseases and illness and also addresses the health care seeking process and healing practices (Krippner 2003). The practice of ethnomedicine is a complex multi-disciplinary system constituting the use of plants, spirituality and the natural environment and has been the source of healing for people for millennia (Lowe 2000). The term ethnomedicine is more accepted and especially the aboriginal populations are in the regular habit of using this with reference to the knowledge of plant or plant part(s) and animal products for the treatment of many diseases. Globally, about 85% of the traditional medicines used for primary healthcare are derived from plants (Farnsworth 1983-97).

Ever since from the ancient times, the tribal peoples have found remedies within their habitat and have evolved different therapeutic strategies among themselves for most of the diseases. After these gradually many of the societies of the world people (not exception of aboriginal people) follow more than one type of medical system to deal with the illness situation. In a developing country like India, where portion of its population is residing in rural and tribal areas and which have their own culture-specific medical heritage, the health policy makers and health care planners, during the conduction work of their scientific health care programmes frequently met with stiff resistance. While local people usually welcome the provision of hospitals and public health programs, the shift to using biomedicine often means that healing traditions are eroded and traditional knowledge lost in the process (Macintyre and Foale, 2004; Macintyre, 2004). This paves great flaw to their native medical system.

Before the execution of ethnomedicine from the tribal community, it is necessary to document and understand this culture-specific medical heritage from its total perspectives. Keeping all these facts and views in mind, the present paper has tried to present two broad aims. First, the study was to assess the richness of ethnomedicinal plant species used and the traditional medical practices of the people. Second, to assess what extent the Kadar people have accepted the modern medicine. To test whether the two systems of health care often operate in parallel or rather opposites.

MATERIALS AND METHODS

Description of the Study Area

The present study was investigated in the contemplation of some aspects of health culture of the Kadar, a tribe of Indira Gandhi Wildlife Sanctuary (IGWS), which lies between 10^0 12.′ and 11^0 7′ Latitude and 76^0 01′ and 77^0 56.5′ E Longitude in Coimbatore district of Tamilnadu, South India. The area of the sanctuary is 958 Sq.Kms., and can be reached through Top slip in Anamalai Hills and Valparai through Pollachi on the Western Ghats of elevations varying from 350-2500 m. The annual rainfall ranges from 500- 5000 mm. The district presents different climatic zones and variable topography which makes it possible for the occupation of many anthropologically significant ethnic groups like, Kadar, Muduvar, Malai Malasar or Maha Malasar, Malasar and Kurumbar distributed over the IGWS.

Methodology

The data was obtained through interviews using both structured and semi-structured schedules, and reviewing both published and unpublished documents. Purposive sampling method was used to interview all ethnomedicinal practioners, and traditional midwives(dhais) among the Kadar tribe in IGWS. Six Kadar settlements were selected for the present study namely Kallar, Kavarkal, Ethakuli, Arumagamkudi, Sundarankudi and Nedumkundru.

RESULTS

Concept of Health Among the Kadar

The Kadar has no clear concept about health. A person is considered healthy when he is not afflicted by any disease, consumes food as usual and carries out his normal functions without any difficulty. Generally the Kadar don't give attention to the disease situation. Their unfriendly habitat tends them to do hard work for getting food. So, only when somebody is seriously ill, will be laid down and allowed to take rest. Then it is the responsibility of the family members to look after and to provide necessary treatment. However, there is no effort to prevent the occurrence of diseases by keeping personal hygiene and preserving sanitary environment. Apparently the Kadar seems to possess good health. Most of the adult people work in the fields throughout the day without any physical constraint. The women folk also engage themselves either in the field or in domestic chores.

The common illness among the people includes, Guinea intestinal worm, stomach order, scabies, pain in different parts/joints of the body, cough, headache and vomiting. The most frequent illness among the adult men is pain in different parts of the body particularly in the joints, among the women is cough, cold and fever whereas the children are mostly the victims of worms, skin disease and stomach disorder. Diseases like polio, diabetes, tetanus, hypertension, hypotension, tuberculosis and cancer etc., are not familiar to the Kadar people. There are no native terms for these diseases but some of the educated people know the names of these. The elderly people maintain that these diseases were unknown among them in earlier days. The names of common illnesses afflicting the people and the therapeutic recipes followed by the medicine men of the Kadar community, and the treatments vary according to the availability of plants in the surroundings. Each plant has its own quality in curing the disease.

Diet and Diseases

In the past, they completely depended upon the forest for food and medicine. Their diet consisted mainly of tubers, fruits, wild vegetables, green leaves, honey, fish, crabs, tortoises and monkeys and the flesh of so many other small game animals which were very nutritious and ideal for good health. The change that acquired in the quality of diet has an adverse effect on the health of the Kadar. For the first time they have experienced the evils like adulteration, pollution, etc., which have telling effect on their health. This paves the way for the origin of new diseases amongst the Kadar. The traditional medicine is helpless to cure this new type of diseases. Since they subsisted on forest produces, there was no problem of adulteration or food pollution. They have obtained a number of medicinal plants also from the forest, which could heal their diseases. The Kadar observes that the occurrence of disease was very rare in the past, when they were following the hunting-gathering mode of life. Availability of game also has decreased due to deforestation and the strictness of forest department. There is a dearth of medicinal plants also. The poor condition of forest tends the Kadar to look for market for food materials and the modern medicinal systems.

Their herbal remedies were effective in checking the few diseases that occurred earlier. In the present period, a number of diseases are affecting the people and traditional medicine is helpless to control them. The Kadar believe that, the change that has taken place in the quality of diet is effectually responsible for the occurrence new diseases. Due to the restrictions of the forest department, Kadar is not able to roam around freely in the forest. The present diet of the Kadar consists of rice, tapioca and other food items purchased from the market and from the ration shops. Most of these food materials are less nutritious and adulterated. Therefore, these adversely affect the health of the Kadar. The deterioration of health due to change in the diet paves the way for occurrence of disease on a large scale.

Overwork and Scarcity of Food

Excessive work and inadequate intake of food are also the reason affecting the health of Kadar. Often, they have to engage in hard work for their survival in the hostile terrains of their habitat. However, after they have started the sedentary life-style, the variety of their diet has decreased largely. Because of the forest department's restrictions, they are not getting many of the traditional food items right from the forest. The food available for them now is less nutritious and chiefly contains starch. Therefore, the lack of a balanced diet plays a complementary role with the excessive work, in the deterioration of health.

Misconcept about the Modern Medicine

Though the Kadar believes that a woman conceives only by the blessings of god, pregnancy is considered as a natural phenomenon. They do not seem to be interested in having regular medical checkup and taking medicines during pregnancy. Only a very few families go for the same in nearby primary health centre(PHC). Generally, the delivery takes place in the house being attended by womenfolk. No male member, including the husband is allowed to enter the delivery room. The old and experienced women of the village, usually relative or mother-in-law etc., help the expectant mother. The service of a trained midwife is not available in most of the Kadar villages. If there is any complication during the time of delivery, the people by and large go for the traditional medicine man and he gives some oral herbal medicine for a normal delivery. In the complicated cases only the Kadar pregnant women move furtively to the nearby PHC. It is very dicky to take the complicated cases to the PHC for the reason that the bridleway is very narrow and perilous.

In the study area there has been more number of complaints amongst the Kadar that they do not have children. Out of 207 married women in the study area 40 (19.32 percent) are not having children. The data clearly illustrates that in the study area the number of barren women are significant. The Kadar has the belief that if they consume the modern medicines they would fail to have the children.

Choice of Medicine

In the selection of medicine no clear preferences towards any system could be noticed. They avail the facilities of both types of medicine according to the nature of illness. The shamans and the traditional medicine men always treat the diseases originating from supernatural causes. Economic constraints and the sylvan isolation very often deter the people for using modern medicine. The results obtained from the Kadar show that ethnomedicine has a definite edge over modern medicine.

Modern Medicine and Diseases

The Kadar claim that the changes occurred in the medical practice also plays a role in the origin of new diseases. In the past, they used to treat diseases with their own herbal remedies. These herbal medicines are non-harmful to the body but increase its vitality. Now a days they are using a number of modern medicines for the treatment of diseases. They believe that even though modern medicines give quick relief from illness these have a number of harmful effects on the body. The traces of modern medicines remain in the body for a long time and cause new diseases. Therefore, the medicine used to recover from a disease, again functions as a casual agent for the origin of another disease.

Ethnomedical Practices of Kadar

In the present paper, an attempt has been made to understand the ethnomedical system of the Kadar. The Kadar has a rich knowledge of ethnomedicine and depends upon it for their health care. List of medicinal plants used by Kadar are given in the Table No. 1. Herbal therapy is a significant component

Table 1
List of Medicinal Plants Used by Kadar Tribe in the Study Area

Scientific Name	*Family*
Ageratum haustomianum L.	Asteraceae
Andrographis paniculata (Burm. f.) Wall. ex Nees	Acanthaceae
Aristolochia indica *L.*	Aristolochiaceae
Asparagus racemosus Willd.	Liliaceae
Boerhavia diffua L.	Nyctanginaceae
Caesalpinia crista L.	Caesalpiniaceae
Canarium strictum Roxb	Burseraceae
Curcuma neilgherrensis Wight	Ingiberaceae
Dalbergia latifolia Roxb.	Fabaceae
Ensete superbum (Roxb.) Cheesman	Musaceae
Entada pursaetha DC.	Mimosaceae
Erythropalum papulifolium Mast. (Arn.) Mast	Erythropalaceae
Hydrocotyle javanica Thunb	Apiaceae
Naravelia zeylanica (L.) C. Syst.	Ranunculaceae
Sansevieria roxburghiana Schultes & Schultes f.	Agavaceae
Sida rhombifolia L.	Malvaceae
Terminalia paniculata Roth	Combretaceae

Contd.

Tribal Name	*Parts Used*	*Uses*
Appichi Soppu	Leaves	Leaf juice or dried leaf powder is applied to wounds for healing.
Kuringi Soppu	Leaves	The leaf extract is given to treat stomachache and snakebite.
Garuda Koddi	Root	Root extract is given to treat snakebite
Sadavalli	Tubers	Tuber paste is applied to forehead for headache.

Mukkaratu	Root	Root decoction is drunk to get relief from all types of hip and joint pains.
Malichikai	Seeds	Seed paste is given to relieve from chest pain and stomach problems
Thelli	Resin	The resin is applied to the skin for all types of skin afflictions
Kattu Manjal	Rhizome	The rhizome paste is applied to wounds, cuts and skin for rapid healing
Eravadi	Stem bark	The stem bark decoction is drunk to control cough. The paste is applied to the anal region for piles. It is also used during bone fracture as a paste.
Kundai	Seeds	Seed paste is applied to body as a refrigerant. It is also a useful purgative
Vethalavalli	Seeds	Seed decoction is drunk to improve body resistance. It is also useful for relieving severe hip and joint pains
Kanaiyan Suravalli Kodi	Root	Root juice is instilled into ears as a good remedy for all types of ear problems
Kaamada Soppu	Leaf	Leaf paste is applied to the body for all types of skin ailments. Leaf decoction is drunk as a remedy for jaundice.
Elivallii	Root and Leaf	Root decoction taken orally for stomachache and diarrohea. Leaf paste is applied to wounds for healing. The leaf paste is also applied to forehead for relieving one-sided headache.
Marul Motha Manji	Root	Root decoction is drunk as remedy for respiratory problems
Chithramlli	Leaf	Leaf paste is applied to hair to get rid of dandruff
Varu Marunthu	Stem bark	Stem bark decoction is drunk to relieve gastric problems

Source: K. Sasicoumar Brumot and T.S. Naidu (2006)

of ethnomedicine of these people. Kadar have preserved their own divination techniques, spells curing ritual as a sole property of the community. Knowledge of ethnomedicine is accessible to only a few selected persons, they could keep them as top secrets and treat them as the most valuable treasure of the community.

The Kadar has been exposed to modern medicine at the same time. Kadar did not accept modern medicine in the early stages of its introduction by the government agencies. Conversely, their negative attitude was changed with the passage of time. On the other hand, after the contact with the advanced population groups, certain new diseases are occurring among them. The Kadar do not know the actual cause behind these new diseases. Therefore, they have no adequate techniques or medicine for the treatment of these modern diseases. Often they depend upon modern medicine for them. However, they continue to utilize ethnomedicine for diseases originating from supernatural causes. Even so, it can be noticed that the Kadar are more enthusiastic in grasping the facilities of modern medicine.

SHORTCOMINGS OF ETHNOMEDICINE

The Knowledge about ethnomedicine is a part of the traditional lore of the community. This secret knowledge about medicinal plants and magical rituals are always transferred orally through generations and there are no written documents to store this knowledge. They follow the age-old medicinal combinations and healing techniques, which they have inherited from their ancestors.

Ethnomedicine often cannot cope with the fast changes occurring in the community. Changes occurred in the habitat, subsistence pattern and dietary habits of the tribals and the close association with non-tribals are made them to bring alterations in their traditional life styles. Along with these changes acculturation, brought forth many new diseases to them. Most of these diseases were not present among them in the past and hence the tribal medicine men are helpless to tackle these. It is quite natural that there are no medicine to check the maladies like pollution and acculturation in nature. The medicine men are not able to diagnose these causes, which are not familiar to them.

The medicine men of present age are not as competent as their predecessors. As the Kadar in the past solely dependent upon the forest for their food and medicine, the medicine men of those periods had a vast knowledge of the medicinal properties of flora and fauna. With the death of the old medicine men, considerable amount of knowledge was lost. There are also some professional hindrances, which retarded the passing of medical knowledge from medicine men to his disciples. Generally the traditional medicine man won't teach all his techniques to his disciples. They thought that if all the medical knowledge were disclosed, the effectiveness of the formula would decrease, so they don't tell to others. Some of the teachers want to reveal this knowledge in their last days. However, very often, they don't get any opportunity to do so and the precious medical knowledge is lost forever.

The expertise of tribal medicine men in the art of the surgery is very crude and not sufficient for the successful treatment of complicated cases. Even though they have a good knowledge in the bone setting technique, they may commit mistakes when fractures are involved.

RATIONALE FOR THE SURVIVAL OF ETHNOMEDICINE

Ethnomedicine is still persisting in the Kadar community even after the introduction of modern medicine since a number of decades. Of course, its former popularity and reliability has considerably eroded and a number of Kadar is now exploiting the facilities of modern medicine in addition to ethnomedicine. However, through a close observation one can find out that traditional ethnomedicine is still viable and it plays a commendable role in the treatment of ailments amongst the Kadar. Some observations, given below, explain the favourable factors for the survival of this system of medicine. To get treated through modern medical system it is very expensive. Though the government hospitals provide free treatment, the attention by the doctors and other staff, and the quality of medicines given are of very low category. For most of the costly medicines, the doctors give prescription notes and the patients have to buy them from the medical shops. Most of the Kadar can't afford this treatment. Therefore they depend upon the ethnomedicine, which is available just at free of cost. The medicine men do not demand any money and all the medicines are available from nature.

Most of the Kadar are of opinion that ethnomedicine is harmless and specifically suitable for the body. As plant and animal materials obtained from nature are used for the preparation of medicine, its function inside the body will be quite natural and rejuvenating. They believe that even though a modern medicine gives quick relief, it retains harmful effect in the body. After healing one type of illness, the harmful principles of the medicine can cause another disease some time later. As a result of screening, modern medicine gets the more complicated and serious cases while ethnomedicine gets only cases of minor illnesses. So, the percentage of success will be higher in the case of ethnomedicine than in the case of modern medicine. Thus, the screening is favourable to the ethnomedicine and contributes to its apparent efficiency.

The practitioner of ethnomedicine is an insider to the community and the patients have personal relationships with him. The healer is related to the patient as a friend, kinsman etc. Therefore, their relationship is very cordial and informal. After diagnosis, the medicine men will explain to the patient the causes and remedies of the illness. Thus along with the healer, the patient also has an active role in the treatment procedure. This will ensure full co-operation of the patient with the healer and their joint effort will bring success easily. The relationship between a patient and a doctor is formal and they are representatives of two different cultures. The doctor will ask a number of questions to the patient about the disease and seldom explain the cause and remedy of the illness. The interest of the doctor in the patient is limited to the disease, its diagnosis and treatment.

MEDICAL PLURALISM

Medical pluralism may be defined as the synchronic existence in a society of more than one medicine systems grounded in different principles or based on different worldviews (Veena Bhasin 2007). In the past there was only ethnomedicine to deal with all kinds of illness situation in the Kadar community. Health has been regulated in such traditional communities by the medicine man or shaman, on the basis of sound ecological factors, although neither the healer nor the patient may have been consciously aware of the underlying basis of treatment. The medicine man derives all his medicines from the nature, which includes plant parts, animal matter and minerals. As medicines are the products from the forest, there is no degenerating effect. All the medicines come from the environment to which the tribal community has adopted themselves.

Thus more than one type of medical system came into practice in the tribal universe. This new innovation created numerous problems in the Kadar community. The philosophy of practice of modern medicine was alien to them. The policy of government to uplift the health condition of tribal through the introduction of modern medicine has a number of good as well as bad impacts on the tribals. Many of them first rejected this new system of medicine. But with the passage of time, they have slowly started to accept it for the treatment of certain diseases. But the modern medicine often could not satisfy all their needs. So, most of the Kadar are now using the more efficacious elements of the native systems of medicine. They select a particular kind of medicine according to the nature and seriousness of their illness.

CONCLUSION

The Kadar tribes are suffering a lot to get proper modern medical facilities as well as their own trditional medicine. Due to the non-interest of the younger generation and the wrong belief of forefathers the deliberation of uses of plants has not been explained to the younger generation. For this reason the younger generation fails to give remedies for all the diseases.

Moreover, the younger generation shows apathy towards the ethnomedicine. In addition to this the erroneous belief, which the Kadar had about the modern medicine create some basic problems here. For example, in the study area there has been a lot of complaints amongst the Kadar that they don't have children. The Kadar has the belief that the barrenness is due to the effect of modern medicines. To prevent this immediate step should be taken.

For the above said fact an immediate action should be taken to impart health education. The main reason contributing to the failure of the programmes is ignorance of the health providers towards understanding the people's beliefs and practice, and the meaning they attach to their health behaviour. It is necessary to document and understand this medical heritage from an emic perspective.

To overahead this reality in the tribal areas a separate medical team, which consists of experienced doctors with internship medical students, traditional healer/shaman and a medical personnel as well as a social anthropologist according to the geographical distribution should be appointed immediately. If we engage them in the medical team the rapport between the traditional healer and modern medical officer would be very easier. Not only that the tribal people could enjoy both the traditional medicine as well as modern medicine without any hesitation, but also the indigenous knowledge continues forever without any disturbances.

REFERENCES

Krippner S. "*Models of Ethnomedicinal Healing*". Paper Presented at the Ethnomedicine Conferences, Munich, Germany. April 26–27 and October 11–12, 2003. cited in LAD Williams, Ethnomedicine West Indian Med J 2006; 55 (4): 215

Lowe H, Payne-Jackson A, Beckstrom-Sternberg SM, Duke JA. Jamaica's "*Ethnomedicine: Its Potential in the Healthcare System*". Canoe Press; 2000, University of the West Indies, Kingston, Jamaica.170.

Farnsworth NR: "*Screening Plants for New Medicines*". In *Biodiversity*. Edited by: Wilson EO. National Academy Press, Washington, DC; 83-97. .

M. Macintyre, S. Foale, N. Bainton, B. (2004), "Moktel Medical Pluralism and the Maintenance of a Traditional Healing technique on Lihir", Papua New Guinea, Pimatisiwin: A Journal of Aboriginal and Indigenous Community Health 3(1).

Veena Bhasin (2007), Medical Anthropology: A Review, Ethno-Med., 1(1): 1-20 (2007) © Kamla-Raj.

K. Sasicoumar Brumot and T.S. Naidu (2006), Medico-Ethnobotanical Survey of Kadar Tribe in the Anamalai Hills of Tamil Nadu, India, in edited volume by Prof. T.S. Naidu, *Tribal Health in Inda: Problems and future Perspectives.*

10 Indigenous Knowledge of Tribal People on Forest: A Case of a Tribal Village in Paschim Medinipur District of West Bengal

Samares Kumar Das

INTRODUCTION

Since ages tribal people have a close relationship with the forest. Most of the critical inputs for their sustenance are obtained from the forest. Thus, forest plays a crucial role in the very survival of tribal community. The ability of the forest to act as safety-net or shock-absorber is most noticeable during crisis situations such as disastrous conditions (drought, famine) and seasonal crisis (off-season). In doing so they develop their own perception, knowledge, experience and belief about the forest.

This knowledge, belief, attitude, value, and experience tribal people have on the forest help in utilising the forest resources sustaining its users' needs while not destroying it. Though tragedy of the commons[1]or commons' dilemma affects the forest adversely leading to over-exploitation and gradual destruction of the forest resources. But this is true when population explosion, external forces and policies, and different parties with divergent interests are involved in the use, conservation, protection and overall management of the forest.

On the other hand, the method of conservation of forest in the form of Biosphere Reserve, National Park, Sanctuary, and Protected/Restricted Area negatively affect the lives and livelihoods of its traditional users. Besides, many acts like construction of dams, buildings, factories, etc by deforestation also adversely affect the lives of tribal people. Thus, people who once had the exclusive right to use and conserve this common property resource[2] (CPR) now becoming destitute losing their traditional rights. All these acts combined with over-exploitation of forest force them to search for alternative livelihood to earn a living making them more vulnerable than ever before.

However, the importance of indigenous knowledge and practices are being recognised and efforts are increasingly being made to blend the modern scientific and technology based approaches with that of indigenous local level approaches for sustainable development (Das *et al.* 2003). Therefore, sustainable management of forest resources involving the local people who are the traditional users of the forest is the need of the hour for the very survival of indigenous people. And indigenous knowledge of tribal people on forest may contribute fruitfully toward sustainable conservation and management of forest resources to a considerable extent.

Thus, time has reached to understand and document the knowledge traditionally possessed by tribal people on forest. And getting an insight into and understanding of the same would add to our existing body of knowledge on the issues concerned. Thereby it may be a great help in formulating and implementing various policies and programmes of sustainable natural resource management that have serious implications for the conservation of forest as well as the very survival of tribal people.

Keeping this in view the present study was conducted to explore and understand the forest-people relationship with the following objectives.

- To assess the socio-economic and ecological profile of the village and associated changes that took place over the years;
- To document indigenous knowledge of tribal people on forest and its resources; and
- To understand how and in what extent villagers are related to and dependent on the adjacent forest.

RESEARCH METHODOLOGY

Field research was carried out in Bansiar village—a forest dependent tribal settlement in Paschim Medinipur district of West Bengal. And forest-people relationship was studied using the principles of Participatory Appraisal of Natural Resources (PANR).

PANR: PANR is a Participatory Rural Appraisal (PRA) based approach of listening and learning from local people as users of the natural resources. It focuses on analysing and understanding natural resources from users' point of view with other aspects as relevant to the resources in question (Mukherjee, 1997).

PRA: Participatory rural appraisal/participatory reflection and action (PRA) can be described as a family of approaches, methods and behaviours that enable people to express and analyse the realities of their lives and conditions (Chambers and Blackburn, 1996). It provides an alternative method for data collection and analysis (Mukherjee, 1997) with an emphasis on qualitative information rather than quantitative information (Reddy, 1999).

PRA Tools: PRA tools like time line, listing, mapping, wealth grouping, narrative, topical interview and observation were used for data collection from individuals and groups of villagers.

Time Line: Time line is used for tracing local changes in different variables over time such as food patterns, wages, days of work, kind of work, survival strategies, changes in vegetation, farming practices, livelihood, quality of life, etc (Mukherjee, 2002). It gives historical profile of an individual, organization, village, institution or country (Kumar, 2002).

Listing: Listing is a PRA tool used for facilitating an individual/group to recall and highlight a list of items, issues, criteria, or activities concerned for further discussion (Mukherjee, 2002).

Mapping: Mapping helps in spatial depiction of habitation patterns, houses, social infrastructure, local resources, etc. It gives a bird's-eye view of a locality and the way people perceive their locality (Kumar, 2002).

Wealth Grouping: Wealth grouping/ranking is a PRA method commonly used for ranking and grouping households and communities on the basis of income, wealth, and other perceivable well-being criteria (Kumar, 2002).

Narrative: In this method, an individual/group narrates an incident, evidence, event, phenomenon, activity, etc as perceived and experienced by them (Mukherjee, 2002) which has some implications for the study.

Topical interview: It is a PRA tool used to generate focused information on a particular topic (Mukherjee, 2002) interviewing through some open ended broad questions and not just answering direct questions (Beebe, 1995).

Observation: It is a method of social science research used for collecting facts and acquiring knowledge seeing phenomena with a purpose (Ghosh, 1992).

Seasonal variations exert a tremendous influence on the life and livelihood of tribal people in many ways. Seasonality, therefore, was an obvious feature of the present study. Seasonality is described on the basis of local months. The corresponding months in Roman calendar are: *Baisakh* (mid-April to mid-May), *Jaistha* (mid-May to mid-June), *Asarh* (mid-June to mid-July), *Sravan* (mid-July to mid-August), *Bhadra* (mid-August to mid-September), *Aswin* (mid-September to mid-October), *Kartik* (mid-October to mid-November), *Aghrayan* (mid-November to mid-December), *Poush* (mid-December to mid-January), *Magh* (mid January to mid-February), *Falgun* (mid-February to mid-March), and *Chaitra* (mid-March to mid-April).

RESULTS AND DISCUSSIONS

Socio-Economic Profile of the Village

The Village: Bansiar village is the home of *Kora* tribe (except one *Santhal* household) descended from Mayurbhanj district of Orissa, as expressed by the villagers. About 150 years ago, only one family started to reside in an area adjacent to the present village. A look into Chart 1 will show where that ancient *Kora* family resided earlier. Around 70-75 years ago, villagers shifted from old place and resettled to the present place. Residents of Bansiar told that except a few, all of the families in the village have direct blood relationship with that ancient family.

The village is surrounded by natural *Saal Ban* (forest) on its three sides (south, east and north). On the west side there is vast agricultural fields which remain fallow throughout the year, except during monsoon season when fields are used for *Aman*/monsoon/wet paddy (paddy cultivated during monsoon season) cultivation (Chart 1).

The village has two settlements; Upar Bansiar and Tal Bansiar as perceived and recognised by its residents on the basis of their relative topographical features. Tal Bansiar is located on the north side of Upar Bansiar at a lower topography (Chart 1).

Physical Structure of the Village: There are a total of 47 households in the village (Table 1). Number of water sources, both private and public, are 14 (10 wells and 4 tube-wells). Water sources serve drinking as well as other household purposes. There is a *Kabarkhana* (cemetery) inside the forest and a church in the village, because the villagers are Christian by religion. It has two grocery shops, one husking machine and a football playing ground, too (Chart 2). The village is still not electrified.

Table 1
Profile of the Village

Number of Households	47 (35 - Upar Bansiar and 12 - Tal Bansiar)
Religion	Christianism
Caste	*Kora*
Language	*Kora*
Origin	Village-Betnuti, District-Mayurbhanj, Orissa
Title	Singh
Human Population	208 (103 Male and 105 Female)
Livestock Population	59 Bullocks , 19 Cows, 37 Calves, 2 adult he-Buffaloes, 80-88 Goats, 20-25 Pigs, 160-170 Chickens, 40-50 Ducks

The village is about 8 km away from the nearest market centre (Belda) wherein 4 km is made up of *Morram* and 2 km (from the village) is *Matir-Rasta* (mud road). As a result, during rainy season, due to muddy condition of road, villagers have no choice but to find their way through *Hir/Aal* (edge of the agricultural field) facing a great hardship.

Human and Livestock Population: Villagers gave an estimate of human and livestock population of their village. Accordingly, there are a total of 103 males and 105 females (total 208) reside in the village. The village has around 59 bullocks, 19 cows, 37 calves, 2 adult he-buffaloes, 80-88 goats, 20-25 pigs, 160-170 chickens and 40-50 ducks (Table 1).

Primary purpose of cattle rearing is for agricultural operations as cows are very rarely milked. Total amount of dung produced by the livestock is poured in *Khad-Gariah* (manure-pit) to get manure to be used in agricultural field. Dung is rarely used to make dung cake to be used as fuel.

Socio-Economic Class: According to the villagers there are three socio-economic classes exist in the village; richest class, middle class and poorest class. Maximum households (27) belong to the second category while number of households belong to first and last category of socio-economic classes are equal; 4 from each category (Chart 2[3]). However, this classification may have different connotations for different societies. Thus, the basis of such classification, as perceived by the villagers in their socio-economic setting, gives an insight and understanding of their classification. Accordingly, they pointed out 8 criteria as rationale behind such grouping of households in their context (Table 2).

Table 2
Criteria for Socio-Economic Classification

1. Agricultural production
2. Agricultural land holding
3. Service
4. Business
5. Ability to hire wage labourers
6. Type of roof of the house
7. Size of the house
8. Working members

Table 3
Time Line on Village Bansiar

Time Reference	*Profile*
150 years ago	One household. Dense forest sheltering tiger, bear, panther, rabbit, peacock.
60 years ago	Unaware that land could be sold. Share-cropping[5] in practice.
40-50 years ago	8-10 households. Wage rate: 2 *Anna* (8 Paise)/day/head or equivalent rice or *Khoi*. Price of rice: Rs. 1 for 6-7 *Ser*[6]. Price of paddy: 50 Paise to Rs. 5 for 40 *Ser* Price of pulses: Rs. 1 for 4-5 *Ser* (*Masur*); Pulses like *Kurti, Moong, Biuri* obtained in exchange of something. Cost of land: Rs. 24/*Bigha* (good quality). Very little work as agricultural labourers. During Bengal famine, 40 *Ser* paddy was obtained in exchange of 5 cows, rice sold @ Rs. 1/*Ser*. People survived by eating boiled tamarind leaves and flowers of bamboo, after - effects of famine lasted for 2-3 years. Long before 1950 Christian missionaries started religious campaign, villagers adopted Christianism since then.
1960-70	10-12 households. Test-Relief Scheme started by the Government to provide employment during off-season, wage rate: 5 kg. wheat/head. Many cattle (around 400) and hen; no duck, pig, goat, buffalo. No household had land ownership, except one. With the help of Forest Department, villagers killed one *Cheetah* (panther) and one tiger.
1970s	Nunaram Singh (an outsider) arrived at the village. 12 households. Except 2 villagers (Joseph Singh and Nunaram Singh) all were illiterate. Some households had ownership of land. Share-cropping continued. Wage rate: Rs. 5-10/day/head or equivalent rice. Price of rice: Rs. 2-2.5/*Ser*. No poverty.

Contd.

Time Reference	*Profile*
1980s	Nunaram Singh went for Adult Learning Training, brought awareness in education.
1990s	Forest Protection Committee formed, issuing of receipt started for collection of fuel-wood from forest [7]. *Saal* leaf collection started mainly to make and sell leaf plate in market which was learnt from *Baiga* and *Munda* castes. Cultivation by tractor started to some extent.
2003 onwards	47 households. Number of cattle decreased. Wage rate: Rs. 32-40/day/head with 2-3 times food. Price of rice: Rs. 5-6/*Ser* (locally), Rs. 7-8/*Ser* (in market) Price of paddy: Rs. 420-500/Quintal. Price of pulses (*Masur*): Rs. 30/kg. Cost of land: Rs. 20,000-22,000/*Bigha*. Timber, fruit, mushroom, fuel-wood availability from forest declined. Atleast one or two educated members per household; one Post Graduate female, also graduates, some of them are convent educated too. Share-cropping abolished.

Source: Nunaram Singh (67 years), Bhaku Singh (65 years), Joseph Singh (60 years) and Bhagyadhar Singh (55 years) of Bansiar village.

Households possessing 10-15 bigha[4] land, having asbestos or tin roofed large house, business, and/or government service are considered as richest. Richest households have a surplus of agricultural produce for selling after meeting the household's need. They never faced poverty. They are able to get their agricultural operations done by hiring wage labourers. A family having 10-12 bighas of land and large house, but has less working members may not be considered as rich in comparison to families that have more of that. Thus, a family which has one member in service, asbestos or tin roofed large house, but has less than 10 bighas of land would be classified as richest.

Middle class households, on the other hand, are those which have 4-5 bighas of land, smaller house with roof made up of paddy straw or *Tali* (tiles), no surplus of agricultural produce and more working members.

Whereas, poorest households possess no or a tiny piece of land, a hut and a few working hands. They mainly earn a living by working as wage labourers in others' field. In order to meet the household's requirement they need to purchase rice on daily or weekly basis which is complemented and supplemented by rice obtained as wage.

Socio-Economic, Ecological, Cultural and Religious Changes: Through the method of Time Line information on various aspects of the rural life were collected from, and analysed by elderly villagers.

Time Line reveals a number of phenomena, events, facts and figures that have immense importance to the inhabitants. A look into Table 3 will show how over the decades changes occurred in various aspects of village life: number of household; wage rates; prices of paddy, rice and pulses; availability and type of work; profile and utility of forest; land ownership; agricultural operations; education; etc.

Forest: The Rich Reservoir of Resources

Medicinal Plants: Table 4 provides a list of medicinal plants available in the forest and their parts used as medicine. In most of the cases roots of the plants are used as medicine while in case of *Isarmuli Gaud* and *Mushakane*, leaves are also used. Besides roots and leaves, flowers (*Maran*), fruits (*Isarmuli Gaud, Bhalua, Garshul* and *Kasha Fal*) and seeds (*Bhalua*) have medicinal value for the tribes of Bansiar.

Among these plants, roots of *Patal Gadur Gaud* and *Isarmuli Gaud* (*Lal* and *Shet*) are used as anti-venom. *Lal Isarmuli Gaud* is used against *Black Khoris* (Indian Kobra) bite whereas *Shet Isarmuli Gaud* is used against *Dudhia* and *Tentulia Khoris* bite. Villagers told that leaves of *Patal Gadur Gaud*, which is otherwise bitter in taste, will not taste bitter if poisonous snake bites.

Table 4
Major Medicinal Plants Available from Forest and their Parts Used

Plants	*Parts Used as Medicine*
Anantamul	Root
Bir Kundri	Root
Kurchi	Root
Maran	Root, flower
Lal Isarmuli Gaud	Root, leaf, fruit
Shet Isarmuli Gaud	Root, leaf, fruit
Mushakane	Root, leaf
Satmul	Root
Patal Gadur Gaud	Root
Bhalua	Fruit, seed
Garshul	Fruit
Kasha Fal	Fruit
Sirkakul	Root

Scientific Name: *Hemidesmus indicus* (Anantamul), *Asparagus racemosus* (Satmul), *Holaorrpena anthdysen* (Kurchi), *Aristolochia indica* (Isarmuli Gaud).

Animals, Reptiles and Birds: The forest is a home for a wide variety of wild animals, reptiles and birds. A list of wild fauna of Bansiar reveals how rich was the forest at earlier times (Table 5). Villagers described to what extent these wild species have decreased in number or abandoned the forest as a result of over-exploitation and degradation of the forest.

Birds like *Titir, Gondur, Bulbuli, Kapot, Saat-Bhai, Kaththokra,* kite, crow, bat and vulture which were found abundant in earlier days could hardly be seen at present, while peacock and wild hens have completely disappeared from the forest. Among the birds, *Titir, Kapot, Saat-Bhai,* wild hen and bat contributed significantly to the diet of the villagers. The only species of wild birds found relatively in large number at present is *Koptur* (pigeon).

Among wild animals, fox, jackal, rat and squirrel are found relatively in large number at present though their number have decreased over the years. *Hadgar* (wolf), mongoose and rabbit are rarely found. Villagers told that they used to catch squirrel, rabbit and rat for consumption as meat. Thus, complete disappearance or rare availability of wild animals and birds have negatively affected the food pattern of tribal people.

Table 5
Major Wild Animals, Reptiles and Birds

Species	*Name*	*Status*
Birds	Titir, Gondur, Bulbuli, Kapot, Saat-Bhai, Kaththokra, kite, crow, bat, vulture.	Rarely found
	Banmurgi (wild hen), peacock.	Absent
	Koptur (pigeon)	Present
Animals	Fox, Jackal, rat, squirrel.	Present
	Hadgar (wolf), mongoose, rabbit.	Rarely found
Reptiles	Khoris (Dudhia, Tentulia and Black), Boda (viper), Chiti (Bena, Pahadiya, Kanthua and Potuliya chiti), Kaal Daandke.	Present
	Go-Saap	Rarely found

Scientific Name: *Alophoixus flaveolus* (Bulbuli), *Dinopium javanense* (Kaththokra), *Milvus migrans* (kite), *Corvus macrorhynchos* (jungle crow), *Pteropus giganteus* (bat), *Gyps bengalensis* (vulture), *Pavo cristatus* (peacock), *Gallus gallus* (banmurgi), *Canis aureus* (jackal), *Bandicota bengalensis* (rat), *Callosciurus pygerythrus* (squirrel), *Herpestes edwardsi* (mongoose), *Lepus nigricollis* (rabbit), *Varanus sp.* (go-saap).

However, still forest is a home for a number of snake species as evident from the Table. *Kaal Daandke* is most poisonous among them. Only one non-poisonous species is *Go-Saap* (giant lizard) which was extensively hunted and killed for consumption, and extraction of oil after boiling it. Oil extracted from *Go-Saap* has a great medicinal value to the villagers. As a result their number has been decreased over the years almost to a stage of disappearance.

Forest Trees, Shrubs and Grasses: A number of trees, shrubs and grasses naturally grow in the forest which are extremely valuable and useful for the villagers. Trees available from the forest provide useful materials like timber, wood, fuel-wood, oil, leaf, fruit, medicine, flower, *Dhuna* (aromatic resin), etc (Table 6).

Shrubs and grasses available from the forest are used to make *Jhora* and *Kaththa* (basket), rope, *Jhanta* (broom), creel, etc for domestic as well as for selling purposes. They are also used as fuel, for feeding livestock and for preparing medicine (Table 7).

Food: Table 8 shows a wide range of food items consumed by the villagers indicating sources from where they are

Table 6
Major Use of Forset Trees

Name	*Use*
Saal	Very good timber for construction of house, door, window. Wood used to make plough, handle of axe and spade, and as fuel-wood. Leaf used for making plate. Oil extracted from fruit used to make home-made soap. Produces *Dhuna* (aromatic resin) used in worship.
Mohua	Oil extracted from fruit used as body oil and to light *Pradeep* (earthern lamp). Flower used to make indigenous wine (*Mohua*). Green fruit (immature) as vegetable, and ripe fruit as edible fruit.
Khejur	Leaf used for making *Chatai* (mat). Ripe fruit as edible fruit.
Piya-Saal	Very good timber for construction of house, door, window, etc.
Kusum	Good timber. Ripe fruit as edible fruit. Valuable oil extracted from fruit.
Dha	Good timber for construction of house, etc.
Aashna	Good timber.
Bahara	Fruit as medicine.
Bhundru	Most preferred fuel-wood. Ash, obtained after burning of fuel-wood, was used as detergent in the recent past.
Kendu[8]	Leaf used for selling which has major use in *Beedi* industry.

Scientific Name: *Shorea robusta* (Saal), *Madhuca indica* (Mohua), *Phoenix sylvestris* (Khejur), *Carthamus tinctorius* (Kusum), *Terminalia belarica* (Bahara), *Buchanania lanzan* (Piya-Saal), *Terminalia tomentasa* (Aashna).

Table 7
Major Use of Wild Shrubs and Grasses

Name	*Use*
Kush	To make rope for selling in market which is used in betel field.
Kharang	To make broom used to stir rice while making *Muri*, for stitching *Saal* leaves together to make plates. A bunch of *Kharang* is sold at Rs. 1 in market. Also root is sold.
Dubla	In worship, as livestock feed and medicine.
Aataan	As fuel-wood, and to make *Kaththa* and *Jhora* for selling and domestic use.
Dodhilata	To make creel and rope (from *Dodhilata* growing on the ground). Rope made from *Dodhilata* growing on the tree is used in betel field. Creel and rope are sold in market.
Bena	To make creel and broom for selling and domestic use

Note: Shrubs and grasses are also fed by livestock including leaves of other forest and homestead trees.

Kush, Kharang, Dubla and *Aataan* are available round the year. *Dodhilata* and *Bena* are available during *Baisakh-Magh* and *Sravan-Kartik*, respectively.

Scientific Name: *Desmostachya bipinnata* (Kush), *Cynodon dactylon* (Dubla).

Table 8
Food Items

Type of Food	*Name*	*Season*	*Source*
Roots	Teeta Alu, Churka Alu,	Aswin-Kartik	Forest
	Bhundu,	Aghrayan-Poush	
	Bir Kundri,	Jaistha	
	Ghee Karla.	Asarh-Aswin	
Meat	Pork, chevon, chicken, duck meat.	Round the year	Home
	Meat of wild birds and animals,	Round the year	Forest
	Shamkhol[9](stork)	Jaistha-Asarh	
Fish	Kalsa, Punti, Garai, Chang, Koi, Magur, Chingri, Pankal, etc.	Asarh-Aswin	Canal, pond, water-bodies, field.
Snail	Jal Genri, Katla, Ganra.	Round the year	Pond, water-bodies.
Flower	Buch (flower and bud),	Falgun-Chaitra	Forest
	Kuchai (flower and bud),		
	Maran (flower).	Sravan-Bhadra	
	Tamarind (flower),	Magh-Falgun	Homestead
	Sajna (flower, bud, fruit).	Falgun-Chaitra	
Leaf (Lush-green)	Assaththa, Neem, Tamarind, Sajna.	Falgun-Baisakh	Homestead
	Harur, Kuchai, Matha.	Chaitra-Baisakh	Forest
Plants	Kalmi, Chimti, Sushni.	Baisakh-Asarh field, forest.	Canal, pond, water-bodies,
	Gima, Tak, Chakanda, Khapra, Buru Gandri, Kantamari.	Baisakh-Asarh	Homestead, field, forest.
Mushroom	A number of varieties	Asarh-Bhadra	Forest, roadside.

Scientific Name: *Barbus stigma* (Punti), *Anabas testudineus* (Koi), *Clarias batrachus* (Magur), *Penaeus indicus* (Chingri), *Colisa fasciatus* (Kalsa), *Tamarindus indica* (Tamarind), *Ficus religiosa* (Assaththa), *Azadirachta indica* (Neem), *Moringa oleifera* (Sajna), *Zingiber zerumber* (Buch), *Ipomoea bonanox* (Kalmi), *Marsiba quadrifolia* (Sushni), *Mollugo pentaphylla* (Gima), *Pila globosa* (Jal Genri).

obtained. As evident from the Table, a number of roots consumed as food are obtained from the forest in different seasons. They also consume flowers, leaves and whole plants of some species, and varieties of mushroom available in the forest. Thus, forest provides bulk of the foods needed for the survival of the villagers.

Seasonal Fruits: An impressive variety of fruits are available in the forest round the year (Table 9). Yield and availability of these fruits, however, have declined over the years. A number of fruits available in the past are not available at present like *Makar Kenda, Tiril, Bhundru* and *Sasa. Bhundru* tree was extensively utilized as fuel-wood as it is the most preferred fuel-wood tree. Moreover, fruit trees that produce fruits at present are found mostly in rudimentary form (except *Taarab*), hence yield less in comparison to the past. And most of the wild fruits are available during the months of *Baisakh-Asarh.* During *Kartik-Poush* no fruits are available. Again from *Magh-Chaitra* some fruits are available.

Table 9
Major Seasonal Fruits Available in the Forest

Season	*Name*	*Availability*
Falgun-Chaitra	Makar Kenda	Not available
Chaitra-Baisakh	Tiril	Not available
	Taarab, Kheerkul	Available
Baisakh-Jaistha	Keeta, Boinchkul, Garshul, Annakul, Mantakul.	Available
Jaistha-Asarh	Jamkul, Sisir Kuda, Tapah.	Available
Bhadra-Aswin	Bhundru	Not available
Magh-Falgun	Sasa	Not available
	Sirkakul	Available

Scientific Name: *Flacourtia indica* (Boinchkul).

In respective seasons it is very entertaining for the school children to enter inside the forest after schooling to eat and get a taste of each of the different varieties of fruits. They like to spend most of their time enjoying inside the forest playing indigenous games, climbing fruit trees, plucking and gathering fruits, and grazing livestock during these seasons.

Livelihood

As evident from Table 10 residents of Bansiar get employment in agricultural fields as wage labourers during two times in a year; *Jaistha-Sravan* and *Aghrayan-Poush*, for sowing and harvesting of *Aman* paddy, respectively. Works available during *Jaistha-Sravan* are ploughing and sowing (men only) and transplanting (men and women both). Whereas during *Aghrayan-Poush* works available are harvesting, carrying harvested crop, threshing and winnowing (men and women both), making *Khar-Gada* (men only), etc. Wage rates in both seasons range from Rs. 32-40 per day per head with 2-3 times food (*Muri*, *Panta* or *Bhat*) depending on the Gram Panchayat wherein they work.

Table 10
Livelihood Pursued by the Villagers in Different Seasons

Season	*Livelihood*
Bhadra-Kartik	Collecting *Saal* leaves for making and selling leaf plates @ Rs. 60-80 per thousand plates (women and children).
Aghrayan-Poush	Work in agricultural field as wage labourers @Rs. 32-40 per day per head with 2-3 times food (men and women).
Magh-Baisakh	Collecting *Saal* leaves for making and selling leaf plates @Rs. 70-100 per thousand plates (women). Making and repairing roof of house, digging, carrying manure to the agricultural field, etc as wage labourers (men).
Jaistha-Sravan	Work in agricultural field as wage labourers @ Rs. 32-40 per day per head with 2-3 times food (men and women).

During *Magh-Baisakh* women have no work in agricultural fields while men get irregular employment in different kinds of works mainly in others' households. These works include making and repairing roof of the house, repairing *Khar-Gada* (paddy straw stack) of previous year, digging *Khad-Gariah* (manure-pit) and carrying *Gobar Sar* (dung manure) to the agricultural fields by bullock cart for cultivation of *Aman* paddy during *Jaistha-Sravan*, and other miscellaneous household works. They do these works as wage labourers. Men and women sometimes are employed by the Gram Panchayat for construction and repairing of village roads. During these months, women mainly engage in the collection of fuel-wood, fuel-leaves and *Saal* leaves from the forest. From *Saal* leaves women and men prepare leaf plates which they sell in market @Rs. 70-100 per thousand plates. According to the villagers, during *Magh-Falgun* cost of *Saal* leaf plates rises to a maximum of Rs. 100 per thousand plates. Collection of *Saal* leaves, and making and selling of leaf plates seem to be one of the most important livelihoods for the villagers, especially for the poor.

Bhadra-Kartik seems most difficult time for the villagers. During these months no work is available as wage labourers (both for men and women). Women and school children start collecting *Saal* leaves, fuel-wood, fuel-leaves, while men either engage in livestock grazing or in other household works or offer a helping hand to women to stitch up *Saal* leaves or spend idle time with nothing to do at all.

Analysis of livelihood pursued by the villagers reveals that round the year they depend on the forest resources to complement and supplement their livelihood. Dependence is more during the months of *Bhadra-Kartik* and *Magh-Baisakh*, especially during *Bhadra-Kartik* when there is no work as wage labourers. Villagers also expressed that for grazing their stock they heavily depend on forest during *Asarh-Kartik*.

SUMMARY AND IMPLICATIONS

Thus, through the method of Participatory Appraisal of Natural Resources (PANR), using the principles, methods and tools of Participatory Rural Appraisal (PRA), relationship between natural resources and its traditional users can be explored and understood.

In a nutshell, the study reveals that still forest is utilized, and considered essential for the very survival of local people though magnitude of contribution has declined over the decades. Residents adjacent to such forest (spreads over Paschim Medinipur district of West Bengal) are sustained not only by agriculture but by the forest to a large extent. These people do depend on agriculture but forest must be there to complement and supplement it.

Ill-being and well-being of the people are directly related to the condition of forest. Any physical and ecological changes in the forest will cause changes in rural socio-economic life.

Therefore, the paper calls for an immediate attention and action to conserve and check further deterioration of such a treasure trove of resources sustaining its relationship with its dependents.

REFERENCES

Beebe, James (1995), Basic Concepts and Techniques of Rapid Appraisal. *Human Organisation*, Vol. 54 (1).

Chambers, Robert and Blackburn, James (1996), The Power of Participation: PRA and Policy. IDS Policy Briefing, Issue 7. Institute of Development Studies, University of Sussex, Brighton, UK.

Ciriacy-Wantrup, S.V and Bishop, R.C. (1975), Common Property as a Concept in the Natural Resource Policy. *Natural Resource Journal*, Vol. 15.

Dadibhavi, R.V. (2001), Management of Common Property Resource: Some Policy Issues. *Kurukshetra*, Vol. 49 (2).

Das, S K; Samajdar, T; Khandekar, P and Dana, S.S. (2003), Common Property Resources and Rural Dairy Production. *Indian Dairyman*, Vol. 55 (10).

Ghosh, B.N. (1992), *Scientific Method and Social Research*. Sterling Publishers Pvt Ltd, New Delhi.

Hardin, Garrett (1968), The Tragedy of the Commons. *Science*, 162.

Jodha, N.S. (1986), Common Property Resources and Rural Poor in Dry Regions of India. *Economic and Political Weekly*, Vol. 21 (27).

Jodha, N S. (1990), Rural Common Property Resources: Contributions and Crisis. *Economic and Political Weekly*, June 30.

Jodha, N S. (2000), Wastelands Management in India: Myths, Motives and Mechanisms. *Economic and Political Weekly*, February 5.

Kumar, Somesh (2002), *Methods for Community Participation*: A *Complete Guide for Practitioners*. Vistaar Publications, New Delhi.

Mukherjee, Neela (1997), *Participatory Appraisal of Natural Resources.* Concept Publishing Co, New Delhi.

Mukherjee, Neela (2002), *Participatory Learning and Action with 100 Field Methods.* Concept Publishing Co, New Delhi.

Reddy, V. Ratna (1999), 'Wealth Ranking' in Socio-economic Research: Substitute or Complement? *Indian Journal of Agricultural Economics,* Vol. 54 (1).

NOTES

1. In his famous article 'The Tragedy of the Commons', Garrett Hardin (1968) stated that when many people use a finite resource at a time there is every chance of destruction of that resource. Everyone wants to get more and more of the resource surpassing all others. As a result a situation of competition arises in the society leading to over-exploitation of the resources. For example, if a grazing land is used by many livestock owners in common, there will be a tendency of every livestock owner to gain maximum of that resource through grazing of animals as much as possible before anyone can exploit it (Das *et al.* 2003).
2. Property/resource used in common by the members of a particular community having the social sanction to exclude other groups and communities like forest, river, community grazing land, wasteland, pond and well (Ciriacy-Wantrup and Bishop, 1975; Jodha, 1986, 1990 and 2000; and Dadibhavi, 2001).
3. Chart 2 shows the features of Upar Bansiar not of Tal Bansiar.
4. Local units of area measurement: 2.5 *Kotah* = 1 Decimal, 50 Decimal = 1 *Bigha.*
5. In share-cropping, total cost of cultivation is borne alone by share-cropper (*Bhag-Chasi*) while total produce is divided equally between land owner and share-cropper.
6. Local units of weight measurement: 4 *Chhatak* = 1 *Poa*, 16 *Chhatak* = 1 *Ser*, 40 *Ser* = 1 *Mon*, 1*Mon*= 37.5 kg.
7. One family is entitled to collect one bundle of fuel-wood on payment of Rs. 6-14 per day for one month in a year. Once in 10 years Forest Department cuts forest trees. After selling, money is divided between Forest Department and villagers in the ratio of 1:2. Total money alloted for the villagers is divided equally among the beneficiary households. In the year 2002 each household got Rs. 400.
8. *Kendu* leaf is precious as it is used in *Beedi* industry. Villagers do not make *Beedi.* They sell *Kendu* leaf to some middlemen (*Mahajan*) @ Rs. 10-15 for 100 leaves which is ultimately used to make *Beedi.* Whereas middlemen sell those leaves to their *Mahajan* @ Rs. 50 for 100 leaves. Now villagers no more want to be exploited by the middlemen. Consequently, the local government body has started to revive this important but unorganised forest based livelihood by organising local people through the formation of cooperative societies.

9. A large migratory bird. During rainy season (end of *Jaistha* to first of *Asarh*) a flock (10-12) of *Shamkhol* (stork) comes to stay in the forest. During this time they are found foraging inside the forest. Villagers do not know from where they come. However, villagers told that meat of *Shamkhol* is tasty and an adult *Shamkhol* yields around 2-3 kg. meat.

11 Zeme Naga Ethnomedicine

Babul Roy

INTRODUCTION

North Cachar Hills District (24^0 58′ - 25^0 47′ N and 92^0 32′ - 93^0 28′ E) is the homeland of an important Naga tribe called Zeme who today counts for about 9,000 souls (for ethnography see Bordoloi and Sharma-Thakur 1988; Bower 1945, 1950; Das 1986; Dutta 1993; Kabui 1994; Kamkhenthang 1984; Roy 1995, 1998, 2003; Saha 1988). This region is still relatively cut off from mainstream India, and the inhabitants still lead to a great extent a self-sufficient existence. Although modern medicine had been introduced in early 20th Century, the local people still found largely dependent upon their traditional system. Materials used as medicine by the Zemes and their health and illness perception already has been discussed (see Roy 2001, 2002 2004). The present article further elaborates the different substances that are used by them as medicine and their underlying therapeutic principles.

FOLK TAXONOMY AND NOMENCLATURE OF BIOLOGICAL MATERIALS

All languages perceive diversity by grouping things into different categories of greater and lesser inclusiveness and by labeling them with distinctive linguistic terms (Brown 1977).

In *New Ethnography*, folk systematics and nomenclatures are elicited, which give better insight into the native mind. The Zeme use different biological materials as ethnomedicine, such understandings would be inevitably of great significance.

'World' in Zeme perception is differentiated into two broad categories, *viz. makeringbe* (living beings) and *magechaibe* (non-living beings). The plant world is divided into a number of contrasting classes, *viz. hingbang* (tree), *heria* (creeper), *nzei* (any plant like radish, carrot, etc.), *timpat* (any plant that grows into dense bushy overhead due to creeper like growth of top shoots like *Bougianvillea spectabilis)* and *pui* (all those plants that are reproduced by sucker like banana). All unwanted weeds in agricultural field are known as *heu*. This term is also used as synonym to obliquely refer to any useful medicinal plant. It is believed that medicinal plants are sacred and not to be addressed directly. Animals are categorized into *marekaune* (animals), *henea* (snake), *nruipoine* (bird), etc. The man constitutes a separate category distinct from all other living creatures.

Zeme Naga recognizes some hundreds of species of both plants and animals with distinctive term. Nomenclature particularly in case of plant species is quite elaborate, and is made in such a way that from the very name itself most of the salient characters of the species become clear. Several adjectives as suffix describing distinctive features of a species are added to its principal name. In most cases, the category term (e.g., *bang*–tree; *ria*–creeper; *heu*–herb, etc.) is added as suffix: For example, *hereu-bang* (*Rauvolfia serpentina*), *nrangchiambe-ria* (*Vitis quadrangularis*), and *gari-heu* (*Eupetorium odoratum*). But, whenever a plant is referred to in the context of its appropriate use, the part used is also added as suffix to its principal name: For example, *hereu(bang)-ma*, where *hereu(bang)* is the name of a medicinal plant and *ma* meaning root, indicating root to be medicinal. The name of the eye-catching part of a plant (e.g., flower = *pa)* is also added in certain cases as suffix: For example, *dekhai-pa-bang* literally meaning '*dekhai*-flower-tree'. There could be more than one suffix for any particular species describing its different features. However, while speaking, generally only one suffix, which is the most relevant at that point of time, is used. Often two suffixes are used together, but never more than two are used at a time. There are also exceptions, depending upon phonetic sweetness often adjectives are used as prefix instead of suffix, and sometimes not at all used.

PLANT MEDICINE

Like many small-scale communities without having much occupational specialization (see Kiev 1962), the Zemes do not have any professionally exclusive personnel performing specific duties in the field of medicine and treatment. The Zeme medicine man (or the shaman) is rather an ordinary man just like any other fellow. Of course, in some cases individual medicine man acquires special qualities for which he gets some extraordinary recognition. And there are scopes for innovative use of medicines. Individual medicine man often works out his formulae of combination and proportion at which different medicinal ingredients are to be mixed up for a particular cure.

Zeme Naga uses a large number of plant species to cure different ailments (see Roy 2001, 2002). To cure diseases like stomach pain, diarrhea, dysentery, cut injury, septic infection, fever, malaria, bone displacement, muscle cramp and different kinds of skin infections, traditional medicinal remedies are known. They use a large number of plant species to cure stomach complaints. Medicinal plants like *gajing-bei, gangkereu, hapiau-pa-bang, hereu-ma-bang, kampi, kanchabeneu-bang, nunechi-bang, teutak-bang, turechi-bang*, etc., are commonly used for curing dysentery and related complaints. A good number of herbs are used to stop bleeding from fresh cut and to cure septic infection. The common medicinal plants used in such cases are *bangainchi, gari-heu, henaktikpe, namsia-heu*, and *tain-ria*. The *Rauvolfia serpentina* is one of the few most widely used medicinal species in Zeme medicine. It is locally called *hereu-ma-bang* literally meaning the 'medicine-root-tree'. Extracts from young leaves of pineapple (*Ananas comosus*) is used to cure a kind of infertile tongue infection caused by fungus. To cure goiter in its initial stage, the Zeme recommend leaf juice extracted from *bakut* (*Scoparia dulcis*). The dose is recommended upto two to three times a day until the patient is recovered.

The people use a number of *Zingiber* sp. in curing different ailments. *Hegawang* literally meaning 'king of medicines' (*Hega* = medicine; *wang* = king) is one such species believed to have medicinal properties in curing numerous complaints. The high quality medicinal properties and its extensive uses in Zeme medicine perhaps have earned such a name for it. Several other *Zingiber* sp., *viz. gangkereu, hegembega, hepo-bei, kebeugelikpe*, etc. are also considered very effective. Malevolent spirits are believed to be afraid of *hegembega* as it burns them. A Zeme often kept pieces of the rhizome of this species in his/her personal possession to avoid spirit encounter.

ANIMAL MEDICINE

Several animals and their by-products constitute important ingredients of Zeme pharmacopoeia. Of the different creatures that the people use, the tiger, bear and porcupine are most common. For medicinal use, porcupine is hunted during rainy season, when forest is rich with vegetation. The stomach of the animal is removed along with its contents, which is then dried under the sun for future use. It is believed that since porcupine eats different vegetations, a small piece of its stomach and its contents do possess properties of many herbs. A small bit of the dried porcupine's stomach is consumed to get relief from several ailments like stomach pain, influenza and malaria. Different organs of tiger and bear are used to cure several ailments. It is commonly believed that the different parts of tiger can strengthen the corresponding part of its consumer. Elephant's tusk and rhinocero's horn are also considered to have medicinal value. Bone of gibbon (*kepe*) is used as amulet to cure arthritis. Flesh and blood of fox and jackal are taken to get protection from sorcery and witchcraft practices. The medicine called *reheudilungbe,* which is a mixture of spleen of man (nowadays not used), tiger and bear, is used to cure specific ailments resulted from black magic and witchcraft practices.

Zeme Naga believe that many health complaints are curable by magical blow and massage. In case of throat problem due to the pricking of fish bone, it is believed that only some specific persons can cure such complaint by magical massage. A person who has once killed an otter (*krem*) by breaking its neck acquires the power of the animal by which it swallows live fish.

Zeme Naga consume different species of birds and fowls to cure different ailments. Flesh of birds like eagle and kite, which fly high in the sky and move in circular path, is considered best to cure headache and reeling. Following recovery from any ailment, if the body of the patient swells up, soup of a white colored fowl is considered good for health. A species of fowl called *nrui-pegue-kakedal-pejat* i.e., 'hen having feathers twisted backward' is consumed to cure stomach pain called *bungpui-teube* in which case pain moves backward. In both these cases the preparation is done in magical way, and the entire preparation is required to be taken by the patient himself. In normal cases, following recovery from illness chicken soup (*nrui-gi*) prepared by boiling young chick is recommended.

The most interesting use of bird in Zeme medicine is to cure a disease manifested in the form of a boil like eruption on eye-lid locally called *nruirun* after the name of a bird. The bulging projection on the posterior of the bird is actually referred to as *nruirun*. The disease is morphologically similar to it. To cure this particular eye ailment, a magical trick is performed as follows: A straw is collected from the bird's nest; one of the ends of the straw is burnt in fire; the curer then holds it (pointing the burnt end) close to the affected eye-lid of the patient and pretends to hit the affected region by bringing it nearer (which he never does actually). As the curer pretends to strike the affected eye-lid of the patient, he utters addressing it: "*either move out or I shall burn you with this*". He repeats the process as well as the utterance for several times (three, five or seven). It is believed that thereby the disease gets frightened, and so ultimately moves out relieving the patient.

OTHER MATERIALS AND TRICKS USED AS MEDICINE

Zeme Naga consider honey as having medicinal properties. The people give oral dose of honey to cure *milaisube,* a kind of infantile fungal infection on tongue. It is believed that bees collect honey from different flowers, and many of which being medicinal a drop of honey contains rich pharmaceutical properties. Similar logic has been forwarded in *Ayurveda* and also in many other systems of traditional medicines (Ambasta 1988:91-93). In traditional Roman medicine honey is considered to be an excellent ingredient in wound dressing (Scarborough 1996:43).

Zeme Naga also use different non-biological ingredients as medicine like rock-powder, rock-salt, sacred-water, gunpowder, phosphorus (extracted from fire stick), kerosene oil, kitchen shoot, etc. To cure toothache gunpowder is used, which is taken on a lump of cotton and poultice upon the affected tooth. Kerosene oil and red phosphorus together are used to cure a number of diseases. To cure a problem of nose bleeding locally called *mineukahejaibe,* the patient is allowed to inhale smoke produced by burning of dried cow dung. To get quick recovery from fire burn, a coating of egg albumen is given over the effected region. To cure wound caused by animal bite and cut injury, the remains of fermented rice from which rice beer has been extracted is applied. Similar practices also have been reported from among other Naga communities (see Dennehy 1927), and from other parts of the world. Like Zemes, the Peruvian peasants believe liquor and other fermented drinks to strengthen the body, and have the capacity to purify blood much as do the various herbs (Fabrega 1972:246). If someone among the Zemes gets a cut injury by a stone, the concerned stone causing the injury is boiled and the water is drunk for cure.

Zeme Naga traditionally practice minor surgical operations to cure a number of ailments. Traditionally recognized ailment called *mipikanchakpe* or *tingseibasiakbe* in which case toes swell up and irritate which is understood to be caused by exposure to damp soil during rainy season. To cure this, a minor surgical operation is performed. For that each of the affected toes is fastened tightly at some point just below the tip with the help of thread so that the blood flow is minimized. And as the blood turns blue due to lack of oxygen, a needle is pierced into each of the fingertips removing some of the so called polluted blood. Following this, threads are let loose completing the operation. In many other cases (e.g., headache), such blood letting practice is done as an appropriate measure of cure. Similar practices have also been reported from many traditional systems of cure, particularly from South East Asia (Berndt 1947; Stanhope 1968; Webb 1933; Wedgwood 1937). Young (1976) has discussed such a practice from an African community.

PRINCIPLES OF FOLK MEDICINE

Hot/cold model of humoral system, which was the basis of Greek traditional medicine, is found as the conceptual basis of many folk medical traditions world-wide (Logan 1972, 1973, 1977, 1991; Morris 1989; Morti-Ibanez 1965; Reichet-Dolmatoff *et al.* 1961; Simmons 1955; Wellin 1955; Wiese 1976). The Indian and Chinese systems of medicine are based on the same principle (Morris 1989; Morti-Ibanez 1965). Besides the hot/cold model of humoral system, there are other therapeutic principles. According to Browner (1985:29-30), since in most studies investigators have given overemphasis to hot/cold theory, they unfortunately overlooked the significance of other therapeutic principles in ethnomedical system. He discussed therapeutic principle derived from sympathetic magic or analogical thinking among the native people of San Francisco.

Analogical thinking or principle derived from sympathetic magic is the predominant basis of the Zeme cultural interpretation of medicine. In many cases such principles are explicit and explained by the people, when in many other cases these are clearly derivable (see Roy 2001). In fact such principles are found involving many other things (e.g., food prescription and proscription) among the different groups of Naga tribes and sub-tribes. Sema Naga consider owl (*Glaucidia* sp.) and nightjar (*Caprimulgus asiaticus*) as idiots as they prefer darkness to light. Therefore, it is considered that eating of these creatures may impair one's intelligence (Hutton 1921). Crow (*Capricornis sumatraensis*) is locally considered to be a very restless creature as it rarely sleeps in the same spot and rarely lays eggs in a particular place. The Naga women do not eat the meat of crow for fear of acquiring similar habit (Mills 1922:77). Similarly, the Nagas prohibit eating of birds having screaming and scratching nature, and women are not supposed to eat flesh of mischievous animal like monkey, which is prone to stealing from granary (Fero-Luzzi 1975:397; Mills 1937:110). Nagas of Manipur prohibit meat of male animals to girl, women as well as to young men as the practice may stimulate libido (Hodson 1911:184; Hutton 1921:92; Mills 1937:111), as male animals are believed to be sexually active.

Tiger is strong animal so by principle of analogy any of its organs should be strong. And homeopathically anything strong should have the capacity to induce strength. The Zeme consider that consumption of tiger's organ can make the consumer's corresponding organ strong and it is based on analogical thinking. Similarly such underlying logics are very clear for the local consideration that dog's meat can cure dog's poison and snake's one snake's. The people take eagle's meat to cure headache and reeling. The eagle flies high in sky in a circular path and the human head that lies anatomically on top, reeling or moving circularly, are analogically similar.

Zeme Naga consume a variety of mango (*mbachi*) and the rhizome of a *Zingiber* sp. called *hepobei* or *mitungduigabeheu* to induce milking on lactating women. They equate both these items with female breast as the terminal ends of them are pointed like the nipple. The people prohibit any underground tubers and several fruits that grow facing downward during ailment. It is generally believed that a disease emerges out gradually and then moves out from the patient's body in the process of curing. Therefore, consumption of such fruits may influence the disease to go downward (becoming serious) instead of coming up (curing). Among the inorganic substances that the Zemes use as medicines, kerosene oil and red phosphorus together are used against a host of ailments. The analogical basis derivable in this regard is that both these items together produce fire, which on getting entry inside the patient's body also does the same and consequently burn down the disease-causing agent.

DISCUSSION AND CONCLUSION

It is increasingly being understood that forest dwelling tribal folks possess rich knowledge on various wild resources especially medicinal plants (Benz *et al.* 2000; Caniago & SieBert 1998; Voeks 1996), which could be potential source for our many precious future drugs (Blancy *et al.*1995: 744; Das 1994:240; Farnsworth 1988; Johnston & Colquhoun 1996; King 1992; Stiles 1994). The shocking experience, however, is that many of these indigenous communities are now undergoing fast elimination in terms of losing their culture and folkloric wisdom as they are being exposed to outside world (Leach 1994; Plotkin 1988; Rocheleau 1995, *cf.* Caniago & SieBert 1998), and their knowledge is being eroded under the forces of acculturation and modernization factors followed by language loss (Benz *et al.*2000). Forest conversion and land degradation are again affecting the continuity of traditional medical knowledge, particularly by reducing species availability (Caniago & SieBert 1998). We may surely soon come to regret the demise of these tribes and their wisdom from which modern human communities have much to learn, particularly in agriculture and medicine (Myers 1984:162).

Of late, ethnobiological study has gained serious attention from several quarters: Anthropologists, Biologists, Ecologists, Conservationists, etc. Nevertheless, for true convergence of different disciplines in understanding people and their cultural knowledge of natural resource use, it is still at its infancy. Mere description of plant names with some sketchy notes on local uses obviously looks to be incomplete, if not distorted reporting. Anthropological investigation has given emphasis on cultural context of traditional use of medicinal plants and animals, but not yet assumed any well defined conceptual engagement. Browner (1985) has been critical to say that since most scholars had given overemphasis to hot/cold model of folk therapeutic principle they have virtually ignored to explore other possible folk conceptual systems. For sheer industrial purpose of discovering new plant based drugs, mere cataloging of plant species could serve the purpose well, but would be always lacking for documentation and conservation of indigenous knowledge and practices. Ignoring associated cultural context often may lead us to nowhere in our effort to understand the local system of medicine. Sukuma magic medicine could be an eye opener (see Cory 1949). The Sukuma-Nyamwezi group of people of Sukuma land avail several species of plants as medicine. However, among them no medicinal plant is fixed for any particular ailment condition. Instead, a plant as medicine is derived out following certain analogical rule calculated on the basis of the nature of the patient and the category of purpose. For Sukuma people, any description of medicinal plants without taking into accounts the cultural beliefs and folk therapeutic principle would be a total mistake. Johnston & Coloquhoun (1996) rightly pointed out that ethnobotanical study not only identifies products of commercial value, but more importantly they provide a framework for the integration of such findings into development initiatives and identification of key habitats for conservation. To which it may be added that such studies most importantly contribute in documenting the fast vanishing indigenous oral tradition, which in turn would help conservation. To understand cultural context of medicine use, we need a through and holistic investigation. Therefore, if ethnobotany owes more to Botanists, it does not owe any less to Anthropologists. Both, the identification of plant species and understanding of cultural context of their use are equally important.

Zeme Naga uses of plants and animals as medicine are deeply intertwined with their magico-religious world and various social symbolic practices. Analogical reasoning and homeopathic choice are found to be the principle basis of Zeme medicine as found among many other communities (see Browner 1985; Cory 1949). These principles are predominant and much more clearly understandable involving animal medicines. However, it does not mean that Zeme medicines lack utility. Often cultural explanation and empirical knowledge of use may have no true relationships. In many cases of Zeme medicine, particularly in the case of plant medicine, the pharmaceutical effects are evident. Many of the herbs used by them also constitute part of the Indian traditional medical system. And curative properties of many of them have already been authenticated scientifically. Such as *Rauvolfia serpentina* used by the people is a widely used medicine in *Ayurveda* (Krishnamurthi 1969:382-83). The cooling and healing effects of *Bryophyllum* in burn injury, as described by the Zemes, are well known in India. Slightly toasted leaves of *Bryophyllum pinnatum* are used throughout India for wound, bruises, boil and bite of venomous insects (Manjunath 1948:233).

Among several Naga ethno-cultural groups analogical principle is found structuring the native perception involving many other things, and involving food prescription and proscription (see Fero-Luzzi 1975:397; Hodson 1911:184; Hutton 1921; Mills 1922:77). Dimasa Kachari, another tribe sharing space with Zeme Naga, exhibits many similarities in terms of analogical interpretation of ethnomedical ingredients (see Roy 1998). Further studies among other tribal groups perhaps would conclude that such principle is more widely prevalent in this region, at least among the groups who share common racial and ethnic history.

On their uses of animal as medicine, the Zeme Naga come very close to many South East Asian communities. The Zeme belief that whichever part of a tiger is consumed, qualities related to that particular organ can be possessed is quite common in China, Taipei and in many other Mongoloid regions (see Anonymous 1994; Deka 1995; Frick 1957). Bloodletting practice as curative measure, as found among the Zemes, also has been reported from elsewhere in South East Asia (Berndt 1947; Stanhope 1968; Webb 1933; Wedgwood 1937). Zeme Naga racially being Mongoloid undoubtedly has come down somewhere from S.E. Asia, the original homeland of this race. Their similarities to such a great extent in using different animals as medicine and in certain curative practices with South East Asian traditions suggest for age old continuity.

To conclude, the Zeme Naga of N.C. Hills use a large number of biological materials of both plants and animals as medicine. Truly speaking, the people are very extensive in using plants and animals as medicine. And quite certainly, the whole range of Zeme traditional medical knowledge could not be explored. But, it would be of great success if this study stimulates further interest on this line. When the people are recently undergoing rapid changes and losing their traditional wisdom at an equally rapid pace, this documentation certainly would contribute in conservation of their indigenous medical knowledge for posterity.

REFERENCES

Ambasta, S.P. (Ed.) (1988), *The Wealth of India: A Dictionary of Indian Raw Materials and Industrial Products, 2(B)*. New Delhi: Publication and Information Directorate, CSIR.

Anonymous (1994), News Report published in *The Sentinel* Vol. XII (6).

Berndt, R.M. (1947), Wuradjeri Magic and "Clever Men". *Oceania* XVII (3): 327-65; XVII (4): 60-86.

Benz, Bruce F., J. Cevallos E., Francisco Santana M., Jesus Rosales A., and S Graf M. (2000), Losing Knowledge about Plant Use in the Sierra De Manantlan Biosphere Reserve, Mexico. *Economic Botany* 54(2): 183-191.

Blancy, A, and Julie Ann Miller (1995), Research updated I. *Bioscience* 45(11): 741-47.

Bordoloi, B.N. and G.C. Sharma-Thakur (1988), *Tribes of Assam, Part II*, Guwahati: Tribal Research Institute, Assam.

Bower, Graham U.V. (1945), Cycle-migration of the Zeme-Nagas, North Cachar Hills, Assam. *Man in India* XXVI: 50-52.

__________ (1950), *Naga Path*. John Murray, 50 Albemarle St., London.

Brown, Cocil H. (1977), Folk Botanical Life Forms: their Universality and Growth. *American Anthropologist* 79(2): 317-42.

Browner, C.H (1985), Criteria for Selecting Herbal Remedies. *Ethnology* XXIV (1): 13-32.

Caniago, Izefri and Stephen F. Siebert (1998), Medicinal Plant ecology, Knowledge and Conservation in Kalimantan, Indonesia. *Economic Botany* 52(3): 229-250.

Cory, Hans (1949), The Ingredients of Magic Medicines. *Africa* 19(1): 13-32.

Das, Indraneil (1994), Evaluating Biodiversity: The Batu Apoi Experience. *AMBIO* XXIII (4-5): 238-42.

Das, S.T. (1986), *Tribal Life of North Eastern India*. Gian Publishing House (Delhi: India).

Deka, T.C. (1995), Whither National Animal: The Tiger. *GURSA Bulletin*, Gauhati University (Assam: India) 2(1): 1-5.

Dennehy, H.G. (1927), Naga Medicine. *Man in India* 7:196-203.

Dutta, K.N. (Ed.) (1979), *Assam District Gazetteers*, U.M & N.C. Hills District. Govt. of Assam (India).

Dutta, P. (1993), *The Zeme Nagas of Assam Hills: A Short Profile*. Assam Institute of Research for Tribal and Scheduled Castes, (Guwahati, Assam: India).

Fabrega, H. Jr. (1972), Health Maintenance Among Peruvian Peasants. *Human Organization* 31(3): 243-56.

Farnsworth, J.D. (1988), "Screening Plants for New Medicines", pp.83-97 *in* E.O. Wilson, Ed., *Biodiversity*. National Academy Press, Washington.

Fero-Luzzi, Gabriella Eichinger (1975), Food Avoidances of Indian Tribe. *Anthropos* 70:385-427.

Frick, Johann (1957), Medicinal Uses of Substances Derived from the Animal Organism (in Tsinghai). *Anthropos* 52(1-2): 177-98.

Hodson, T.C. (1911), *The Naga Tribes of Manipur*. London: Macmillan.

Hutton, J.H. (1921), *The Sema Nagas*. Oxford University Press (India).

Johnston, M. and A. Coloquhoun (1996), Preliminary Ethnobotanical Survey of Kurupukari: An Amerindian Settlement of Guyana. *Economic Botany* 50(2): 182-194.

King, S.R. (1992), "Pharmaceutical Discovery, Ethnobotany, Tropical Forests, and Reciprocity: Integrating Indigenous Knowledge, Conservation, and Sustainable Development", pp. 231-238 *in* M.Plotkin and L. Famolare, Eds., *Sustainable Harvest and Marketing of Rain Forest Products*. Island Press, Washington DC.

Kabui, Gangmumei (1994), The Zeliangrong Religion: Its Theology and Philosophy-Some Observations. *Journal of Indian Anthropological Society* 29(1-2): 173-78.

Kamkhenthang, H. (1984), "A Note on Religious Belief of the Northern Chin (Zemi)", *in* Sebastian Karotemprel, Ed., *The tribes of North East India*. Vendrame Missological Institute: Shillong.

Krishnamurthi, A. (Ed.) (1969), *The Wealth of India: A Dictionary of Indian Raw Materials and Industrial Products*, Vol. VIII. New Delhi: Publication and Information Directorate, CSIR.

Kiev, Ari (1962), The Psychotherapeutic Aspects of Primitive Medicine. *Human Organization* 25:10-15.

Kurup,G.U. (1974), "Mammal of Assam and Mammal Geography in India", *in* M.S. Mani and W. Junb., Eds., *Ecology and Bio-geography in India*. b-v Publishers, The Hague.

Logan, M.H (1972), Humoral Folk Medicine: A Potential Aid in Controlling Pellagra in Mexico. *Ethnomedizin* 1: 397- 410.

__________ (1973), Humoral Medicine in Guatemala and Peasant Acceptance of Modern Medicine. *Human Organization* 32(4): 385-96.

__________(1977), Anthropological Research on the Hot-Cold Theory of Disease: Some Methodological Suggestions. *Medical Anthropology* 1(4): 87-112.

__________(1991), Locus of Illness Control Beliefs Among Brazilian Herbalists: Findings and Methodological Recommendations. *Human Organization* 50(1): 82-88.

Myers, Norman (1984), "Disappearing Cultures", in Edmund Hillary, Ed., *Ecology 2000*. Michael Joseph Ltd., London.

Manjunath, B.L (Ed.) (1948), *The Wealth of India: A Directory of Indian Raw Materials and Industrial Products*, Vol. I .New Delhi: Publication and Information Directorate, CSIR.

Mills, J.P. (1922), *The Lhota Nagas*. London.

________(1937), *The Rengma Nagas*. London.

Morris, Brain (1989), Ayurveda and the Myth of Indian Spirituality. *Man and Life* 15(3-4): 103-22.

Morti-Ibanez, Felix (Ed.) (1965), *Pictorial History of Medicine*. London: Spring Books.

Rao, A.S. (1974), "The Vegetation and Phytogeography of Assam, Burma", *in* M.S. Mani and W. Junb, Eds., *Ecology and Bio-geography in India*. b-v Publishers, The Hague.

Reichet-Dolmatoff, G and A. Reichel-Dolmatoff (1961), *The People of Aritama*. Chicago: The University of Chicago Press.

Roy Burman, J.J. (1996), A Comparison of Sacred Groves Among the Mahadeo Kolis and Kunbis of Maharashtra. *Indian Anthropologist* 26(1): 37-45.

Roy, Babul (1998), *Socio-Cultural and Environmental Dimensions of Tribal Health: A Study among the Dimasa Kacharis and the Zeme Nagas of North Cachar Hills in Assam*. PhD Thesis (Unpublished), Gauhati University, Guwahati–781014 (Assam: India).

__________(1995), An Anthropological Peep at Zeme Religion. *Bulletin of the Department of Anthropology*, Gauahti University (Assam) IX: 51-60.

__________ (2001), Folk Medicine and Folk Therapeutic Principle Among the Zeme Nagas of N. C. Hills in Assam (India). *Curare* 24: 161-64.

__________ (2002), Folk Medicine Among the Zeme Nagas of India, In: *Handbook of Ethnotherapies*, Eds. Christine E. Gottschalk-Batschkus and Joy C. Green, Institut fur Ethnomedizine, Germany.

__________ (2003), Evolving Gender Relationships Among the Zeme Nagas of North Cachar Hills (Assam). *Journal of Indian Anthropological Society* 38:9-20.

__________(2004), Folk Perception of Disease and Curative Measures Among the Zeme Nagas of North Cachar Hills in Assam. *Journal of Indian Anthropological Society* 39:57-66.

Roy, Babul and A.N.M.I. Ali (1997), "Shifting Cultivation and Forest in North East India", *in* K.C. Mahanta, Ed., *People of the Himalayas: Ecology, Culture, Development and Change*. pp. 135-143. Kamla-Raj Enterprises: Delhi.

Saha, N. (1988), "Ethnographic Study of the Zeliangrong Tribe of North East India", *in* Sebastian. Karotemprel, Ed., *The Tribes of North East India*. Vendrame Missological Institute: Shillong.

Scarborough, John (1996), Drugs and Medicines in the Roman World. *Expedition* 38(2): 38-51.

Simmons, O.C. (1955), Popular and Modern Medicine in Mestizo Communities of Coastal Peru and Chile. *Journal of American Folklore* 68:57-71.

Stanhope, J.M. (1968), Competing Systems of Medicine Among the Rau-Breri, Lower Ramu River, New Guinea. *Oceania* XXXIX (2): 137-45.

Stiles, Daniel (1994), Tribals and Trade: A Strategy for Cultural and Ecological Survival. *AMBIO*, XXIII (2).

Voeks, R.A. (1996), Tropical Forest Healers and Habitat Preference. *Economic Botany* 50(4): 381-400.

Webb, Theodor (1933), Aboriginal Medical Practice in East Arnhem Land. *Oceania* IV (1): 91-98.

Wedgwood, Camilla H. (1937), Sickness and Its Treatment in Manam Island, New Guinea. *Oceania* V (1-2): 64-280 & 281-307.

Wellin, E. (1955), "Water Boiling in a Peruvian Town", *in* B. Paul, Ed., *Health, Culture and Community*. New York: Russell Sage Foundation.

Wiese, H. Jean C. (1976), Maternal Nutrition and Traditional Food Behavior in Haiti. *Human Organization* 35(2): 193-200.

Yonuo, A. (1982), *Nagas Struggle Against the British Rule Under Jadonang and Rani Gaidinliu 1925-1947*. Leno Printing Press: Kohima (India).

Young, Allan (1976), Some Implications of Medical Beliefs and Practices for Social Anthropology. *American Anthropologist* 78(1): 5-24.

12 The Story of Kamli: A Birhor Medicine-Woman

Bulu Imam

The Birhors constitute one of the primitive tribal communities in the world. They still live very close to nature though during recent time their reciprocal association with nature has been threatened, to a large extent, owing to multiple factors like deforestation, climatic change, grazing, implementation of government forest policy etc. Their integrated intimacy with the natural surroundings is conditioned by age-old tradition and their basic philosophy of life has been oriented accordingly. The Birhors, in course of time, have developed a full-fledged idea on the medicinal aspects of variegated herbs that grow wild in the jungle and these have been patterned into their cultural traditions. It is a pre-agriculturist's medicine and not like the Oraon and the Munda ethnobotany which consists of the use of the common everyday plants, the variations in prescriptions comprising the main data. The Santal medicine studied by Bodding is more of jungle plants perhaps, since the Santal stand at the edge of the hunting period and commencement of the agricultural cycle. But it is to the Birhor that we must turn to understand the uses of thousands of the very smallest forest floor plants which are in imminent danger of being wiped out in many places in and bordering Chotanagpur with its epicentre in Hazaribagh.

An understanding of Birhor approach to medicine will be incomplete without understanding their oneirology or dream significance. The Birhors consider dream as instruments to alter the future and not indicators of a psychological interpretation of the past. So, dream is a medicine too. If the Birhor dreams of a bird, insect or reptile during the night and keeps quite about it then if a friend visits him the next day he will consider him as the *rais* or ancestor spirit of his parent, more particularly the *demon*. But there are contradictions too. For example, the nature of the visitor will specify the particular demon spirit of the ancestor. But if the Birhor tells someone of his dream, then the whole power of the dream is lost. These myriad natured rais and other paraphernalia, in order to become tangible, have to be passed from father to son, especially among the Birhor *baiga* or medicine-men who hold the sacred traditions of the tribe in trust.

Birhor medicine-men - the *Mati* or the *Baiga* - are tradition-bound personalities; their roles to the society are regarded as indispensable, their presence is the trade or the residential unit keeps the latter away from any evil influence; they are called in and are approached to solve diversified problems in relation to the troubles in connection with the individual health as well as the health of the community. They are trained up according to the social norms and traditions which come down through generations. Birhor traditional medicines have recently been brought to the modern market and the selling of herbal medicines to the people of other communities has become the essential source of income of some Birhors. Side by side with medicine-men the Birhor women have come forward to train themselves as per tribal tradition. Here a life-sketch of a particular Birhor medicine-woman, whom I know intimately, is being presented here so that we may have an insight into the process which bring into being a tribal doctor and continue the tradition of tribal medicine.

Kamli Birhorni represents a vanishing breed of humans. She came from Hupad in the west. Her father's name was Sanichar Birhor, or Sanichar Burha (old man) as he was commonly known. Her mother was Rudhni Birhorni. She had one other sister and three brothers. She came to the tanda of Demotand where she presently lives five miles out of

Hazaribagh on the highway to Ranchi from a far off, she says. The year she remembers was 1972. She had been married in Parasnath in Jharkhand, the sacred hill of the Jains, at the same time as her younger brother Bansi was married. Bansi also lives here in Demotand now. Kamli's first husband's name was Bhadwa Birhor and he died in the month of Jitia (November), in 1971. When she came to Demotand the place was lovely and wild and the Birhors lived a purely carefree and nomadic existence living all year round in their leaf houses called *kumbas* and moving with the seasons. Two or three times a year the entire tanda or village was shifted. She came to Demotand with her then ten year old daughter Somri by her first marriage, having married again in Demotand.

Kamli recounts nostalgically the memories which she retains of her parents and the family which she grew up in as a child. Originally from the jungles south of Koderma in the great Deborh ranges, she was familiar with wilderness and the unknown. After her first marriage she came with her husband from Parasnath to Harli-Peto, then Baraoni, Chandwar, Paota, Morangi, and when he died on the way, she moved into this part of the Hazaribagh jungles which in those days was teeming with game and medicinal plants. Medicine was her professional mainstay after her husband's death, for in the Birhor family all members are "breadwinners", even children. Birhors are consummate hunters and gatherers moving all day with nets and traps and string baskets in search of food and medicine. The family used to move to Kundalbaghi, Hupad, Chapua, and finally from Hupad to Demotand. God, she says, taught her jungle medicine. *This is very significant*. Bansi says that their parents taught them the basic knowledge of medicine or *jari-buti* as it is referred to by them, or the "knowledge of roots and their properties". Kamli's eldest daughter Somri, has now come back after her marriage to Demotand after many years living in the jungles thirty miles away to the northeast with her husband's tanda. Somri lost her two beloved sons Bujulal aged six and Babulal four, and this broke her heart, and she and her husband left their tanda near Barkatha to come here to Kamli, whose home they are sharing. The Birhor mother-in-law is a loving one and Somri's little family feels welcomed. Kamli's son Sukra lives here also. My wife and I visited Kamli here in April 1975, the month Sukra (Friday) was born. I have rare photographs in black and white taken on that day reproduced here. Today Sukra is a young man who shares his earnings and lives with his mother, but he is still unmarried. Now the rooms are bigger than the Kumba and all live in the same government two-room cum-veranda housing, Somri's children call her by her name, as she refers to her own mother by her name. Somri's husband Mangru has given tier two children, who are alive, a son named Bishna and a daughter, Rudhni who is named after Somri's grandmother, Kamli's mother. Her husband's mother's name is Sugni, his father is named Rondo.

Kamli takes up the story, "My mother taught me all that I know about medicine", she says with emotion. She is a frail 57 years and life and time have taken their toll of Kamli's health, but she is supremely happy and self assured. She continues about her mother:

> "She used to take us with her to the jungle". Our family tanda was in Magadh-desh (Gaya district), near Koderma". (This is in the great Deborh jungles referred to). She continues, 'We are from Magadh, the biggest of all the Birhors, the Maghadhi. The hills of Rajauli, Singar, Ekwalpur, Deborh Buru (Buru means mountain god), these were very good jungles which we lived and hunted in with our parents. The jungles there have many big animals. There were a lot of birds and wild animals including tigers. The jungles were also full of wild medicines, especially the creeper *Chandwa-ghari* or *Bholan-jhari* which is used for catching girls. The girl cannot run away once she is taken to the creeper which a young man may plant in his courtyard. She will fall down unconscious, and only by breaking off a branch can the girl be wakened from her swoon. The man must of course know how to do this".

She continues, "My father died in Charhi and my mother died in Kundalbaghi in 1982. My father died when I was seven years old and Bansi was then only five years old. I went to my husband's home in Parasnath shortly after this. I was married by my mother Rudhni and my stepmother (Saitin), Kario Didi. I called my mother Barki Ma and my stepmother Chotki Ma.

Chotki Ma died in Bargadi beyond Domchanch in Chortumbhaij only last year. My mother Rudhni's mother's name was Jhungo Birhorni, and her mother's father was Barka Birhor and mother was Rishni Birhorni. They lived in the Deborh jungles from the time of their parents".

"With Jhungo Nani (grandmother) and my mother and Kario Didi I first started to learn the skill of recognizing and knowing the properties of the jungle plants for making medicines from them, and how to know them by sight with or without leaves, in their flowering or dormant state for it is difficult to know where they are when the leaves are not on them for only in the rainy season do some plants flower. My uncle Babulal taught me how to sell medicines in the bazaar (market), and so I started to sell my medicines collected and prepared with the jungle roots and wild herbs and the different parts of birds or animals or the epiphytes from the different trees. I began to sell medicines in the Sunday market in Charhi and the Monday market in Kuju, and even went as far away as Ramgarh and even on occasion to Ranchi to sell my medicines. I have even been as far as Bermo, Chaas, and Jarangdih in the coal mine areas selling medicine. All types of medicines were bought by the Muslims, Bilaspuriyas, Thakurs, Kurmees and others, and they used to pay a good price".

Kamli's youngest daughter Kui, who is six years old, comes to where we are sitting and shyly joins the group. Her eldest daughter Puniya whom she affectionately calls "Munia" died last year at only twelve years of age. I say "eldest" referring to the children by her second marriage. Munia's death broke her heart, for even though she is an expert medicine-woman she could not save the child. There are times when Birhor medicine may need supplanting by advanced medicare in a hospital as the time when Babulal broke his ribs and I had him admitted in a local hospital, or the stomach ulcer operation I had done for a Birhor child in agony in the Matakdura tanda. But these are exceptions. Kamli believes she can no longer conceive having taken the powerful steroid Paan-ko-jari root of the Bengal paan (*Piper betel*) is believed to be a very powerful steroid taken either by itself, or with other roots. Once taken the steroid effect cannot be withdrawn. I had contacted the National Institute of Family Planning at Delhi and was told that the steroidanagram of paan-ko-jari is 20%, that is, a 20% negative steroid capability and 80% superstition value (S. K. Bose).

Bhola, Kamli's husband, is alive and well. Sukar and his younger brother Chotkul live in the family, and Kui is her mother's closest companion after Munia's death. Kui too is now learning the jungle medicine. All four children are from Bhola. Somri is the only child from her first marriage. All the children are learning the medicine. Somri is already an expert in medicine. Little Kui is starting to bring in medicines from the scrub jungle of Saal behind the tanda while Kamli is away at market and to, in this way, replenish the stocks. When Munia was alive she too helped her mother in this way. Somri has been a couple of times to the Hazaribagh District Court compound where Kamli sells medicine five days a week. One day she sold as much as forty rupees worth of medicine. The most popular medicine was Jadu-muni a medicine for catching men! She tells me this with no trace of shyness. She says :

> "The woman gives to the man the Jadu-muni medicine and he is caught in her love trap for her. He will even allow the woman to beat him if she wishes." This is naturally a very popular medicine with the men, and in Burma I believe it was called the "Poongi Pill" by the European community.

After Kamli, now Somri will take over selling medicine since she has a readymade place for herself after Kamli retires or dies, since the Birhor are not a long-lived people. Somri says she and her husband have left Koriatand for good after the death of their children and they will settle down permanently at Demotand tanda. Mangru and Somri have now two children, Bishna aged ten and Rudhni, four. Kamli is a fulfilled grandmother.

On an average I have figured out that Kamli earns about fifty rupees a day which is quite a lot. She daily takes her place at 10 a.m. in a line of other Birhor medicine sellers in the Courts compound. Slowly the line has shortened. Somra of Matakdura, Budhni of Sijhwa, Karmi of Demotand, Bhuneswar of Bhuswa, Sukar also of Bhuswa, Babulal of Demotand, Sukar's wife Budhni of Bhuswa, Narang guru of Sijhwa, have each fallen out of line and returned to their ancestor spirits, Now the line comprises Kamli, Baburam, Chedi from Demotand... Kamli calls the man selling tooth medicine beside her "butcher". Tomorrow Sukar and Somri will join the line. An old medicine man from Kundalbaghi named Tuti Boho comes sometimes. He is her husband's cousin and he is nicknamed "Budhu" which means stupid, but now he is also too old to join the line. Her husband's mother, or her mother-in-law Titinga Burhi is a real charmer in her late sixties. She knows all about this medicine business but refuses to go commercial. She is after all the great-grandmother with three generations of medicine women under the patronage! Back at the tanda Titinga Budhi has her own medicine bag which contains a wide variety of roots and herbs and bits of bone, hair, dried meat and other assorted paraphernalia. What are the ailments these bags of tricks can cure?

Kamli tells us, "There are many plants in the jungles. Each has a medicinal property in some of its parts. Khaksa root stops menstrual bleeding and Morom-Dah and Pathal-Konda roots are very good in treating women's complaints. For diabetes mixture is made from the Kamraj and Chiriakanda rhizome. Arthritis is cured by taking the crushed Gaithia root with milk. Chiriakanda is excellent for reducing inflammation of hydrocile if ground up with oil and applied during night time. I have many patients with indigestion and I give them Sikajori, the same medicine which Narang Guru from Bhuswa makes up with eighteen roots. Mine is more effective as everybody knows".

Anyone who has seen Kamli selling her medicines will know that she is a wonderful saleswoman. She continues, "A good tonic is made from the Bhojraj root, Hemraj wood, Tejraj stem, Satawa bark, and Simarkanda root. For snakebite many roots can be used including the Saram Lutur and Isror roots ground up and administered orally, or the Tali Baha bark or Tirsul root. Many persons come to me with continuous headache problems and I give them Jinda-Lakri which is wood from the Tejbaal tree which contains oil. It is ground up and mixed with hot mustard oil and applied on the forehead. For the Adhkapari or half-headache I give the wood of that name which is lighter than the dove's breast feather, to be hung by a thread from the ear on the opposite side to balance the fluids, Paan-Ko-Jari as you know is the most powerful steroid known. Naran Guru uses ten roots and a wild flower to prepare it. But I make it simply with one root. The tail of the Sambur deer is made into an oil for application in hernia cases and relieves the constriction. Bon Piyaj or Kulu Kanda is made up in oil to cure eczema and itch of all kinds. Most oral medicines are administered on an empty stomach in the early morning, and according to the prescription they may have to be taken with black pepper corns or misri sugar, or the milk of a black cow. In rare cases a black pigion is placed on the patient's head while administering the medicine as in cases of epilepsy."

I have ascertained that indeed the jackal has a horn - this was a bone of contention among several naturalist and sportsmen friends when I told them the Birhors collect the cone of grey hair, the Sia-singhi (literally : Jackal Horn) from the ground when the male jackal cries "Fee-a-ow" on a moonlit night. Sterndale mentions it at page 118 of Mammalia of India, 1929 Edn., Thacker, Spink & Co., Bombay and Madras. The Sia-Singhi belongs to the leader of the pack. It is a potent charm which Singhalese call Narricomboo. This is to my knowledge its first mention in regard to the Birhor knowledge. The Birhors believe a Sia-singhi will grow if placed in vermilion powder or Sindur. Kamli then continues with her story:

> The Sia-singhi is the horn of the jackal which drops when the jackal howls to the full moon. It is a powerful charm for good luck. The Eiksirha pod is also a good charm that is tied to a child's waist by a black thread to avoid hydrocele. Many people get filaria nowadays. In the monsoon a thick white mushroom grows in trees called Ooth. Mix it with hot oil and apply it to reduce swelling. For treating dysentery Bhengraj is very good. For coughs and colds I make people chew the Barki-jari which is a bitter type of bark. If there is a very high fever then I give the Ghorbaaj root to eat, or the Charki-jari or Kapurni stem crushed in water. Kapurni is also a powerful reliever of pain and it is put into a fresh wound. For snakebite or severe

pain I give Raj-gurumba. For persons afflicted with fits or epilepsy I give the Saramlutur root and the Karilakhan stem. Both these are trailing plants and hard to find during summer. They are administered with milk from a black cow. For diabetes the Kewakanda and Chiriakanda roots are good and I make a tonic with these to cure diabetes."

In the other tandas there are others like Kamli, both men and women. I have taken her as a typical example of the best. She says :

"I give the deer navel chord ground up well to cure epilepsy, or if I have it the humerous bone of the common river otter, or a piece of donkey's bone or a piece of monkey's skull. Any of these will do but they have to be ground fine and given in water preferably during the attack. Or you can use the rhizome of the Pathal-Bando in streams near the big rocks for vegetarians. Hathajori and Premjori are powerful love potions. You may add some Jogmohni seeds also and some Laihaoni-Ghas. I mix it in oil, but I advise scented oil. You touch the other person with it only. The best sexual stimulant is Haser. I sell a lot to the men. But my best sales are medicine for asthma for which I give Bon-Piyaj and Bowad (wild ginger) with ten crushed pepper corns. For deep coughs Kanta-saru and Danta-hasura for toothaches, which is why I sit next to the "butcher"! Ralli root sucked cures whooping cough, and Kirni empties the stomach of worms. I cure gonorrhoea with the Ghuraiinch root."

Mainly Kamli's prescriptions are from plants. Others use deer horn (for epilepsy), monitor lizard jawbone (for tetanus), peafowl leg bone (to stop singing in the ears); elephant bone (for driving off evil spirits), etc. Kamli is content and says that she will now not move from Demotand. Despite damage to the forests she says that the medicinal plants are not damaged, these being on the forest floor, small herbs and creepers, rhizomes and tubers, which form the basis for Birhor ethnobotany. Her personal requirements are few: a little tobacco and lime, a length of ribbon for her daughter, even these considered as luxuries. For one with so few wants simple things become precious, and with Schumaker we may say, "Small is beautiful". Whether ethnobotany amongst the Bushmen of the Kalahari desert or the Tirio Indians on the Sipaliwini river in north Amazonia the simple plants coupled with ancient therapeutic knowledge point to a rare resource base of human kind which can save millions of dollars in research and save untold suffering for millions. There can be cures here for cancer and AIDS or other problem sicknesses ravaging the modern world. After all the basis for Vincoleucoblastine to cure leukemia came from the humble periwinkle, as antibiotics came from foot trodden moss or the cure for malaria from cinchona.

Somri is in no hurry to have Sukra married who she had carried on her back, and Titinga Burhi also feels Sukar should not marry just now. Her husband's brother Babulal was my great friend and the one who taught me much of Birhor ways and medicine. He was Kamli's uncle and also taught her the medicine trade, He died recently and for me a close, and great friend, has passed on to the hunting grounds, where I hope to meet him some day Babulal used to say that Titinga Burhi carded him on her back! That was to show how old she is. The interior of Kamli's house resembles a cave dwelling, smoke blackened walls tell of cooking without a chimney. Warmth exudes from the clothes hung from a pole and the string nets hanging from pegs in the walls, the string baskets and the smell of living things. Tragedy enters here to pass for this room is a caravanserai of generations, the gift of a ceaseless survival knowledge which is irreplaceable, requiring constant weaving through the changing hands of each generation, and a way and view of life vanishing forever from the planet earth. Kamli stands as a guardian of that spirit that will not give in, she says :

> "In the olden days, man, monkey, fruit, animals, vegetable, entered the mind of stone. Plants are the creation of Bhagwan (God) as food for healthy living, and a balance between our collective common needs and individual desires. Bhagwan is in all things."

Once Kamli told me the great rock on the crest of the Sitagarha hill nearby is a petrified giant. I believe it. Below the hill I found an anthropomorphic status (maha-deva) exactly resembling the hill crest. Kamli comes from a tribe as old as the hills of Hazaribagh which are today being mined for stone chips and bombarded with heavy artillery of the army for shooting ranges. The Ora Bonga in the tandas has not yet said a word.

Both Ora Bonga and Maha Deva stand under the heavens for no roof of clay must cover them. Thus, the guardian spirits forever guard Kamli and her clan living on the edge of the forest.

13 Indigenous Knowledge for Sustenance: An Introspection of Tribal India

Amitabha Sarkar and Samira Dasgupta

In India different communities live in different eco-setting and for sustenance they utilize the immediate natural resources with their traditional knowledge and technique. The ecological setting reflects the technology, worldview and the belief system of the communities as a whole. Their economic pursuits are usually linked with the ecology, environment and technology, which allow them to adjust themselves with the local situations.

With the advent of globalization the tribes of Indian sub-continent even in the secluded, remote corners are also aware of the fast changing economic and technological scenario and the consequent socio-cultural impact on their society. Infact, concepts like globalization and global village indicate that the world has become more and more easily accessible and open to any one. This process has made the ethnic groups of contemporary world increasingly more interdependent, susceptible to the market forces and also flexible to the changing currents. Globalization refers to a more advanced stage in the process of development of the world economy through the establishment of worldwide information technology and communication networks (Saxena, 2003). The tenets of globalization are also affecting traditional socio-cultural pattern of interaction and inter-relationship among the tribal people of India, who are a repository of vast and varied indigenous knowledge.

To our mind indigenous knowledge (IK) is the product of interaction between a community with its immediate environment and this environment is both physical and social in which they live and maintain their subsistence in a sustainable way. When we say indigenous knowledge (IK), we refer to the unique traditional, local knowledge that has developed and has been acquired by a group of people living in a particular niche and the knowledge is transmitted from one generation to another primarily with the help of oral tradition.

The knowledge system is embedded in the folklore of a community that is not only time tested but it also helps them to interact with the components of their eco-setting. It is believed that indigenous knowledge (IK) is a pivotal factor in their subsistence mechanism. Each aspect of life of a community in the rural, hilly, forest clad area, or in a riverside area is supported by the body of indigenous knowledge that offers them a survival strategy. In the light of modernization and cultural pluralism in Indian culture their rich indigenous knowledge equips them to exist with their traditional cultural markers even in the midst of the thrust of modernization.

In India there are altogether 461 tribes (Singh, 1994), of which about 172 are segments. Majority of them, that is, 402 live in hilly terrain. Out of these 461 tribes, 226 live in dense forest, 113 live in plateau, 48 live in high altitude, 46 in valleys, 14 in island, 10 in semi-arid region, 21 in coastal region, 1 in desert and 227 in the plains. This speaks of the diverse physical and cultural setting in which the tribal people of India exist (Sarkar and Dasgupta, 2000).

The present paper highlights how indigenous knowledge is used in various facets of life by the inhabitants of the Sundarbans in the southern part of West Bengal, among the tribal groups of Abujh Marh hills in Chhattisgarh, among Birjia and Mal Paharia of Jharkhand and Toto of northern part of West Bengal.

ROLE OF INDIGENOUS KNOWLEDGE FOR SUSTENANCE

Sundarbans Region of West Bengal

During our extensive field work in various islands of the Sundarbans especially which are under South 24 Parganas district of West Bengal (incidentally a part of the Sundarbans falls under North 24 Parganas district; previously there was only 24 Parganas district in West Bengal), it is observed that 44% of the total population belongs to Scheduled Caste and Scheduled Tribe (Saha, 1999). Majority of Sundarban inhabitants (about 75 to80%) are engaged in cultivation work on reclaimed land and that too single crop, that is, only paddy is grown. Apart from cultivation the other important economic pursuits are fishing, practicing pisci-culture, woodcutting and honey collection by *bauley*(wood cutters as well as *gunin versed with chants)* and *mauley*(honey collectors*)* respectively. Besides there are peoples who are involved in collection of shrimp (*meen dhara*) and in this economic pursuit a child of 10 years old to a person of 60 years old are involved and during peak season their average contribution to each family is Rs.450 to Rs.500/- per month. About 55-60% agricultural labourers are landless and in this category we find the scheduled castes and scheduled tribes. Their per capita earning clearly suggests that they exist below poverty line (BPL).

In this area the following ethnic groups viz., Brahman, Kayastha, Patit Brahman, Paundra Kshtriya (or Pod), Namasudra, Bagdi (both Duley and Tetuley –these sub castes are endogamous in nature), Napit, Kamar, Kumar, Sadgope, Goala, Tilipatnis, Hari, Kaibrata, Kapali, Jalia, Tior, Dhoba, Jogi, Suri, Kaora, Chandal, Rajbanshi and tribal people like Munda,Bhumij and Oraon together with Muslims and Christians are found. A large number of immigrants from Bangladesh live in this area, and almost all of them are involved in fishing as a major source of earning.

The Scheduled Castes and Scheduled Tribes play a vital role in the composition of population in the Sundarban region. The scheduled caste population according to 1991 census in south 24 Parganas district is 906447 and sex ratio is 1000: 947 while Scheduled Tribe is 59457 and sex ratio is 1000: 939. The Scheduled Caste population in North 24 Parganas district is 1,22,3982 and sex ratio is 1000: 932, the Scheduled Tribe population is 1,78,952,their sex ratio is 1000: 967 (Mondal, 2003). There is altogether 6-major Scheduled tribe in the Sundarban region. These six tribal groups are Bhumij (89%), Munda (82%), Oraon (63%), Santals (66%), Kora (92%) and Mahali (90%) etc. It is found that Bhumij are chiefly located in Sandeshkhali, Gosaba, Hasnabed, Canning and Raidighi. Oraon are found in Raidighi, Sandeshkhali and Canning Police Station. Santals are concentrated in the police station of Haroa, Canning, Gosaba, Hasnabad and Sandeshkhali (Das, 1981).

It is seen from the aforesaid discussion that the present day Sundarban inhabitants are basically immigrant population inhabiting the various islands of the Sundarbans. In course of their settlement at Sundarban within this long span of time (record shows that these islands were populated as early as the early 18th century when labourers were engaged for clearing jungles and for reclaiming lands–criss-crossed by rivers and rivulets and often interconnected by canals). Since then the people in the Sundarbans have adopted their life and culture with the demand of local environment. The adaptive strategy, which has developed among various ethnic groups at this delta environment, is obviously one of the means of survival strategy.

The fieldwork was carried out in various islands of Gosaba block of Sundarban, which is considered the gateway of Sundarbans. In Gosaba block there are nine islands with 14 Gram Panchayats, while one island is uninhabited.

As per 2001 census the population strength of various islands of Gosaba are as follows:

It is reported that in the Sundarban forest every moment is full of insecurity and uncertainty for the people of the Sundarbans who enter the forest for collection of honey and cutting of fuel wood. The tribal people like the Munda, Oraon, Bhumij, who have been brought from Chotanagpur region in Bihar now Jharkhand or from Mayurbhanj of Orissa, have tuned their life style on the basis of their experiences acquired in this area. The knowledge and experience have helped them to live in this Sundarban region where the climate and topography are different from their natal region.

Table 1
Island wise Population of Gosaba (As per 2001 Census)

Islands	*Population*	*Total Population*
Gosaba and Rangabelia	17167+13806	30973
Bipradaspur, Sambhunagar and Pathan Khali	13952+13501+16060	43513
Bally I and Bally II	11644+16280	27924
Kachuakhali	11977	11977
Radhanagar – Taranagar	21078	21078
Amtali	15304	15304
Kumirmari	16193	16193
Chotamulla khali	18419	18419
Satjelia and Lahiripur	16684+20699	37383
Char Amlamethi	Uninhabited	
Total		2,222764

Honey collection is a seasonal operation starting from the month of *Chaitra* (March–April) and it continues atleast for three months. With the end of the season of *neem*(margosa*)* flower it is the time when the bee-hives are stepped in honey, as all the flowering plants and trees in the Sundarban forest (such as, *khalsi* (*Aegialitis carniculatum* (L), *keora* (*Sonnevatia apetala,*) etc, are full with bloom. The *mouleys* (honey collectors) locate the beehives tracing the velocity of the northerly wind. During collection of honey *hental* (*Phoenix paludosa*) leaves are used as broom, chappals and shoes are used to protect them from piercing of sting of bees. For collection of honey, they set fire to the mixture of the dried and fresh *hental* leaves and with the smoke of the burnt leaves the bees are driven away. After setting fire they hold it in favour of wind. As soon as the smoke reaches the honeycomb, it irritates the bees and finally the bees leave the beehives and after which they collect honey. The *mauley* of this region collect honey one or two days before the full moon or new moon days; otherwise they may find the honeycombs empty.

It is to be noted that a social regulation is empowered here by the fact that whenever they dig out any tuber from the earth, they should not take out the whole portion out of it. Always they leave some portion of roots of tuber in the earth for allowing it to rejuvenate. Young bamboo shoots are delicious item of food to them. Often they cover the young bamboo shoots with an earthen pitcher. The bamboo shoots grow in a circular fashion inside the earthen pitcher (*handi)*, which looks like a cabbage. Though it is delicious, they usually avoid preparing it frequently, as it hampers the growth of bamboo.

The fisher folk (Hindu, Muslim, Christian and tribal people like Bhumij, Munda, Oraon etc) of the Sundarbans use various kinds of net for their catch which depends on (a) nature of catches, (b) depth of water, (c) colour of water and (d) bubbles created by a shoal of fish in the water, size of fish etc. In this profession, they use varieties of fishing nets for various types of catches as given below, which mainly depends on their indigenous knowledge that have been acquired over generations.

During both full moon and new moon periods, the intensity of tide and ebb is very high. The tide on these two days is called *kotal.* The *kotal* on the full moon day is regarded as a *madi* or female *kotal* and that of the new moon day is called *madda* or male *kotal.* The force or intensity of the male *kotal* is more than a female *kotal.* There is a myth behind it. It is told that the female *kotal* wants to run away from male *kotal* and the male *kotal* runs behind her to catch hold of her. The effect of the *kotals* is continued till next three to five days. After that gradually it becomes minimized. The tide with lesser force is called *marani* tide and *marani* ebb. Catching of crab also depends on nature of *kotal.* The crabs come with the tidal water towards the bank of the river, locally called *khari* and take shelter in the potholes of the riverbed. During low tide the local people dig out the crab by an iron stick. Often, it is observed that they hang a small fish (*chuno machch*) tied in a thread, attached with a stick or a branch of twig by the side of the river on the bank, very close to a hole when a crab gets attracted and comes out of the hole, the crabs are caught. There

Table 2
Use of Indigenous Knowldege for Fishing

Local Name of the Fishing Net	*Name of the Catches*	*Nature of Water etc.*
Benti Jal	Chapra (Prawn)Chuno Machch (Small fish)	Found in low water near sand-bank
Char pata jal	Bhetki, Phansa	Coastline of mangrove and sand bank
Khal Pata jal	Chapra (prawn), Chuno machch, Bhetki, Datney, Kan machch, payra toil.	Where estuary of river becomes dry and low deep of water in estuaries and canals.
Kumo jal	Kan, Payratoli, Bhetki, Koibhol	Different tree twigs are used in covering the area for catching fish
Kalsi Jal	Bhetki, Jawa bhetki, Payra, Datney	Nets are tied with big tree on both the sides of creeks or rivulets.
Monofil Jal	Khayra, Parsey, Prawn (big size viz. Bagda, Galda etc)	With the help of bamboo, fishing nets are spread over the creeks and canals.
Galsa Jal	Sheley, Jawa, Bhetki, Bhola Bhetki (big size)	Nets are spread in the water with the help of *gorapi* (made of iron and used as anchor) where current in the river exist.
Bhesal Jal	Chapra Prawn, Parsey, Phansa	Use search light in the boat then by seeing light shoal of fish are attracted, then nets are spread from inside water.
Khepla Jal	Prawn, Parsey, Phansa and various small fishes (chuno machch)	Nets are thrown from ground knee deep water.
Don Barsi Jal	Fishes like Mochan, Medh, Kan, Sheley, Murali etc.	For deep water. Use bait in fishing hook. Prawn, *loteh* or *nereh, sita pati* etc. fishes are used as bait.

Table 3
Herbs and Plants Used as Therapy

Name of the Disease	*Herbs/Plants used*	*Method of Use*
Cough and Cold	(a) Leaves of *manasa* (*Anemopsis californicia,*)plant, salt or honey. (b) Leaves of *tulsi(*basil*)* plant and honey	(a) The juice of leaf is extracted and then mixed either with salt or honey and the mixture is taken for cure. (b) The leaves are grinded and mixed with honey and taken.
Cuts/ Wounds	Leaves of Marigold plant and sundried rice	The leaves are ground along with the sundried rice and then applied it to the cut.
Abscess, boil	The roots of *kelki* plant	The roots are ground and then applied
Bone injury or sprain	Stem of the Harjora plant (*Acanthus ilicifolius L.)* or The leaf of *nischindi*(*Vitex negundo L)*	The stem is ground and then applied to the wound and bandaged tightly Or The leaf is crushed and applied to the place. It gives relief from pain
Stomach troubles, dysentery	Thankuni(*Centella asiatica(L)urban)* leaf, mustard oil	The leaf is grinded and mixed with mustard oil and then taken with hot rice
Headache	Telakucho leaf(*Coccinia grandis(L)*	The juice of the leaf is applied to the affected parts of forehead
Sprain	Turmeric and mustard oil	Paste of turmeric added with mustard oil, heated and applied to the affected zone.

are various types of crabs, which also depend on nature of *kotal* as well as *tithi* (determined through almanac) such as *tele, chiti, nona* and *hero* etc. The *chiti* crabs grow more in summer, the *tele* variety is found during monsoon, and while the *nona* and *hero* crabs are available throughout the year in the river.

In this delta environment the rural folk of the Sundarbans mainly depend on nature (physical environment) for curing their ailment. They use local herbs and plants. The knowledge they have acquired in this respect is developed from oral tradition due to a prolonged interaction with their immediate niche. This knowledge is also handed down by the shamans who possess special skill to identify the medicinal and other kinds of plants.

APPLICATION OF INDIGENOUS KNOWLEDGE: COGNISANCE OF ENVIRONMENT AND WORLDY OBJECTS

The rural folk of the Sundarbans including the tribal people identify their habitat as their own world. All their views, ideas, activities are based on the geographical environment in which they live now. They have nearly forgotten their own legends, stories and myths about their origin, the universe and have taken and adopted new way of life in their present place of habitation at Sundarban. The tribal people coming from Bihar (Jharkhand) and Orissa have been gradually assimilated in this new physical and cultural environment.

According to these people of the region there are chiefly three seasons, namely *garam* (summer), *varsa* (monsoon) and *thanda* (winter). It is told by the Munda and the Oraon that with the performance of *Sarhul* they feel that the summer season is approaching. Again with the blooming of flowers like *khalse*, mango and neem trees they are confirmed that the days of scorching heat are very close. During summer season when they observe that the ants, especially the black ants, are moving in rows towards a safe and comparatively high land from a low lying place with eggs in their mouth, they get the signal of the advancing rainy season. Again, the frog's croaks are the confirmation of the rains. If there is plenty of mango production they get assured that the sufficient amount of rainwater will help them in cultivation and they will get bumper crop. When they find the tamarind production is high, they become afraid of 'excessive rain', which lead to a flood like situation. Similarly, when they observe that the crabs crawl on plants and snails are seen to climb on plants and trees it is definite that there will be flood.

They have developed a cognitive sense from their empirical knowledge of environment, because they are closely associated with the natural environment for their livelihood. When they observe that there is wind blowing from the northern direction, the date palm trees are ready with juice in the morning. If there is mist and they feel cold, they say that winter season has arrived. According to them during winter season if the wind blows from the southern direction, they confirm the appearance of fog on the next day.

They believe that in a rainy season at the time of sunset if the sky becomes red, they apprehend for rain. When they see that there are two stars, called as *jele* and *jeleni* found in the same line in the *nairit* (south-west) corner of the sky, they are sure about the possibilities of rain with thunderstorm. Similarly, when they see any water vapour encircling the moon, they are in the habit of forecasting rain. The water vapour circle is locally known as *paras* or *chander sabha* or *pani mandav.* If the circle is found to encircle the moon from a closer distance they forecast rain in distant places, while during reverse condition they apprehend rain in nearby places.

Another signal for rain they get from the *jhinjhi poka* (twinkle of little creature), which lives on the top of the tree; when they come down in a row, there will be rain. During night they calculate the time through stars and crowing. Cawing is the signal of dawn while hooting is the sign of midnight.

Abujh Maria–A Primitive Tribal Group of Chhattisgarh

The Abujh Maria, a primitive tribal group of Bastar district of Chhattisgarh state, are chiefly *penda* (shifting hill) cultivators. The life and culture of the Abujh Maria are also cherished under the lap of forest environment. Behind all shadow of beliefs, some kind of ethno science is reflected which in turn controls their livelihood and surrounding niche. With this native wisdom they not only exploit the natural resources for sustenance but also conserve and preserve their bio-diversity. An in depth study of folk medicine from an emic point of view will help in understanding the cultural symbols (Tribhuwan, 1998). Ethno-medicine speaks of the beliefs and practices relating to health and disease, which are derived from indigenous geo-cultural environment and not derived from the knowledge taught by the modern medicine (Dasgupta and Sarkar, 2005). Anthropological data on ethno-medicine is instrumental in understanding the health related beliefs of the Abujh Maria as well as the mechanism adopted by them to conserve the surrounding bio-diversity. They utilize the resources of a particular territory and also protect the resource base to sustain their future generation. Every Abujh Maria village has a *tallur,* sacred grove, which is also the seat of the village deity. This obviously suggests the importance shown by them to the surrounding flora where rituals are performed on relevant occasions. The sacred grove is also a portion of original forest most of which has been cleared to establish the village.

The abode of Abujh Maria, a little known primitive tribal group, is a vast tract of forest resources. The Abujh Maria are depended on their specialist like *leske* (medicine man) and *sirha* (sorcerer) who possess a thorough knowledge of plants, herbs and roots and of their territory. The *leske* or *sirha* gets some hints through his/her magical power about some black magic or sorcery to harm a person. The *leske* or *sirha* prescribes remedies, if they fail to identify the actual reason or culprit, he takes the help of 'log god' or *pen* deity (clan deity) who by his/her divine power identifies the witch or wicked person responsible for the mischief and also prescribes methods for healing. Generally, some forest leaf or root with some magical quality is prescribed to get rid of the effect of black magic; but in almost all the cases a ritual offering to the deities is obligatory.

Table 4
Indigenous Knowledge Being Health Care Practice

Use of Local Herbs/ Plants/Seeds	*Name of the Disease*	*Method of Use*
Turguma fruit, Katta or Kota fruit	Headache and Stomach pain.	Boil the fruit in water then consume the fruit or fry the fruit and consume.
Harra (*Terminalia chebula*)	Cold, Cough and fever (Local Name : *Muta pasinta*)	Grind it in water then keep it soaked in water for at least 2 hours; then drink the water. It is taken 2 to 3 times in empty stomach.
Kohka or velva seed (*Semicarpus anacardium*)	Headache and wound (Local namej *Tala naunta)*	The seed is slightly broken and heated. The oil of the seed comes out and is applied on the forehead/wound. The wound will be healed.
Beng podia tuber	Blood dysentery (Local Namej *Neturpota*)	Ground and soaked in water overnight, taken in the morning.
The root of *duli* tree	Diarrhoea (Local Namej *Tatti/ pet darna)*	It is ground and soaked in water overnight, taken in the morning.
Pendra root	Body pain (local namej *mendur nainta)*	Ground and taken.
Pittereka fruit (green small sized)	Eye trouble (Local namej *kondang putingta)*	The fruit is taken as a medicine, which is available in forest.
Tora seed oil (mahua seed)	Cold, cough and cracks in the skin	Warm oil is massaged all over the body.
Karanj Seed (*Pongamia glabra)*	Skin disease	Extracted oil is applied on the effected parts of the body.
Chiraita (*Swerita chirata*)	Malaria, blood purifier	Grinded it and soaked in water overnight and the water is taken.

Contd.

Use of Local Herbs/ Plants/Seeds	*Name of the Disease*	*Method of Use*
Sannhemp seed (*Crotrolaria junea*)	Barrenness (Local namej *Banj*)	It is taken after grinding.
Balbairang or Barbreng (*Embelia ribes*)	Wormicide	Root of the plant is ground and taken.
Mud of ant hill	Sprain	Collected the mud and it is heated and then anointed at the place of sprain.
Bark of *neem* tree (Azadirachia indica)	Irregular menstruation	Bark of *neem* tree is grounded and soaked in water for a few hours and then the water is drunk.
Arjun bark (Terminalia arjuna)	Chest pain	Bark is soaked in water overnight and water is taken.
Gunchee (*Abrus precatorius L.)*	Skin disease	The seed are pounded with water and the paste is applied.
Iswarmul (*Aristo lochia indica)*	Snake and rat bite	The whole plant is ground and consumed.

In the above table a list of locally available herbs, plants and seeds with their curing power are presented. This is how the knowledge system of the Abujh Maria helps them in surviving without paying any heed to the modern medicare system.

The above data on indigenous health practices by the Abujh Maria clearly reflect that their own concept of disease and their way of treatment are directly influenced by local herbs, plants etc. in their neighbourhood. The *sirha* or *leske* who actually knows the medicinal plants always try to conserve these in their ecological niche by imposing certain norms and restrictions. Since these medicines are the products of the forest, there is no degenerating effect. Moreover, use of herbal medicine is curative rather than preventive.

Apart from the indigenous health care practices the Abujh Maria socio-economic life is also guided by indigenous knowledge where myth plays a key role. Abujh Marias are traditionally *penda* (slash and burn) cultivators. Ownership of land here is firstly on the village basis and then on the clan deity basis. Sometimes the village site is abandoned for various superstitious reasons such as death, disease or any calamity. After cultivating a land for two to four years, they shift to another plot of land leaving the previous land fallow for its regeneration and for allowing the soil to regain its fertility.

They move from one hill to another. When all the land of that particular hill are cultivated and exhausted, they leave the total hill area and shift to another hill, which is also under the control of the same clan deity. In this way they used to shift from one hill to another and again come back within 15-20 years to the old *penda* plot. As they have to move from one patch of land to another in an interval of four years, they have a requirement of a vast land but there is a sharp territorial demarcation of each and every *pen*'s (clan deity) area and again each *pen*'s territory is divided among the Abujh Marias according to their respective *kattas* (clan). (Each *pen* consists of number of *kattas* who are considered as *dadabhai* or *bhaiband* group and marriage within the same *dadabhai* group is strictly prohibited). In this backdrop the *katta* members are bound to cultivate within their own territory that ultimately results in a land limitation and it indirectly has an impact on their family size. Average family size of the Abujh Maria is 4.92 members. Practice of *penda* cultivation and movement of one patch of land to other in an interval of four years clearly suggest that they are aware by dint of their traditional knowledge that the fallow land will be rejuvenated with the requisite elements in the soil content and thereby would be fitted for cultivation.

Abujh Maria of Abujhmarh hills of Bastar, who live in association with hills and forest, have their own world. They are least bothered to know anything beyond that limit. Each and every aspect, object and happening around them is thought, understood and explained in their own way through certain myth, stories, songs and legends. They count their months and days according to the position of the moon. The full moon day is regarded as the fifteenth day of the month. They have twelve months that are divided into three seasons. When the *mahua* and *palash* flowers bloom, the mango tree start flowering, they get the indication that the summer season is coming. During summer season new *chhind* (date palm) leaves grow. When they find that new leaves begin to flourish in the *mahua* tree, there is no flower in the tree, they understand that monsoon is approaching. When *sulphi* or sago palm tree are ready to provide sweet juice, paddy is ready for harvest, they can realize that winter is very close.

BIRJIA–A PRIMITIVE TRIBAL GROUP OF JHARKHAND

The Birjia – a less known primitive tribal group of Chotanagpur plateau of Jharkhand state are nurtured in the cradle of nature. Environment is one of important factors which influences the needs, customs, behaviour and mental make up of the people, that is, the culture of people. This becomes more determining in case of the tribes who live in the forest and for whom environment has a direct bearing on their sustenance pattern and the possession of wisdom is the product of the immediate environment (Dasgupta, 1994).

The Birjia were traditionally *beonra* (slash and burn) cultivators, iron-smelters and basket weavers. Dasgupta (1994) has shown in her studies how through IK they have classified and divided the whole year into three seasons like, the *garmi* (summer), *barkha* (monsoon) and the *jara* (winter). Blooming of sal and *mahua* flower is the symbol of summer season. When sal flowers begin to fall and when frequently wet cloud is seen in the sky they think that rainy season is coming soon and within a few days after the performance of *soharai* they believe that winter is approaching. Their occupation varies according to season such as, during *garmi* (Feb-June) they are engaged in basketry, wood cutting, bamboo cutting, collection and hunting. During, *barkha* (June-Oct) they practice chiefly agriculture, labour work, collection, cattle herding while in *jara* (Oct-Feb) they do basketry, bamboo and wood cutting, collection, agriculture and hunting (occasional) etc.

Birjia settlements are found in undulated land of hilly terrain and accordingly for sustenance activity they have developed their own indigenous knowledge for cultivation in such kind of hill slopes. Infact in those patches of land they prefer to do *beonra* cultivation, the main cereal are *marua* (finger millet) and *gondli* (a kind of millet). Now a days they practice coarse variety of paddy cultivation in the hill slopes. They also make various types of *tokri* or *tuki* (basket) and *soup* (winnowing fan) of various sizes and shapes. Baskets are made by bamboo splits and bamboo is collected from neighbouring forests. They collect *pani bansh* from the forest for basketry because the splits of this type of bamboo is more suitable for basketry work than other types.

With the help of indigenous knowledge they prepare various kinds of *fundas* (trap) for hunting which also varies according to the nature of animal to be caught. They generally hunt *hiran* (deer), *lagna* (wild goat), *ban suar* (wild boar) by *tir-dhanush* (bow and arrow) and *tangi* (axe) while, *kutunga funda*– a noose trap generally used by them in their *beonra* field especially to catch a *jik* or *sahi* (porcupine). There is a noose in the trap placed slantingly at an angle so that when a porcupine enters the field, its head goes into the noose and the noose becomes tight when it tries to run away. Then it is caught. They use *sim funda* trap to catch the *jangli sim or* wild fowl. When such foul comes out of the jungle to the field to eat the ripe crop, it is caught in the *funda,* spread over the field as a protection from the fowl. Therefore, *sim funda* serves them in two ways, namely, first to protect the crop from the fowl and secondly, to catch the fowl for consumption.

Collection of forest produce plays an important role in their sustenance activity. They use digging stick (*rambha*) for collection of various tubers from earth. They select a place for digging a particular spot after observing the herbs or creepers or leaves growning there. The most important of those tubers are *gethi* (Dioscorea bulbifera, Linn), *nakoa* (Momochroria vaginalis, (Burm), *kulu* (Eterculia urens, Roxb), *baiyang*(Dioscorea glabra), *baser* (Indigofera linifolia) *sakar kanda* (Ipomoea batatas), *pitharu* and *duru* (Diocorea belophylla) and *sakhina kanda* (Alocasia indica, Schott). Often they exchange the edible tubers in the weekly market with rice grain. Along with these they also collect several vegetables and grasses for their livelihood. They also collect various types of *putu* (mushroom) such as *bans khukhri, beng puttu* from the forest for their own consumption. The *gethi* tuber is of bitter taste and *nakoa* tuber causes an irritating sensation. So these tubers are at first sliced and then boiled. The boiling takes some period when the water is changed for at least six times and only then it becomes ready for consumption. Kulu tuber, which is very poisonous and intoxicating, are made edible after a lengthy process. At first these slices of *kulu* are boiled in water for a long time. Then those are taken in a *nachua* (basket) and kept in flowing water of the stream for one or two days so that the poison of the tuber is washed out. In each case they always keep some portion of the tuber beneath for further rejuvenation. This IK helps in the conservation practices in their ecological set-up.

Birjia prefers application of Indigenous knowledge for treatment of diseases. Disease among the Birjia is regarded as the effect of evil eyes caused due to malevolent spirits. They have much faith on the magic done by village *manti* or *deona* (medicine man) and the locally available herbs, plants, roots and tubers etc. are noted hereunder.

Table 5
Use of Plants in Ailments

Name of Disease	*Plant in Use (Local Name, Botanical Name)*	*Process of Application*
Rautana/ Jendraina (Fever)	(a) The bark of *karam* (Adina cordifolia)	The bark of *karam* tree is crushed and soaked in water. It is then boiled in water, added with some salt and then taken
	(b) The bark of *gethi* tuber (Dioscorea bulbifera)	Bitter bark of *gethi* tuber is crushed and taken with water.
	(c) Ghoti tuber (Vernonia roxburghii)	When fever continues for several days, *ghoti* tuber is rubbed on the stone and taken with water
	(d) Bark of Mahua tree (Bassia latifolia)	Bark of *mahua* tree is ground and taken with water.
Khuktana (Cough and Cold)	(a) Root of *tin patti* tree (Desmodium polycarpurn) or fruit of *ban-bhanta* tree (Clesodendrun indicurn)	The root of *tin patti* tree is taken with water orFruit of *ban-bhanta* tree are tied on the neck of the patient as *totakha* (an empiric medicine)
	(b) Bark of *harra* tree (Terminalia chebula)	Paste of bark of *harra* tree is taken with water.
		Black pepper corns are ground mixed with water and taken.
Khojli/ Funsuri (Eczema)	Mahua seed oil (Bassia latifolia)	*Dori* oil (oil of *mahua* seed) is massaged and take bath.

Contd.

Samangha- Sutana (Headache)	(a) Root of *putri* (Croton roxburghii)	Root of *putri* tree is rubbed and applied on the forehead.
	(b) Root of chakkoar tree (Hibiscus sabdariffa)	Root of *chakkoar* tree is rubbed and taken once daily in the morning before sunrise.
	(c) Turmeric and garlic	Turmeric and garlic are ground together and applied on the forehead.
Datahasua (Tothache)	(a) Root of *rangaina* creeper (Solanum xanthocarpum)	Root of this plant is crushed and made into paste and applied to the affected tooth.
	(b) The leaves of *auragait* tuber (Papilionaceae plant)	The leaves are crushed on the palm and applied on the affected parts of teeth.
Kurainhasua (Chest pain)	(a) Fruit of *bansemi* tree (Dolichos lablab)	Dry fruit of *bansemi* tree is crushed into powder and taken with *ghee*(clarified butter).
	(b) Bark of *arjun* tree (Teminalia arjuna)	Bark of *arjun* tree is made into paste and then applied
	(c) Bark of chhatiani tree (Alstonia scholaris)	Bark of *chhatiani* tree is crushed into paste and applied.
Suantana (Stomachache)	(a) Root of *aithu*((Grenia tiliacfolia)	The rot of *aithu* tree is crushed and taken with water.
		Ashes are spread on the stomach and the place cauterized with a hot sickle where the pain is most acute.
	(b) Root of *tin patti* tree (Desmodium polyarpurn) or root of *marodotto* (Helictores isora) or bark of *tilsa* (Sterculia urens)	The root of *tin patti* tree or root of *marodotto* or bark of *tilsa* tree is crushed to powder and then taken with water

Contd.

Dautana / Babadtana (Worms in stomach)	(a) Root of *munga* sag (Moringaceae olifera)	The root of munga sag is crushed and taken.
	(b) The root of *dhandhapoj* (Ougeinia dalbergioides)	The root of this plant is crushed and given to a child to get cured from worms.
Suobai (Blood dysentery)	Sarai (sal seed)	Sarai seeds are crushed and taken without water.
Chheraina / Aonkatitana (Dysentry)	(a) Bark of *telsa* tree (Sterculia urens)	Bark of mango tree is crushed and taken with water. Bark of telsa tree is crushed and taken with water.
Gethia (Rheumatism)	Root of *champa* (Michelia champaca)	Powdered *champa* root is taken with water.
Haddi tutna (Fracture of bone)	The *harjorni* leaves (Cissus quardrangula, Linn)	The *harjorni* leaves are tied on the affected part and its paste is applied on the fractured portion. Then the bone is tied with the support of bamboo, wood and rope for a fortnight.
Sujak (Blood in Urine)	Root of Setha (Annona squamosa) or *karhi* root (Capparis decidua)	As per availability the root is crushed into paste, mixed with water and taken.
Garra Girana Ko (Abortion)	Young shoots of *dhandhapoi* (Rivea hypocrateriformis)	After crushing the young shoots of the plant, it is taken with one-quarter bottle of *mahua* liquor.
Garmi (Syphilis)	Tikhur *kanda* (Curcuma angustifolia) or the root of *kapasi* (Thespesia lampas) or Champa (Michelia champaca)	As per availability it is crushed and then taken with boiled water.

Apart from these there are certain food items, which also possesses some medicinal effect on their body and as a result keep their body fit. Some of those are-

- Futkal Sag (Desmodium heterocarpum), *chakor ka sag* prepared with *kanji* (rice gruel)– It helps a person to get rid of constipation and stomach upset.
- They also eat *munga sag* (Moringaceae oleifera) to keep their body fit to refresh themselves. It also protects them from blood pressure and small pox.
- Putu or *beng sag* (mushroom)– It is very nutritious and it helps to keep stomach normal.
- Papita (papaya)– It helps to avoid constipation.

MAL PAHARIA–A PRIMITIVE TRIBAL GROUP OF JHARKHAND

The Paharia embracing Mal Paharia, Sauria Paharia and Kumbharbhag Paharia are usually confined in their habitat in Damin-I-koh area of erstwhile Santal Pargana district (now Dumka district) in the state of Jharkhand.

The term Paharia includes, Sauria, Mal Paharia and Kumbharbhag Paharia. In Dumka district the Mal Paharia are mainly concentrated and local administration identify them as Paharia who are of one of the Primitive Tribal Groups of Jharkhand. According to Risley (1981 reprinted), the Mal Paharias are Dravidian tribe inhabiting the Ramgarh Hills of the erstwhile Santal Parganas. Until recently they lived by hunting, gathering and *kurao* (shifting cultivation). Dalton writes that the Mal Paharia "appear to be altogether unconnected with the Raj Mahal hill men". The Mal Paharia are altogether distinct in appearance, customs and languages from the Sauria Paharia or Maler who occupy the Raj Mahal hills proper. It appears that the natural surroundings of the Mal Paharia like those of Sauria Paharia are mostly afforested hills. The fear of the unknown and the unknowable, the denizens of forest and hills, streams and springs has crystallized their belief system which in turn generates various malevolent and benevolent spirits who are propitiated with offerings and sacrifices by their priest–*deheri*.

The Mal Paharia live in hills and jungle. In olden days there was thick jungle in their habitat. They had plenty of food in their vicinity. Hunting and collection of forest products were very important among their occupations. After the declaration of forests as national property by the government, their right on the forest products is restricted. Again as per impact of several developmental programmes and for several other reasons forest area has shrunk. As a result, they have started feeling shortage of food as their hunt and collectable items are not sufficient today. Now-a-days hunting as an occupation has lost its importance and charm. They hunt occasionally specially as an event of recreation and also in connection with certain rituals and festivals and in performance of certain magic. In hunting they generally go in a group even sometimes accommoding other communities of the village in the hunting group. They hunt porcupine, hare, boar, birds, jungle cat, cock etc. They use bow and arrow and different types of nets and traps. A very common type of trap is *lumbhar funda,* used to catch jungle cat and *lumbha* or hare. The members of the party share the flesh of hunted items. If there is a big hunt by the Mal Paharia hunting party of the village, they arrange for a grand feast in their hamlet.

In spite of certain restrictions imposed on them, they believe that forest is their own property. They enjoy the rights of collection of forest products collectively. There is no demarcation or binding in the collection of forest produces among them but when a tree grows in between the cultivable land of two different families, the family takes the product of the tree whose field is closer to the tree. Forest products till date have very important position in their economic life. It provides them their house building materials such as wooden logs, bamboo and grass etc. They collect *roa* or palm leaves to prepare the frame or structure of the thatch of the hut. They use bamboo especially for cross framing. There are two varieties of bamboo namely the *jungle bansh* (bamboo of jungle) and the *kheteir bansh* (bamboo of cultivable land). The bamboo collected from jungle is with thinner circumference in comparison to the *kheteir bansh;* but it is stronger than the *kheteir bansh*. It (*jungle bansh*) is also used to prepare various types of baskets, *sup* or winnowing fans etc. items of daily use. Baskets prepared by this variety of bamboo last long.

They collect *sarai* grass to prepare rope to tie logs and bamboo whenever needed in house making and for caning of cot. The ordinary variety of grass is known as *kheir* . It is also of two varieties. Those grown in the jungle are thicker variety and the *kheir* of the cultivable land is of thinner variety and known as *patla kheir*. They also sell those in the market. They collect *bena* grass to prepare ful jharu (broom). A bundle of which costs Rs.8/- to Rs.10/-. They collect seeds and leaves of *banahata* (or *dhol langra* in the Mal Paharia language) – a local plant from jungle and sell those to the businessmen at local market at the rate of Rs.2/- per piece. Dye is extracted from these plants and these are used for various commercial purposes. These have medicinal value also.

They collect fuel wood, bamboo from forest. They sell one *bhar* (30-35 kg) of *lakri* (wood) at the rate of Rs.40/-. They collect *rolabari* or *sakhoa* wood for construction of house at the rate of Rs.25-30/- per piece. The price varies depending on the thickness and maturity of the log. They collect several minor forest products such as *sal* leaves, *bidi* leaves, *sal* twigs, various type of fruits, flower, seed, leafy vegetables, mushroom, various types of tubers etc. from the jungle. They prepare dishes and bowls etc. from *sal* leaves, prepare charcoal by burning firewood and sell those at the local weekly market from where they purchase vegetables, salt, oil, spices, soap (*murga sabun, sitko bar* etc.), rice grain, pulses and kerosene and other commodities needed daily. They earn Rs.200/- approximately in a month from the collection of jungle products.

As per their Indigenous Knowledge they have classified their cultivable land and practice cultivation for sustenance accordingly. They have primarily three types of land that are categorized according to their position. Those are again divided according to qualitative differences within these and it is completely an emic concept governed by their traditional wisdom.

Table 6
Use of Indigenous Knowledge in Collecting Edible Items for Sustenance

Season	*Collected Items*
Garmi/Garam (Summer) End of February to 1st week of June	Leafy vegetables j kodra sag Flower-mahua, sakhoa (sal), kachnar Fruit-kathal (jackfruit), aam(mango), imli(tamarind), kendu (bidi), khejur (date palm), jam, piyar, amsipra (guava) etc. Seeds j mahua, sakhoa
Barish/ Barsha (Rainy season) June to 1st week of October	Leafy Vegetable j Sola, Kana, Kundla, Netia Fruits j Sarifa Other Items j Various types of mushroom such as j murga chhati, kamar chhati, agomas/ agowas, loa, parba, sugi, saranda, bansh chhati etc. Kondki j a potato like tuber locally called as abo or au. Various other types of au/abu such as chirkia, jaria, bhakta, mahua, tigo, chambo, jorwa, kosiyar, churka, foba, bharnari, boa, bokoya and etc and young bamboo shoot.
Jara/Jare (Winter) Octoberj February	Leaves and leafy vegetables j bidi pata, nakoa sag. Fruits j ber/kul, aola, behera, haritaki, kendu, bheloa etc. Various types of au/abu as mentioned earlier grow during rainy season, ripen during December-January were eaten.

Bhitto land– It is again of two varieties – the (a) Pahari Bhitto and the (b) Gharendi Bhitto.

Pahari Bhitto– It is situated at a very high position in the hills. They cultivate *ghangra/barbate* (a variety of legume), *makai* (maize), *bajra, surthi, kudrum, kosra, arhar, kurthi* or *sarguja,* (all varieties of cereals and pulses) and *til* (oil seed) in this type of land. They have to depend solely on rainwater for cultivation in this type of land.

Gharendi/Garendi Bhitto– It is the land attached to their own houses which commonly known as *bari.* They also have *bari* but that is of a different variety. In *garendi* land, they cultivate *ghangra, surthi,* gehu (wheat) and *makai* with some vegetable such as *jhingi, bhindi, kudrum* etc. They also cultivate some *rabi* crops such as *sorso* (mustard) and various types of vegetables such as *mirchi, muli, began,* tomato etc. This type of land is situated at the lower level where water retention capacity is more than that of the *pahari bhitto.*

Ghait or Kurab– This type of land is situated on the hill slopes locally called as *ghait* where during first year, they cultivate *barbate or ghangra*(beans) also known as *kawai.* Next year, in the same land they cultivate *baro garendi* or maize of bigger size, *arhar*(pulses), *bajra, surthi* and also a little quantity of *ghangra.* During second year, the same land is called as *bari.* In this type of land they cultivate for two years. During the first year they cultivate *barbati* only by slash and burn cultivation method, which is known as *kurao* cultivation. During first year they cut smaller plants, bushes and grass and keep those in the field for a few days till those get rotten. Then they dig a number of holes with *khonta* or dgging stick at least of 2" to 2½" depth. They sow *barbati* seeds in those holes. They fell some big trees and keep those in the field as support for creeping during the growing of *barbati* plant. Barbati seeds are sown in July–August. It grows upto September. In October there will be inflorescence. During the festival of Durga Puja in the month of Aswin(Oct-Nov), they take a variety of legume and roam in the fair held for the festival with an intention to show it to a large number of people. They have a belief that the production depends on their ability to show the legume to more number of people. After that they keep those at the boundary of the *ghait* where they have cultivated.

During November-December they harvest *barbati*. They put fire in the land. The trees felled earlier in the previous cultivation are all burnt. The land has no plant but ashes, which act as manure. They cultivate *garendi* or *makai, bajra* or *alna, sutri* or *kakro* (a kind of pulse), *kundram, bambaru, muto, metro/ matro, kang*. They plant *san* and *kushi* in the boundary to act as hedge. They also plant different varieties of sag or leafy vegetables such as *jhinga* sag, *kadima* sag, which they also consume. All the items are sown during *ashar* (June-July)) and except *arhar* (pulses) all those harvested in *aswin* (September-October). Arhar is harvested in *aghan* (November-December). They eat *san* flower and *kushi* fruit. Kushi fruit is very poisonous. Prior to the preparation of *bhat* from *kushi* fruit they wash it for at least five times. It also has some medicinal values. *In case of scorpion bite, the kushi fruit is broken and pounded on a stone and applied at that particular cut or place of bite; this will cure the patient within one hour.*

In the *ghait*, traditionally they used to cultivate for successive two years. Then they used to leave it as fallow land for next twenty years. Now as the jungle area is being depleted day by day and as the plots are divided again and again resulting to smaller plots to accommodate all the Mal Paharia families, they are unable to keep any land fallow for twenty years. Only after a gap of three to four or at the most six years they return to the same plot. In cases of emergency for owner, he approaches another person with a request to borrow a piece of land from him for two years. In lieu of that the original owner will get two bottles of liquor and a portion of the product cultivated in that land. This practice is known as *talmil*.

Khet- The third variety of land is known as *khet*. The *khet* is again divided into four different varieties namely *bhadai khet, badh, sorka* and *bohal khet*. The *bhadai khet* is situated at the topmost height where they sow varieties of paddy grains during June-July and harvest during September-October. The next variety of *khet* – the *badh khet* is situated at a lower position, next to *bhadai khet*. Here also sowing is done in June-July and harvesting in October-November. The third variety of *khet* – the *sokra khet* is situated at a lower position than the *badh khet* having a little more water retention capacity. In this type of land sowing is done in the month of July-August and harvested in the last week of November. The last variety of *khet* is *bohal khet*. It has the capacity to store maximum water. It is situated at a low level where automatically water comes down due to **gravitational force** and is stored there. In this type of land sowing is done in July–August which is harvested during December. In this type of land they cultivate *kalipankaj and swarna* varieties of paddy. Sarna or *swarna* can be cultivated in slightly high *sokra khet* as they are able to grow in less water.

INDIGENOUS WAY OF MANURE AND INSECTICIDES PREPARATION

These people accumulate cow dung and put earthworm in it. Ultimately it becomes manure. Mal Paharias call it *ishar khad*. They also prepare compose *khad* by leaves and cow dung deposited in a 3 feet deep pit. When it is completely filled up, it is closed by mud and kept for at least one month. By this time it gets rotten. During the time of cultivation, it is taken out and added to the soil. Another very important manure is named as *matka khad*. It is prepared in a *matka* or big earthen pot. At first half of the vessel is filled up with cow dung and the rest half is filled up with cow's urine, water and ½ Kg of molasses. Then it is closed for six days. On the seventh day the lid is opened and the whole substance is stirred with the addition of more water. Then it is sprinkled over the cultivable land.

The Mal Paharias also know how to prepare organic insecticides by accumulating *neem* leaves, *karange* leaves, *akowan* leaves in a vessel specially of clay added with cow's urine and a little water, and the pot is then closed. After six or seven days they open the lid of the pot and extract the decomposed leaves. Then they sprinkle that processed water on the plants specially affected by insects.

TOTO–A PRIMITIVE TRIBAL GROUP OF JALPAIGURI DSITRICT, WEST BENGAL

The Dooars–a sub Himalayan region of West Bengal is having a beautiful scenic beauty due to the location of forest, tea plantation and wild life. The Totos, small Mongloid, underdeveloped tribe are the inhabitants of this region. They are found only in Totopara of Madarihat police station of Jalpaiguri district of West Bengal. A study by the author in 1985 shows that they were 785 in number (Male 407 and Female 378). They numbered 1184 in 2001 census. They have chiefly two types of relatives (*neoscha*), namely *miphu papaya* or consanguineal relatives while *samdi/ pami-bei* are affinal relatives (Sarkar, 1993).

The Toto prepare their log houses, which are made of bamboo splits with bamboo platform, known as *nakosa*, where they apply their traditional knowledge. Since their abode is on the hilly undulated terrain, they construct their house on a raised platform. The houses are built on wooden or bamboo posts about five to six feet above the ground. The materials of the house are procured from neighbouring forest. The roof is generally two sloped and thatched with grass. For climbing on to the platform (*dui*), a tree trunk or thick wooden plank piece (*kaibei*) is placed in an inclined position from the ground to the floor of the *dui*, the *kaibei* is having groove for using it as a staircase.

In order to get a plain surface in the house the Toto construct their houses on a raised platform, more so, because in their habitation area there are numerous leach, snakes and scorpion and monsoon is very strong in this area. To get protection from the flowing water resulted from heavy rain as well as leach, construction of houses on raised platform is very much logical. Moreover, in all the Toto families there are good number of livestock like fowl and pig, which are kept below the bamboo platform, *dui*, of the house.

The basic constraints among the Toto regarding their agricultural activities lies in the poor arable land. This limitation has been due to the presence of high slopes on the

Table 7
Use of Plants in Ailment

Name of Diseases	*Plant in use (Local name, botanical name)*	*Process of Application*
Skin disease	Lotodabai (*Cassia alata, Linn*)	Paste of leaves and fruits applied to affected area.
Ulcers and headache	Daising (*Cordia dichotoma*)	Juice of the leaves applied on ulcers and also as remedy for headache
Stomache trouble	Lungdi (*Gluchidion assimicum*)	Juice of the bark is taken.
Cold and disorder of digestive system	Makaibi (*Drymaria cordata*)	Juice of the plant is used as laxative and also taken in case of disorder of digestive system. Leaves roasted and inhaled, which gives relief from cold.
Check bleeding from wound	Duba (*Cynodon dactylon*)	Grind the plant and apply its juice in the affected region
Diarrhoea	Sadhimodi (*Emilia son- chifolia*)	Juice of the root is used.
Bleeding of Gums	Dirisai (*Kirganelia reticulate*)	Juice of the leaves is applied to the affected region.
Scorpion bite	Langaya (*Polyalthia simiarnm*) or Ahmiche (*Amaranthus viridis*)	The bark is ground and applies as paste or juices of the leaves are directly applied.
Fever	Pagra (*Laportee erenulate*)	Juice of the root is taken
Cough and Cold	Kising (*Phlogocanthus thyrsiflorus*)	Juice of the leaves and roots are taken
Blood pressure, Labour pain and fever	.Korengdabei (*Raurolfia serpentina*)	Juice of extracted root is taken to reduce blood pressure and to increase the uterine muscular contractions during delivery. Powdered root is taken to get relief from fever.

hills, rocky soil and absence of irrigation facility. In the vast unfriendly terrain the Toto apply their native knowledge and understandings for the cultivation of cash crops like ginger, drumstick and areca nut.

The Indigenous Knowledge is also applied during any ailment. The Toto do not prefer to take any alien medicine. They believe that the evil spirits cause various diseases among them and to get rid of such they practise magic or exorcism. They offer puja to appease their ancestral God – **Mahakal**. They often consult *jhankri* (a local Nepali medicine man) during crisis that gives them herbal medicine along with prescription of offering white or black chicken in order to please the spirit. Now a day with the change of time they also consult local PHC (Public Health Centre). The common diseases among the Toto are dysentery, fever, cold and cough, carries in teeth, ulcers etc.

CONCLUSION

From the aforesaid discussion it reveals that with the advent of rapid changing scenario, the subsistence mechanism of the marginalized communities especially tribal folk are being threatened.

Study of indigenous knowledge is one important dimension in New Ethnography that started in American Anthropology in the middle of the twentieth century. This has helped ethnographers to assess the knowledge of an ethnic group to interpret the nature and the natural phenomena, analyse the flora and fauna around them and how these people utilize the nature in the best interest of their livelihood-as their survival strategy.

Sundarban's tribal folk (in the southern part of West Bengal), the Abujhmaria (of Chhattisgarh), the Birjia and Mal Paharia (of Jharkhand) and the Toto (of northern part of West Bengal) are the five communities or locales that have close interaction with their immediate biotic environment. They have developed a survival strategy by making use of their Indigenous Knowledge System in their two most important aspects are economy and welfare. The best way the IK can be utilized is to support the subsistence economy—whether hunting or fishing or agriculture. This knowledge of the people helps them to classify the land according to topography and to identify the forest area where specific animals are found or utilisation of the arable land where cash crops are grown. The traps to catch different kinds of fishes are known to the people.The designing and constructing of the traps have been done after prolonged and close set direct observations on the movements and nature of the animals. Similarly, through their close acquaintance of the herbs and trees in the forest, the medicinal value of the plants, the medicinal and commercial importance of the flora are known to the people. This knowledge not only rests with the common people but also with the shamans who are aware which plant can drive away which kind of evil spirit. The indigenous knowledge also helps the people to prepare organic and inorganic manure, prepare agricultural land and produce cash or cereal crops in appropriate plots. Classification of fertile and fallow land, male or female tide or good and bad indigenous manure are done without any formal training or any exogenous teaching. This situation has been made possible only by the tradition based close interactions with nature which instigated the development of an intrinsic knowledge pattern. This traditional knowledge handed down from generation to generation has naturally provided them the potential experience to exist in a specific set up and thereby devised various native ways of working and understanding patterns.

REFERENCES

Choudhury, N.C. and Biman K. Dasgupta (1975), "The Lois of Manipur:A Study of Inter-Ethnic Relationship", Jr.of Indian Anthropological Society,Vol.10.No.2, pp.153-158.

Das, Amal Kumar (1981), "Trend of Population", in A Focus on Sundarban, ed.A.K.Das &et al, Calcutta:Editions Indian.

Dasgupta, Samira (1994), Birjia: Society and Culture(A Study in Cultural Ecological Perspective), Calcutta: Firma KLM Private Limited.

Dasgupta, Samira and Amitabha Sarkar (2005), Reflection of Ethno Science: Study on the Abujh Maria, New Delhi: Mittal Publications.

Mondal, Asim Kumar (2003), The Sundarban of India:A Development Analysis,New Delhi; Indus Publishing Company.

Risley, H.H. (1981), (reprinted) The Tribes and Castes of Bengal, Vol.II, Calcutta:Firma Mukhopadhyay.

Roychoudhury, Bikash (1977), " The Fishing Communities of Chilka:

A Study in their Eco system", Journal of Indian Anthropological Society, Vol.12, No.2.

Saha, Bikashkanti (1999), Mangrove Tigerland Sundarban, Calcutta:

Intelsoft.

Sarkar, Amitabha (1995), " Ethnic Conflict: Unrest Among Autochthons of Jharkhand", Social Change, Vol.25. No.4.

Sarkar, Amitabha and Samira Dasgupta (2000), Ethno-ecology of Indian Tribes: Diversity in Cultural adaptation, Jaipur: Rawat Publications.

Saxena, Ranjana (2003), " Globalization and Culture", in Culture Studies: Themes and Perspective, ed. Chandan Kumar Sharma, quoted by Desmond L Kharmawphlang & et al In 'Globalization: The Khasi Perspective', Indian Folklife, Serial No. 22, July,2007.

Singh, K.S. (1994), People of India, Vol. III, The Scheduled Tribe, Delhi: Oxford University Press and Anthropological Survey of India.

Tribhuwan, R.D. (1998), Medical World of the Tribals, New Delhi: Discovery Publishing House.

14 Horticulture on High Slopes: Knowledge System of the War Khashis of Meghalaya

Sumit Mukherjee

INTRODUCTION

It is an omnipresent historic truth that the major indigenous groups in India live in the relatively less productive habitats with restricted resource base. In the north-eastern part of India one can easily find that the high mountains, difficult slopes, less fertile plateau surfaces, unhealthy tropical forests, etc are all inhabited by numerous tribal groups. On the other hand due to prolong interaction with their own habitat these people have achieved optimum management of the natural resources whatsoever available around them. Hence it is obviously interesting to observe the tangible elements of their traditional technology linked to their environmental wisdom and deep perception, the intangible part. This, on eco-cultural perspective, is indicative of their territorial affinity in general which in tern define a cultural group in its basic form.

The War Khasi represents one of the five subgroups of the Khasi tribe of Meghalaya. The Khasi are one of the oldest inhabitants of the north-eastern India (Bareh, 1967) occupying the oldest habitable landmass of the region – the Meghalaya plateau. The war Khasi habitat in particular is certainly the most unique in the Khasi hills. They dwell in the southern slopes of the central Meghalaya plateau. The resultant landmass of the several long continued phases of geo tectonic movements has been developed into a highly dissected topography under the rapid erosion of torrential rivers fed by heaviest rainfall of the world. In fact Cherrapunjee bounds the war region on its west and Jaintia hills on the east with north–south extent from the central plateau axis up to the international border with Bangladesh.

RI-WAR- THE WAR COUNTRY

The war people are traditionally categorized into three sub-regional groups e.g. the real war who occupies the Ri-War (war country), a narrow belt with several ridges abruptly culminating at the Surma valley, the War Phlang resides over the middle altitude Sohra platform covered with grassland renowned for world's highest rainfall area and the War Synteng villages in and around Dawki bordering Jaintia hills.

The altitude ranges from 250 to above 4500 ft. as the plateau drops step wise forming at least three platforms. Topographically prominent feature of this region is highly inclined valley walls of 2000-3000 ft. vertical exctent locally known as *Podwar,* from which it is believed that the inhabitants are called war and the region Ri-War meaning the country of the War people. The flattish hilltops in between are called *Rygnko.* Most of the annual rainfall occurs from south-west monsoon during May to September. Air temperature varies widely from milder conditions over the northern high plateau above 900 m. to the seemingly hot humid in the low southern hills and deep valleys. In most parts there is a short dry winter between November and January followed by dry pre-monsoon months (March to April) characterized by very strong winds. January is the coolest and August is the hottest. Dr. Hooker in 1850 narrated the richness in floral diversity as the riches in India and probably in all Asia (Simon, 1981). The plateau top or Ringko is almost devoid of large trees due mainly to its highly porous soil layers. At present only the relics of healthy forests are found protected as either sacred or community forests mostly in the upper catchments of rivers and streams.

The War people, through their traditional knowledge and belief system and indigenous technology, have developed a

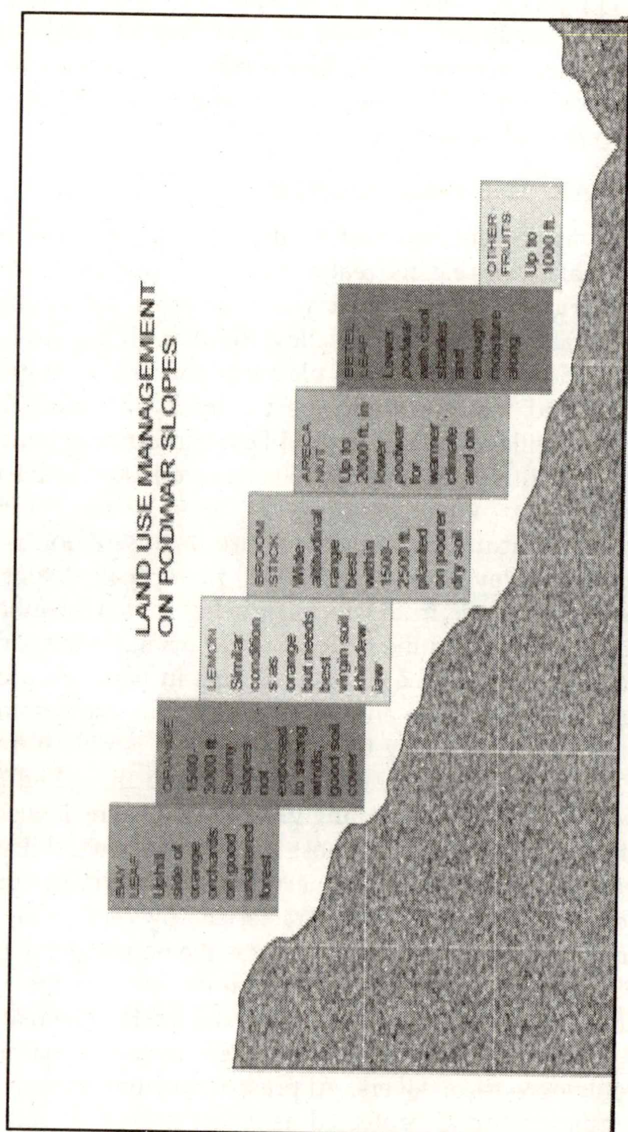

Land Use Managemenbt on Podwar Slopes

Month	**Gregorian**	Jan	Feb	Mar	Apr	May	Jun	Jul	Aug	Sep	Oct	Nov	Dec
	War Khasi	*Kyllalyngkot*	*Rymaiang*	*Lbre*	*Jaiong*	*Jymmang*	*Jylliew*	*Naitung*	*Nailar*	*Nailur*	*Rysaw*	*Naiwieng*	*Nohprah*
Season	Gregorian	Winter		Spring		Rains				Fall		Winter	
	War Khasi	*Tlang*		*Pyrem*		*Lyiur*				*Synrai*		*Tlang*	
Orange ***Soh Mynthra***		Harvesting Completed		Flowering		Maturity period						Harvesting starts	
Lemon *Soh Kwit*			Flowering		Maturity period			Harvesting starts and mostly over before Orange					
Areca nut *Kwei*				Harvesting period									
Betel leaf *Tympaw*		Growing period		2nd Harvest		Minor or intermediate harvest		1st Harvest		Growing season			
Bay leaf *La Tuson*				Harvesting starts after Orange								Weeding and pruning	
Broom stick *Lynnai*		Harvesting			Weeding		Stumps are burnt after every 2-3 years						

War Khasi Calendar for Plantation Agriculture

unique natural resource management through generations. The well knitted social organization has certainly contributed towards the success of their rural economy. Mawlam, a typical War Khasi village in the interior of the Pynursla block of East Khasi Hills district, was studied to understand and record the prevalent traditional management system of these people. The village is located far from the urban impact and majority of the villagers are still practicing the traditional Khasi religion. At this instance only the details of the horticulture of orange, a practice surviving since time immemorial, has been dealt with.

CHALLENGES OF HIGH SLOPE

The village Mawlam is situated on the intermediate level of the *Ri-War* at around 3500 ft. above mean sea level. Along the southern slopes of the eastern valley wall of the Um-rew river the narrow flat ridge top or *Ringko* runs north-east to south-west and deeps sharply on either sides into the *Podwars* (in War dialect *pud*=steep valley walls on either sides of the *wah*=river). The *Ryngko* land is used as homestead while the *Podwars*, forming almost 80% of the village area, is devoted to all kinds of economic activities. It was observed that the slopes of more than 20 degrees inclination are usually termed *Podwar*. In the village such *Podwar* lands are dipping even above 50 degrees with a continuous vertical fall of 2000–3000 ft. these slopes are mostly under thick green cover either with natural vegetation or various permanent plantations. In the depth of these narrow gorges the air remains warmer than in the upper parts helping the growth of a variety of trees and crops.

Due mainly to the higher altitude and high slope cultivation of common food grains like paddy in the traditional *jhum* fields were uncommon in the Ri- War. Moreover the long tradition of horticulture in this region did not allow shifting cultivation to be continued as traditional mode of land use (Dasgupta, 1984).

It is interesting to observe that the otherwise difficult highly inclined Podwar lands provide the main support to the village economy, which is primarily the commercial plantation.

The War villagers meticulously judge the Podwar lands by altitude, amount and direction of slope, availability of water, soil type, vegetation cover etc. to select the suitable micro-environment for various fruits and crops. All the major plantation crops like orange, lemon, betel nuts, betel leaf, bay leaf are grown in the podwars only. Under the traditional tenure system the orchards are raised mainly on the private lands like Ri-Kynti (individual ownership) and Ri-Seng (clan ownership). The Ri-reid (community owned) land of the podwar is mostly used for jhum cultivation though small portions of individual podwars are also under jhum. Therefore, there are two sets of management systems in vogue in the podwar lands in terms of holding and type of agriculture e.g. subsistence level jhum field and commercial orchards.

The highest part of the slope, just below the ringko with less moisture in the soil and lower air temperature, is planted with broom stick and also the bay leaf plants on better soil conditions. In fact broom stick grasses are being planted on both old and new jhum-fallow plots for last 20 to 22 years or so. But this grass has occupied plots across and along the hills with poorest soil conditions. The orange orchards are developed roughly from 3000 ft. altitude downwards along with lemon. A strip of about 300–500 ft on either side of the river floor is occupied mainly by the areca and betel plants which are inter-cultured (sometimes including black pepper). Owing to a higher requirement of water the betel leaf climbers are planted close to the perennial source on the slopes e.g. streams and springs. Various fruit trees like papaya, guava, mango, jackfruit etc. are also grown successfully on the lower podwars having soil moisture.

ORCHARDS OF ORANGE

In Mawlam village horticulture is practised as the main mode of sustenance. Majority of households (63.5%) in the village has one or the other type of horticulture and all such horticulturist have orchards of orange.

The orange grown in the southern Shillong plateau has a very long history and famous for its excellence. Dr. Tanaka, a

Japanese expert, attributed the origin of orange to the Khasi hills itself (Simon, 1991). The *'soh niamtra'* or the Khasi orange is identified as Khasi mandarin species and believed as the only orange in India propagated directly through seeds. In the War region till date, villagers only depend on their traditional wisdom and techniques in every stages of orange growing. Systematic exploratory survey of mandarin orange showed that Citrus indica is one of the most primitive species of citrus available in the region. Other promising natives so far identified and commercialised in Northeast India are cytron (C. medica), sweet lime (C. lamittoides), sour orange (C. aurantium), sweet pumalo (C. grandis), sour pumelo (C. megaloxycarpa), Khasi paida (C. latipes), and rough lemon (C. jambhiri), etc (Yadav, 1998).

The orange and lemon (*soh kwit*) plants are grown through elaborate process involving two nurseries. The seeds are collected carefully from the most mature and healthy fruits and then dried completely in the sun. The seeds are then directly placed inches beneath the soil in a small nursery plot within the homestead during December to February (Chart–1). The first nursery or *share-shyieng-soh* is fenced properly to save from domestic animals. The plot is watered regularly and is covered with leaves to retain moisture in the top soil which helps germinating the seeds. *Dieng-soh-niamtra* or the small saplings are transplanted to the second nursery when those become 3-4 inches tall.

For the second nursery a warm slope in the lower *podwar* preferably with shallow rocky soil is selected purposively. This type of soil *'daw-maw'* is found suitable because it does not allow roots to penetrate deeper and hence the final transplantation becomes easier. After four to five years of growth the plants become mature enough to finally shift at the actual place fixed for the orchard called *bri-soh-niamtra*. The villagers partly clear the forested slope to remove the undergrowth and other small plants.

The young orange plants are planted at 6-9 feet intervals depending upon the gradient of slope. The large shady trees that act as the wind barriers are left in the new orchards and are gradually being lopped off synchronized to the growth of the orange plants. The Khasi mandarin takes around 5 – 8 years to flower and at about 20 years of age the plant becomes fully mature to bear maximum fruits. The quality and quantity of fruits decline with aging and lack of proper maintenance. It was reported by the villagers that some orchards have orange plants more than 70 years of age.

The harvesting of orange starts from the orchards at the lowest parts of the *podwar* because fruits at the higher altitude have a longer maturity period than in the lower warmer slopes. In the month of October the fruit starts becoming reddish in colour but actual plucking can only be started around middle of November. Hence the War people call this month *Ri-saw* means a land full of red colour. The harvesting continues up to February. According to the villagers' statement the quality of fruits are available in the middle part of the *Ri-War* at a village named Wakhen located further north near Lyngkerdem in the Rumkheng river gorge (at an altitude of 2500 ft), the sweetest orange in the world. It was recorded by Gurdon (1975) that a full grown tree yields as many as one thousand fruit in a season.

The first major pruning and weeding is done during and after harvesting. They spread those dead branches on ground to add green composite manure to the soil. Till today they do not use any chemical fertilizer common to other orange growing regions in our country. Every year flowering starts within one month after completion of harvesting i.e., in the month of March, early spring season or *'Pyrem'*. In the month of October or *Risaw*, the fruits start becoming orange in colour and the villagers clear the undergrowth in the orchards. The clearing of the tree trunk from mosses and other parasitic plants is also done to keep each tree healthy as they believe. But the experienced orange farmers in the village pointed out that as some of the farmers do not maintain this hygiene routinely the whole regions gets diseases and pests. During our study period it was found that per tree production was at a low as 50 to 120 oranges only. The villagers reported that a damaging pest locally called *'kasain'* had severely attacked the whole orange belt. They have nothing to do towards its control but only observed with curiosity that the pest has a somewhat similar life cycle to that of a butterfly. This caterpillar like pest first appear and feed on leaves and later bore holes in the stem and damage the fruit as well. They simply insert a stick into the hole to plug it for stopping the movement of the pest out side. Finding this crude method insufficient to check the crop damage recently they have appealed to the State Agriculture Department to render help. Later it was learnt from the concerned department that so far nothing could be done as it was almost impossible to spray pesticides over the orchards on the high slopes without the help of an air born spray machine. A few spells of untimely rains, which is not uncommon, during maturity period always inflict damage to the crop.

FRUITS OF PRAYER

So the helpless villagers perform a ritual in the sacred grove of the village during March (Lber) before the start of flowering. The traditional War villagers practising *'Niamtre'* (traditional religion of the Khasi) belief that by appeasing certain guardian spirits like *'Ka Jymngiew'*, a female spirit, who brings good luck or one of the four main village spirits namely 'Mawkhan', 'Maweh', 'Mawknoe' and 'Shynteng' such natural damages can be stopped.

A TRADITION TO LIVE

The unique elements of the indigenous mode of raising orchards by the War Khasi people and its long continued history of success certainly demands more attention and in-depth study. Already a group of scientists from the Horticulture Division of Indian Council of Agricultural Research, Meghalaya (Yadav, 1998) and some others have substantiate the sustainability and economic viability of horticulture in different parts of the State which was understood and undertaken by these War people long back. The study suggested horticulture on the hill slopes owing to several favourable agro-climatic conditions and commercial prospects: i) the Northeast India is the diverse gene pool of large number of horticultural and plantation crops but the potentiality is yet to be managed for sustainable economic development; ii) orchards will bear fruits not only for the market but also in preserving the valuable top soil on high hill slopes facing world's heaviest downpour; iii) increasing biotic pressure on land resources form traditional jhum cultivation can be lessened by substituting those with permanent horticultural plantations and iv) when applied at large it will act as the key to empower the rural tribal population in particular and rural economy in general. This is tern take off the pressure from cities and towns by controlling the rural to urban migration. In addition to horticulture the prevailing ecological condition is found suitable also for plantation of ornamental, medicinal and aromatic plants. The Khasis carry a rich traditional knowledge on herbal medicine which will be boosted and kept alive by growing endemic medicinal plants which are also in demand throughout north eastern part and even across the border in Bangladesh.

The commercial horticulture was highly boosted up after the construction of the first highway through this region connecting Guwahati in Assam to Shylhet in Bangladesh during the last part of the nineteenth century. But the closer of the Indo-Bangla border after independence hampered the trade of orange a lot. The present scenario of the once famous War orchards seems rather gloomy mainly due to the attack of pest and also due to a probable shift in the occupational preference among the younger generation. Hence to carry on the long glorious history of growing oranges by the great ancestors is needed to be relayed on to the hands of the present day trained horticulturists of the same community to cope up with the newer problems. On the other hand the still viable components of this unique traditional system of horticulture could be guided by the appropriate modern developed methods. As a step further, similar ecological niches in the north-eastern part of India can be tested with the same variety of orange applying the same traditional technology of the War Khasi people which will help preserving the indigenous variety of the orange and the related knowledge system as well.

REFERENCES

Basic Statistics of North Eastern Region 2000, North Eastern Council, Shillong, Ministry of Home Affairs, GOI.

Basic Statistics of North Eastern Region 2000, North Eastern Council, Shillong, Ministry of Home Affairs, GOI.

Dasgupta, B. (1984), The War Khasis of Meghalaya, Anth. Survey of India, Kolkata.

Gurdon, P.R.T. (1975), The Khasis, Cosmo Publication, Delhi.

ICAR (2002), Agricultural Research Data Book, ICAR Research Complex, NEH Region, Barapani.

Simon, A. (1991), Gazetteer of United Khasi and Jaintia Hills, Govt. of Meghalaya, Shillong.

Yadav (1998), Status and Prospects of Horticulture in NEH Region, Division of Horticulture, ICAR Research Complex, NEH Region, Barapani.

Singh, R.L. (1971), India: A Regional Geography, National Geographic Society of India, Varanasi.

15 Indigenous Marine Fisheries Regulations and Management of Sundarban Coast, West Bengal, India

S.K. Pramanik and N.C. Nandi

INTRODUCTION

The unregulated expansion of fishing fleets and round the year fishing in the coast waters of Sundarban lead to gradual depletion of stock of marine fish species. The increasing dependence of coastal dwellers on fishing and the mounting demand for fish are mainly responsible for overfishing in this region. So, knowledge of indigenous management practices and regulations, which have already vanished or are fast vanishing largely due to non-fishermen participation in the trade, are discussed hereunder in designing appropriate management system and ecologically sustainable utilization of resource.

Fisheries management today is no more solely about fisheries biology or about population dynamics of the fish stocks but about human beings, about management of fisheries more than anything else (Chong 2000: 26). The emergence of conflict among fisherfolk prompted countries to develop rules and regulations as part of their fisheries management (Martosubroto 2002:4). Marine Fishing Regulation Act (1980) aims "to protect the interests of different sections of persons, especially those engaged in fishing with traditional craft; to conserve fish; to regulate fishing on a scientific basis, and to maintain law and order" (Mathew 2002: 39). In the absence of any legal mechanisms to address all these aspects of marine fisheries management of Sundarban coast, this paper is communicated with a view to appraise the winter dry fish trade of this region and to highlight some thoughts to decide and develop a marine fisheries resource action plan in harmony with socio-cultural values of coastal fishermen community.

BACKGROUND INFORMATION

The Sundarban region is rich in fishery resources and constitutes one of the chief supports of the capture fisheries in India. The total geographical area of Indian Sundarban is about 9630 sq. km. It includes mangrove forest area of about 2180 sq. km., populated area of about 5363 sq. km., coast line of 64 km. long and inshore and estuarine fishing area of 2085 sq. km. are the estuarine rivers, tidal creeks, canals, sea-shore and mud-flats. The present level of exploitation of the fisheries resources of Sundarban is about 73800 mt. out of 164000 mt. in West Bengal (1997- 98). The numbers of mechanised and non-mechanised fishing boats for the year 1997-98 are 1418 and 2080 respectively. The winter bag net fishery of this region accounts for 46-86 %of the total yield in Sundarban (Mitra

Table 1
Distribution of Fishing Camps, Crafts, Gears, Fishermen and Fishworkers of Winter Marine Dry Fish Centres of Sundarban Coast During 1993-94

Items	*Jambu-dwip*	*Kalis-than*	*Bak-khali*	*Fraser-gunj*	*Sagar*	*Total*
Fishing camps	31	18	36	38	116	239
Mechanised boats	55	31	27	41	95	249
Non-mechanised boats	83	36	54	76	170	419
Bag nets	279	148	173	180	476	1256
Fishermen	1425	708	212	285	920	3550
Fishworkers	2481	526	420	598	1392	5417

Note:
1. Large offshore fishing camps found in Jambudwip and Kalisthan.
2. Medium-size camps located at Kalisthan, Frasergunj and Sagar.
3. Smaller inshore fishing units established at Bakkhali, Frasergunj and Sagar.
4. Fishworkers include male, female and child workers.
5. Women workers exclude children below 12 years of age.

et al., 1997). The main concentrations of this winter fishery are Jambudwip, Kalisthan, Bakkhali, Frasergunj and Sagar Island (Table 1). It is believed that the progressively increasing fishing efforts have led to the decrease of CPUE and make the Sundarban fisheries vulnerable.

MANAGEMENT CONSTRAINTS

The marine fisheries of Sundarban suffer from several constraints as follows:

Demographic Problem

The unprecedented growth of population is the root of the severe stress in the fishery. In 1951, the population of Sundarban was 12 lakhs and in 1991 and 2001 it has reached about 32 and 42 lakhs respectively. Thus the population has increased about 30 lakhs within a time span of only 50 years (Census 2001). This alarming growth is due to high birth rate as well as infiltration from Bangladesh and migration from other districts.

Open Access to Fisheries Resource

Sundarban coastal fisheries enjoy open access system and there is no limit on the growth of fishing efforts, which lead to serious overfishing. So, solutions to this problem should seek limited access system. The rational fishery management practices necessitate the transformation of common property to some kind of limited entry system. Indonesia follows a system of open access fisheries and common property management, which has led to overexploitation without any thought given to maximum sustainable yield. The users carry out destructive fishing for short-term profit. The result is environmental degradation and habitat destruction, and a fall in fishery resource potential. This has of late become a serious problem (Basuki, 2002:34).

Destructive Fishing Gear

Introduction of small meshed harvesting gears for capturing shrimps in estuaries and coastal waters of this region has resulted in the exploitation of juveniles, sub-adults and spawners of many fish species as well as other organisms in the food chain. So, mesh size should be regulated to prevent the loss of biodiversity as well as stress to the ecosystem.

Onslaught of Foreign Vessels

The onslaught of foreign vessels with sophisticated fishing appliances causes a great damage to the coastal marine resources of Sundarban. Many Thai, Bangladesh and Sri Lankan fishing vessels and fishermen are arrested every year for alleged intrusions into India and neighbouring waters. During the 1981-1992 period 1,503 Thai fishing vessels were arrested by seven different countries (Phasuk 1994:119) including India (61), and Bangladesh (6) bordering Sundarban region.

Indiscriminate Trawling

Indiscriminate trawling by modern vessels with fine meshed nets leads to depletion of stock of many species in the coastal water of Sundarban. As a result, such trawlers can be referred to as destructive fishing craft leading to loss of bioresource and ecological imbalance. The non-targeted by-catch is an inevitable component in trawl fishing.

INDIGENOUS REGULATIONS AND MANAGEMENT PRACTICES

Non-participatory Regulations and Management Practices

The age-old traditional socio-cultural values and management practices helping in preservation of fishery resources of Sunderban coast are as follows:

Social Practices: The social system of caste based occupation even in post independence period was effective in checking the mobility of caste-based occupations in this region. Only the persons belonging to the fishing castes were known to pursue fishing as their occupation. Now a days the rigidity of caste system no longer exists and as a consequence persons from non-fishing castes gather in the marine fisheries sector of Sundarban. Both fishing (70%) and non-fishing (30%) castes are overcrowding the occupation.

Religious Practices: Religious injunctions, even in 1980s, acted as important measures to conserve fishery resources. People in Bengal would not partake Hilsa, for example, from Durga Puja (Sept.-Oct.) to Sri Panchami (Jan-Feb.) (Hora 1954). This period coincides the spawning period of Hilsa. Thus, this sort of fish taboo creates the favourable environment for breeding. It very naturally indicates the specific effort for saving the species from destruction. Furthermore, in many houses in West Bengal fish is not consumed on a particular day in a week (Tuesday/ Thursday/ Saturday) due to religious prohibition and thus helping in the conservation of fish species.

Belief System: Several fish species (skates, rays, Bombay duck, etc.) earlier were considered non-edible because of superstition. This belief system helped preservation of species as well as ecological balance. But now, all fish species including juveniles, whether liked or disliked by the people are extensively harvested and used as fishmeal and poultry feed (Pramanik and Nandi, in press).

Ethical Values: Fishermen consider it a sin to destroy indiscriminately the stock of fish species, Fish is not only an item of consumption but also an item of worship to them. They have a strong conservationist ethic towards the fishery resources. Fishermen of Bengal, like their counterpart in Kerala, view the ocean (fishing ground) as community asset and life-giving system rather than hunting ground (Kurien 1995:163). It seems that ethical values of fishermen communities enhance conservation of fish biodiversity. Thus the value attitude system of these traditional fish workers in Sundarban region is set in such a depth-oriented background that all of them consider it is their sacred duly to conserve the fish species.

Participatory Regulations and Management Practices

The gradual increase of fishermen with fishing fleets and consequently the scarcity of space both in the fishing ground (sea) and in the camp site (beach) have aggravated the problems of crowding and gear conflict. The coastal fishermen solve their problems by indigenous regulations as follows:

Regulation for Setting Up of Fishing Camps: As the participants are numerous and space is insufficient, the usual practice is first come, first serve. The possession of a particular plot for successive years enables fishermen to acquire tenancy right, which gradually develops into transferable right. It limits over-crowding and unlimited entry of other castes in this occupation.

Regulation for Setting Up of Fishing Nets: Fishermen, in the matter of setting up their fishing nets at the places of their choice, plant wooden/ iron posts in the sea with the signal at the top to mark their selected fishing grounds so that the other fishing units can easily recognise it. The system of deciding the matter by lot is also in vogue (Pramanik and Nandi, in press) for peaceful existence in the fishing ground.

Regulation for Group Fishing: In Sundarban, fishing groups are formed on the basis of variety of fishing gears and fishing techniques. The bag net fishing is done in a body at particular portion of the sea during particular period of the year. Similarly, gill net fishing is done collectively at a different place in the sea. To avoid the possibility of gear conflicts between fishing groups/ units; fishermen use separate fishing zones in the fishing ground.

Regulation for Entry of New Fishing Units: The new fishing unit can set up fishing camp on the beach only when it gets permission from the Fishermen's Association functioning on that beach. The association selects the sight and determines the quantum of land/ plot to be allotted. So, new entry is always subjected to the approval of Fishermen's Association, which prevents unrestricted expansion of fishing pursuits.

Regulation for Signaling System: Fishermen use signal in the fishing ground for their safety. They use green flag in case of submerged nets and white flag in case of floating nets. A fishing unit facing danger is required to use red flag. They use flag of different colours during the day whereas at night lights of corresponding colours are used.

Regulations for Settling Disputes: Fishermen's Association makes rules to avoid breach of peace both on land and in the fishing ground. In case of any dispute between the fishing units the matter is brought to the notice of the Fishermen's Association for solution. The decision of the association is binding.

SUGGESTED GUIDELINES FOR FORMULATING MANAGEMENT MEASURES

To prevent fishing pressure and to achieve scientifically sound, socially acceptable and ecologically sustainable fisheries development in this region indigenous regulations and management practices need to be supplemented by formal rules and regulations. Inventory, planning, development of data bank, review and researches on fish stocks, recruitment potential etc. are required at regular interval as management aids. The suggested guidelines to this effect are as follows:

TOWARDS REDUCING THE DEPENDENCY ON FISHERIES

To Control and Limit Entry into Fisheries

- *Introducing Closed Season:* Introduction of closed season for 4/5 months during the spawning period of estuarine fish species of Sundarban appears to be urgent. Trawling, which scrapes the depth of the sea and destroys the fish spawns, may seasonally be banned. However, scientific assessment of fish stocks and researches on recruitment potential of the commercially important species of fishes, prawns and crabs are needed.
- *Regulating Destructive Fishing Gear and Mesh Size:* The regulation of destructive fishing gear and regulation of mesh size of nets of Sundarban coast is expected to guard the fishery resources from overfishing as well as to prevent immature and under-size fishing.
- *Implementing Compulsory Licensing System:* Compulsory licensing system for all types of capture fisheries operating in the coastal areas of Sundarban should be introduced together with effective enforcement mechanism.

To Encourage Exit of Fishermen from Fisheries

- *Giving easy access to financial institutions for alternative livelihood:* Easy access to financial institutions is to be given to fisherfolk to encourage them to exit from fisheries into alternative livelihood practices.
- *Providing training and extension services supporting alternative livelihood:* Adequate training and extension services including technical advice and supporting help need to be provided to the fishermen to encourage them to resort to alternative occupations including integrated fish culture.
- *Raising Educational Standard of Fishermen Communities:* The young generations of the coastal fishing families do not come out of the fishing occupation because of the lack or low standard of education. So, their educational level may be uplifted to opt for other occupations.

To Provide Economic Diversification in Fishing Communities

- *Promoting of Small Scale Industries:* Promotion of small-scale industries such as dairy, goattery, poultry etc. may be made for economic diversification of fishermen communities
- *Promoting Woodbased Handicrafts:* Leaf and wood based handicrafts, which has immense scope in Sundarban as well as in India, may be given priority with proper training and financial support.
- *Establishing Sea Food Processing Centre:* The establishment of seafood processing centres in this part of the country will promote economic diversification of coastal fishermen communities

Towards Development of Data Bank

The want of relevant data creates formidable barriers towards formulating management policies. Stock abundance study along with species-wise analysis of catch composition, recruitment, growth and mortality is required to assess and regulate overfishing from time to time.

To Strike a Balance between Social System and Ecosystem

To achieve effective management a balance must be struck between maintenance of the social system and the ecosystem. The balance must consider the valuable anthropogenic (skills, social networks, knowledge, family stability in fishery dependent communities) and ecological elements (water quality, pollution effect and sustainability of fishery resource and habitat) giving equal weightage to these major aspects.

Adoption of Co-management Model

Co-management model emphasizes a say of the user groups in the management of resource (Jentoft and Kristofferson, 1989). So, while formulating management plans in marine fisheries sector of Sundarban, adoption of co-management model to ensure fishermen's participation in the process should be taken into consideration.

DISCUSSION

The social practice, religious practice, belief system and ethical values of the coastal community of Sundarban have contributed to the sustainability of fishery resources. The fishermen of Kerala also, Kurien (1995:163) reports, realize the need to revive, strengthen, and enhance their cultural belief in the context of fisheries management. Ulluwishewa (1995:132) also observes that some traditions, beliefs, values and ethics of the traditional society have contributed to the inland fishery resources of Sri Lanka. He further reports that the villagers of his study area, like the coastal people of Sundarban, avoid or dislike to eat some species such as eels (*Anguilla* spp.) and Teppiliya and some species are not eaten in certain periods of the year.

The right to fish carries with it the obligation to do so in a responsible manner. It sets out principles and standard of behaviour for such practices and aims at effective conservation, management and development of living aquatic resources (Sinha 2001:18). Many fragile coastal ecosystems are facing severe threats of degradation and overexploitation of a few target species. The factors responsible for their plight have been studied and suitable options suggested for their conservation. However, many such options are beset with hindrance owing to social, economic and political reasons. Often the cost of enforcement of legal restrictions is very high, particularly when there are large number of resource users.

Jentoft (1999) and Chong (2000) have stressed that fisheries management is about the governance of human behaviour, not fish behaviour. It is, therefore, imperative to understand the proper needs and behaviour including belief as well as value system along with self-made rules of the fishermen for better fisheries management (Pinkerton, 1989; Smith, 1990; McGoodwin, 1990; Suseno, 2000).

The present study has revealed that the fishermen of Sundarban formulate rules for them to supplement the traditional code of conduct for maintaining peace and avoiding gear conflict in the fishing ground. In the Sundarban coast, owing to absence of legal provisions, the emphasis is given on the voluntary compliance of the indigenous rules made by the Fishermen's Association. It is true that force can not ensure compliance of the rules to a large number of resource users of Sundarban coast. A management regime, says Devraj (1996: 177), based on social acceptance, with the power of moral persuasion from within the group of participants, is the only way to manage widely dispersed resources which are shared by a multitude of small scale fishermen and various other users. So in order to ensure conservation of resources and preservation of peace in the fishing ground fishers of Sundarban cooperate voluntarily among themselves like the fishermen of Indonesia and Sri Lanka (Siregar 2002 and Stirrat 1988).

CONCLUSION

The existing indigenous management practices and regulations are not sufficient/ efficient enough to cope with the current problems confronting the marine fisheries of Sundarban coast. Legal regulations with enforcement mechanism to improve and strengthen the existing system of management practices need to be formulated on the basis of the suggested guidelines.

In formulating polices for fisheries management the fishermen's involvement in the regulatory process must be ensured in the light of co-management model which has been successfully implemented in Norway and other countries.

REFERENCES

Basuki, R. (2002), Maau Dabau Bakuok (MDB): A Traditional System of Management of Fisheries in Bakuok Lake, Kamper Community, Riau Province. In: Y.S. Yadava (ed.), Traditional Fisheries Management Systems in Six Provinces of Indonesia – North Sumatra, West Sumatra, Aceh, Jambi, South Sumatra and Riau, BOBP Report 2002/ 89, 38 pp.

Chong, K.C. (2000), Operationalising the Code. Bay of Bengal News, 11(18): 25-27.

Devraj, M. (1996), Coastal Biodiversity – Conservation and Sustainable Management. In: N.G. Menon and C.S.G. Pillai (eds.) Marine biodiversity conservation and management. Central Marine Fisheries Research Institute, Cochin, 225 pp.

Hora, S.L. (1954), Proverbs and Popular Sayings Current in Bengal. J. Asiat. Soc., 20(1): 19-27.

Jentoft, S. (1999), Healthy Fishing Communities: An Important Component of Healthy Fish Stock. Bay of Bengal News, 11(14): 19-20.

Jentoft, S. and T. Kristofferson (1989), Fishermen's Co-management: The Case of the Loften Fishery. Human Organization, 98(4): 355-364.

Kurien, J. (1995), Collective Action for Common Property Resource Rejuvenation: The Case of People's Artificial Reefs in Kerala State, India. Human Organization, 54(2): 160-168.

Mathew, S. (2002), Small-scale Fisheries Management in India: Need for Paradigm Shift. In: H.E.W. Seilert (ed.) Interactive mechanisms for small-scale fisheries management: Report of the Regional Consultation. FAO Regional Office for Asia and Pacific, Bangkok, Thailand. RAP Publication 2002/ 10, 153pp.

Mcgoodwin, J.R. (1990), Crisis in the World Fisheries: People, Problems and Policies. Strandford University Press, Strandford, CA.

Martosubrato, P. (2002), Towards Strengthing Coastal Fisheries Management in South and Southeast Asia. In: H.E.W. Seilert (ed.)

Interactive mechanisms for small-scale fisheries management: Report of the Regional Consultation. FAO Regional Office for Asia and Pacific, Bangkok, Thailand. RAP Publication 2002/ 10, 153 pp.

Mitra, P.M., H.C. Karmakar, M. Sinha, A. Ghosh, and B.N. Saigal (1997), Fisheries of the Hooghly–Matlah Estuarine System: An appraisal. Central Inland Fisheries Research Institute, Barrackpore, West Bengal, 49pp.

Pinkerton, E. (ed.) (1989), Co-operative Management of Local Level Fisheries: New Directions for Improved Management and Community Development. University of British Columbia Press, Vancouver.

Phasuk, B. (1994), Fishing Effort Regulations in the Coastal Fisheries of Thailand. Proc. Symp. on Socio-economic Issues in Coastal Fisheries Management. RAPA Publication, Bankok, 442pp.

Pramanik, S.K. and N.C. Nandi (1999), Coastal Marine Fisherfolk of Sundarban and their Indigenous Management Practices. Proc. Nat. Seminar on Integrated Coastal Zone Management, Kolkata, pp.183-190.

Pramanik, S.K. and N.C. Nandi (2004), Dry Fish Production Profile of Indian Sundarban. Classical Publishing Company, Delhi.

Siregar, S. (2002), Marine Fisheries Managemnt under the "Panglima Laut" (Sea Commander) System in Aceh Province. In: Y.S. Yadava (ed.), Traditional Fisheries Management Systems in six Provinces of Indonesia. BOBP Report No. 89, 38 pp.

Sinha, N.K. (2001), Key-note Address. In: Yadava, Y.S. (ed.) Report of the national workshop on the code of conduct of responsible fisheries. BOBP Report No. 90, 166pp.

Smith, M.E. (1990), Chaos in Fisheries Manageent. Maritime Anthropological Studies, 3: 1-13.

Stirrat, R.L. (1988), On the Beach: Fishermen, Fishwives and Fish Traders in Post Colonial Lanka. Hindustan Publishing Corporation, Delhi, 170 pp.

Suseno (2000), Some Thoughts on Coastal Community Development and Fisheries Management in Indonesia. BOBP, 11(16): 28-30.

Ulluwishewa, R. (1995), Traditional Practices of Inland Fisheries Management in the Dry Zone of Sri Lanka: Implications for Sustainability. Environmental Conservation, 22(2): 127-132.

16 Bio-piracy and Bioprospecting of Traditional Knowledge: Can Ethics Influence Equity?

D.C. Nanjunda

'Biopiracy is understood as the unauthorized use of the genetic resources and the indigenous knowledge of communities by others who have neither taken permission from the communities nor entered into any kind of contract with them'.

INTRODUCTION

Nature of Traditional Knowledge

The notions of traditional Knowledge, indigenous knowledge and indigenous peoples have acquired wide usage in international debates on sustainable development as well as those on intellectual property protection. However, the concepts of traditional knowledge, indigenous knowledge, and indigenous peoples are widely used but there are so far no universally adopted definitions. Different persons define them differently depending on their intellectual persuasion and professional interest. And many often use the concept of traditional knowledge interchangeably with that of indigenous knowledge. Stephen Brush has defined indigenous knowledge as *"the systematic information that remains in the informal sector, usually unwritten and preserved in oral tradition rather than texts...[It] is culture specific, whereas formal knowledge is de-cultured."* One may well ask whether Brush's definition of indigenous knowledge and his distinction between such knowledge and that which he terms "formal knowledge" stands repeated empirical testing. First, he reduces (perhaps Unconsciously) Knowledge to information and as such misplaces the "practical or skills aspect" of indigenous knowledge holders: one who possesses knowledge usually has skill and experience in the particular problem domain but one may possess information without experience and skill.

Traditional Medicine

Traditional Medicine (TM) plays a crucial role in healthcare and serves the health needs of a vast majority of people in developing countries. Access to 'modern' health care services and medicine may be limited in developing countries. TM becomes the only affordable treatment available to poor people and in remote communities. World Health Organization (WHO) defines traditional medicine as *'the sum total medicine as the sum total of all the knowledge and practices, whether explicable or not, used in diagnosis, prevention and elimination of physical, mental or social imbalance and relying exclusively on practical experience and observations handed down from generation to generation, whether verbally or in writing'.*

Health care providers worldwide including major pharmaceutical giants are turning to incorporate many of these into their mainstream activities. As traditional medicines are largely based on medicinal plants, indigenous to these countries, where the system has been bogus for several centuries, the effort is on accessing them either directly or through the use of modern tools of breeding and cultivation, including tissue culture, cell culture and transgenic technology. Traditional or indigenous medicine encompasses knowledge and practices used for diagnosis, prevention and cure. A greater part of indigenous knowledge refers to the properties of natural materials especially medicinal plants, animal parts and minerals (Sindiga 1995). Due to the extensive use of plant materials, traditional medicine is associated with herbalism. However, animal-based medicines also play a significant role in healing practices of many traditional health practitioners in India.

In addition, traditional medicine encompasses a great variety of methods of diagnosis and treatment, including physical, mental and spiritual therapies. The application of such methods is largely influenced by the culture and beliefs dominate in a particular community to the extent that they may be ineffective when applied in a different context. Thus traditional medicine includes knowledge concerning medicines and their use (appropriate dosage, particular forms of administration, etc.) as well as the procedures and rituals applied by healers as part of their traditional healing methods.

A new world of drug designed has opened up with the sequencing of the human genome. Scientists are using this knowledge to better understand the functions and interactions of proteins, leading to more effective strategies in designing molecules to block or enhance the actions of proteins involved in many disease processes. This collaboration of genetics, biochemistry and organic chemistry has given rise to many new potent pharmaceuticals targeting many diseases; however, there is one major drawback in this vision of future health care. The large number of potential drug targets elucidated has already outgrown the supply of potential drug candidates.

Combinatorial chemistry is a relatively new technology that has allowed chemists to greatly increase production of new synthetic compounds, but it has its limits. Even combining the efforts of classical land combinatorial organic chemistry with another new technique called rational drug design computerized modeling predictions of potentially active molecules-has not been able to keep up with the demand for new molecules to test against the newfound drug targets. If you asked me what I lay awake at night worrying about today: It's not genomics. It's not genetics. I lay awake worrying about chemistry," commented Peter N. Good fellow, Senior Vice-President of Discovery at SmithKline Beecham.

With this shortfall of chemical compounds to analyze, the pharmaceutical industry has begun to look again at plants as a principal source of potentially bio-active molecules. This change in attitude is ironic since plants were, before the era of synthetic organic chemistry, one the most popular place to harvest potential drugs in Western medicine. Furthermore, 80% of the world, mostly the 'undeveloped' regions, still rely on the indigenous medicinal knowledge of local plants for their medical needs.

Plants as a Source of Pharmaceuticals

It is well known that plants are an abundant source of medicinal drugs. Between 25% and 50% of current prescription pharmaceuticals come from plants, either directly or through modifications of biochemical templates harvested from the plants, and the value of drugs to the U.S. pharmaceutical industry coming from plant species is estimated at over 30 billion US$ per year. Aspirin, digitalis, cortisone, taxol, ephedrine, curare and few vaccines were all initially plant-derived, to name but a few.

A natural ecosystem like a rainforest acts like its own chemical laboratory, with each species experimenting over time with various chemical defenses to ensure survival in the world of natural selection. They have been synthesizing these compounds for millions of years to protect against predators, infection, pests, and disease. This makes plant species an excellent reservoir of bioactive compounds with the potential for application to treat human diseases. However, it has been estimated that fewer than 5% of tropical plant species have been examined for their medicinal value. This huge untapped potential, plus the increasing need for new molecules to test, has generated increased interest in the pharmaceutical industry for novel plant-derived compounds. In 1983, there were no U.S. pharmaceutical firms involved in research of plants found in developing countries. Today, there are over 200 corporations and U.S. government agencies studying rainforest plants for their medicinal capacities.

Bioprospecting or Biopiracy?

With this increase in what is known as 'bioprospecting,' however, another political, economical and human rights issue has arisen.' The notion of 'biopiracy.' Bioprospecting is the "exploration, extraction and screening of biological diversity and indigenous knowledge for commercially valuable genetic and biochemical resources." This practice is not new, however. For decades, plant collectors from industrialized countries have ventured southward in search of valuable genetic material for agricultural plant breeding, but no money changed hands in the process, nor was recognition given to the indigenous farming communities who selected, maintained and improved traditional crop varieties. This type of practice has become known as biopiracy, which refers to "the theft of intellectual property, such as genetic resources or traditional plant medicines, from poor communities by multinational companies.

A similar type of prospecting is now occurring in the pharmaceutical industry. Many drug companies are obtaining vast numbers of plants and chemical compounds derived from plants from developing countries mainly from India and screening them for potential use as pharmaceutical agents. Although this will probably lead to many new disease-fighting drugs, and thus substantial profits for the pharmaceutical industry, there are currently no regulations in place to ensure that the source countries of these plants will be adequately compensated.

How are the pharmaceutical companies obtaining the plant species from the developing countries? According to one report, biotechnology companies are sending scouts around the world–often posing as tourists–to discover plants that potentially have commercial value for the drug industry. Under the guise of ecotourism, local people are employed as 'nature interpreters' to guide visitors in biodiversity-rich places, and to share with them their indigenous knowledge about biological resources and how to use them. These scouts then collect the identified plants and bring them back to their companies for testing.

It has also been reported that locals in developing countries smuggle species of plants out of the country and sell them to pharmaceutical companies for analysis. In Sri Lanka, for example, a botanist was intercepted by customs at the airport trying to smuggle out plant extracts in his suitcase. In the same month, customs officials discovered a container-load of Kothalahimbutu–an herbal medicine believed to control diabetes–being shipped to Japan through a firm owned by a wealthy Sri Lankan.

Once the plants have been analysed, the pharmaceutical companies can patent any potentially active compounds as their own discovery, thereby preventing the source country from having any legal claims to royalties from the sale of the drug. In essence, they escape paying any financial compensation knowledge first originated. One could argue that these countries should simply patent the drugs themselves; however, they generally do not have the requisite scientific equipment to analyze the chemical components of their indigenous plants, nor the capacity to pay the international patent fee of 60,000 USD per patent. Therefore, they are unable to compete with the wealthy pharmaceutical companies trying to patent their indigenous medicines (Patrick, 2002).

Recently, however, there have been two court rulings in favor of the rights of the indigenous countries. Product patent are normally given only if they fulfil the criteria of being new, specify the process of production, and have commercial value. If there are discrepancies in this process, the patent can be contested in court, as in the case of the U.S. patent for turmeric, which was successfully challenged by India on the grounds that its medicinal properties have been well-known since ancient times. Similarly, an American firm acquired the patent for a fungicide derived from the seeds of the Neem tree, which flourishes all over Asia, Africa, Central and South America, and is used for many purposes, including as an insect repellent for crops. This patent was revoked by the European Patent Office in May 2000 on the grounds that is was not a new technology. Although these rulings seem encouraging, many countries do not have the wherewithal to fight the multinational pharmaceutical companies in long court battles, and so without change to the current system, the developing countries will probably lose in the end.

If unpaid royalty payments were being made to developing countries and indigenous peoples for the plant varieties and local knowledge used by multinational food and drug companies, those providers would be earning an estimated 5.4 billion USD a year, says a report commissioned by the United Nations Development Programme (UNDP). Examples of countries not receiving their full share of these royalties include Tibet, India, SriLanka, South Africa, Samoa, Madagascar, Ecuador, Mexico and the Philippines.

Finding Solutions to the Problem

Owing to the lack of adequate compensation for the countries supplying the medical plant species, the question of what can be done to bring about change to the current system needs to be addressed. First, we need to assess exactly what the developing countries desire in terms of compensation. Besides an agreement for royalties on sales of pharmaceutical products derived from the plants, an immediate reciprocal exchange would also be very important, since research conducted in any given location may never lead to a commercial product. Without the commitment of immediate compensation by the pharmaceutical companies, it is possible that the developing nations could derive no benefits from their knowledge and assistance if no products ever make it to market. Besides direct financial contribution, it would also be beneficial to provide immediate compensation in the from of supplies and services to the local peoples and to ensure that at least a part of any funding goes to support environmental protection in the regions supplying the plants in order to ensure long-term stability of the natural ecosystems.

A study reprot prepared for the UNDP discussed potential strategies to assist indigenous peoples in claiming biodiversity as their own property and to claim financial royalties owed to them by industry. The proposed steps in this new "intellectual integrity framework" are as follows.

- Consultation with indigenous communities to learn what steps they wish to take to preserve biodiversity and to properly acknowledge their contributions.
- New deposit rules that would identify biological 'inventions' as to their origin, including names of

individuals or communities in developing countries, when they are deposited in gene banks or when patent application is made. Failure to provide such 'passport data' could nullify a patent.

- A rule that would make any material in gene banks and cell libraries collected from indigenous communities off-limits for patent claims by others.
- Appointment of ombudspersons in industrial-country patent offices to investigate complaints from indigenous communities and their national governments. This person would have authority to delay patent approvals and require review of patent applications.
- Tribunals that could resolve disputes between indigenous communities and patent claimants.
- The creation of a fee structure in each patent jurisdiction that would pay for expenses incurred by indigenous communities for deposits, tribunals and legal representation (Jain, 2002)

Some Companies are Trying Help

Although some pharmaceutical companies are exploiting developing countries for their resources without compensation, there are others who have made strides to reciprocate financial rewards to these nations in the form of investments and promised royalties. Shaman Pgarnaceytucaks us a U.S. company that discovers and develops novel pharmaceutical agents from tropical plants with a history of medicinal use. At its induction in 1990, Shaman instituted internal guidelines for reciprocity to indigenous cultures and countries that contributed knowledge and resources to its medicinal plant discovery efforts. Shaman outlines short-, medium-, and long-term support measures in its guidelines, which serve to provide financial, infrastructure, technology, and sustainability support to the peoples and countries from which it derives its pharmaceutical products.

Although Shaman's efforts are to be commended, it has been reported that some local peoples are less than satisfied with the overall experiences with Shaman. In Tanzania, locals expressed disappointment that Shaman did not live up to its reciprocity standards. The report goes on to state that if Shaman had spent more time trying to understand and adhere to the local healers' perceptions and priorities, the company could have easily made the healers more satisfied with respect to their own wishes and needs.

Another pharmaceutical company that has made efforts to reciprocate compensation is Merck and Company. In 1991, Merck invested over 1 million USD to Costa Ruca's Instituto Nacional de Biodiversidad (INBio) bioprospecting project. INBio agreed to collect and provide samples from so- called 'wild' plants, insects and microorganisms to drug-screening scientists at Merck laboratories for medicinal assay. If the compounds prove useful and any resulting drugs make it to market, Merck will give INBio an undisclosed share of the royalties, of which 50% will be set aside for conservation projects through Costa Rica's National Park Fund (Internet Resources).

Thus far, however, the Merck-INBio agreement has not produced any major revenue-producing drugs. Regardless, Merck has provided continuing support for the project; published report states that, as of 1999, Merck had invested more than 3.5 million USD to the project. Despite Merck's efforts, this level of financial compensation is relatively insignificant compared with what the pharmaceutical industry, as a whole, realistically owes to the indigenous countries for the knowledge and biological resources they have supplied for many years.

The Gaps between Traditional Medicine Areas and Existing Modern Patent Law

Currently, some 95% of patents in the world are held in developed countries. At present, international patent law and most national conventional patent law protection requirements of novelty and inventive steps do not seem to be applicable to traditional knowledge and biodiversity. For example, there is no act under patent law which could be used to protect the non-medication of traditional therapies, such as manual therapies and spiritual therapies. Because of the lack of database and the same medicinal plants growing and being used in various countries and continents, it is very difficult to identify the founder.

Pharmaceutical products can be protected by the existing conventional patent law. However, herbal medicines and herbal products are quite different from chemical drugs. They are very difficult to be protected by the existing patent law.

For example, there are only three key prosecutable subject matters in order to get patent for pharmaceutical products in the conventional patent law:

1. Patent for discovering new chemical components;
2. Patent for know-how in producing the products;
3. Patent for the trademark

In addition to patent law, knowledge on herbal medicines could also be protected by keeping it a secret!

Firstly, the above-mentioned means are without little or no compensation to the custodians of this traditional knowledge and without their prior informed consent. Secondly, herbal medicines have been defined by several WHO guidelines that they include crude plant materials, such as leaves, flowers, fruit, seed, stems, wood, bark roots, rhizomes or other plant parts, which may be entire, fragmented or powered. The products, which chemically defined active substances have been added, including synthetic compounds and/or isolated constituents from herbal materials, are not considered to be herbal medicines. Therefore, it is impossible to get existing patent law protection for herbal medicines through the discovery of new chemical components.

Thirdly, the major dosage forms of traditional herbal medicines are directly derived from their herbal preparations, which include powdered herbal materials, or extracts, tinctures and fatty oils of herbal materials. They also include preparations made by steeping or heating herbal materials in alcoholic beverages and/ or honey, or in other materials. The production process and major dosage forms of traditional herbal medicines is normally very simple. There is almost no know-how available to protect this by patent (Awadh ,2004).

Biopiracy today is facilitated by international organizations like the WTO, World Intellectual Property Organisation (WIPO), the Convention on Biological Diversity Conference of the Parties (CBD COP), and the United Nations' Food and Agriculture Organisation (FAO), the TRIPS chapter of which allows anybody to patent anything, regardless of whether the subject of the patent claim has been acquired legitimately or otherwise. The other international convention, the Convention on Biological Diversity (CBD), which deals with biological resources, is a pro – community convention which recognizes that local communities are the owners of the biological resources and the indigenous knowledge developed by them. IPRs and private monopolies over biological resources and related traditional knowledge can have direct negative effects on India's food security, biological diversity, the protection of traditional knowledge, and the rights of traditional communities such as farmers and forest dwellers.

The recognition of sovereign right of nations over their genetic resources is an advantage to the gene-rich yet technologically poor developing countries like India. This gives India, which holds most of the genetic material and indigenous knowledge base an opportunity to get maximum benefit. For example, they point to cases in developed countries where excessively broad patents have been granted over genetic biodiversity. NGOs also argue that the current international intellectual property system has failed to provide for benefit sharing. They are pressing to introduce mechanisms into the international intellectual property system to address these issues.

The free flow and trade of genetic resources has been replaced by a wide range of national and international legal instruments that seek to regulate access, control and use of genetic biodiversity and to protect traditional knowledge. Of particular concern is the recent trend to extend intellectual property rights (patents and plant breeder's rights) to plant genetic resources. Genetic resources and traditional knowledge also play a fundamental role in many contexts.

Some of the main elements that developing countries have been highlighting as part of the proposed arrangements include: (i) the protection of genetic resources through measures which prevent the grant of patents over genetic resources; and (ii) the protection of the innovations of indigenous and other traditional communities. The first case reported in India for IPR benefit sharing is with the Kanis, Kerala, India: The indigenous Kani community eat the seeds of a wild plant (arogyapacha), which boosts energy and helps people through periods of physical exertion. Instead of being exploited, the tribal community receives a fair share of the benefit derived from using its knowledge.

IPRs do not cover the traditional knowledge base of local communities. This allows MNCs to exploit the resources and use the knowledge of indigenous communities to manufacture high-value products without acknowledging traditional communities. This led to a furore in India especially in our scientific community, industries and NGOs which asserted that MNCs have no right to exploit our indigenous knowledge and research commercially. The patent on turmeric was revoked on the basis of novelty. Patents on Neem, Amla, Jar Amla, Anar, Salai, Dudhi, Gulmendhi, Bagbherenda, Karela, Rangoon-ki-bel, Erand, Vilayetishisham, Chamkura(common names of few medicinal plant in India) all need to be revoked. The strategy is identified on *sui generis rights* (Community Intellectual Rights). The argument for sui generis law is that current IPR laws operate in a discriminatory fashion and that laws enacted should better reflect the realities of people's lives.

There is a wide gap in the availability of information in countries like the United States for patent examination purposes pertaining to traditional knowledge base from biodiversity-rich countries. The insistence on written published information, as opposed to oral knowledge, could make challenges to such patents difficult. The need for greater scrutiny of patent applications pertaining to biological resources, and the need to consult the source of the biological resource and knowledge pertaining to the same is, therefore, imperative. Efforts towards documenting peoples' knowledge in Biodiversity Registers, if structured carefully, could help to establish "prior use" of a particular resource/ product derived from it. Documentation of traditional knowledge has therefore to be seen in the national interest before any move is made to make community knowledge accessible globally. Surely we can stall this documentation of traditional knowledge till effective safeguards are put in place. Between 1992 and 2000, China revised its patent laws twice to ensure intellectual property control over its unique system of medicine. Sui generis legislation giving indigenous peoples' rights unknown (outside) the common law is the most viable option. Currently, there is no requirement under patent laws of most countries for the holder of the patent, or any intellectual property rights for that matter, to share the benefits with those who had collected, preserved or initially identified the biological material as potentially worthy of investigation. The TRIPS Agreement that seeks to harmonize the Intellectual Property laws of various countries does not mandate this either (Ganesan, 2004).

The fact remains that foreign patenting cannot be challenged if a written/published credible document is not available. All the 165 members of the WIPO and inter-governmental organizations like European Patent Office would pay attention to strength to IPRs in developing world. The Patent (Amendment) Ordinance issued on 8 January 1998, does not allow Indian Medicine System Patentable. Currently traditional knowledge systems fall under public domain and are not included in the Indian system of medicine. India should, therefore, include medicinal plants used by the tribals and indigenous community under Indian Medicine Central Council Act, 1970. In the 4th Conference of Parties (COP) to the CBD held in Bratislava recently, the focus was on the sharing of benefits derived from biological resources with indigenous and traditional communities. The Government of India is under obligation to the WTO–Trade Related

Intellectual Property Rights (TRIPS) Article 70(8) and (9) to amend its patent act of 1970 so that it can meet international requirements. The Patent Amendment Bill of 1995 was a step in this direction. Having failed to amend the Patent Law, the US took India to the Dispute Settlement Body (DSB) for non-compliance of TRIPS agreement. India should therefore, take necessary action to amend its Patent Law. R&D institutions should encourage filing of patents. Currently India's share of the world patent is only 0.25%, while Japan has 25% followed by the US with 12%. Filing of patents in India has drastically improved recently. India should adopt the policy of selective prioritization of research and scientific screening of plant products/natural resources-based products as the world market for pharmaceuticals, agrochemical and seeds exceeds $250 billion.

CONCLUSIONS

Despite the allegations of 'biopiracy,' it seems that bioprospecting, with its potential, as a rich and important source of new therapeutic leads for drug research and discovery, is here to stay. Collaborations between pharmaceutical companies and the countries supplying the indigenous knowledge and medicinal resources could offer an important new revenue source for impoverished developing countries; however, future bioprospecting endeavors will require sensitive handling to avoid accusations that Western drug companies are plundering indigenous knowledge. Therefore, efforts to establish fair and equitable partnerships between the pharmaceutical industry and the developing countries are imperative to ensure sustainable, mutually beneficial relationships.

In the same time the intellectual property rights is one of the important means in protecting the benefits of traditional knowledge. It needs to be further developed and expanded. Patent law, however, is not only means in protecting the benefits of traditional knowledge. Each government should develop its own means to protect the benefits of the knowledge of traditional medicine. There is no doubt that these discussions will share ideas and information to facilitate our Member States to develop their own practicable systems, means and regimes for the protection of Intellectual Property Rights in order to achieve fair and equitable benefits in sharing traditional knowledge. Traditional knowledge would markedly contribute to the development of economics and health care in 21st Century.

REFERENCES

Awadh A. (2004), Medicinal Plant and Pharmaceutical Industry, African Journal of Traditional, Complementary and Alternative Medicines; 1:72–76.

Farnsworth, NR. Screening Plants for New Medicines. In: Wilson EO., editor. Biodiversity. National Academy Press, Washington, DC; pp. 83–97.

Ganesan S. (2004), Ethnomedicine and Economics, Indian Journal of Traditional Knowledge; 3:299–304.

Ignacimuthu S, Sankara Sivaraman K, Kesavan L.(1998), Medico-ethnobotanical Survey in Inida. Fitoterapia; 69:409–414.

Jain, SK. (2001), Ethnobotany in Modern India, Phytomorphology Golden Jubilee Issue: Trends in Plant Sciences. pp. 39–54.

Patrick OE (2002), Herbal Medicines: Challenges (Editorial). Tropical Journal of Pharmaceutical Research; 1:53–54.

Rajan S, Sethuraman M, Mukherjee P.K. (2002), Ethnobiology of the Nilgiri Hills, India. Phytotherapy–Research; 16:98–116.

Sandhya B, Thomas S, Isabel W, Shenbagarathai R. (2006), Ethnomedicinal Plants and Drug Manufacturing, African Journal of Traditional, Complementary and Alternative Medicines; 3:101–114.

17 Pattern and Perspective of Dingi: The Indigenous Boat in Sundarban Region

K. Basu

INTRODUCTION

India is perhaps unique in the boat typological knowledge. It is evident from various documents that sea faring activities have been evolved from ancient time and gradually reached the consent stages. Trading activities among countries such as Lakshadeep, Srilanka, South India, Bengal, Indonesia and medieval Arab were carried out through boats. Besides Danish records, other records on sailing in the countries mentioned above have also corroborated the fact on evolution of boat typology. Archaeological records since pre 14th century found in Southeast Asian countries reveal that Ship structures of that time are of one specific technical tradition. These ships were built by raising planks on each side of a keel-piece that shows clear signs of having evolved from a dugout base. This typical technique of ship structure signifies that there is a structural development from an earlier simple dugout canoe, from which planks were progressively raised. This technique therefore appears to have been in general use in Southeast Asia. This is confirmed by its survival under a variety of forms in scattered areas over most of the region, from Hai-nan, and Viet-nam to the Philippines and Eastern Indonesia in some cases well into the 20th century. South East Asian vessels appear to be belonging to the lashed-lug and stitched-plank tradition. The stitched-plank technique is associated to lashed-lugs when the planks with which hulls are built held together with way stitches made of vegetal fiber passed through holes and drilled near the edges (generally within the seams, not visible outside the hull). In some of the older remains from archaeological sites as well as in most modern craft, this stitching of the planks together appears to have progressively given way to dowelling. This is usually done by adding locking pins to prevent the planks from drifting apart. The compressed hull structure is unique in Asia (but very similar to that of early Scandinavian boats). It is revealed in Bengali Literacy composition during 17th to 18th century that in the religious center such as Navadvipa and in oral tradition that boat technology existed wherever there was intercontinental trading. According to historical and archaeological data, Asian indigenous people are identified in ship building tradition and it traces various stages of evolution it has undergone, during the past two thousand years. The evidence shows an original, structurally unique technical assemblage which was developed earlier in Chinas or Indian Ocean neighboring area. With the advent of civilization man moved from one place to another place, by means of various mode of communication. *Boat* was one of the vital means of water transport. Earlier man easily used this means of transport for their trade and also shared and exchanged their cultural behavior. Before sailing of boat a series of rituals were practiced, which are deeply embedded in the socio-cultural behaviour of a community.

Empirical studies have reflected that ecology plays a vital role in determining and maintaining the cultural life style of a community. In different ecological settings, different types of traits are displayed which results a distinctive economy, social organization, religious beliefs and practices. The people have to compromise with nature for survival. In the context of Sundarban delta the people came from different ecological backgrounds and adapted to a new ecological situation for their survival. Dingi plays a vital role, for their transportation, economic life, and as well as recreation. Here, I have tried to bring out the role of *Dingi* in the society as an alternative means of transportation for meeting their economic needs. The inhabitants of Sundarban are solely dependant on Nature. In course of time natural calamities and rise in population posed several threats to their survival.

According to the different scholars men coped up with the harsh ecological condition for their sustenance. According to *Ratzel*, 1899; *Sempel*, 1911 the environment determines a culture and on the other it is expected that the environment limits a culture (*Kroeber*, 1969; *Toynbee*, 1947; *Fordes* 1934). One cannot ignore the impact of environment on life and culture and the inter-relation and interdependence between man and his environment. According to, *Vayda* and *Rappaport* (1968), an ecosystem comprises all the living organisms and non-living environmental elements such as soil, water, climate, etc. that interact with each other within a spatially defined area.

PHYSICAL GEOGRAPHY

Sundarbans present a unique bio-climatic zone. The biosphere falls within the Indo-Malayan realm and the Indo-Gangetic plain bio-geographical region. It forms the southern most portion of the Gangetic delta and extends along the sea-face of the Bay of Bengal, from the estuary of the Hoogly on the west, to the river Meghna (now in Bangladesh) on the east. The biosphere reserve is situated on coastal Bay of Bengal between 21^{0}32' and 22^{0}40' North Latitude and between 88^{0}95' and 89^0 East Longitude, bounded by the Dampier-Hodges Line in the north, Bay of Bengal in the South, Bangladesh in the east and river Hoogly in the west . The estuarine delta consists of forests, tidal channels, creeks, nallahs and islands. Besides this, the area is full of endangered wild animals, birds, rich terrestrials, aquatic resources and a good number of unique floras.

The total area of the Biosphere Reserve is 9630 sq. km. Out of this, forest area is 4263 sq. km. and the remaining 5367 sq. km. is of human population. Sundarban forest happens to be the only mangrove tiger land of India and the protected Royal Bengal Tiger reserve covers an area of 2585 sq. km. Sundarbans Tiger Reserve under core area is 1330.12 sq. km. The Indian portion comprises of a total of 102 islands, out of which 48 are forest land and rest 54 have human population.

The mangrove ecosystems are unique but fragile and most productive for maintaining the ecological balance. This biosphere reserve was declared as a "World Heritage Site" in 1987. Sundarbans, in the coastal area of West Bengal is well known for having a most interesting and extensive bio-diversity mangrove habitat, flora and fauna. The mangrove plants and mangrove dwelling fauna in the delta and estuarine mouth of the river Hooghly are unique and important. The biosphere has about 81 species, including trees, shrubs and herbs (*Naskar, K.R* 1999). Most of these plants are endemic in the inter-tidal high saline deltaic areas, for having their special adaptation in these physiologically dry soils. Additionally there are many kinds of shrubs and other brushes, which thrive in the saline environment. These mangrove forests, brushwood and bushes play a significant role in maintaining ecological balance by preventing and withstanding soil erosion by both the rivers and the sea.

THE PEOPLE

The Sundarban delta is covered with forests and surrounded by river and sea. The land is inhabited by the multi ethnic groups who have migrated from different part of India, including East Pakistan (now Bangladesh). The inhabitants have come from different ecological set up and entered in a new ecological condition for their survival. The colonization was started by the British in the early 18th century. In 1903, Sir Danniel Hamilton, established his Zamindary over three islands namely Gosaba, Rangabelia and Satjelia. He brought people for establishing settlements mainly from Chhotonagpur, Mayurbhanj, Midnapur, Purulia, Ranchi, for cutting trees for timber and land reclamation. Along with these laborers, other non-tribal communities like Mahishya, Mahatos, Poundra-Kskatriya, Namsudra, Bagdi, Tantubay, Kamar and Doms came for making the land cultivable.

In 1947 a sudden influx of migrants from East Pakistan (now known as Bangladesh) mainly from districts of Jessore,

Khulna, Barishal and Bakharganj also added to the population of Sundarbans. The migrants belonged to Raj-Banshi, Namosudra, Poundra etc. and Malo (fisher folk), Jele besides other castes.

Again another group of community came to occupy the area in 1971. They came from Bangladesh. These displaced persons forcibly occupied the wasteland, and such a big chunk of population created a pressure on this region. In course of their migration, these migrants were either rehabilitated or illegally settled adjacent to the Bio-sphere reserve. Hence the total population comprising the migrants of 1947 and the additional entrants of 1971 became dependent on the ecological reserve of the Sundarbans. Since the area is mostly covered by rivers having saline water with tidal susceptibility and most of the time the saline water penetrated into the cultivable lands of the migrants. In such eventuality, the inhabitants were forced to think once alternative modes of sustenance and they adopted "the country Boat" as the only medium of survival.

They used boat not only as a means of livelihood and sustenance but for fishing, honey collection, transportation for local communities as well as for the tourists also. The mode and tune of economic activities was thus related to the boat as a means of shaping the livelihood of the families. For collection of honey, fish, crab etc their only means of transport is country boat, which is locally known as *dingi*. At the time of fish collection they use *dingi* boat, but comparatively bigger in size. For the transportation they used motorized boat locally known as *bhat-bhati*. *Betnai* –this type of boat was used for carrying timber, goods etc and it is bigger in size. But today this type of boat is not found in the Sundarban area. Jele batari is a boat which is very long in size, the middle portion of is narrow in shape and it is used for recreation- which locally known as Baich. Boat racing competition is held at the time of Durga puja at Kachu khali, Molla khali Gosaba etc. To reiterate boat plays a vital role in their sustainable economic concerns as well as recreation. The study was conducted at Dayapur village of Gosaba block of South 24 Pargana.

The people of Sundarban used to depend on their age old experience i.e. their traditional knowledge of making a boat. At the time of boat making they fallow traditional measurement units like *'hat'* means one "cubits". 1 cubit is counted from elbow to the tip of the middle finger. Similar term used is *'pad'*. *'Pad'* is considered as closed up to thumb nail. The *'pad'* is the main measuring unit of the boat makers. According to their concept, the unit *'pad'* depicts the boats length, and its width, as well as loading capacity of the vessel. For example, one *Pad* boat, means length will be 3 ½ *hat* (cubits), length of 6 *pad* boats will be 21 *hat* or cubits and its width will be 87" (the local boat maker consider the width of boat, 1 *pad* = 14", 6 *pad* = 14Í6 = 84". For covering the boat, six planks or *takta* are required for either side of the boat. The plank will be six inches in width, which is covered on the both sides horizontally. The vocabulary term *pad* is communication media for the boat business. The charges of boat making depend upon the number of *pad*. Local price of 1 *Pad* is Rs. 400/. For making the boat they purchase the wood from nearby local market. In early days they used to collect wood from jungle for boat making. The boat makers are so expert with their professional skill that they can easily calculate the width, length, and *joot* accordingly. *Joot* is an important measurement to help the boat making. On the basis of *joot* the boat makers calculate number of planks, size of the boat and other accessories required. The strength of the boat is determined by the *joot*

PREPARATION FOR BOAT MAKING

Religious ceremonies are observed by the communities before starting the boat making to appease some god and goddess who are believed to be benevolent and malevolent in nature. The common belief is that by worshiping and appeasing these god and goddess the process of boat making will be smooth and it will save them from evil spirits. For safe construction generally the boat maker prefers to start the work of boat making on Tuesday and Saturday. On such auspicious day the boat owner performs the rituals and sails a wooden piece on the river with a belief that his new boat will bring him good fortune. He appeases mother goddess Ganga or Mangal-chandi along with his friends and relatives.

On the same day the boat maker offers prayer to Brahma, Vishnu, and Mahershwra .The boat maker puts vermillion marks at three places of the central place of the main frame of the boat i.e. *dara*. The boat owner offers a bowl (*punnya patra*), which is filled with betel leaves and nuts along with rice, new cloth and one coin. The boat maker washes the *'dara'* and wipes it with the help of a new cloth locally known as *gamcha*. It is locally called *pattan*.

During boat making they follow some rules and regulation related to boat technology. At the time of boat making, they divide the construction work in different stages as mentioned in the age old process of boat making.

First Stage

On that day, main structure of the boat work gets started. (i). A long wooden plank is fixed between two wooden poles .This wooden plank is locally known as *danra*. The distance between two poles is set as per the required measurement. The wooden plank is supposed to be one and half inches thick and three inches width and the length depend upon the size of the boat. (ii) The boat maker fixes the plank between two wooden poles to give it the shape like a bow or chord shape. One twinned string is set at the upper portion of the pole from one pole to another pole as per the required measurement which depends upon the size of the boat. The function of the twinned string is to help the measurement and leveling of both the side of the boat. (iii) They measure the total length of plank and divide it into two equal halves. After measuring the centre point, the plank is fixed between the two poles with the help of iron nail. The centre point is locally known as *dara*. Both sides of the wooden poles are locally known as *khuti*. (iv). The total length i.e., stem to centre point i.e., *dara*, and *dara* to stern is equally divided and marked on both side of the wooden frame. They mark the place fixed with chalk "Í" (like into sign) or with the help of iron nails. Now they wait for ten to fifteen days and observe the accurate measurement and shape of the plank or any problem in the boat frame and perform necessary correction. It takes 10 to 15 days to perfectly align the frame of the boat. Right measurement and achieving the accuracy in the frame measurement of the boat plays a vital role.

Second Stage

The second stage work is related to *joot* calculation. Joot is a crucial measurement system of the boat technology. On the basis of the *joot* measurement the boat maker decides how many wooden plank i.e.*takta* are required for the boat. It also decides the load bearing capacity of the *boat* .The *Joot* is considered as the center point of the boat i.e.*dara* .The vertical height of the boat is called *joot*. The measurement of *joot* is proportional to the size of the boat, and it helps to calculate the numbers of wooden plank or *takta* required for the boat. After calculation of *joot*, the boat maker sets up the planks horizontally as per the requirement of the boat.

- Then the boat maker starts setting the wooden planks horizontally one after another as per requirement. The wooden planks are then stitched with the help of iron nails. After completion of plank setting on both sides of the boat, the covering system starts which is locally known as *patali*.
- One wooden plank is fixed just for completion of the upper part of the *patali* of the boat from rear to front side of the frame. The system is locally known as *nabo-dali*.
- The third stage of the plank setting is *dali*. The *dali* is used to gain more strength for the boat, which is fixed from both the sides i.e., from *galui* to *pachha* of the boat. The boat maker takes care of it. For fixing the *dali*, he avoids the centre point i.e. dara because the joint place of the *dali* is supposed to be set up in the place of *dara* otherwise the strength of the boat will be decreased.
- The *malom* is the final and last step of stitching plank system of the boat which preferably happens to be 2" to 2 ½ " thicknesses and more than 6" breadth. The

boat maker fixes the two wooden planks from two end points of *Gochha* of the boat. It is also noticed that the *malom* plank saves the boat from the waves.

- *Malom bit* is a narrow wooden frame fixed as supporting part of the *malom* which is generally used for strengthening the boat and saves it from wave.
- *Chandi Kath:* - The final stage of the boat making work is related to the main structure of the boat. The structure of the boat reflects 12" to 18" size of wooden frame on both the side which is called *chandi kath*. The front side is used for offering the puja before starting for sail. The back side is used for navigation and paddling of the boat by the *majhi*.

Third Stage

The inner part of the boat is made in the third stage that consists of a small wooden frame.

Gochha is a small wooden frame fixed to join the planks of boat with the help of iron nails. The method of tying up depends on the size of the boat. For example if the boat is six *pad*, the boat maker fixes eleven pair of wooden frame (11×2). Six *pad* boat means it is of 21 *hat* or cubits length and 87" width that requires 11 pairs of *gochha*. These are set on both sides of the body of the boat for strengthening it. It is done within 1 *hat*/cubit or 1 ½ feet or 18". It consists of 2" to 2 ½" width and its length differs from *pachha* (back side) to *golui* side (front side).

Bank is a term used for numbers of small wooden frame to be fixed in the boat as per requirement. The boat maker generally fixes the *bank* in between two *gochhas* for strengthening as well as to increase the durability of the boat. The preferred wood for this purpose is that of *Babool* tree.

Koldali refers to long wooden plank generally measuring five inches wide and two inches thickness, which is attached to the upper part of the boat. It is seen that the *koldali* is fixed leaving fifty-four inches from left and similarly fifty four inches from the front side of the boat. The function of the *koldali* is mainly to hold and strengthen the boat. It acts as a support to the *gochha*. If the boat is of 6 *pads* i.e. 21 *hat* or cubits , the total area of *koldali* is 16 *hat* lengths, total 5 cubits are from both sides of the boat, one side will be in 2 and ½ cubits distance. .

Gunro is the long wooden plank fixed on both sides of *koldali* of the boat. The setting of *gunro* depends on the measurement .The *gunro* is preferably made with eucalyptus tree. It measures 1 ½ " to 2" in thickness and 5" to 6" in width and length extends from rear side to back side of the boat. It supports the wooden platform which is locally called *patatan* of boat where the people can easily walk.

Jugo is fixed on both sides at the end of *gochha* and usually limited to four in numbers. The function of the *jugo* is to anchor the boat with the help of rope. The small gaps between the joints are packed with cotton or jute. Generally they use jute or resin to put the joint places protected from the water. Besides, they also use coal-tar, locally called *alkatra* as final stroke of the boat for prevention from decomposition in view of constant water contact.

At the time of last and final function of the boat making, it is observed that, on at day the boat maker hand over the boat formally to the owner. On the same day, it is a custom that the owner, as recognition of boat maker's skill and efficiency awards prizes to him with new cloth (dhoti) or gamcha, tumbler or dish of bell metal depending on his economic condition. Besides these rituals a feast is organized in which all the kith and kin of the boat maker are invited.

During the first day of the voyage, the boat owner performs a function to ensure the safe voyage, and for this Biswakarma puja is performed in the front side of the boat known as *galui*, Maa kali puja is performed in the middle portion of the boat known as *dara* and Narayana is worshiped in the back side of the boat locally known as *pachha*. It is believed that these divinities will protect them from all sorts of mishap. The Brahman priest performs this puja when the boat is set for sailing.

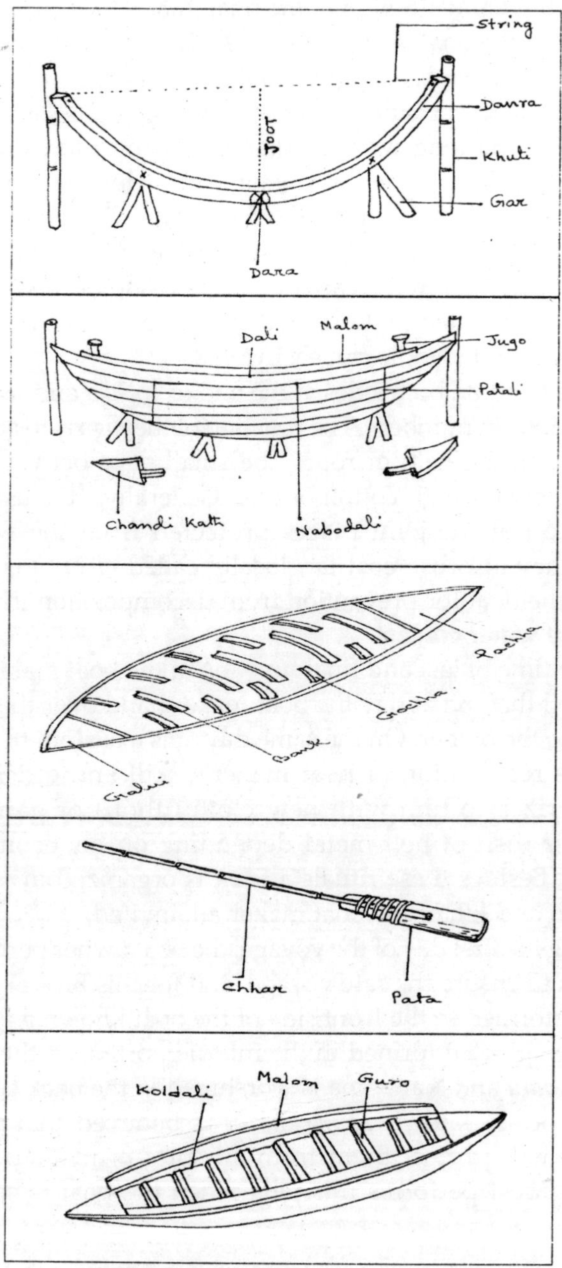

Sketch of Different Parts of the Boat (Dingi)

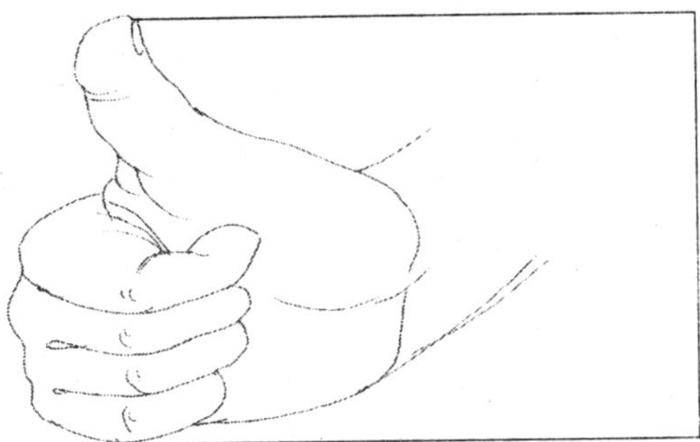

Traditional Measurement of *Pad*

SOME SPECIAL TECHNIQUES OF BOAT MAKING

The carpenter follows certain rules and regulations during boat making, acquired from age old experience and inherited from generation to generation.

- The main frame of the boat is called *danra*. The total length of the *danra* is divided into two halves. The centre point of the boat is referred as d*ara*.
- Total length of the *dara* is again divided into two halves, and the half-length measurement put on both side of the *danra*. Two wooden poles are fixed at both ends of *danra* with the help of iron nails.
- The length of the p*ad* is equal to the length of thumb nail. The p*ad* is used to measure length, breath and to determine the load capacity of the boat.
- The j*oot* is the centre point of the d*anra*. The measurement of j*oot* determines the number of *plank, goccha, kol dali,* etc.required to perform the work. .
- The lower surface of the boat is called *tala*. The measurement of *tala* is calculated as half of the total number of *pad*. This method of measurement is not strictly followed for all types of boat.

MEASUREMENT OF BOAT

The methods used for measurement of the boat are herewith cited below. This is as per the traditional knowledge of the boat maker of Sundarban.

The measurement of six-pad boat and its different parts are as follows:-

An Example of Six Pad Dingi (Measurement)

Pad is the numerical unit of measurement, having different connotation in *joot* measurement, *pad* is considered as 6" whereas at the time of width measurement of the boat *pad* is considered 14".

1 *Pad* = 6" *Joot*.

If one *pad* is equal to six inches joot then 6 *pad* boat = 6Í6=36" *joot* (considered as the strength of the boat)

1 *pad* = 14" (inches) width, locally called *ber*. 6 *pad* boat will be 14Í6 = 84" width. Width of the boat is measured from middle portion to the inner side of the boat extending from one border to another border.

Length of the boat is measured as cubit. If 1 *pad* = approx 3 ½ *hat* (cubit) length, then 6 *pad* will be 21 *hat* .Breadth of the boat is measured according to the total width which is divided by . 84"/ 2 = 42", it is half inner portion of the boat from *dara* to one border of the boat i.e. up to *malom*..

Takta setting is dependent on breadth of the boat. Total *takta* required for 6 *pads* boat are twelve numbers, six *pads* on each side.

If 1 plank = 6" (inches), then 6 planks will be 6Í6 = 36". This 36" is the measurement of the *patali*.

1 *Dali* will be 6" the total takta and *Dali* measurement will be 36"+6" = 42".

Gochha- 11 pair gochha is required for 6 *pad* boat, which is put on the inner part of the boat with 15" distances.

Bank- 11 numbers required, which are set between two *gochhas*.

Guro- 11 numbers required, which are set on both sides of the *koldali*.

Malom- two numbers of *malom* required, which are set on left of *kodali* within 2½ cubit on both sides of the boat.

Baitha- is used for paddling the boat. It is made of one long bamboo stick locally called *cahhar,* attached to one U shaped wooden plate locally known as *pata*. The measurement is generally considered 54" for *cahhar* and pata will be 36".

During the course of boat making, both the boat owner and maker ensure that no scythe is found around the vicinity. The superstition is based on the fact that the function of scythe is contradictory to the function of boat. As a scythe always cuts backward, while a boat always moves forward. In case of any death of the family member the boat maker postpones the work.

Knowledge about Water, Wave, and Season

Prior to undertaking the study of evolution of boat and dependence of people of Sundarbans one should understand the cosmology, myths, rituals, social behavior and history of the entire socio-economic life of the delta. People of Sundarban depend on this cosmology which reflects in their economy like fishing, wood cutting, crab collection, honey collection, etc. It has been observed that the people of Sundarban are accustomed with the seasonal and lunar system for resource collection and procurement from both terrestrial and aquatic sources. For all such activities the means of transportation is boat. During activities related to river or sea the people depend on weather condition, lunar system, as well as wind variation. People appease some god and goddess during their sailing or collection of forest resources. The Banobibi, Dakshnia Rai, Shahajangali are regarded as the central authority of the biosphere and Mangalchandi, Ganga, and Kali are revered as the authority of aquatic field.

People are accustomed to their age-old experience in the field of sailing and resource procurement. As per their conception, the seasons are divided broadly into three categories namely *Garam kal* (summer, March to June,) *Barsa kal* (rainy, July to October) and *shit kal* (winter, November to February). *Garam kal* is considered the period during Chaitra to Jaistha, *barsa* ranges from Ashar to Kartik and *shit kal* from Agrahayan to Falgun months. People procure prawn, crabs and Parse fish throughout the year. During the summer as per the order of the forest authorities fishing is prohibited .During this time it is permitted for honey collection. This is exclusively done in the month of Chaitra and Baishakh. However, women and girl children collect Bagda meen (spawn of tiger prawn) from the river bank round the year, locally known as "*char*".

Rainy season is considered as the best time for fishing. They also collect crabs in small quantity. During the month of Bhadra, hilsa fish is available but it depends upon the weather condition, while the water remains blackish in colour for a few days. During the months of Falgun and Kartik women also go to jungle for crab collection. They go to sea at high tide and return home during low tide.

Winter season is considered as the best time for collection of crab, prawn and bagda meen (from deep river). The species of fishes mainly available are Mochan or Air, Chakul, Rupamoti, Chele, Parse, Chanda, etc. During this season hilsa fish is also available for a couple of days.

INVOKING LUNAR CALENDER FOR SUSTENANCE

The inhabitants of Sundarban are very much dependent on the environment and available natural resources for their livelihood and sustenance. Depending on the position of the moon they perform fishing of various kinds of fish and crabs in the creek and river. As per their experience the lunar system is indicative of the position of water level of river or creek during high tide and low tide which in turn predicts the

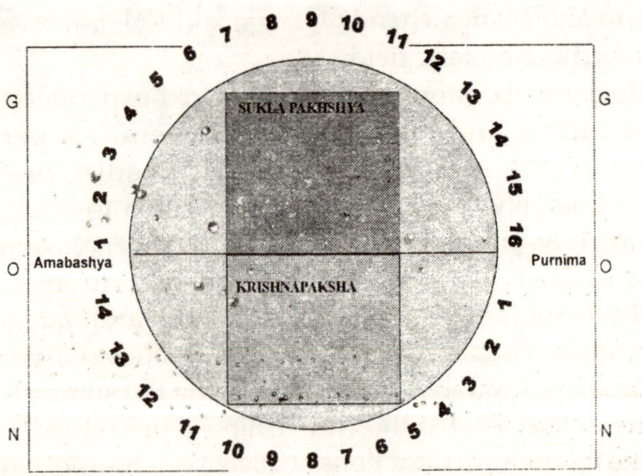

availability of aquatic resources. The lunar system is locally known as "*tithi*". Each month is divided into two halves or fortnights (*paksha*).One fortnight (*paksha*) is brighter, i.e., *Suklapaksha* and the other fortnight is darker, i.e., *Krishnapaksha*. In the fortnight periods, the darkish moon is known as (*amabshya*) and the full moon is known as (*purnima*).

Now each paksha is divided into three categories as per their traditional knowledge. The period *Suklapaksha*, is calculated as the 1-15 days and locally known as "*Gonmukh*". During the Gonmukh, the river and creek water levels remain high and saturated; current gradually decreases with high tide in the river or creek. It is the best time for fishing and collection of crabs. Within this *gonmukh* period 14th day of *Krishnapaksha* to 5th day of *Suklapaksha* is considered as *Barogon*.

The second part mentioned as "*Marani*", which is from 6th to 9th days of the *Suklapaksha*, is the best time for Bagda meen collection mainly done by womenfolk at the river side. During this period, river and creek are generally calm. These days are not suitable for fishing.

The third part is colloquially known as "*Barogon*" or "*Bharakotal*". It is from the 14th day to 5th day of *Suklapaksha*, i.e., *Amabashya*. During this period the river or creek water level reaches an optimum level and there is strong under current. It is the best time for fishing different types of fishes and crabs.

Similarly the darker moon period '*Krishnapaksha*' is divided into three parts. From 1st to 5th day, it is locally referred as *Gonmukh*. In this period the river or creek water level is high and the surface water becomes saturated. It is the best time for collection of fish and crab. "*Marani*" or *marakotal* starts from 6th to 9th day of the both *paksha*. During this period the river or creek is generally calm. It is observed that in both the "*Marani*" they prefer to be at home because the time is unsuitable for fishing or collection of crab.

The third part of the calendar is known as "*Barogon*" or *Bharakotal*, which starts from the 10th day to 14th day of the *Krishnapaksha* that is up to Amabashya. It is the best time for of fishing and collection of crabs because of the of strong under current in the sea. The people follow the traditional way of cylindrical system, which is part and parcel of collection of aquatic resources like fish and crabs from river and creek.

WIND VARIATION AND RESOURCE AVAILABILITY

Speed, velocity and direction of the wind determine the economic activity of the people of Sundarban. They consider wind movement broadly into two types, *Dakshiner hawa* and *Utturer hawa*. According to them the month or period from Chaitra to Aswin (April-October) is referred as *Dakshiner hawa* and is considered as the best time for collection of honey and fishing.

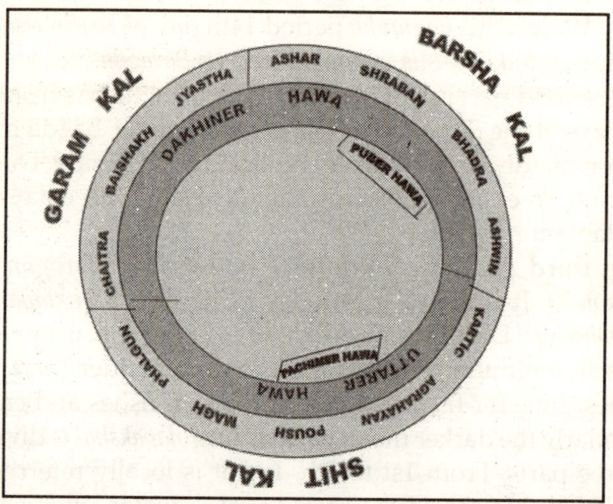

During rainy season (Shravan and Bhadra months) the wind blows from eastward direction, locally referred as *puber hawa* and is unsuitable for any type of collection. The river turns very rough and water level becomes very high, with undercurrent and whirlpools. Such situation does not permit the voyage. During this time they generally prefer to go to *khari* (creek). Similarly, they consider the month Kartik to Falgun as *Utturer hawa*. During this period they collect different types of fish, crabs, etc. Water level at the river and creek is calm and this is considered as most suitable time for collection activity. During the *Utturer hawa*, the two months of Agrahayan and Poush are not suitable for any collection activity because west ward wind occasionally blows in these two months, and is locally known as *Paschimer* hawa (westward wind). During this time river turns very rough and there is strong undercurrent which damages the road and embankment.

The forecast for wind variation is calculated on the day of Shree Panchami and Kojagori Laxmipuja. Collection of honey is started by the *Bouley* .They check and test the direction of winds on the night which they consider as "*Prohor*". Time around 9 p.m. is considered as *Protham prohor*, midnight is considered as *Dittiya prohor*, and 3 a.m. onward is considered as *Tritiya prohor*. As per their experience, they can locate the bee hive, based on the direction of wind blow .Generally the people practise an age old traditional ritual in the night of Sree Panchami, when they light lamp in an earthen pot and follow the direction of wind. The movement of the flame indicates availability of beehives. The *Bouley* organizes this ritual but other members also follow this ritual either in the night of Kojagori Laxmipuja or during Sree Panchami. They consider that the bee always moves against the wind, i.e., "leeward".

The forest goers also identify the presence of tiger easily. In this case wind also helps them. The tiger too moves against the wind to sniff its prey. Direction of the wind and weather condition play a vital role for economic life of the people of Sundarban in this regard.

TABOOS AND RESTRICTIONS

The people who are to visit the terrifying forest for their sustenance regularly observe various taboos and other restrictions. Honey collection is a very challenging job and for which they strictly follow certain specific measures to keep themselves away from the danger of consequences. Honey collection is referred to as "*mahal*" and those who collect honey from jungle are referred to as "*mouley*". There is perennial danger of tiger attack during honey collection. Numbers of cases are recorded with regard to injury and man missing. It is found that beehives are chiefly found in trees like Khalsi, Garjan, Bani, Geoa, Keora, etc. and the best quality of honey is collected from *khalsi* flower. Those who collect fish are known as "*Jele*" and those who collect wood from jungle are called "*Bouley*". Collection of honey and wax is completely seasonal, and it starts from Chaitra (March–April) to Vaisakh (April to May).

The symbolic identity of Bonbibi, Dakhin Rai, and Shahjangali plays a crucial role in the forest and economic life of the people of Sundarban. From ancient time people associate them with the mother cult culture. People from all caste and creed worship and appease the mother goddess. Both in case of post and pre journey, the team members perform offerings and worship Bonbibi and seek her blessings to keep themselves safe in the forest. They believe that her supernatural powers can protect or save their lives from all sorts of hazards and unusual events. Both the Hindus and Muslims worship the same deities despite belonging to different religions. The goddess of the forest "Bonbibi" is worshipped in almost every village.

Women follow some taboos for safety of their family members at the time of *mahal* that are as follows.

Before sunrise they finish all their daily ablutions like bathing, combing hair, applying oil, use of soap, cleaning the house and cooking, etc. Also, they atert themselves in not seeing any cooked utensils during the day, not wearing vermilion on their foreheads, not squeezing wet clothes in the day and not sweeping courtyard and house, etc. On Fridays, the women observe fasting and offer special prayers. They also abstain from doing any form of stitching and cleaning of cloth. They do not sleep during day time. Those women whose husbands go for collection to the forest can have their bath and apply vermilion only during the darkness but before their husbands leave for forest or on their return. Men also follow certain taboos like shaving and hair cutting by village barber following the death rituals, assuming any probable death of family members in their absence. They do not enter the jungle on Fridays; instead stay on boat. No onward journey is performed on Fridays for *mahal* as a mark of respect for Bonibibi. The concept of purity includes no defecation on the ground in the jungle but on leaf or other substance. Before journey they do not eat or carry bananas, bottle gourd, gourd and radish. They do not eat anything which is burnt or roasted even and instead it has to be boiled, fried or cooked otherwise. These beliefs and practices have come into existence over a period of time and are strictly observed.

SUMMARY

From the above few pages it can be said that Dingi together with its typolitical pattern plays a vital role in the socio-economic life of the people of Sundarban. The preparation and technique of the boat making is an indigenous method and had evolved over the period of time. It is also observed that the technique of boat making is undergoing changes. Similarly, they also have adapted boat technology and which is used to earn money as secondary source of economic support. So, boat is the life line of the people of Sundarbans.

In conclusion it can be said that the multi ethnic people of Sundarban delta is governed in their fishing activity and Dingi typology by forces of nature and the unknown spiritual world associated with it as per their conceived superstitious belief, evolved through the generations due to and subject to the cause and effect phenomena. The superstitions are so strong in view of environment of hostile forces, that every step of their fishing activity and dangi making is associated with it, to place the unknown forces lest they, cause harm. They are supplementary fisher folk and they take every precaution, spiritual as well as environmental, and material, to make their activities successful as far as their intelligence, developed through years of experience would permit.

REFERENCES

Bennet. W. John (1976), *The Ecological Transition. Cultural Anthropology and Human Adaptation*. Pergamon Press Inc. New York.

De. Barun (Ed.) (1994), *West Bengal District Gazetteers, 24 Parganas.*

Debnath. H.S. (2004), *Sundarban Biosphere Reserve*. Botanical Survey of India.

Hunter, W.W. (1998), *A Statistical Account of 24 Parganas*. Govt. of West Bengal.

Raha, R.K. (2004), *Indian Sundarban– An Overview Sundarban Biosphere Reserve*. Wildlife Wing, Forest Department.

Ray Choudhury, B. K. (1980), *The Moon and the Net*. An. S. I., Kolkata.

Journal of South-East Asian Studies Vol–XI. No-2 September-1980, Singapore University Press.

18 Traditional Knowledge and Health Care Practices among the Chuktia Bhunjia Tribe of Orissa

Bhubaneswar Sabar

Health is an important phenomenon for human survival. In order to have socially and economically productive life, health is man's natural condition. It is also an indicator of human development. It is affected by socio-economic status, family composition, custom, belief, life styles and use of available medical facilities (Clement, 1932; Foster, 1978; Choudhuri, 1986, 1990). Every human society irrespective of its simplicity and complexity has its own beliefs and practices concerning diseases. They evolve their own system of medicine and methods for coping up with diseases and eventually create a body of its own medical system. This system is known as traditional medicine, often known as ethnomedicine, folk medicine, popular medicine, and so on. Since last few decades there has been increasing research in this field that has developed a special discipline called 'community medicine' in a broader field of medical sociology/anthropology.

Ethno-medicine focuses on the nature of illness as it is conceived by the natives, their own methods, criteria of classification of diseases (etiology), the causes and cures, types of therapists and healers who seek to alleviate illness and their skill and social roles, preventive measures, the relation between medicine and religion, cultural aspect of ethno-medicine and also ethno-psychiatry (Hughes, 1968; Foster, 1978). It also deals with the relationship between the healers and clients; behavior of healers and training and efficacy of their treatments.

Among the pre-literate/tribal societies, various kinds of events are attributed for the cause of illnesses, the most common being the supernatural forces. Due to such belief the tribals are invariably found to repose faith in divines. So the health practice of these communities is merely based on magico-religious theory of disease causation and they seek device through supernatural forces. Clements (1932) identifies five basic categories of events or situations said to be the causes of various illnesses: (1) Sorcery, (2) breach of taboo, (3) intrusion of disease object, (4) intrusion of disease curing spirit, and (5) loss of soul. Foster's dualistic classification as 'personalistic' and 'naturalistic' medical systems is also marked in the folk system of medicine. In personalistic system illness is believed to be affected by the action of supernatural being like deity or gods or a non-human agent such as ghosts or an evil spirit, or a human agent like witch or sorcery where as in naturalistic system illness said to be caused by the disturbance in equilibrium of the impersonal and in sensate elements in the human body (Foster, 1978). On this background this paper attempts to delineate the traditional health care practices of Chuktia Bhunjia tribe residing in Sunabeda Wildlife Sanctuary of Nuapada district, Orissa. It also touches upon the reasons for the continuation of such practice.

METHODOLOGY

Data pertaining to this study were collected from four villages located in Sunabeda Wildlife Sanctuary during April to October, 2006. Data were collected from laymen, magico-religious practitioners, and herbalists through interview scheduled containing open ended question in order to document their knowledge on different diseases and treatment methods. An attempt was made to find out associated rituals, festivals and taboos pertaining to treatment of diseases. Emphasis was given to the medicine men and disease specialists for gathering medicinal plants; however laymen were also asked. The extraction of medicinal plants and medication methods were closely observed. A focus group discussion was also conducted combining both the laymen and medicine men in order to understand their perception on this traditional practice, feasibility of change and any constraints facing with the accessibility of the medicinal plants. The discussion also gave an insight of relationship between the patients and medicine men that helped analyzing sustainability of the practice.

CHUKTIA BHUNJIA

There are 62 tribal groups found in Orissa of which Bhunjia is one. It is recognized as primitive tribal group (PTG) in the state. They are also distributed in Bindranawagarh and Dhamtari sub-divisions of Raipur district in newly formed Chhattisgarh State. In Orissa they are largely found Nuapada (ex-Khariar) district which was earlier forming a part of Central Province (Dube, 1948; Dubey, 1961). They are divided into two broad social groups: Chinda Bhunjia and Chuktia Bhunjia (Russel and Hiralal, 1916; Dubey, 1961, 1963; Pattnaik et al. 1984; Mishra 2002). Chinda Bhunjia, otherwise known as Oriya Bhunjia, are found in and around the plain area and fallow the Oriya culture and thus considered acculturated section of the society. Chuktia Bhunjias, on the other hand, exclusively inhabit in the Sunabeda Wildlife Sanctuary along with other communities namely Gond, Paharia, Kultha (an agricultural community), blacksmith and dom (scheduled caste). The Kultha and blacksmith are reported to have been migrated from plain area in 1960s. Bhunjia are Kolahrian category (Russel and Hiralal, 1916) who speak their own dialect "Bhunjia"-(a mix of Oriya and Chhatisgari) among themselves and use regional language for inter-group communication.

In Sunabeda Wildlife Sanctuary they have been distributed in 16 villages (9 revenue and 7 hamlets), which comprise 519 households. Their total population in this plateau is 2174 (1085 (49.91%) male and 1089 (50.09%) female). their sex ration is 1004. Out of the total population, 758 (34.87%) person are literate. 559 (51.52%) male and 199 (18.27%) female. (Population Census, CBDA, 2001).

Chuktia Bhunjia family is nuclear in nature. They are also an endogamous group. Hunting, gathering, and fishing, collection of minor forest produces and slash burning cultivations (*Bewar*) are their main economic pursuit which is self sufficient in nature. Most of them do not have agricultural land and live with encroached land. They are animistic in nature. They worship gods and goddesses including their ancestral spirit. Goddesses *Sunadei* is the propitiate deity apart from other deities worshipped in specific purpose. They celebrate various festivals most being related to agriculture.

HEALTH FOR CHUKTIA BHUNJIA

The concept of health varies from social groups to groups even between the same groups living in different territories. They understand health, diseases, causes of illness, and treatment mainly in cultural terms. They integrate their medical knowledge into the conceptual frameworks of their societies and all members share the same theories of ideas and treatment. Unlike other people the Chuktia Bhunjias define health in term of the capability of a people to work. They decide health and illness according to his ability to perform his/her regular works like attending household work, and agricultural duties. They identify illness through visible symptoms or acute bodily discomfort. They persist longer duration symptom as severe illness and attribute unseen spirits for it. They also perceive health in term of blood contain in the body. They consider red blood is good and sign of healthy body. They believe that as the person grows older red blood turn to blackish red and the quantity of blood decrease indicating lesser strength and decreased health status.

Before proceeding in detail of the health care system of Chuktia Bhunjia it is important here to make a point of reference that their health seeking behavior is determined by their customary norms. It is reported that their customary norms does not allow their women to have an access to phenomenon including modern medicinal facility. However, male members also do not prefer the same. Being a very typical culture geared society they always try to retain their traditional custom. In this regards when any family prefer qualified doctor or nurse the family is ostracized from the society, viewing it as modernisation or Hinduisation. This social ostracism perhaps forces many people to remain at the hitherto of traditional system. It is also observed that the house pattern particularly the kitchen room plays a dominant role in which women are the mere followers. They worship their tutelary deities inside it and if any outsiders, including other community of the same village, touch it they immediately set it fire and construct a new one followed by sacrifice of a hen. It is the main cause for which they do not want to be touched by any outsiders, the qualified doctor here, which may contaminate them and as well as their kitchen room, as the women are most of the time engaged with kitchen activities.

ILLNESS AND BELIEFS SYSTEM

Like other tribal communities, the Chuktia Bhunjias attribute supernatural forces or what Foster call 'personalistic agents' for any kinds of illnesses, albeit change in environmental condition is hardly accepted. The personalistc agents include ancestral deities (*duma*), evil spirit (*Masan*) and sorcery (*Pangan*). They classify evil spirit into two broad categories: *Masan* and *Chirngel*. They believe that when a person dies in evil spirit he/she becomes *Masan*. They also believe that when a pregnant woman dies she becomes *Chirngel*. In such case, they do not immerse her in the place of their general cremation. She is either cremated in the jungle or on the bank of river stream. Ancestral spirit is often attributed for illnesses. They worship *Mata* (goddess of chicken pox) and *Chhatigudi* (goddess of scabies) to protect them from any kind of illnesses in a regular interval. Failure of worshiping them is believed to cause diseases. If anybody get injures by falling from trees, they also attribute it to the evil spirits. They belief that older the trees more the chance of evil spirit thus afraid of going to such places during noon and evening. The unmarried persons are believed to be more attacked by such spirits. So they suggest not going outside particularly during in noon. Illness caused by ancestral spirits (*dumas*) is not so harmful which they believe only affect to the family members. They believe that when they forget to offer new crops and if unpolluted women touch the place of worship the spirit attack them. In such case the head of the family offers little liquor to appease the spirits. They also believe in sorcery (*pangan*) as a cause of illness, albeit not reported have applied due to fear of *Sunadei.*

HEALTH PRACTITIONERS

There are two health practitioners found among the Chuktia Bhunjia: *Gunia* (magico-religious healer) and *Baiga* (herbalist) are found. *Gunia* treats diseases through various religious methods. His role is resorted when the causes of illness is attributed to what Foster (1978) call 'personalistic agents'. *Baiga,* on the other hand, is herbalist whose treatment is resorted when the cause of the illness is identified as a natural substance or disturbance in body composition. His medicines preparation and exploitation of medicinal plants/herbs fallow certain taboo and precautions. However everybody possesses some or little knowledge in treating ailments, the Chuktia Bhunjias always consult the Baiga. Very often *Gunia* also use plant medicine in treating the patient. *Baiga* and *Gunia* are related to each other. *Baiga* is consulted when *Gunia* fails to treat certain disease. Both the positions are hereditary. Besides, there are other disease specialists found in the sample village such as (1) Bone setter; (2) *Gardi* (specialists in curing snakebite); (3) diseases specialists; (4) Dai (traditional birth attendant) (Table 1).

Table 1
Diseases Specialists from Sampled Villages

	Bone Setters		*Gardi*		*Disease Specialists*		
Village Name	*Male*	*Female*	*Male*	*Female*	*Male*	*Female*	*Birth Attendant*
Sunabeda	2		14	1	3		2
Koked	1		5		1	1	2
Gadbhata	1	1	7		1		1
Gadgada	1	1	6	2	2	1	1

In the sample villages 7 bone settlers were identified. They are specialized in curing bone fractures both of human and domestic animals. Their therapy is absolutely manifested by herbs. The technique and technologies developed is purely local.

Gardis are specialists in treating snake bite. A total of 35 *Gardi* were identified in the sample villages. All the Gardis interviewed have learnt this knowledge from a non-tribe. Once the case of snake bite is passed on to one *Gardi*, it is circulated among them. They immediately come to cure the patient. They bring *Kochila* (*Strychnos nuxvomica*) bark, *Patalgarud (Rauwalfia serpentine*) and *Akashgarud* (*Redermachera xylocapa*) fruits with them. They chant mantra by holding the patient in a sitting manner. Some of them paste the bark and fruits herbs separately and pour the juice, according to needs, on the nostril. They render their service with a great solidarity. They do not charge any fee. Interesting to say that they do not accept anything even little water or a *bidi* at patient home until the patient is cured completely.

There are 9 disease specialists found in the sample villages. Most of them have possessed knowledge on gynecological problem and its treatment. Of the total two were female who have extensive knowledge on the fertility and menstruation disorder. Among the male they have knowledge on abortion and sterilization. All the specialists cure the diseases by means of plant medicine.

Traditional birth attendants (Dai) are seen universally in all sample villages. She involves in spiritual as well as physical health care of mother and child. She helps the women in delivering child. She makes the new born baby bath. Immediately after delivery, she gives the boiled *Kulath* (Horse gram) to the woman believing it recovers blood that is lost during the delivery. Three birth attendants were interviewed to understand the technique, process, and their role in delivery; however, few more were available in the sample village. They could not explain what they exactly do in stead of taking care of the child and mother. All the Dai interviewed have learnt this knowledge through their mother-in-law. They render their services purely on voluntary basis. They family gives some grain, a saree and a coconut on or after purificatory ritual (*Hanichhia*).

SOCIO-ECONOMIC PROFILE OF THE HEALTH PROVIDERS

Table 2 shows the detail socio-economic profiles of the sampled health providers.

From the table it is found that out of 62 health functionaries, no health practitioner is aged less than 30 year. 25 (40.32%) were in the age group of 30-40 and remaining were above 40 years. Few women health practitioners were also found who work along with male practitioners. Only 14.52% of them are literate. All the health provides depend on forest produces for their livelihood. All of them practice slash and burning cultivation. Very few of them hold land *patta* and majority are landless with encroached land. Except 2 *Baigas* and 2 disease specialists all work with communitarian value. 27.42% of them have gained this knowledge from their father. Only *Gardis* that constitute 56.45% of sample gained the knowledge from a non-tribal. 3 (4.48%) have acquired it automatically.

As far their societal status is concerned they enjoy the special status and are highly respected. They not only provide health care but also important public functionaries in many socio-political institutions in the society. Disrespect them in any forms may results illness. It is also observed that when they visit any of the families for any purpose people offer them *bidi* and local liquor. At the time of family festivals such as marriage, it is expected that the head of the household personally invites them. They do not refuse anybody to handle any case even during night time. They are not expected to lens and fees in cash or kind of the service he renders. Family members of the patient recognize the traditional practitioner sooner or later. As the token of appreciation of their service, people offer them cloth, grain, and paddy.

GUNIA AND DIAGNOSIS PATTERNS

Gunia is medico-religious functionary of the Chuktia Bhunjia. 5 *Gunias* were identified in the sample villages. All the *Gunias*

Table 2
Socio-Economic Profile of the Health Practitioners

Health Providers	*Number Identified*	*Average Age*	*Sex*		*Primary Occupation*	*Education*	*Learned Methods*	*Average Years of Served*
			M	*F*				
Magico-religious healers	5	51.6	5	0	Agriculture	Illiterates	Father	15.8
Herbalist	8	49.4	7	2		Illiterates	Father	17.34
Bone Settlers	3	42.6	3	2	Agriculture	Illiterates	2 (Father)1 (Imitation)	18.17
Snake bite specialist	35	41.23	32	3	Agriculture	27 (Illiterates)8 (Literates)	Non-tribal Master	13.43
General Diseases Specialist	5	50.6	3	2	Agriculture	1 (Literate)4 (Illiterates)	2 (Father)3 (Experiment)	21.03
Birth attendants	6	43.7	0	6	Agriculture	Illiterates	Mother-in-Laws	22.53

were formally interviewed to know their knowledge on spirit affect and healing processes. They adopt the following methods in treating the patient attacked by evil spirits.

- When a person is affected by evil spirits his/her pulse become cold and the patient appear restless. His/her ways of talking is different from the normal individual. In some case when *Gunia* reaches to the patient house, the spirit becomes calm. After noticing the cause he immediately chants mantra inscribing the name of popular Gods and Goddesses simultaneously throwing un-boiled rice in the face of patient.
- To identify the spirit attacked the *Gunia* presses the little finger of the patient. The spirit immediately tells the motive of coming to his/her body. He orders the spirit to go out of the body. If the spirit reluctant to go, the *Gunia* drives away the *Masan* by some means like beating with broomstick, iron chain, making smoke by burning rubber, dried red chilies, etc. In complicated cases the gas of burnt dried chilies is forcefully given to the patient to drive the evil spirit away. Sometime he pours the juice extracted from *tulsi* (*Ocimum sanctum*) leaves and applies the kajal on patient' eyes to drives the spirit away. This medication causes burning sensation in the eyes and tears roll down the eyes of the patient relieving the spirit too.
- When the ancestral spirit attacks the *Gunia* finds out the cause and suggests the head of the family accordingly. In some case the spirit demands some rituals and sacrifice of hen or male goat. They most of the time appease the spirits by offering liquor and giving flowers of different colour.
- In case of sorcery or black magic, *Gunia* does not handle the cause lonely rather is assisted by other *Gunias* and *Diharis* (Shamans). They fix a date to throw the spirit away from the body. They prescribe to arrange black goat, black chicken, a mirror, kajal, comb, sindoor (vermilion), and different variety of

millets. During night the patient is asked to sit on the spot specially arranged for this purpose. They chant mantra, bid the drum and sing the song so that the patient automatically dance and tells the name of the spirit, his/her motive and the procedure to appease her. This process is known as *Kulanacha*. In the same night, they take the patient to a river stream or the jungle and tell him/her to go away from the patient body. They catch the evil spirit through mantra and keep in a *tani* (pottery). The *tani* is then buried followed by fixing four iron points around it and sacrifice and offering the materials suggested. This method is locally called *Talen*.

HERBALIST AND PATTERNS OF TREATMENT

As said earlier, *Baiga* is the herbalist in Chuktia Bhunjias society who administers herbal medicine to cure diseases caused by natural agents and bodily discomforts. However, his treatment method is endowed with certain norms and beliefs. He possesses enormous knowledge on the medicinal plants. The medicines prepared by the Baiga are the extract and mixture of the plants' root, bark and leaves (Table No. 3). When the Baiga unable to treat any diseases he suggest the patient to consult qualified doctor. So we find the close proximity among patient, Baiga and qualified doctor as found among the patient, *Gunia* and shaman as represented in figure below.

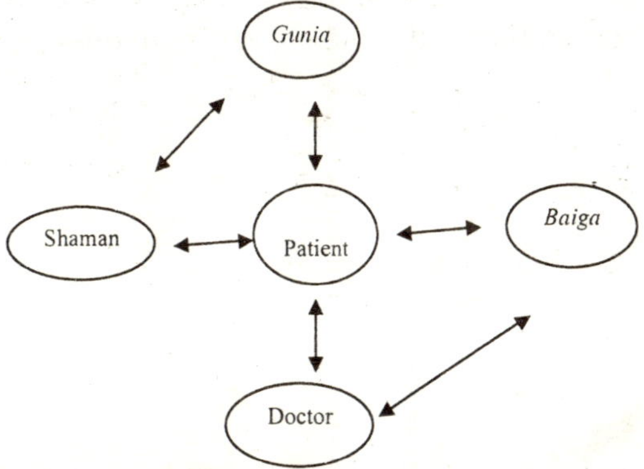

Figure 1: Relationship between Patient and Health Practitioners

Table 3
Medicinal Plant Used By Herbalists

Diseases/ Ailments	*Plants/Herbs Used*	*Part Used*	*Methods of Medicine Preparation*	*Application*	*Precaution*
Dental pain	Bankithoko (*Thespesia lampas*) Chitki (*Sida rhombifolia*) Ramdatum (*Smilex zeylanica*)	Whole parts of all the plants	The plant is first washed in cold water and is grinded in a stone. The paste is orally applied below the cheek and upper site of the mandible.	Most of the time herbalist suggest the patient to use the twig of these plants as tooth brush	
Eye redness	Jam (*Syzygium cumini*) Sihna (*Lagerstroemia parviflora*)	Leaf Leaf	Leaves are first washed and is grinded to extract juice	Juice is filtered into a new cloth and then poured into the eyes.	
Delivery expedition	Basanga (*Adhatoda vasica*) Tipiri (*Leonotis repetifolia*)	Root Leaf	Root is grinded with 7 black peppers Leaves are grinded to make paste	It is given to her to drink with water.	
Dog bite	Kukur miria (*Geodorum densiflorum*)	Bark and Root	Bark and root are grinded together finely	Paste is given to the patient twice a day before meal. The paste is also applied on the part affected.	This is also cured by mantra therapy where the poison is removed through steel plate.
Skin abscess	Boro (*Zizipus mouritina*) Dhub (*Cynodon Dactylon*) Mandar (*Hibiscus Chinensis*) Bansuli (*Gredia sapide*)	Leaf Grass Leaf Leaf	All the species are used for it, but separately. The paste made from all plant is considered beneficial. It is first washed in cold water and grinded in a stone to the paste.	The paste is orally applied on the affected part and a clean cloth is covered tightly.	

Contd.

Abdominal pain due to irregular menstruation	Batudi kanda (*Euliphia nude*)	Fruit	The raw fruit is grinded with 5 black peppers	The paste is given to the women twice a day for 7 days.	
Ear ache	Kuder (*Catatrophi gigantia*)	Bark	The bark is rubbed against a stone to extract juice	The juice is poured into the ear so as to get rid of it. Sometimes white pulp and come out from ear. They also cure it by applying medicine made from it.	
Excessive bleeding during mensturation	Raktabidar (*Christella semigagitata*)	Root	Root of the plant is first washed in cold water. Then either rubbed against a stone or grinded. The pulpy paste is then filtered.	Consumed at morning with cow milk.	Must consume after bath and should not cohabit during medication.
Avoid child birth	Binmulia (*Cusuita reflexia*) Brahmi (*Centalla asiatica*) *Vitex Penduncularis*	Root Bark Bark	Fresh root is first washed in water and grinded with 9 black peppers	Grinded paste is given to the women to consume at morning time.	Should not cohabit during this period.
Alti	Raw turmeric and neem	Leaf	Raw turmeric and neem leaf is grinded.	After the bath, the affected part is first itched with hand and the paste is orally applied on it.	Should applied after bath otherwise the medicine does not works out.
Migraine	Bhuikadam (*Sphaeran thus indicus*), Patalgarud (*Rauvolfia serpentine*); Kaikeyi (*Combretum nanum*)	Root Seeds Roots	Generally the first one is given as it is easily found. It is too cold. The root is grinded in a cord.	The paste is given to the patient before meals. The root paste mixed with cord is applied on the patient forehead.	

Contd.

Diabetes	Kalihari (*Gloriosa suberba*)	Root	Root and fruits are grinded to make the paste	The mixture paste is orally taken twice a day after meal.	Should not take sugar and honey
	Balaraj kanda (*Lannea acaulis*)	Fruit			
Menstrual disorder	Lal muter (*Caesalpinia salpan*)	Root	Fresh root of the plant is grinded with 7 black peppers	Grinded paste is given to the women to consume in empty stomach.	
	Sunderi (*Mallotus Philippenis*)	Seeds & Fruits	It is mixed and make paste		
Asthma	Basak (*Adhatoda Zeylanica*)	Leaf	—	The patient is suggested to consume the leaf in the form of smoke.	The medicines should be taken in full moon day.
	Menzati (*Lowsonia Inermis*)	Bark	The bark is grinded to extract juice		
Pitbemar (jaundice)	Bhuiamla (*Phyllanthus fraternus*)	Bark	All the three medicines are mixed together and is grinded to make paste.	The paste is given to the patient after meal. It is generally given during afternoon.	
	Dumer (*Ficus racemosa*)	Root			
	Menzati (*Lowsonia Inermis*)	Root			
Headache	Castor oil	Oil		The paste is applied on the forehead of the patient.	
	Amaltas (*Cassia fistula*)	Bark	The bark is grinded to make paste.		
	Keukanda (*Costus Speciosus*)	Tuber	The tuber is properly washed and grinded with cord. After crushing the keokada it is mixed with cord.		
Dysentery	Bhuamla (*Phyllanthus fraternus*)	Bark	The bark is finely grinded with 7 black peepers.	The paste is orally taken in empty stomach at morning.	
	Raktamandar (*Erythrina cariegate*)	Bark & Leafs	Equal proportion of bark and leaves are grinded.	The paste is orally given to the patient in empty stomach at morning.	

Contd.

Diarrhea	Bhuineem (*Andrographis peniculatus*)	Seeds	The cleaned seeds are grinded to make paste.	A tea spoon is given to the patient.	It is believed to be caused by supernatural so they first appease the malevolent spirits by offering liquor and sacrificing goats.
	Dalim (*Punica granatum*)	Fruits bark	The bark is crushed to make a paste	The paste is given to the patient in empty stomach	
	Kochla (*Strychnos nuxvomica*)	Bark	-do-		
	Lemon (*Citrus indica*)	Fruit	The juice is extracted and sometime mixed with salt.	-do-	
Burning	Dhup (*Shorea robustus*)	Resin	The white resin is finely grinded and is mixed with ghee.	It is applied on the affected part of the patient.	Patient should not take bath for some days.
Snake bite	Patalgarud (*Rouvolfia Serpentine*)	Fruit	The fruit is grinded to make paste and the paste is mixed with water	The mixture is then poured into the nostril of the patient.	This is purely cured by the mantra therapy with great taboo from the part of the specialists.

HOUSEHOLD THERAPY

The Chuktia Bhunjias also treat certain aliments themselves which have reported acquired by long term experiences and observation. They follow certain specific techniques in treating the ailments but always supported by plant species. Chicken pox is most important ailment cured by household therapy method. They belief it caused by Goddess Mata. The affected person is respected by everybody with the belief that it is bless of Goddess. Patient remaining untouched unless it is cured. It is cured by giving the gas of *Sal* (*Shorea robusta*). The head of the household put a little resin in fire put in a leaf cup made of *Palaş* (*Butea Monosperma*) or *Kurei* (*Holoptelea integrifolia*). He also simultaneously applies apply milk and liquor made of *Madhuca indica* flower. Another ailment cured in house is diarrhea to infant (*Kirum*). It is believed caused by increasing salt proportion in the body. It is cured by giving fruit juice of *Bhuineem* (*Andrographis paniculata*). They also treat abdominal pain in the following method: The patient is laid on a bed. An earthen lamp (*Bati*) is kept over the bally and the Bati is covered with an aluminum jug (*Gadu*). The *Gadu* pulls the skin and after one hour it automatically removes from the bally. This process is called *Upka*.

Similarly when an infant suffers from fever, the head of the household bring a *Barish kanda* (*Gloriosa superba*) particularly on Sunday. The tuber is grinded and put in a bucket of water. Then an iron that is fixed in plough tip is heated. The heated iron is place on the ground and the water bucket on the roof. The water is put on the head of the infant in such a way that it would also pour into the iron. It is said that the evaporated gas from the iron come to the infant and he/she gets cure. They also apply the root paste of the *Gloriosa superba* on the abdomen of the infant. It is also treated by orally massaging the root powder of *Arakh* (*Calatropis gigantean*) plant taken on full moon day. The juice of sacred basil is used for cough; however, few people tie worm salt beneath the abdomen. They apply the hot pulp of Bhelwa (*Semacarpus anacardium*) seeds to cure feet cracking. All the people are habituated of applying leave paste of neem (*Azadirachata indica*) and raw turmeric paste to cure scabies. Very few of them also apply oil extracted from *Karanja* (*Carissa carandas*) seeds. The Chuktia Bhunjia also believe that spider sometime urines in human ear due to which white pulp comes out from ear. They treat it by applying the gas of wax of *Madhuca indica*. They first put the wax in fire till it become reddish brown. It is then put in a jug of water so that gas comes out from it. The affected ear is immediately faced toward the container in such a way that the gas can enter into the ear. It is done three times till the pulp comes out completely. They also treat bleeding and ringworm by applying leaf paste of *Biskhapri* (*Tridax procumbens*) on the affected part.

PEOPLES' VIEW ON TRADITIONAL MEDICINE

From the study it was found that the Chuktia Bhunjias do not prefer qualified doctors rather *Gunia*, Baiga, and diseases specialists for treatment, however, a government hospital is located in Sunabeda village. Their society does not allow them to rely on qualified health specialists, particularly in women related diseases, which they conceive disrespect to their tradition and is considered modernization. It was found that the eyewitness, life experience, beliefs and social acceptability have made them to prefer their traditional medicine men. Most of the diseases are treated on Sunday. There are also certain beliefs on the part of the patient, i.e. they belief that herbal medicines do not work if taken without bathing. All the Baiga interviewed said that easy availability of medicinal plants and faiths of the people have made their service sustainable. The non-tribals from the plain areas also consult them for treatment. Hospital record shows that very few Chuktia Bhunjia depended on it. Those who have opted were only for ailments like cough, sneezing, and affect on body. It was also reported that the clearing of the forest patch by the forest department has gradually threaten the medicinal plants and herbs. The forest department in these days restricting them to collect medicinal plants because the sanctuary has now been declared as protected areas and tiger project. Lack of communication facilities, zigzag roads and the expensive of modern medicine force them to rely on traditional health providers; however young masses are ready to accept the modern system of medicine. The intervention of the non-tribal medicine men from plain areas has also threatened the very existence of medicinal plants.

CONCLUSION

It was found that the health functionaries play very crucial role in the treatment of diseases in this society. They always believe on supernatural forces for any kind of diseases and behave the patient accordingly. They follow various techniques in treating the patients. Their health practice is manifested by culture, traditional, customary norms and more by local forest. There are certain norms followed for the treatment of diseases as well as collection of medicinal plants for this purpose. They use very simple technologies for the collection of medicinal plants most of which are plucked in hands. The free collection of medicinal plants and reciprocal treatment process of the health practitioners have made their practice cost-effective. Besides, laymen also recognize the medicinal plants, though they lack medication process. Given the positivity of traditional medical practice by this community care must be taken to conserve the medicinal plants. It will help them retaining their traditional practice. Outsiders must be restricted from entering the Sunabeda Wildlife Sanctuary who are found responsible for the commercial exploitation of the medicinal plants. Further given the declining traditional knowledge due to certain factors care must be taken to preserve it. It will help them surviving sustainably.

REFERENCES

Brochure of Sunabeda Wildlife Sanctuary (2001), Forest Department, Government of Orissa.

Chaudhuri, B.D. (1986), "Tribal Health: Socio-cultural Dimension", New Delhi: Inter India Publication.

Chaudhuri, B.D. (1990), "Cultural and Environmental Dimension on Health", New Delhi: Inter India Publication.

Clements, F.E. (1932), "Primitive Concept of Disease", *American Archaeology and Ethnology*, Vol. 32, pp. 185-252.

Dube, S.C. (1950), "Inter-relation of Tribes", *Man in India*, Vol. 30, No. 2 & 3, p.73.

Dube, S.C. (1948), "The Arrow Marriage", *The Eastern Anthropologist*, Vol. II, No. 1, pp. 22-26.

Dubey, K.C. (1950), "Possible Origin of Bhunjia and Other Ethnic Relationship: A New Hypothesis", *The Eastern Anthropologist*, Vol. IV, No. 1, pp. 49-58.

Dubey, K.C. (1963), "A study of Bhunjia settlement", *Vanyajati*, July, pp.132-135.

Foster, G.M. (1978), "Medical Anthropology", New York: John Willey and Sons.

Hughes, C.C. (1968), Ethnomedicine. In David Sills (ed.) *International Encyclopedia of Social Sciences*. London: McMillan.

Mishra, S.K. (2002), "Chuktia Bhunjia Sankriti O' Lokasahitya" (*Oriya*), Bhubaneswar: S.T. & S.C. Research and Training Institute.

Pattanaik, et.al. (1984), "Life in Sunabeda Plateau: The Anthropology of Bhunjia of Kalahandi, Orissa", Bhubaneswar: ST, SC Research and Training Institute.

Russel, R.V and R.B. Hiralal (1916), *Tribe and Caste of the Central Provinces of India*. London: McMillan.

19 Wood Craft and Traditional Wisdom among the Nicobarese of Katchal Island

K.M. Sinha Roy

INTRODUCTION

India is the motherland of numerous communities, who have always been identified with their traditional wisdom to signify their rich cultural heritage. The craft is one of such important media through which one's own traditional wisdom can be reflected to the outside world. In reality, craft has always remained apart of human activities of both technical and manual, concerned with one's feelings, emotions and expressions. And craft can never be isolated from art.

The craft originally derives from an Anglo-Saxon word 'craft' i.e., *strength, skill*. In second sense 'craft' is synonymous with *guild,* which is applied to occupational association. Anthropologist prefers to signify craft as 'technology' to refer to the process of manufacture and 'material culture' for the artifacts related with the crafts (International Encyclopedia of the Social Sciences; vol. 3; 1968). Eminent scholars opined that 'craft' is an art or skill or manual art (Bark; 1978; 34), man's creation (Chottopadhaya; 1975) and technical activities (Crowley; 1968), which always mingled with creator's feelings, emotions and expressions. On the other hand it can be said that the craft is an integral component for regulating one's own social function, economic and religious performances.

There are three distinct types of crafts which have evolved through the years. *Firstly,* the folk crafts objects, which are created by the people for their personal use. *Secondly,* which have been developed around religious centers. *Thirdly,* the commercial craft, which are made in specialized, centers and for which a complete mastery over the technique is necessary (Dhamija; 1977). It is truism to say that the growth of the crafts in society was the sign of the cultivation of sensitivity and the stirring and mellowing of humanism and the performance of any kind craft essentially need to be a person, who have a knack or aptitude and acknowledge skill to his performance. Craftsmanship obviously emerged and unfolded itself in the peace and refulgence of the countryside, where the community living in close intimacy with nature, with its many splintered mien and in tune with its changing rhythm of the day, of the night, the varying seasons and the life cycles, evolved a culture of its own in harmony with environment.

Here an attempt has been made to analyze the superb quality of Nicobarese traditional wisdom, which very much is reflected through their crafts objects-canoe (hori). How their social and religious organization mingles with the craft have been brought into light..

Material and Method: The fieldwork of the present study was carried out in the four villages namely, Kapanga, Jhoola, West Bay, Ponda of Katchal island of Nicobar district (Table 1). Katchal belongs to central Nicobar group of islands, which is situated in the South-West of Kamorta, Nancowry, Teressa, Bompoka between 7° 53' and 8° 7' north latitude and 93° 30' east longitude respectively. It lies under the Nan-cowry tahsil. The area of this island is about 62 square miles and reaches a height of 835 feet on the eastern side, which consists of hills of ecatereous sandstone and marble slate formed in deep seas during the tertiary period. The total island is covered with dense tropical rain evergreen forest. The villages are situated near the seashore for easy accessibility. Katchal is one of the developed islands with many amenities laid on. It has good soil and good landing facilities that offer tremendous scope for growth and development of plantation.

Number of Individuals

Village	*Number of Households*	*Male*	*Female*	*Total*
Kapanga	36	120	96	216
Jhoola	27	82	63	145
West Bay	35	107	90	197
Ponda	40	135	120	255
Total	134	813	444	369

People: Katchal island is inhabited by multi-ethnic groups, like the Taamil, the Ranchiwalas and the Nicobarese, who are the most dominant group considering the number of 2491 souls out of a total population of 5072(census 1991).The Nicobarese settlement is spread over from East Bay to upper Katchal. The names of such settlements are like the following (i) East Bay,(ii) Kapanga, (iii) Jhoola,(iv) Jhansin, (v) Lakapah (vi) Chongipoh, (vii) West Bay (viii) Katahua, (ix) Chana Lakul. (x) Kuimikion, (xi) Ponda, (xii) Intuha, (xiii) Cape Albany, (xiv) Kilotha, (xv) Upper Katchal.

Their main occupation is rising of coconut, arecanut and rearing of pigs. The islanders have kept the plantation as their main activities while these have retained cultivation as their secondary activities. Cultivation in this island is limited to rice, tapioca, sugarcane, cane etc. They believe that land is sacred as because it is protected by their ancestral spirits, which also keep an eye on the gardening activities of the people. Most of the Nicobarese families depend on horticulture. Due to the impact of modernization some of them involve in white-collar jobs as alternative occupation.

The Nicobarese of Katchall island are following both types of religion i.e., animism as well as Christianity. It is observed that almost every one of them has a belief that a kind of spirit exists in natural objects like forests, hills, mountain and sea. In order to appease these spirits, they initiate certain process by means of wood curving, a mode of craftsmanship, which is governed by the forces of nature and the unknown spiritual world. Principally, the Nicobarese employ their traditional wisdom of craftsmanship in the field of canoe making, which is related to transport, economy and recreation.

Methods: The data are collected through observation, informal interview with the individuals and group discussion. The various phases involved in procuring the raw materials and the corresponding craft techniques are documented through sketches. In order to elucidate the richness of their craft, the perceptions of local people have been considered.

History of Origin and Development of the Craft: It has already been mentioned in earlier text that the Nicobarese have a close affiliation with the nature, the making of dugout canoe is observed certain rites and rituals, which is governed by their traditional beliefs and practices. Technologies and skills for canoe making are evolved to suit the local demands and pattern which never disturb the harmonious balance of nature. How the techniques of canoe making first evolved in their mind is a matter of study. But as per the age-old view, the techniques of canoe making had been borrowed from the traders of China, Burma, Ceylon and Malaysia. According to their opinion, in earlier period, there was a trade relationship between the foreign traders (China, Burma, Ceylon and Malaysia) and the Nicobarese inhabiting in Car Nicobar and Nancowry island, and on the basis of which the Nicobarese were employed as labourers there (Sahay, 1976: XIX: II). During that time, the Nicobarese were required to help for repairing their boats and acquired and developed the skill in the techniques of canoe making. In course of those activities the Nicobarese realized how the vessel could be of beneficial use towards their survival. They started to employ their acquired techniques for making of canoes. Thus the craftsmanship of canoe making became an important activity to the Nicobarese people.

From the above mentioned illustration, it is clearly revealed that the principal variety of craftsmanship of wood carving in the Nicobarese society is primarily based on their necessity. It has also been observed that when the Nicobarese are really in need of such kind of craft, they adopt the teacher which is neither of their regular practice nor used by the members of every household. Dugout outrigger canoe is one of such important craft, which is closely associated with their socio-economic life. Previously, it was a practice that at the time of canoe carpentry, the Nicobarese used to invite other Nicobarese brethren from Chowra, Teressa and even from Car Nicobar, who have expertise in canoe craftsmanship. It was conducted through bartering of some consumable and non-consumable items (Pigs. Yams, Tapioca, Cloth Timber etc). But nowadays, this kind of practice does not retain its value. It is also important to mention here that at present the Nicobarese of every island have some knowledge of canoe carpentry.

Findings: The tradition of wood carving in India existed in ancient times. The early stone-curved temples, which have survived the ravages of time, bear witness to the influence of wooden structures on which they were based. Each region developed its own style of wooden structures and carvings. Because wood seems to be a favorite material of the people and were influenced by the local tradition, its availability and suitability of use. In relation to every folk tradition, wood carving always finds an expression for manufacturing the ritual objects. Times are closely associated with the life of the people.

The Nicobarese of Katchall island also has the tradition of manufacturing wooden crafts. Among them, the dugout outrigger canoe (*hori*) is most important one. An attempt has been made to correlate the canoe with their ways of life. Traditional calendar is another wooden craft, which has also been affiliated with the movement of their outrigger canoe in one hand and disclose the traditional wisdom on the other.

TECHNIQUE OF PREPARATION OF THE CRAFT

Before giving into the further details of canoe preparation and its technique, it is worth to mention here that there are three prevalent types of canoe in Katchal Island.

1. Chowra model *Reviso.*
2. Kendal model *Regi-long.*
3. Katchal model *Reuoay.*

Generally, the Chowra and Kondul model canoe are large in size; approximately the length of it is 10-12 metre long and can accommodate 15 or more persons at a time in the open sea. Katchal model of canoe is comparatively smaller than that and can accommodate five to six persons with commodities. Women and children are not involved in this job. The men are principally engaged in the craft of canoe manufacturing.

TECHNIQUES OF CANOE MAKING

1. The middle point of the canoe, irrespective of the size, is taken to start with measuring the circumference at it and then divided into half. This measurement gives a V-shaped formation to the log, where the walls of the canoe remain one inch in thickness.
2. Then the total length from the base of the bow to that of the stem is divided into three equal parts for fixing the two booms where the parts correspond with each other. The length of the boom is the length of one part of the three equal parts. the two booms are inserted through three points and affixed by means of bamboo or cane strips. The knots are tied in a criss-cross manner.
3. The float is then fixed at the outer ends of the boom to the spars, which are the criss-cross apparatus and affixed to the boom ends to suspend above the water level on which the canoe remains floated.
4. The float tapers to a pointed end in the front side, while it is thicker and broader at the rear.
5. The normal immersion depth of the empty canoe in the water is equivalent to the height between the point where the stanchion meets the spars and the vertical point below it on the float.

All these five steps are the best examples of their traditional wisdom in the craftsmanship. According to them, these five techniques have been learnt from their forefathers. For making a canoe, firstly, a suitable tree is selected and felled. Thereafter its branches are separated from the tree trunk. This activity is locally known as *Infant*. Then the appropriate length of log is cut as per their requirement. The system of traditional way of measurement is locally termed as *Tanaka*. It is a customary rule that the smallest size of canoe will be of two *Tanaka,* locally known as *Inlay*. The medium sized canoe will be of four *Tanaka* termed as *Insane* and the big size canoe will be of eight *Tanaka*, locally known as *Infuana*.

Preparation of Canoe: At the beginning of canoe carpentry, a number of chicken and piglings are being sacrificed in the jungle and the oozing out blood is spread over the trunk. Adult members of the immediate household and the clan members actively participate on this occasion, which is marked by merry making in the form of sacrificing chicken and piglings. At the time of making canoe, first of all, they cut the tree trunk horizontally as if an even and smooth flat surface has come out. In the next step, they start to chisel the wooden particles from one side of the trunk to the other side, with the help of axe and chisel. This system is locally known as *Uhalla*. After completion of *Uhalla*, the measurement of the inner side of the canoe is taken. Here also they strictly follow the traditional rule of measurement.

Their main occupation is rising of coconut and arecanut and rearing of pigs. The islanders have kept the plantation as their main activities, which they have retained for cultivation as their secondary activities. Cultivation in this island is limited to rice, tapioca, sugarcane, cane etc. They believe that land is sacred as because it is protected by their ancestral spirits, which also keep an eye on the gardening activities of the people. Most of the Nicobarese families depend on horticulture. Due to the impact of modernization some of them involve in white-collar jobs as alternative occupation.

The Nicobarese of Katchal island are following both types of religion i.e., animism as well as Christianity. It is observed that almost every one of them has a belief that a kind of spirit exists in natural objects, like forests, hills, mountains and sea. In order to appease these spirits, they initiate certain process by means of wood curving, a mode of craftsmanship, which is governed by the forces of nature and the unknown spiritual world. Principally, the Nicobarese employ their traditional wisdom of craftsmanship in the field of canoe making, which is related to transport, economy and recreation.

(a) Total length of the log is divided into half, which will be the enter point of the canoe.

(b) They measure the total diameter of the log from outside which is divided into half. Now the half of the length of the diameter is made into a 'V' shape at both ends of the inside of the canoe after keeping one inch thickness at the side walls of the canoe. Now, about 6 inches are kept apart in both ends. After which the 'V' shaped pattern is inserted at both ends. The total interior portion is then scoped out with the help of axe, chisel and the outer surface is given a convex shape. They are keeping in mind that 1-inch thickness should always be retained in the sidewalls of the canoe. This is the rough shape that they give to the canoe at the beginning of the canoe construction. The whole system is locally recognized as *Saniva.*

(c) In the next step, the total length of the semi-prepared log is divided into three equal parts.

The measurement of each part is taken to measure each boom, which is to be fixed to one side of the canoe. This activity is called *Hafuknga Muah.* Now the two inner points divide the canoe into three equal segments. Two booms (long, thin pole) are to be fixed through round holes, which are made on the sidewalls of the canoe. This activity is locally called *Iffash.*

The performance of iffash is followed by two more rituals, before taking out the canoe from the jungle to their settlement. While arranging transportation of canoe to their settlement, they invite their friend and relatives to join them in the jungle. A chicken is then killed and its blood is smeared on the right arms of those who actively take part in bringing the canoe out of the jungle. The chief craftsman of the canoe is then garlanded with a cut-off-leg of a chicken in order to establish his supremacy. After that the chicken is used for preparation of a good dish.

The remnants of grooved out wooden chips are strewn and heaped on which water of green coconut is sprinkled with the idea that the said heap is scattered by the wild boars.

When the canoe is brought to the settlement, it is first kept inside the *nyihupol,* the community hall for observing animistic rituals. In the *nyihupol* they prepared a model of the canoe with the help of coconut phony (cover of the coconut flower). Then they prepare an item of food, which is a mixture of ground rice and grated coconut flesh, *hinleuon*. This process is known as *hinleuon*. Then the outer portion of the canoe is decorated by engraving some designs and two separate wooden structures are fitted to two ends. This process is known as *iseuas*.

After that, a portion of the canoe is grooved by inserting nails in order to gauge the thickness of the wood used for canoe. This is also done to bring a uniform thickness of the canoe. The holes are then closed with small pieces of wood so that there is no leakage in the canoe. This is known as *taniva*. After *taniva*, the inside as well as the outside of the canoe is fumed by means of torch made of dry coconut leaves, which expands the canoe and gives it a black colour. Then the inner side is smeared with the water and flesh of green coconut which is named as *suny*.

Finally all accessories like sails, outrigger etc. are fitted in the canoe in a traditional way. The front of the outrigger is generally thin and the back portion is comparatively thick. This is done for free and smooth voyage. At the time of launching into the sea, there is a ceremony to appease the devil or the evil spirit by sacrificing a piglet or a chicken. The most interesting part of the technique of canoe making is that the canoe is simply a dugout type where no keel is present. This helps the canoe to sail easily with the wind.

COMPONENTS OF THE CANOE

Boya (Hintaha): It is made of a kind of soft wooden log, which is used as an outrigger for the balancing the dugout canoe.

Paddle (*Kayal*): *Kayal* is made of a plain piece of wood. It is generally 3 feet long and 6 inches in breadth. It has a shaft with double blades. Sometime it is found in big size. It is manipulated by hand only. The same *Kayal* is also used for steering the canoe. It can be switched from side to side as per the convenience of the sailors for propelling the canoe.

Sail (Hinteha): The sail is triangular in shape made of cloth, which is sewn together. It is attached to the mast by a rope, which is further fixed as to adjust the sail at a particular angle for sailing, when so required. This way they insert the movable spore to manipulate the sail together with all knots and paraphernalia for fixing it.

Tinyial: Adjacent to the side wall of the canoe a plank is to be fitted vertically from the outer side from bow to stern, on both the sides of the canoe. This may even be made by a thin piece of wood, and is meant to keep the waters away from splashing into the canoe.

TOOL AND IMPLEMENTS OF CANOE CARPENTRY

Inluny: It is an iron axe having an iron head with tapering sharpen working end in one side. A wooden or bamboo shaft is inserted through the neck of the iron head. The Nicobarese use it to cut the tree and give it a desirable shape for canoe making.

Kinleuoh: It is a wooden implement with a sharp pointed iron head, which is inserted into a wooden shaft head by means of a protruding iron pin, at a right angle to the wooden shaft. Normally it is used for chopping.

Tininich: It consists of a sharp pointed iron head slightly bent in shape. The iron head is inserted into a wooden shaft by a protruding iron piece in the middle of the iron head.

Saneas: Saneas has a curved pointed iron pin for owing design to the canoe. The working head is socketed to a wooden stick.

Hinleuon: It consists of an iron plate. It is generally used for separating the wood and shaping the sides of the canoe walls for to a smooth finish.

Sanuk: It is a particular portion of a tree branch having an angular shape. On its head, an iron blade is attached and used for cutting, chieselling of wood for various purposes.

Socio-Religious Belief and the Crafts: During the process of preparation of their crafts, the Nicobarese observe certain beliefs and rituals. This highlights their traditional wisdom in one hand and gets rid of evil spirits on the other.

Hahumsicaich: This particular ritual is related to canoe building. This ritual is celebrated just prior to the initiation of canoe manufacturing. The chicken or piglets are sacrificed and the blood is poured over the particular tree trunk. Leaves from different plants having cultural significance, are tied around the trunk of the tree to be cut. Then the evil spirit is appeased by sacrificing chicken and piglets, which are then roasted over the fire and eaten by the participants.

Moot: It is a ritual initiated when a portion of the top of particular tree trunk is sliced out, and a wooden pole is inserted at the centre of it by hammering it into the raw wood. On the top of the pole green coconut, coconut leaves are tied; chickens and pigs are sacrificed. The chickens and pigs are kept with their blood. This is done with the concept that the tree trunk, and subsequently the 'canoe' do not develop any crack and also to ward away evil eye.

Hanvich-Nyih: After completion of the canoe preparation, a ceremony, locally known as *hanyich-nyih* is performed in front of the canoe owner's house. Here the canoe is decorated with coconut leaves, coloured cloths and tender coconuts. Every family member participates in the function. The owner of the canoe sacrifices one or two pigs. The pigs' blood is mixed with coconut paste and is then smeared on the canoe, particularly on the decorated parts. The family members smear the remaining part of that mixture over their bodies. Thereafter, the pigs are roasted and every members of the family eats a piece of it. A piece of pork is also tied to the canoe. Here is a belief prevails that the evil spirit would be appeased with his share and would not commit nuisance during their voyage. The people believe that this ceremony would help them to have a safe voyage.

CRAFTS AND RELATED TABOOS

During the course of canoe carpentry, the people follow some taboos for the betterment of the crafts as well as for their society.

1. *Ungfang:* The choiceable tree for the canoe preparation is cut during the dark quarter nights and not otherwise. As it is believed that during that period, if

any tree is cut, that would not be infested with insect. This system is known as *ungfang*.

2. *Chich:* When a wife is pregnant, any kind of participation of her husband in any social or constructional activity in relation to the canoe carpentry is tabooed. This period is extended upto first three months of his wife's pregnancy.
3. *Hanikahayoa:* Consumption of any kind of food or green coconut and peeling off the coir from the coconut is tabooed before the departure for fishing. Only the green coconuts can be taken in the canoe. There is a belief that if it is not done properly, there will be a poor catch of fish. This system is locally known as *hanikahayoa*.

HINROVO KAHE (TRADITIONAL CALENDAR)

The Nicobarese of the Katchal Island use their traditional calendar (Fig.1) consisting of seasonal variations, weather conditions and knowledge of the sea for fishing, transportation and other daily activities. The upper part of the calendar reflects seasonal variation and the lower part indicates condition of the sea on the basis of tide, current, wave etc.

The first part indicates that there are four seasons in a year;

Months	Season	Characteristics
May June July	*Sumhav*	a) West wind b) Heavy rain c) Very bad weather for fishing and journey
August September October	*Ilui*	a) South wind b) Heavy rain c) Not good for journey d) Fishing activities mainly in daytime
November December	*Foul*	a) East ward wind b) sometimes rainy weather bad. This weather is not suitable for fishing and transportation or undertaking a journey and hence these activities are generally avoided during this spell.
February March	*Kuikaba*	a) Northward wind. b) Very good weather for fishing, journeys and other activities.

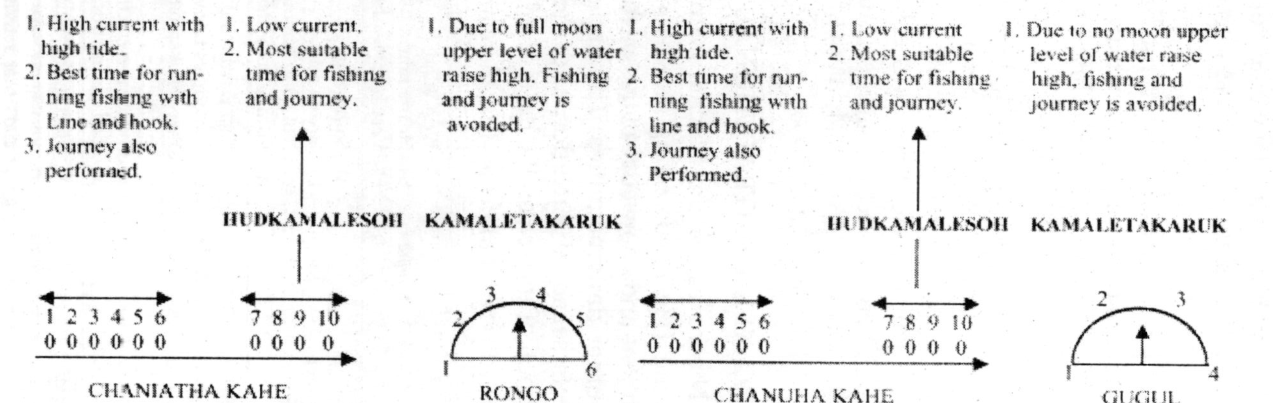

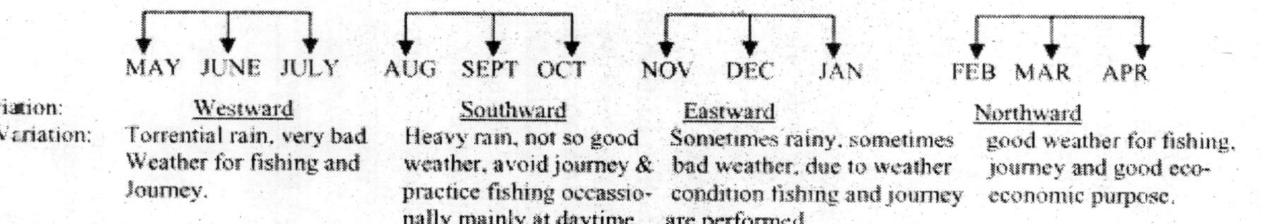

Figure 1: Traditional Calendar : Nicobarese of Katchal
HINRÖVÖ KAHE

The Nicobarese have their own way of dividing a calendar month. This is primarily based on the full moon and no moon periods. Their fishing and journey are directly related to these phases.

They broadly divide a 30 days calendar into two phases. The first is the 16 days duration towards full moon (*karuk*) and the next 14 days towards no moon (*gugal*). *Kåruk* is further divided into *Chaniatha kahe* of 10 days duration and *Kamletakaruk* of next 6 days.

The first six days of *Chaniatha kahe*, according to the Nicobarese, is not safe for mid water fishing and journey because of high tide and high current of the sea water. They take part in line and hook fishing and perform journey within the village only during this phase.

The next four days (*Hudkamalesoh*) is best suited for fishing and journey because of the low current in the sea water whilst it remains calm.

The last six days of *Karuk* (*Kamaletakaruk*) is the period when the pull of the full moon is strongest, the water level rises. Fishing and journey is usually avoided in this phase.

The *Gugal* period is also divided into *Chanuhakahe* (the first 10 days) and *Kamaletakaruk* (the next 6 days). The nature and criteria of these division are similar to the *karuk* period.

A small wooden pegis usually put on the hole of the calendar, which indicates the particular month of the year and particular day of the month.

The Nicobarese of Katchal island have a few folk songs which are sung in connection with the movements of their canoe.

KANASO UNG YNONG NYI

Harou	kayal	hi	lakhelo	kayingo
Chi- ot	kayalo	men	ngin	cho ook
Hinlo	nguat	ung	yiong	choh

"Quick! Quick! Give out the oars for fishing soon we have to go".

Free Translation

We don't have oars we tell you so. start the canoe with coconuts green, for soon to fish we have to oar. We will start right on to row when the tide goes low.

Kum	ching	kona	kui	ngen	on	no	ye	u	i	
N	o	tong	to	ngen	no	y e u	I	ka	an	nee
Han	to	ung	yango	ngin	on	roho				
Chit	oo	no	nen	cho	tong	to	ngen	to	teong-on	

Free Translation

Choose out the best tree and locate the fishing lane. Reach the place and say ye so men. The canoe members ask whether they have reached the place. The tree's there, we surmise we have, but the name of the tree we cannot trace.

Mat	fot	chu	kon	sayeuh	no	snatore		
Oiy	lum	nit	kan	chuno	yang	supefas		
E	yap	cho	tit	loi	chuno	lap	yon	he

Free Translation

The day or time when those men will return.
There will be joy at home by turns.
We will be aware, will go with care, and safety earn.

Kasi	saningo	me	t e r o n		kaneh
K o h e m e		yo	pusa	rema	
J o h e m e		pasio	pore	ureh	u r e h

Free Translation

Hi, let's go, let's go fast and hurrying.
The time ripe for betting, we'll go betting.
We must be first; our canoe should first be reaching.

The wooden craft, canoe (*hori*), principally attached with their society at large. In every sphere of life from economic pursuit, recreation, canoe plays a vital role. The way of making the wooden craft, canoe, always reflects their traditional knowledge, which is mingled with their indigenous belief and practice as a whole.

Due to the immense influence of Christianity the pattern of social life of the Nicobarese has been changed over the years. But even then, in some aspects of their social life, traditional practices dominate the recent ones. The wooden craft, canoe, and its craftsmanship is based on traditional wisdom. It is observed that though modern technology influence their society in one hand but the traditional techniques still exist in their society on the other.

REFERENCES

Adair, John (1944), *The Navajo and Pueblo Silversmiths*; Norman; University of Oklahoma Press.

Bark, W.D. (1978), *Primitive Art & Crafts*; New Work; University of California Press.

Bunzel, Ruth. L. (1929), *The Pueblo Potter: A Study of Creative Imagination in Primitive Art*; New York; Columbia University Press.

20 Island Ecology, Society and Dynamics of Resource Utilization: A Case of the Nicrobarese Society of Katchal

Umesh Kumar and Samir Biswas

INTRODUCTION

Islands are unique ecosystems of the world because of their well-defined boundary and broad resource base both terrestrial and aquatic. The insularity of the islands, typical resource and interface between land and sea make islands suitable for ecological studies. The islanders have the advantage of utilizing resources of the islands as well as that of the adjoining sea. Human survival in the islands depends not only on what type and quantity of natural resources are available there but also on the way these resources are used. Therefore, human adaptation to the island environment has peculiar form and processes. The Nicobarese of Katchal have adapted themselves to the island environment in a manner where social organization and religion are outgrowth of the practical system for making a living, rather than their cause. Thus a close connection can be drawn between the ownership and management of resources and social organization in the Nicobarese society.

AREA AND PEOPLE

The Andaman and Nicobar archipelago is like a chain of pearls in the Bay of Bengal. There are as many as 319 islands in the form of more or less an arch and have an area of about 8293 sq.km. spread over a length of 700 km. The islands are situated between 6° and 10° N latitudes and 92° and 94° E longitudes in the Bay of Bengal. The 10° channel with a uniform depth of 400 fathoms and an approximate width of 128 km separates the Andaman group of islands from the Nicobar. There are altogether 19 islands in the Nicobar Archipelago out of which only 12 are inhabited. The inhabited islands can be divided into three groups viz. (1) northern group consisting of only Car Nicobar island (2) central group consisting of Chowra, Terresa, Bompuka, Camorta, Nancowry, Trinket and Katchal and (3) southern group consisting of Little Nicobar, Pulomilo, Kondul and Great Nicobar. Except in the Great Nicobar where the Shompen tribe of Mongoloid stock and a few ex-army personnel are living, in all the other islands the main population is Nicobarese. The Katchal Island is situated in the south-east side of Kamorta, Nancowry and Bompoka islands between 7°53′ and 8°7′ N latitudes and 98°18′ and 98°30′ E longitudes. The total area of the island is about 62 sq.km. and comes under Nancowry tehsil.

The present study was carried out before tsunami in the year 2000. Katchal was one of the worst effected islands of Andaman and Nicobar archipelago. There were altogether 24 villages in the Katchal of which twenty villages were uni-ethnic and four were multi-ethnic. In the aftermath of tsunami which struck the Andaman and Nicobar Islands on 26th December 2004, there exist now only four villages. They are namely Slow Tegree (uni-ethnic), Oil Palm (uni-ethnic), Mildera (multi-ethnic) and Beach Dera (multi-ethnic). Also the sea water has advanced over a large area in the west Katchal. The total population of the Nicobarese before tsunami was 5321 (Census, 2001), out of which 345 lives were lost and 4310 were missing in the aftermath of tsunami. (Sinha Roy & Datta Chaudhuri, 2007).

Climate:- The island has a semi-equatorial climate. Two monsoons pass over the Katchal in a regular annual cycle. Taking these and the spells intervening them five seasonal phases can be distinguished, namely,

- the south-west monsoon, from June to September
- period of transition, in October.
- the northeast monsoon, from November to January.
- period of dull in February and March and
- the warm season of April and May.

The southwest monsoon brings heavy and extensive rain that facilitates planting of food crops. The northeast monsoon is comparatively week but rain during this period helps in extending horticulture activities beyond wet days. The average rainfall in the island during the year is approximately 260 cm. One finds calm and pleasant weather only from January to April. The climate is hot and humid with the maximum temperature between 30° Celsius and 33° Celsius with an approximate humidity of 80 percent.

Flora and Fauna:- The tropical climate and fertile soil have favoured luxuriant growth of vegetation. The natural flora in the island consists of mangrove forest, pandanus, casurina, silk cotton, cane creeper, fish poison tree (*kinyaya*), neem, bamboo thickets etc. Besides, due to a long history of outside contacts many plants have been introduced in the Island. These are mainly coconut, areca, banana, jackfruit, mango papaya, pineapple, yam, tapioca, lemon etc. Generally the islanders get all the timbers they need from their own groves and forest. Where there is paucity of such resources their requirement is met through inter-island trade. The avian and faunal life of Nicobar group of islands is not exotic. Among them are wild pigeons, python, green snakes, imperial pigeons, pigs, dogs, oxes, cats, rats, poultry birds, turtles, land crabs, sea cucumber, variety of fish etc.

People:- The Nicobarese is the generic name for indigenous people of Nicobar Islands. The term seems to be derived from the name of these islands which the Nicobarese as *takasstto*.. The island community inhabiting different islands of nicobar identify themselves by different terms such as Tarik (native of Car-Nicobar), Som-poi (native of Chowra), Som—Tehiong (people of Teressa), Som-Payuh (inhabitant of Katchal), Som-

Onhet (native of Nancowry), and Som-Long (inhabitant of Great Nicobar). Racially there are no differences among them. Mathur writing about the physical characteristics of the Nicobarese says that the people have in general Mongoloid features (1967: 42). E.H.Man (1889: 367) has emphasized the racial affinity between the Nicobaries and the Indo–Chinese. Grierson writing about the Nicobarese language says that Nicobarese also belong to Khmer branch Austro-Asiatic sub family that seems to form a connecting link between the Munda languages and Mon. (reprint 1967:32,33). Each island constitutes a social system and the interaction amongst its population is direct and face-to-face. Everyone knows every other. Here interaction means cooperation (Hillery, 1968:34). In the island cooperation between and amongst families is not on the basis of individual settlements but on an entire island basis. Familial cooperation between and amongst families of the island during the life cycle as well as in economic activity is the *sin qua non* of the Nicobarese community of Katchal.

Occupation:- The basic occupation of the Nicobarese is horticulture and chiefly consists of raising plantation of coconut, areca nut, yam and other vegetables and fruits, making copra and fishing. The main stay of their economy is coconut followed by piggery. Besides these, when necessary they also make or repair fishing canoes, and make articles of handicraft such as mats and baskets. Of late owing to spread of education, many Katchal islanders are in service and holding jobs in both public and private sectors.

RESOURCE MANAGEMENT AND SOCIO-POLITICAL SYSTEM AND RELIGION

The literal meaning of resources management is the use of resources in a manner through which one meets his needs without disturbing the recuperative rate of resources. The islanders of Katchal are successfully doing it. In the Nicobarese society of Katchal the resource management is achieved through the island's social structure, economic organization, political system and religion.

Social Structure

Nicobarese society of Katchal is a well-organized entity. Every inhabitant of the island has a strong attachment with the village of birth. Each islander who traces their descent from a common ancestor belongs to a descent group which is known as *ramage* in northern group and *kamunchiase* in central group. The *kamunchiase (ramage)* is a six level generation group related through consanguinity. The *kamunchiase* is exogamous in nature. After the marriage, either husband goes to live with her wife or wife joins his husband's *kamunchiase*. Through negotiation it is decided who will join whose family after marriage because leaving one's *kamunchiase* and joining another *kamunchiase* on account of marriage is considered to be depletion in the number of working hands. Both *kamunchiase* wants an increase in the number of working hands. As a logical corollary to it, when the husband joins the *kamunchiase* of his wife, his position is inferior to that of her wife in the *kamunchiase* and vice versa. The *kamunchiase* consists of a number of agnatic kin groups called *tu-het* in northern group and *nitakaru* in central group of islands. In other words, the *kamunchiase* usually consists of more than one household. A lesser group has a separate *nitakaru (tu-het)* but the land, plantation and gardens are generally not separated.

The resources of the island are controlled and supervised by the *kamunchiase.* In the social structure of the Nicobarese of Katchal island the individual can not accumulate and usurp any property or produce of garden. The distribution and allocation of resources like land, supervises gardening activities etc. are done by the head of the *kamunchiase.* The size of gardening plots makes relocation easy and convenient. A big piece of land is divided into a number of sub plots and each sub-plot is used by a family. He also supervises day to day reciprocities of food, constitute canoe making teams etc. between *nitakaru.* In an island situation and from the view point economy, it is always very prudent that that management of resources and related activities are not left to the individual. This way the economic interest of weakest and less intelligent is protected. Thus the socio-economic functions of the *kamunchiase* ensure the survival of *nitakaru* in particular and the entire island society in general.

At *kamunchiase* level, there is possession of common plantations and gardens. The *kamunchiase* works as an integrated economic unit for the production of food crops, copra, and grow piggery and poultry. The chief economic value of the land lies in its use, that is, the potential capacities of the *kamunchiase* to use the land for different economic purpose. The wealth of the *kamunchiase* does not depend on the area of the land it owns. Rather it is the productive capacity of its members that can increase the production. In absence of any individual title of ownership, its economic foundation is not perturbed. More importantly, the material resources are drawn out sufficiently when the *kamunchiase* works as an integrated whole under the leadership of the head of a *kamunchiase.*

The bonds between one *kamunchiase* and another are affected through mutual economic aids. For example, if a *kamunchiase* requires to cultivate a particular variety of plant for which there is no extra land, the head of that *kamunchiase* approaches the head of another *kamunchiase* of his village or a friendly one of another village to get a share in the garden for the plant which is to be cultivated. If the extra land is available, the request is complied with. At the time of gardening, the people of donating *kamunchiase* go to help that *kamunchiase,* which has received land for cultivation, in the garden preparation. But such usufructuary relationship in the use of land is declining with increasing population. The introduction of money has brought about a subtle change in the value of common ownership. Cash economy now getting ground, labour of the *kamunchiase* spent in output of copra is readily changed into money.

Form the study it appears that social organization of the Nicobarese is an outgrowth of the practical systems for making a living, rather than their cause. Thus a close connection can be drawn between the ownership and management of resources and social organization in the Nicobarese society.

Village Council

The village council in the island is an outgrowth of an earlier informal political system that existed a few decades aback. Earlier each island of the Nicobar used to have one chief. But the old system was replaced by the village council in the early quarter of twentieth century by British Government. Therefore the present set up is attributed to British administration.

There is a functional difference between the village council and social organization. Every *kamunchiase* in the village organizes and maintains social and economic activities as separate entities. But the affair that concerns the entire village and those between one *kamunchiase* and other are controlled and issue thereto decided by the village council. The village council acts as legislative, adjudicative and executive body in the island. The main aim of the village council is to provide an orderly life and help the people in getting their basic needs satisfied. One of the ways through which the village council achieves its objective of resource management is through the economic and judicious use of resources. The council exercises regulation over the entire landmass of the island, but with regard to the use of the land, it is the head of the *kamunchiase* who regulates the allocation and use of the land. However, even here, if the council wants it can interfere and impose its decision. The council controls the spread of the settlement. For the school, dispensary, Govt's offices and quarters, the council earmarks the area after much consideration. For raising the ceremonial hut the formal approval of the council is needed. Similarly before burying or cremating a non-tribal person, the permission of the council is necessary for it is the council, which decides where the dead should be cremated or buried. Regarding the use of the forest the permission of the council is needed for it approves which part of the forest should be exploited.

Any violation of norms in utilization of land and forest is considered as an economic offence. Any economic offence is considered as an offence against the community. Under such situation the council gives the punishment which may range from simple economic penalty to excommunication.

Spirits and Shamanism

Prior to the occupation of these islands by the British, the people of the Nicobar group of islands were animistic. At the beginning of twentieth century Christianity entered into the Car Nicobar. Due to the effort of Rev. Gabriel and his fellow faithful, the Christianity made its presence felt in the Katchal in fifties. Today, in Katchal about 90% of islanders are Christian and rest of 10% are still following their traditional religion. The impact of Christianity on traditional religion is not so much as to shatter its system of adaptation but it has certainly effected the position of the *Menluena* and their popularity is on wane. However, people of both faiths have adjusted themselves with each other. The Christians of island implicitly regard Christ as one amongst the benevolent spirits. In facts it happens with first generation of converts because they have only normal understanding of Christianity and partial affiliation towards it. All the life cycle ceremonies amongst the Christians are performed according to the two traditions. Firstly it is performed according to the Christian tradition then by the native tradition. An analysis of both the traditions helps us to understand as to how both have mixed together without disturbing the symbiosis of man, nature and spirits.

For the Nicobarese, the religion is an adaptive mechanism to nature. The Nicobarese has their own cultural construct of nature in which they belong to a scheme of hierarchy to which both spirits and dead relatives who have become spirits belong. Propitiation of the spirits before the initiation of any economic activity is necessary and it, in turn, has caused the development of symbiotic relationship with nature whose outer manifestation is spirit-worship. Writing about the religion of Nicobarese, Richard Temple says, "Fear of spirits and ghosts is guide to all ceremonies and the life of the people is very much related with ceremonies and feasts of all kinds (1903)".

Concepts of Spirits and their Forms:- The Nicobarese believe that spirits regulates the entire universe. The Islanders conceive three categories of spirits. They are (1) malevolent spirits (2) benevolent spirits and (3) the ancestral spirits which may be benevolent or malevolent depending on the nature of the dead when they were alive. The malevolent spirits are more powerful than benevolent spirits. These three categories of spirits are known as *Iwi*, *Sia and Ma-la-ha* respectively in the central group of islands.

The *Iwi* are considered as very powerful and the islanders attribute to them different powers like control over climatic condition and the environment. The non-physical forms of *Iwi* take the shape of forces of nature like a gush of wind, cyclone, monstrous waves in sea etc.

The pivot on which the old religion' revolves is *shaman.* They are called *Menluena* in the central group of islands. They are the bridge between the supernatural and the mundane. The people still believe that *Menluena* control the forces of nature. More importantly people believe that they not only control the spirits but also act through them. They are specialists in ethno-medicines also and in fact are witch doctors too. In the Islander's cultural construct of nature, man is embedded in nature and spirits possesses nature. Interaction between man and nature take place through *Menluena* who helps propitiate spirits.

Beliefs and Management of Resources and Environment:- At the beginning of every economic activity like gardening fishing, while making fishing and large outrigger canoes, while starting on a voyage to other island, the *Iwi* are appeased necessarily with sacrifices of pigs and chickens. People believe that if they do not appease the *Iwi,* anything unwanted and unexpected may happen to them. Further, there are some taboos connected with economic activities, which have to be strictly observed, otherwise the wrath of the *Iwi* may strike the offender in any form. For example a women during the menstrual period, and people after a death in their families are supposed to be under pollution; they are tabooed to enter their gardens, touch their fishing canoes, and equipments, To ward off the pollution and to bring them to the normal state of harmony with the cosmos they require sacrifices of pigs and chickens to the *Iwi* spirits.

Months	*Economic Activities*	*Ceremony*
February-March-April	During these three months garden is cleared, leaves and twigs are burnt; new garden is prepared for new plants that are to be planted	*Kuikapa*- This festival isrelated with clearing of garden
May-June-July	During these months, coconuts *(Uyav)*, sweet potato, (*Kubang and Kani)* areca nut *(Hiyah)*, banana *(Sia)* etc. are planted. Thereafter crab catching begins.	*Vani-ayom*- This ceremony is related with the fencing of garden and plantation. *Kanacha*- It is held every year in the last week of plantation. *Isa-Yuang-Unviha*: This festival is also related with the crab catching and celebrated in the month of May. If viewed climatically, it is the time when the crabs are found in abundance. Secondly it the time when the monsoon sets over the island. The crab catching ends with *Idfat* festival. *Panuha-Minlan*: This festival is related with catching of crab. It is celebrated in the month of June. *Panuha* is the name of the festival and *Minlan* is the name of the red crab.
August-September-October	It is the season of making racing canoes *(Reui)* and fishing spear (*Mi-am*). Some plantation is also done during this period.	*Idfat*- it is generally held in the month of October. It means plantation is over and they are washing themselves over. If *Idfat* is not held they would soon grow old and die. Two or three *Idfat* are held every year. The last *Idfat* is held between October and November and the pig is sacrificed on the last Idfat in goal ghar *(Nyihopol)*. After *Idfat* no plantation is done . *Hahumsicaich* j It is related with canoe making.
November-December-January	Fishing activities in open sea begins. It continues up to march. It is also the season of making outrigger canoes.	*Kanaochilu or Anucha*-This ceremony is related with fish catching .The date for it is fixed on last *Idfat*. During this festival, which is held on moon lit night, people venture into sea in their outrigger canoe and fishing is done by spear with the help of mashal (torch). This festival continues for about 10 days. Sail is not hoist on the canoe. It ascertains the onset of northwardly wind and is indicative of good weather condition also.*Yanata-kanyaum*-It is also an important festival. On this day young men do fishing with the help of hook, line and net. They also use the frits of *tivila, yoanhoa and kinyav* trees to poison the fish.

Since the Nicobarese construct of nature is intricately related with spirits, their every economic activity begins with the propitiation of spirits and it is marked by a particular ceremony. They are as indicated in the previous page.

ECONOMIC AND ALLIED ACTIVITIES

The literal meaning of the resource management is the use of resources in a manner through which one meets his needs without disturbing recuperative rate of the resources. The Islanders or Katchal are successfully doing it. In the Nicobarese society of Katchal the resource management is achieved through the island's social structure, economic organization, political system (Island council) and religion.

Horticulture

Of the total land available in Katchal, approximately 60 percent land is under horticulture, 30 percent under forest and 10 percent under settlement. As discussed earlier, two categories of land ownership are found in Katchal Island. They are the land on which Island Council has control and is covered by such thing as the ceremonial hut, burial ground, school, dispensary etc., while the forest and gardening land owned by them are other category of lands and are owned and administered by the *Kamunchiase.* Of all economic activities, the horticulture particularly the coconut plantation is most important activity. Horticultural garden needs harrowing, weeding and application of manure at regular interval for good crop. However, the Nicobarese are never seen to follow the said process. It does not mean that they are indifferent about good production of coconut. In fact aforementioned task is carried-out by the pigs. Piggery is the second most important economic activities after plantation. Each Nicobarese household keeps a good number of pigs. While roaming in the garden, pigs turnover the soil in search of roots. The turning over of soil kills the weeds. Besides, the excreta of pigs serve as manure. It is how the three stage process of harrowing, weeding and manuring is accomplished.

Water Related Activity

Since the time immemorial the Nicobarese of Katchal have been inhabiting the island, it has helped them understand the moods of sea and its relation with seasons. Accordingly they have developed a seasonal calendar, which helps them in fishing and making journey.

Fishing

The fishing activities of the Nicobarese can be divided into two categories viz. daily activity and seasonal activity.

The fishing activity, which is carried out daily, is generally performed near the coast while the other one is seasonal and begins with some ceremonies. The methods of fishing followed by the Islanders are the hook-and-line techniques, spear fishing and torchlight fishing. Groups as well as individuals do hook-and-line fishing.

Spear fishing is of two types. They are:

- *Simple Spear Fishing:-* In this method fish is killed with a long spear in the shallow sea water.
- Dive-fishing:- It is mainly done by a group in open sea. Every one carries a spear attached with a long and strong rubber string. Success depends on alertness and perfection. Torchlight fishing is also a group activity. It is carried out in open sea. The light attracts the fish.

Canoe Making

Like other Nicobarese, Islanders of Katchal also make outrigger canoe. This activity takes place between the months of February and April. It is the period when the open sea fishing comes to an end and people prepare themselves for the next season. For canoe making generally the trees of Borneo mahogany, white Bombay and wild jackfruit are used. The canoe making is associated with a festival known as *Hanumsicaich.* Similarly when the canoe is ready for sail the *Hanuich-Nyi- Rsuax* festival is performed in front of the owner's house.

Housing

The houses in the Island are unique in design and generally of high standard. It is remarkable that these people had learnt to make good houses very early in the history.

Broadly speaking, the houses are of three types- (a) dome shaped round houses on silts (b) Rectangular houses with sloping wagon type roof on silt and (c) pacca houses.

The dome shaped round houses look like giant beehives and is oldest. In these houses, the roofs and the walls are continuous and one hemispherical top serves both the purposes. The entrance to the house is by means of an opening at one edge of the floor on which a ladder is kept to climb in and out of the house. The floor is made up of horizontally laid split bamboo or areca nut, owing to this it is easy to clean the floor. An analysis reveals that their houses particularly dome shaped houses are an index of climate, made up of locally available materials and an epitome of their social requirements and religions faith. Environmentally, the dome shaped houses are index of climate. They are able to withstand the force of a cyclone as it deflects the force of winds in all directions.

Besides the lofty dome shaped, there are the rectangular wagon type of houses also. The rectangular houses are also on silts with floor raised about 6 to 8 feet from the ground level. But they are not as grand as the circular houses.

RECIPROCITY AND RESOURCE MANAGEMENT

In Katchal the social and economic system still depends on the traditional system of gift, exchange and reciprocity. The significance of gift giving in such societies goes with three essential aspects, viz., (i) obligation to give presents (ii) obligation to receive them, and (iii) the obligation to repay the gifts received (Rappaport, 1968). Mauss (1954) call this as 'total presentation'. The same system of gift giving is found in socio-economic system of Katchal. Here the thing, which is given, is not important but the act of giving, receiving and repaying is important. Following salons partially the type of reciprocities practiced by the Katchal Islanders within the island could be categorized into (i) generalized reciprocity and (ii) balanced reciprocity.

It has been observed that generalized reciprocities occur quite often within *nitakaru*. In this sector the obligation to repay is not strictly adhered to. Here the exchange of food, material, equipment and services is very frequent. At the inter-*nitakaru* and inter- *Kamunchiase*-level, the obligation to repay is more than in the previous sector. The ceremony of 'ancestor' worship comes under inter-*nitakaru* level while 'pig festival' comes under inter- *Kamunchiase* category. Here co-operation in terms of men, material and services are provided to the head of the tuhet who is organizing it. It is done so because it is beyond the capacity of the host families to feed the invites from their own resources. Thus an examination of reciprocities and exchanges in the island suggests that it is in fact a way of resource management.

CONCLUSION

The island situation of the Katchal has contributed to the development of organic relationship between man and nature. The most important element in the system of resource management in Katchal Island is the social structure of Nicobarese in which the decent groups *(Kamunchiase)* exercise authority over land and forest and are responsible for distributing usufructury right to the individual families. Family, in turn, is responsible for making full utilization of resources in cooperation with other such units. Religion in the form of spirit worship is an adaptive mechanism to nature where the propitiation of spirits, prior to the use of resources, is considered necessary. It has led to the development of a symbiotic relationship with nature resulting into the sustainable use of resources.

However in the aftermath of tsunami which had struck the Andaman and Nicobar archipelago on 26th December, 2004, the Nicobar group of islands was worst affected and Katchal was one of the worst hit islands. The magnitude of devastation in term of loss of life and destruction of property were immense. The colossal loss of lives has resulted into loss of expertise in different spheres of material culture and belief system. Now there is probably no *Menluena* alive in the entire island in the aftermath of tsunami. It will take a long time before this void is filled in.

REFERENCES

A & N Administration (1966), *Statistical Hand Book, A & N Islands.* Port-Blair.

Bodley, John (1976), *Anthropology and Contemporary Human Problems.* Cunnings, California, p. 99.

Bonnington, M.C. (1931), *Census of India, Andaman and Nicobar Islands,* Part II & Vol.-II, Kolkata, I.

Government of India (1909), *Imperial Gazetteer of India, Provincial Series: Andaman and Nicobar Islands.* Kolkata.

Government of India, 1991.

Grierson, G.A. (1967), *Linguistic Survey of India.* Vol-I Part-1, Kolkata, pp. 32, 33.

Hillary Jr. George A. (1968), *Communal Organization: A Study of Local Societies.* Chicago, Univ. of Chicago Press, p. 34.

Kloss, B.C. (1971), *Andaman and Nicobars* (reprint). Vivek, Delhi

Man, E.H.B. (1889), "The Nicobar Islanders" in the *Journal of Anthropological Survey of India and Ireland,* Vol. XVIII, London, p. 367.

Mathur, K.K. (1967), *Nicobar Islands.* NBT, New Delhi, p. 42.

Mauses (1984), *The Gift,* Cohen and West Ltd., London.

Netting Robbert, MCC (1972), "The Ecological Approach in Cultural Study", in *Current Topics in Anthropology,* Vol. I.

Rappaport, Roy, A.B. (1967), "Ritual Regulation of Governmental Relation among New Guinea People" in *Ethnology,* 6, pp.17-31.

Rappaport, Roy, A.B. (1968), *Pigs for the Ancestors.* Yale University Press, New Haven.

Sahalin, M.D. (1968), *Tribesmen.* Prentice Hall, New Jersey.

Sinha Roy, K.M & Datta Chaudhury, S.S. (2007), "Tsunami 2004-A Disaster Unparallel: A Case Study of Katchal and Nancowry Island" in *Tsunami in South Asia* published by Anthropological Survey of India, Kolkata.

Shyam, N.K. (1977), *Social Structure of Car Nicobar Islanders.* Anthropological Survey of India, Kolkata.

Temple, R.C. (1903), "The Andaman and Nicobar Islands" in *Census of India,* Vol.III. Kolkata.

Temple, R.C. (1903), *Census of India, Andaman and Nicobar Islands.* Vol.III. Part II, Kolkata.

21 Role of Indigenous Knowledge among the Apatanis for Sustainable Living

Arnab Karar and Suvendu Kundu

INTRODUCTION

Among many virile and colorful tribes in Arunachal Pradesh, the Apatanis' are one of them. They live in a small intermountain valley known as Ziro or Apatani valley since time immemorial. The valley is situated at the distance of 160 kms. from State Capital Itanagar. Ziro, rightly called 'A rice bowl of Arunachal Pradesh', is surrounded by lofty green hills from all sides. It is the districts headquarter of Lower Subansiri district. The customs, culture, tradition, social, political and economic pattern of the Apatanis are unlike those of the other tribes of the region. A strong tribal sentiment, a consciousness of their basic separateness, a pride in their institutions and customs, and a passionate attachment to their small homeland, turned by incessant labor into a veritable garden, unite all Apatanis and set them apart from the surrounding populations which represent to them the outside world (1962, Haimendorf). Apatanis are gifted with exclusive utility items, the cane and the bamboo. The Apatani believe that there is no life without bamboo. They build their huts solely of bamboo and pinewood. Therefore, an integral feature of their villages is well stocked and carefully tended bamboo and pine groves. Arunachal Pradesh has a vibrant craft tradition and every tribe excels in craftsmanship. Cane and bamboo is an important craft of this area, and the workmanship is of a very high order. The Apatanis are expert workers in cane and bamboo. They make beautiful baskets, bags, hats and even jewellery that speak expressively of their skill. Bamboo is used for basketry. Basket making is a major craft in these areas. They produce baskets, grain holders, rice beer containers, haversacks, food plates, etc. from bamboo. From cane, they produce headgears, cane belts, anklets, chairs, tables, wardrobes, toys, etc. Their domestically produced articles from bamboo and cane meet all their requirements in basketry. The Apatani maintain their traditions by remembering their legendary and mythical beginnings (*http://www.newworldencyclopedia.org/entry/Apatani*). The present article of the indigenous bamboo and cane culture of the apatanis highlights the relationship and involvement of the apatanis with their environment, jungle, land to bear the customs and indigenous culture from generation to generation. Bamboo and cane are such two items of apatanis which is used in every aspects of their daily life routine. Empirical data are collected during my fieldwork at Apatani villages of Ziro, Arunachal Pradesh and secondary data were collected from the library.

OBJECTIVE

The paper intends to examine how bamboo and cane is enmeshed in the life and culture of Apatani as well as its socio-religious significance in their life in action.

METHODOLOGY

This article is the result of my fieldwork among the Apatanis during the time of my fellowship tenure at Anthropological Survey of India. Data were collected from both primary and secondary sources. A variety of techniques were used to piece together several information regarding social cultural life of the Apatani tribe. The fieldwork was done in phased manner in the year of 2008-09. The present authors employed several techniques for collection of empirical data, viz., Direct, firsthand observation of the daily behavior of several tourists. Conversation with varying degrees of formality, from the daily chitchat that helps maintain rapport and provides knowledge about what is going on to prolonged interviews, which can be unstructured or structured depending upon the need. Interview schedules to ensure that comparable information is available for everyone of interest to the study. To conduct the historical method for recording the past events, because it involves very deep and intensive investigation of material that already exists. To conduct the Narrative technique which helps the investigator to gain preliminary and generalized knowledge about the topic inquired.

BAMBOO CULTIVATION IN THE APATANI VALLEY

An Apatani must have his own bamboo and pine groves which are usually located near the village though they may sometimes be located farther away. It is the duty of the men folk to maintain these bamboos and pine grove. Engineering in the field of natural culture of cane and bamboo development is equally flourishing in domestic economy of the Apatanis by cultivating plenty of bamboos with a meticulous care in homestead.

They grow a variety that is locally known as "bije" (*Phyllostachys bambusoides*). It is a medium sized, straight stemmed, non-clump with bow shaped leaves, male bamboo that stands up well to cold winters with seasonal frost and occasional snow. It is the Plateau's characteristic and is not found in the surrounding areas. Over the centuries the Apatanis have evolved an indigenous farming system with a very high degree of energy and economic efficiency, partly due to effective recycling of organic wastes and crop residues (1997, Singh A.K.). The legend tells that these bamboos and pine trees were brought from their homeland Miido Supung. Bamboo and pine groves are essential parts of an Apatanis' holdings. In between the bamboo and pine groves and the settlements are located dry lands where the Apatanis grow maize, tobacco and millet. This type of land can be owned by the poor Apatani also. There are different species of bamboo in the valley like Phyllotachys bambusoides, Chimnobambusa callosa (*Tabyo*), Dendrocalamus hamiltonii (*Yahi*), Bambusa tulda (*Hijo*), Cephallostachium capitatum (*Yabin*), Pleiosblastus simony (*Tajer/Taping/Tapyu/Tadar*) etc. (*http://lowersubansiri.nic.in/html/forestpractice.htm*).

IMPORTANCE OF THE BAMBOO AND CANE IN THE SOCIO-CULTURAL LIFE OF APATANIS

Arunachal Pradesh has a vibrant craft tradition and every tribe excels in craftsmanship. Cane and bamboo is an important craft of this area, and the workmanship is of a very high order (http://www.ignca.nic.in/craft151.htm). With the nimble fingers and deft hands, the Apatanis produce exotic designs and colorful verities of household articles of cane and bamboo for domestic as well as commercial use. The luxuriant and magnificent cultivation of bamboo by the Apatani people of the valley facilitates the making of various construction purposes and household furniture and articles, which are associated to them in their daily life. The constructional purposes include the factors like building of houses, granaries, fences, ramparts, embankments of rivers and streams, creating religious altars, household crafts and articles etc. which are associated with the socio-economic, socio-cultural and socio-religious life of Apatanis. Such necessity has, however, compelled the Apatanis for careful cultivation of bamboos in plenty in their homestead.

SEVERAL USES

Everywhere the significant usage of bamboos and cane for construction materials, hunting gears, decoration object, domestic usage, agriculture purposes etc can be witnessed (http://www.amazingarunachal.com/artscrafts.html). Cane and bamboos are utilized for various purposes. These are sliced, trimmed and seasoned according to their need. Split bamboos are shaped flat and dried in the sun for a month increasing its durability for matting their walls and floors. Trimmed strips of bamboo and cane are dipped in the water before use for flexibility. Bamboos dipped in water for a month makes these seasoned and such bamboos cannot be infected by insects and termites when used latter for any purpose. An

Apatani must have his own bamboo and pine groves which are usually located near the village though they may sometimes be located farther away. It is the duty of the men folk to maintain these bamboos and pine groves because all the building materials come from here. Thus bamboo and pine groves are essential parts of an Apatanis' holdings. In between the bamboo and pine groves and the settlements are located dry lands where the Apatanis grow maize, tobacco and millet. This type of land can be owned by the poor Apatanis also. The constructional purposes include the matters like building houses, granaries, fences, ramparts, embankments of rivers and streams, creating religious altars, house-hold crafts and articles etc. which are associated with the multiple factors of life of Apatanis.

The mats are useful household articles for carpeting and drying of grains in the sun and fire place like *Piiping*, *Pakhe*, and *Perre*. *Pakhe* are used for drying millets, chilies and tobacco on the fire tray. *Piiping* are used for drying rice and husked millets as well as for rice beer preparation. *Perre* are used for drying grain and stock of rice grain in the time of harvesting in the fields. The mats are also used as tents at the time of festivals. These are used as sleeping mats. Generally sleeping or floor mats are made of hydro reeds called *Pepu*. Rain shield called *Yattii* is made up of bamboo or cane strips by twilling in two layers with durable leaves which are inserted in between for protection against dripping of rain. The upper part is concave and triangular shaped and is rested on the head. The lower part is flattened and rectangular shaped and is rested on the body. Many types of weapons like bow and arrows and animal traps and other agriculture tools like handle of spade, hoes, rain shields, besides weaving tools and fowl cage are made of bamboos and canes.

Of late, the Textile and Handicraft Department, Ziro has introduced the new items of household furniture and articles made from bamboo and cane such as chair, table, hand bag, cup and other decorative show cases and articles.

A sacred basket called *Supung yagii* woven from cane splits is decorated and designed with chequer in lozenge shape. It cannot be used other than religious purposes. *Supung liiha*, a sacred bowl, used for carrying rice flour to smear the altar, sacrificial animals and distributing rice flour to the members present during ceremony. Apatanis have measurement baskets made up of bamboo or cane in different sizes to measure grain and other goods and are named in accordance to its size. They are *Piilyee yagii, Puyeh yagii, Paro yagii* and *Pachu yagii* used for measuring quantities during barter system and at the time of *Murung* festival.

The other varieties of Bamboos found in the valley are also useful for making various household articles and for construction purposes. But these are not as durable as the bamboos cultivated in homestead. Of course, bamboos like *Taping – Tajer* is used in certain religious ceremonies and *Yabing* is a medicinal plant. The water content in *Yabing* bamboo and its shoots are good for stomach trouble like dysentery and diarrhoea.

CONCLUSION

The Sub-Himalayan climate with moderate sunshine and rainfall makes the valley a paradise for many varieties of plants and animals. The soil and salubrious climate of the valley also provide for luxuriant growth of crops and vegetation including Bamboo and Pine trees.

It can be said that the bamboos cultivated by the Apatanis have characterized the high order of cultural and socio-economic development of the society. However, many items of household crafts and articles have been substituted by mill made items. It is high time for the society and the Govt. to preserve these vanishing heritage articles in the form of material or documentation in the midst of changes.

REFERENCES

Singh A.K. (1997), 'Apatanis: A Study in Ecology and Change', The Journal of the Anthropological Survey of India, Vol.46 No. 3.

Haimendorf C.F. (1962), 'The Apatanis and their Neighbors', Routledge and Kegan Paul Publication, Great Britain.

External link

New World Encyclopedia (http://www.newworldencyclopedia.org/entry/Apatani)

Official Website of Lower Subansiri District (http://lowersubansiri.nic.in/html/forestpractice.htm).

Arts and Crafts of North-East (http://www.ignca.nic.in/craft151.htm).

Amazing Arunachal – God's Masterpiece on Nature's own Canvas (http://www.amazingarunachal.com/artscrafts.html).

22 Knowledge and Practices of Ethnomedicinal Plants among the Kamar Tribe of Chhattisgarh

Nilanjan Khatua

The traditional beliefs and practices regarding indigenous health care system vary from society to society and region to region. The *Traditional Medical Systems* provide major health care in the remote, inaccessible rural areas where tribal people generally live in. Folk Medicine, Tribal Medicine, Indigenous medicine, Alternative Medicine and Ethno-medicine are some of the names by which these systems have been identified in the discipline of *Medical Anthropology*. The study of indigenous medical features of a particular ethnic group is known as ethno medicine. 'Ethno-medicine' is a new emerging sub field in *Medical Anthropology* (Hughes : 1968) which is the direct descendant of the initial interest that anthropologists took in the medical systems of the primitive and non-literate societies. The extensive knowledge of wild edible and medicinal plants lies with the tribal societies, the use of which secure and sustain the people to a great extent. The tribal people collect a variety of leaves, fruits, roots, tubers, barks, seeds from their habitat and make use of these in their daily lives for their subsistence and health management. The *present paper aims* to explore the existing traditional knowledge in utilization of ethno-medicine including plant and animal products etc., among the Kamar tribal community and to find out the pattern of use of those plants.

The Kamar are traditionally shifting cultivators and expert hunters. Collection of minor forest produce and basketry are their perennial economic activities. Agricultural labour, forest labour, fuel wood selling, charcoal selling are the seasonal economic activities on which the Kamar subsist only for a part of the year. They have adopted settled cultivation to a great extent abandoning their age-old practice of shifting cultivation. Now hunting as a traditional occupation has little role in the Kamar economy. Now-a-days, hunting is merely a recreation for them. This is due to certain restrictions imposed by the government through the Land Revenue Act.

The present paper is mainly based on the fieldwork conducted in the year 1997. This study was conducted in Gariaband block of Raipur district of Chhatisgarh (earlier Madhya Pradesh). The data were collected from seven villages of Gariaband block. These seven villages were Bamhni, Kesodar, Pantora, Mohara, Ambakona, Nawagarh and Baghdogra. The total population of Kamar in Raipur is 14,922 as per survey in 1995 by Kamar Development Agency, Gariaband, Raipur. According to Census of 1981, the total population of Kamar is 17,517 in Madhya Pradesh and 5,939 in Maharashtra.

The Kamar society has its own beliefs concerning sickness and adopts indigenous health practices to treat it. According to the Kamars, the causes of illness are due to wrath of deities, spirit intrusion, magical practices, intake of wrong or less nutritive food and environmental effects. The use of herbal medicine, collected from the various medicinal plants, is widely accepted health care system, practiced by the Kamars. They have a good faith on medicine man (*vaidh*), who gives them herbal medicine for curing illness. Those medicine men have a fair knowledge on various medicinal plants and time and place of availability of such plants in their ecological niche.

In the olden days Kamars' staple food was *Madia (Eleusine coracana)*, a variety of coarse millet. They are unanimous in the view that it is *Madia* that used to keep them young and enable them stand the strains of hard rough life in the wild, hilly areas. It is indeed remarkable that the Hill Marias of

Abujhmarh also have the same opinion about this crop and so have the Baigas of Baiga Chak. The most important wild fruits, which seasonally break the monotony of their diet, are *tendu (Diospyros tomentosa)* and the *char (Buchanania latifolia).* The *mahua* flowers provide another very substantial item of their diet. The ripe *tendu* fruit is either fresh or it is dried and stored for subsequent use. The *char* is also a great favorite with them. They enjoy its sweet and very pleasant pulp; and then break the hard shell and take out the kernel i.e., *chironji* which they equally relish. Char fruits are also dried and stored. Since there is a great demand for *chironji* in the market, the Kamars now break the fruit and take out the kernels for selling these in the market or exchange these in terms of crops or grains. The other fruits, which supplement their diet, are mangoes, *Imli* (*Tamarindus indica*) and *Eugenia jambolana.*

The *mahua* (B*assia latifolia*) flowers provide an important item of Kamar diet. The much welcome *mohua* season starts when its first corollary began falling to the ground. Day after day the Kamars collect these flowers. The fresh flowers are boiled and eaten. They are also dried and stored in large quantities. These dried flowers are necessary for distilling liquor. When no other food is available they are boiled and eaten, that is why they call *mahua as roti (bread).*

Among the Kamars after delivery mother is given herbal medicine by the medicine man (*Vaidh*). Bark of *kanke* (*Flacourtia ramantchi*) and roots of *chhind* (*Phoenix accualis*), after cutting in suitable size, are boiled with water. Sometimes they mix jaggery while boiling. This liquid dose is given to the new mother for a period of three days, which gives her relief from stomach pain. To regain the energy, the new mother takes *pej* (prepared rice with boiled rice water). The mother is under the treatment of hot water bath up to 2 to 3 weeks of delivery.

They believe that if one takes excessive food, then he/she will be surely out of order. If one takes nutritious food with full vitamins, nothing wrong will happen to his/her health. If one takes food frequently and if this food is not properly digested, then there is a chance to store air in stomach, as a result stomachache occurs. Consumption of many green vegetables like pumpkin (*Cucurbita maxima*), bottle guard (*Langenria vulgaris*), kundru (*Coccinia cordi folia*) leads to the disease like Malaria. Food bitter in taste like *neem* (*Azardirachta indica*) and *karela* (*Momordica charantia*) are also good for health and act as medicines. Persons, who consume these bitter items more, are hardly affected by snakebite.

Environmental effect is one of the causes of illness as is believed the Kamars. Certain illnesses are "hot illness" believed to result from ever- exposed to sun or from ingesting 'hot' foods or beverages. Heatstrokes occur due to excessive heat of sunlight. This type of illness is treated by the ingestion of 'cold' foods or by 'hot treatment' such as drinking of hot boiled rice water (*Pasia*) before exposing in the sunlight. Both pregnancy and menstruation are considered to be 'hot states, so women are not allowed to consume *Mahua* liquor (hot food) in these periods.

They have good faith on village medicine man (*Vaidh*) who gives them herbal medicines collected from the various medicinal plants. It may be roots, leaves, barks, tubers, flowers, and fruits of some plants, which are used as medicine by the *Vaidhs*. The medicine men have a fair knowledge of various medicinal plants and time and place of availability of such plants and the use of those plants in curing of various illnesses. They collect the same from hillside, forests and preserve them carefully for future use. This curative health care system is invented by them in order to adjust themselves with their ecological niche for their survival. It is believed that in the past they learnt this art of curing the ailments through experience by trial and error methods and this knowledge is passed on orally and practically from generation to generation.

CONCLUSIONS

The Kamar society has its own magico-religious beliefs concerning illness and adopts indigenous health care practices to treat it. According to them, the causes of illness are due to wrath of deities, spirit intrusion, magical practices, intake of wrong or less nutritive food and environmental effects. Magico-religious performances occupy a prominent place in the treatment of illnesses. The Kamars make use of roots, tubers, leaves, barks, flowers, fruits of various plants as medicine and prescribe such medicines to the sick person. In the Kamar society, these herbal medicines are used to cure the various illness like cold and cough, fever, wounds, throat chokes, snakebite, loose motion, head ache, stomach ache etc. Due to ecological imbalance some of the herbal medicinal plant species are getting extinct from their habitat. Such scarcity leads them to loose dependency on their own health care system. And thereby, they are gradually getting inclined towards the modern health care facilities available nearby.

Some Common Diseases and their Treatment are Listed Below:

Local Name of Disease	*English Equivalent*	*Indigenous Medicines*
Bukher	Fever	The leaves or small twigs of *Bhuinlim* (*Swertia chirate*) crushed and its juice mixed with a little water and given to the patient for Two days.
Malaria	Malaria	The mixture, prepared by the juices, after crushing the leaves of *Patkoria* and *Bhuinlim* (*Swertia chirate*) along with tubers of *Dasmukh*, (*Asparagus racemosus*) is given to the patient.
Patla Saradi	Cold	Tea prepared by *Harra* (*Terminalis citrina*) and *Bahara* (*Terminalis belerica*) fruit. *Tulsi* leaves (*Ocimum sanctum*) with salt are given to the patient.
Khansi	Cough	*Harra* (*Terminalis citrina*) is roasted in the fire and the patient is asked to suck it.
Katjana	Cut	*Amla* (*Emblica officinalis*) Leaves are ground and this is applied on the affected place.
Gala Baithna	Throat chokes	Raw turmeric along with salt is used orally.
Haddi Tutna	Broken bones	Take the creeper *Harsingari* (*Nyctanthus arbortristis*) crush it and apply it to the fracture part, tying it firmly with the support of a bamboo split. The patient gives a coconut to medicine man as per customs.
Sap Katna	Snakebite	The bark of *Koria* tree (*Holarrahena antidysenterica*) is given for drinking the *guni – baiga*, after taking *Ghee* (*Clarified butter*), (1 Spoon), or Curd or Buttermilk (1 Glass), starts sucking the blood from the biting spot.
Khun kam hona	Anemia	Honey, *Dudung* fish is best item for blood increasing.

Contd.

Local Name of Disease	*English Equivalent*	*Indigenous Medicines*
Hat-gor pirathe	Joint pain and pain in hands and legs	They use *Mahua* (*Bassia latifolia*) liquor to get relief from pain. They massage with mustard oil after heating slightly.
Patla tatti	Diarrhea	The seed of *Tilsa* (*Linum usetatissimum*) or *Mizona* (*Celostrus panicularta*) after removing the outer layer, crush it and add water and drink it for 3-4 times.
Ulti-Tatti-me Khun ana	Dysentery	Bark of *Tilsa* and roots of *Aonla* (*Emblica officinalis*) grind these and allow drinking with water.
Hara-tatti	Loose motion	The juicy form extracted after crushing the leaves of *Birsakola*, is given to drink 3-4 times.
Pilia	Jaundice	*Haldi* (*Turmeric*) flower is mixed with water and is given to drink two times in a day.
Dant dard	Toothache	They use the small twig of *Sarfok* (*Tephrosia purpurea*) as toothbrush. The small twig of *Bajara danti* (*Barleria prioritis*) and salt used for brushing
Sir-dard	Headache	The root of *Kukurdanti* (*Grewia hirstua*) grind it and apply on forehead.
Pet-dard	Stomach-ache	The entrails of stomach of *Saipota* (*Animal*) is given to eat with some jaggery.
Pi-lena	Over drunk	Tonic prepared from coldwater with salt is given to drink.
Biri-pina	For get rid of smoking habit	The patient is advised to chew areca nut, *sounf* (*Pimpinella anisum*) and tobacco.
Galla-khar-khara	Throat ache	The mixture of lime and jaggery is applied near glottis.

REFERENCES

Datta, S.K. (2001), Marketing of Wild Medicinal Plants, in *Economic and Political Weekly*, Vol.- XXXVI, No.- 38. pp. 3598-3602.

Hughes, Charles C. (1968), Ethnomedicine, in *International Encyclopedia of Social Sciences. Vol-IX*, New york, The Macmillan Company & The Free Press.

Khan, Hussian. C.G & et.al. (1992), Relevance of Ethnomedicine in *Man and Life*, Vol-18, No. 1&2. pp. 11-20.

Khatua, N. (2005), The Kamar of Chhattisgarh, in *Primitive Tribes In Contemporary India"* Ed. by Sarit K. Chaudhuri & S S Chaudhuri, pp. 131-141, New Delhi, Mittal Publications.

Tewari, D.N. (1984), *Primitive Tribes of Madhya Pradesh*. New Delhi, Tribal Development Division, Ministry of Home Affairs.

23 Kuki Tradition and Shifting Cultivation

George T. Haokip

Kukis living in north-eastern states of India and Chin Hills of Myanmar have rich custom and tradition. Their traditions have relation with their shifting cultivation in the hills. In fact, their rituals have its sources from the practice of shifting cultivation. In that case, it is deeply rooted in Kukis' psyche and it influences the mindset of the tribe concerned. Shifting cultivation for the Kukis is more than sustenance; it is a way of life, the foundation from which emerged their economic and social tradition

INTRODUCTION

In India for many decades shifting cultivation (locally known as Jhum) has been construed as a major challenge to the development of tribal. According to the tenth fifth year plan, shifting cultivation has remained as one of the unresolved issues of planning for tribal development in India. (Govt of India, 2001)

The origin of shifting cultivation is recorded in the Neolithic period dating back to 7000 BC. It is rain-fed agricultural practice for economic sustenance. It is characterized by rotation of fields rather than of crops by short periods of cropping alternating with long fallow periods and by means of slash and burn. Crocklin (1961) described shifting cultivation as use of human labour, use of stick or hoe, short periods of soil occupancy alternating with long fallow periods. Shifting cultivation served as the economic mainstay. The tribals were totally dependent on it for survival. It is widely practised in the north-eastern states of India. In India about 10 million hectares of tribal land stretched across 16 states is under shifting cultivation. Based on satellite image, Forest Survey of India estimate 1.73 million hectares of land is affected by shifting cultivation.

In Manipur, the main reason for fast removal of forest are burning of the forest which constitute 90 percent due to shifting cultivation and hunting of animals whereas felling of tree by the local people for fuel wood hardly constitute 1 percent of forest removal in the state.

STUDY AREAS AND OBJECTIVES

Study area covers the entire hill areas of Manipur which cover 20,082 square kilometres (92 percent) out of the total land area of the state which is 22,327 square kilometres. Kukis are found in the entire four hill districts of Manipur. Kukis concentrate mostly in Churachandpur, Chandel and Senapati districts. Hill areas have cool and pleasant climate. The rainy season starts from June and lasts up to September, and the winter makes its presence felt from November to February. Eventually, the state receives adequate amount of rainfall, its distribution is higher in the hill area than valley. An objective of the study is to investigate and analyse the traditional land use pattern of the Kukis and their relation with the tribal mindset and custom.

KUKIS' SHIFTING CULTIVATION

Kukis are agriculturalists and rice is the staple food, from it reckoned wealth besides food and drink. A Kuki farmer is a careless sower and weeder, but the long gentle slopes with their thick covering of soil give him excellent crops, famine is rare. The cultivators use the land for 2 or 3 years and then leave the site with enough trees standing to regenerate the jungle and the land is cultivated at the interval of about 7-10 years, the jungle then grows up on the abandoned jhums, preventing the soil from erosion by rain.

Shifting cultivation is practised throughout the hills of Kuki region and their village economy too is more or the less dependent on it. It is a well organized and regulated social system of cultivation in the Kuki region. The following stages are adopted in jhum cultivation (Binodini Devi 2006:36):

1. Selection of land with ceremonies
2. Jungles are cleared spreading out the cutting and drying for burning
3. Burning of dried forest
4. Dabbling and sowing of seeds/crops
5. Weeding the crops
6. Watching and protecting the crops
7. Harvesting and threshing the crops
8. Village celebration
9. Following the land

Kukis were one of the earliest to practice wet-rice cultivation. In 1918, Kuki villagers from *Lalpani, Bongbal Khullen, Liwapokpi valley, Vungkok* and from the northwest sub-division had excellent wet-rice cultivation. They had, besides rice, also cultivated pineapple, ember, plantains and jackfruit trees. Later in the 1930s, the Kukis from Khuga valley started wet-rice cultivation.

The Kuki Chief *(Haosa),* who is the owner of the village land and responsible to the welfare of the villagers assisted by his council of ministers, earmarks the site for cultivation. The villagers go to the forest and locate a site and each family would mark by cutting portion of its trunk or tie bunches of grasses in the border of his fields making *'Louchan'*. The villagers for using the Chief's land are obliged to pay certain tributaries.

CUSTOMARY ENTITLEMENT OF THE KUKI CHIEF

The chief also by virtue of being the owner of the land there are customary entitlements that the chief enjoys. Such levies imposed by the chief are:

1. Front leg of the animal killed in his chiefdom;

2. Forced labour from the villagers. It is a free 1-4 days free labour of the villagers;
3. Mithun Levy
4. Sales levy,
5. A levy on a wild honey in the forest.
6. Each house in the village contributes its share of any expense incurred

A payment of tributaries to the chief is a manifestation of their obedience and loyalty to the centralized authority. It is the mechanism in which the chief legally gets obedience and loyalty. It is a material ethic of obedience shown by the villager. It has legal sanction by customary law and thus cannot be objected or disobedience to the practice. It is their culture the same as their life.

There are also other tax given to the Chief and these are sale tax, bird tax, forest tax, etc. Every year cultivation begins in the month of *Tolbol-Lhakhao* (January-March). After clearing the ground field house for shelter, *'Lou-buh'* is built for resting during the weak of toil. The Kukis practiced multi-cropping since the beginning and it is still prevailing. They have also practiced fallow type of cultivation, and as a result, frequently change the site. Rice, beans, millet, job's tear, maize, chillies, turmeric, gourds, sesame, cucumber, pumpkin, gingers, etc are popular crops usually cultivated.

AGRICULTURAL IMPLEMENTS

Tools and implements used for cultivation are simple and required a small numbers. *Chempong (A knife of bigger size), heicha (Axe), tupeh (Spade)* and *tucha (Small spade)* are commonly used implements. They have clearance, weeding and harvesting tools. They did not have any idea of scientific technologies. For the manure the burn down ashes serves as manure. In some fields due to the fertility seeds are sown without digging but in the case of less fertile land, about 2 to 3 inches deep is dug and mixed with ashes. Women are involved in almost all important activities of shifting cultivation. The following are the list of jhuming implement commonly used:

1. A short handle hoe,
2. A dao or bill hook,
3. Wooden mallet to break up the clods,
4. Sickle,
5. A bamboo flail,
6. An Axe

CEREMONIES LINKAGES

Khe-Lhai-Khai Ceremony

This is a test for suitability of land and took place before cultivation began with rice ladder. It is the first test in the new field and performed by the priest, called Thiempu. This was followed by the villagers cutting the trees and clearing the jungle the next day.

Ahtuisan Ceremony

It is done to ascertain if the proposed cultivation land would yield good harvest. In case, the omen is bad the proposed cultivation is abandoned. It is usually done during night time. The *Khe-Lhei-Khai* and *Ahtuisan* ceremony were done to test if the land would yield good harvest.

Tuilutna Ceremony

This ceremony was done to appease the water god if there was spring or rivulet within the site of the cleared land, requesting the god who is the owner of the site, to descend seven layer of the earth and the cultivators shall be on the surface so that cultivation can be carried on. After the ceremony, sowing of the seed begins.

Muchitu Ceremony

The village chief and villagers would go to the site and inaugurate. The Chief's wife would sow the seed first, followed by the ministers and the villagers. It was a ceremony of the whole village after the priest do some ritual on the jhum site.

Kuts

Kuts are associated with the various stages of shifting cultivation. *Mim Kut, Lolhun Kut, Chapchar Kut,* etc. are special ceremonies/festivals of the Kukis and Mizos. It is a tradition handed down from their forefather. Today these Kuts are celebrated at the state, district and area level in Manipur and Mizoram. In Manipur Kut is celebrated on 1st November every year. It is the only festival recognised by State Tourism Department. Modern Kut celebration is marked by organising traditional show, beauty contest and music.

In the traditional Kuki Society the chief as per custom received the following tributaries as tax from the villagers for using the chief land and the service render for cultivation:

Changseo

Chang- paddy rice and *seo*- tax. The chief has overriding power over the utilization of the village land. The system is somewhat similar to semi-feudal type. A villager is initiated a plot of land for cultivation. But, this does not constitute permanent individual ownership of land. The villager or the tenant-at-will as a customary rule pays to the chief a yearly tributaries called *Changseo.* The subscription was like a kind of agricultural tax or fees for cultivating the chief land and it range from payment of 1 to 5 baskets of paddy by every family for cultivation of the land. The Chief however has the right to exempt any village from the payment.

Lou man

Lou man is another payment made by any outsiders cultivating in the chief land. Such a cultivator from outside the village has to pay *louman* periodically. The Kuki chief collect taxes from outside the village if it is under his jurisdiction.

Gamsan

Gam-Land *San*-Rent *Gamsan* is a payment to the chief for the lease of the land. It is another type of payment that villagers upon the cultivation of the chief land pay annually to the latter. The chief is responsible for the security, development and maintenance of his villagers. The villagers in return render absolute loyalty and allegiance to the chief. It is a payment to the chief for the lease of the land. It is another type of payment that villagers upon the cultivation of the chief land pay annually to the latter

The Kuki chief received above privilege for the following reason.

1. In due recognition of the chief authority and legitimacy over the land ownership,
2. In recognition of the service rendered by the chief,
3. In gratification for which they got the privileges of enjoying the amenities of village life,
4. As a mark of respect, and
5. To honour the head of the clans by the younger chiefs in case of the clan chief.

CONCLUSION

Shifting cultivation is deeply rooted in the Kuki psyche, having evolved through the time, and being rooted in customs, belief and folklore. It influences the tribe's mindset. It also influences the cultural ethos of its agrarian society and social fabric. Their observation of various ceremonies/festivals is related to nature. They have given due respect and appreciation from the dwellers for it is the provider of their sustenance and livelihood. Their traditional way of living and the tribal mindset have given respect for environment. Jhum for the Kukis is more than sustenance, it reflects, the reason for existence. Their traditional obligation to the chief is based on the belief that he is the head of the village owner of the land whose rule is legitimately based on traditional authority sanctioned by kinship and customary system that they have inherited through the ages.

REFERENCES

Darlong, Vincent T. (2004), To Jhum or Not to Jhum-policy Perspective on Shifting Cultivation. Guwahati: The Missing Link.

Devi, Binodini P. (2006), Tribal Land System of Manipur. New Delhi: Centre for Manipur Studies and Akansas Publishing House.

Devi, Binodini (2006), Tribal Land System of Manipur, Akansas Publishing House, New Delhi.

Dutta, BB and B. Datta, Ray (eds.) Shifting Cultivation in North East India. Shillong: North East India Council for Social Science Research (NEICSSR).

Éswaraiah, G. (2003), Challenges of Rural Eco System in India', Employment News, 27(50):1-3.

Gangte, T.S. (1993), The Kukis of Manipur- A Historical Analysis. Delhi: Gyan Publishing House.

Sachchidananda (1989), Shifting Cultivation in India. New Delhi: Concept Publishing Company.

Sen, S. (1992), Tribes of Mizoram: Description Ethnology and Bibliography. New Delhi: Gyan Publishing House.

Shakespear, Lt. Col. J. (1983), The Lushai Kukis. New Delhi: Cultural Publishing House.

Shaw, William (1929), The Thadou Kukis. Delhi: Cultural Publishing House.

Tour Dairy of the President of Manipur Derbar, Dated 21.4.1924

Tour Dairy of C. Gimson, Dated 2.8.1937

24 A Note on Ethnomedicine and Magical Practices among the Tamangs of Darjeeling Himalaya

Ganesh Chandra Mallick

INTRODUCTION

In an illuminating appraisal of the literature on disease and treatment in primitive medicine, Mayer (2002) rightly validated the illness or disease as the products of a specific set of historical, economic and cultural circumstances, and with their functioning as aspects of social ideology of the tribal. Thus to understand the nature and the significance of illness in these societies it is necessary to look primarily at certain aspects of the people's conceptions of relation between 'bodily', 'physiological', 'spiritual' and 'social' aspects of the person and of attitudes towards the physically unfit or incapacitated. In this context Grossinger (1982) has rightly defined medicine as institution through which societies deal with mind/body relationship and their ramifications. Sarkar (1986) writes in this aspect, 'it has been argued that successful practice of medicine is dependant not only on the therapeutic skill and diagnostic ability of the physicians but also on their understanding of the socio-psychological and cultural factors'. Thus the modern medical research inquiring into and striving to control the body, mind and psyche, and environment as these bear upon health and illness (Fox 1976).

I am quite aware that my own data on the treatment of disease, collected intermittently in the form of adhoc observations and accounts of informants of varying intelligence and knowledge of tribal therapy, are relatively scanty and have many lacunae, but they are enough to demonstrate that Tamang Shamanic Healing procedures are governed by the same principals and modes of the classifications as their religious rites and moral concepts. My aim here is to reveal the ideas implicit in the Tamang Shamanic Healing procedure and to show that these ideas pervade wider realms of belief and action.

MATERIALS AND METHODS

This study is a contemporary one in the sense that it is based on field experience and on the historical data on the Tamangs in the context of Darjeeling Himalayan Region. It studies the concept about health care among the Tamang population with regard to the socio-cultural aspect of them. The data have been collected from primary as well as secondary sources. For gathering background information various published and unpublished materials have been consulted, while the primary data has been collected through the intensive field study among the Tamangs of the Kalimpong-I P.S. of the district of Darjeeling in West Bengal, India. Personal interview, group interview and observation have been used to draw a general conclusion based on specific situation.

DISCUSSION

The Tamang is one of the largest ethnic communities of Nepal and North-east India. Due to the great influence of Tibetan cultures, Tamangs mostly follow the same tradition- they not only depend upon the physical recovery from the sickness but also look it in the psychological aspect. Dhonden and Tshering (1976) have rightly pointed out in this aspect, 'Tibetan physicians regard the practice of moral laws as the utmost importance in the elimination of both physical and mental afflictions'.

Among them the *'Jhakri'* (local medicine man as well as shaman) plays a great role in this context. Basically he deals the problem of illness or disease or sickness in his magical way as well as ethnomedicinal way.

In this society diseases are supposed to be caused by the two factors- spirit caused and natural illness, but there is no clear-cut demarcation line between them. The natural illness may be mild, like a stomach problem, cut injuries, headache, fever, pyorrhea etc and in that case the *Jhakri* does not always recommend to *chinta* ceremony (magical healing process); he tries to solve these problems through ethnomedical process. But, for the more severe forms of natural illness it seems that the patient's problem may be influenced by spirit and then *chinta* ceremony is prescribed. There is no specific technique to trace out the diseases caused from spiritual or natural way; the diagnostic decision appears to be based on experience of the *Jhakri*. The *Jhakri* intuitively knows in which way he could treat successfully and which way he could not.

ETHNOMEDICINAL HEALING PROCESS

In case of natural illness the *Jhakri* applies the ethnomedicine to solve these problems. This ethnomedicinal concept is deeply rooted in this society and it also influences their cultural matrix. In this context Sarkar (1993) wrote that, 'Folk medicine has its very root in the cultural settings and thus the whole workings and the behavior patterns relating to the healing practices are interwoven in the culture matrix of the people'. This ethnomedical concept of *Jhakri* is fully based on their deep observation and understanding of nature and surrounding environment. Mostly they use herbs for this treatment pattern which are collected from the surrounding jungles but due to deforestation all herbs may not available in time. Some representative samples of these herbaceous medicine are presented here which have been referred by the Tamangs during the survey work.

Joro (Fever)

Used Herbs The *Tinosporia cordifolia* or *Dillenia indica* .

Preparation To prepare the medicine the extracted juice of fruits of anyone of the said trees mixed with sugar and water.

Doses Generally 2-teaspoonful juice is to be taken in 2 times in a day and it continues up to 3 days.

Pakhalo(Diarrhoea/Dyscentry)

Used herbs/ materials *Cannabia sative* and *Allium cepa.*

Preparation Seeds of *Cannabia sative* is dried firstly and then grind it to make powder. More or less 15 grammes of this powder mixed are with one-teaspoonful juice of Allium cepa.

Doses This mixture is to be taken (15g. powder+1tea spoon full juice) thrice a day and continues it up to 3 days.

Margi (Caugh)

Used herbs *Zingiber officinate* and *Nyctanthoe orberfriate.*

Preparation The equal amount of extracted juice from each herbs are mixed in a pot.

Doses Two-teaspoonful of this mixture is taken twice a day and continues it up to 5 days.

Kateko (Cut injuries)

Used herbs *Compaicum annom.*

Preparation These fruits of this herb is ground to dust and then alum is grinded for making dust. Equal amount of two types of powder are mixed in a pot.

Doses This mixture is used externally in the affected area as per need and it is applied twice/thrice a day and continues it up to 7 days.

Chala-ka-Rog (Skin diseases)

Used herbs *Acorus calamus.*

Preparation The extracted juice of that herb's leaves is mixed with equal amount of *Gomut* (urine of cow) in a pot.

Doses This liquid is used externally in the affected area and it is applied at least thrice in a day and continue for 7 days as per need.

Zooleko (Burn)

Used herbs *Stephania hernandifolia.*

Preparation The leaves are slightly grind until a little amount of juice come out from it.

Doses The paste of leaves is externally used in the affected area and it is applied 2-4 times in a day and continues it 3-5 days.

Jue Dukhne **(Body ache)**

Used herbs/materials

- *Cinnamomum camphora* and mustard oil.
- Vermilion, honey, milk, egg, mustard oil.
- Piper *nigrum.*

Preparation

- *Cinnamomum camphora* is grind and mustard oil is mixed with it to preparing it as paste.
- Honey is mixed with milk and then white portion of egg is mixed with it. A little amount of mustard oil and boiling water are assorted into the mixture and stirring this vigorously.
- The leaves of that herb dried at first and then pounded.

Doses

- Two tea spoonsful of that paste is smeared on the body twice a day and continue it for 7 days.
- 300-500 ml of that mixture is taken once in a day and continue 2-4 days
- One tea spoonful of that dust mixed with water and take it 2-3 times a day and is continued for 3-5 days.

Doreko**(Loss of Appetite)**

Used herbs/materials

- *Euphorbia nerifolia,* banana, butter.
- *Geimum sancitum, Zingiber officinate*
- *Raphous sativus,* normal salt
- *Allium cepa,* normal salt.

- Maize, Salt, *Piper nigrum*

Preparation

- Latex of *Euphorbia herifolia* is mixed with banana and butter to make it sticky.
- The same quantity of *Zingiber officinate* and leaves of *Geimum sancitum* are mixed in a pot.
- Underground portion of the herbs cut into small pieces and then normal salt is mixed with it.
- Either juice are extracted from that herbs or these are cut into small pieces and the normal salt is mixed with it.
- The maize is boiled with salt and *piper nigrum*.

Doses

- 50ml of that mixture is taken with rice twice a day and continued for 3 days to 7 days.
- 2 teaspoonful of that juice are taken 2-3 times a day and continues for 7-10 days.
- 75-100grams of that mixture is taken at least 7-15 days, 2 times in a day.
- If the juice is prepared, then it is taken 2-tea spoonful in a day and otherwise 40- 50 grams of that mixture is taken twice a day and continues it for 5 days.
- The boiling grains of maize are taken with tea as per patient's capacity and continues it for 3-5 days.

Kira Tokne (Insect Bite)

Used Herbs

- *Allium cepa* and *Allium sativum*.
- *Syzygium aromaticum* and *Schima wallichii*
- *Allium sativum* and *Schima wallichii*
- *Compasium annuom*
- *Nicotiana Tabacum* and lime.

Preparation

- The juice extracted from both herbs mixed in similar quality in a pot.

- The powder of *Syzygium aromaticum* is mixed with the juice of second herbs leaf or fruit.
- The extracted juice of first one is mixed with the juice of fruits or flower of the second herbs.
- Powder is made from dried fruits of the herb.
- The leaves of the herb dried firstly and then pounded, finally it is mixed with lime.

Doses

Each of the mixtures used externally and it is smeared over the affected area twice a day and continues it 1-4 days as per condition of affected area.

***Bhura-ko-Rog* (Stomach Problem)**

Used herbs

- *Lua macrophylla*
- *Dillenia indica*
- *Pteridium polypodiaceae*
- *Hydrocotyle Umbelliferea*e

Preparation

- The roots of the herb are dried firstly and then grind it to make powder.
- The juice is extracted from fruits or leaves and the powder is made from the bark of the herbs.
- Extracted the essence of the fruit or rhizome by boiling method.
- The juice is extracted from the leaves of the herbs.

Doses

- One teaspoonful of that powder is taken with water twice a day and it is continued for 3-7 days.
- If juice is prescribed then one teaspoonful of juice is taken orally and if powder is prescribed then ½ teaspoonful of powder is taken with water. Both are prescribed to take twice and continue for 3-4 days.

- ½ teaspoonful of this essence is taken 2 times a day and continued it for 3-5 days.
- One teaspoonful of this juice is taken orally with cold water 2-3 times in a day and continued for 3-5 days as per requirement.

MAGICAL HEALING PROCESS

The *Jhakri* for the more severe form of natural illness or spirit caused illness suggests the *Chinta* ceremony. In such cases he observes the patient and takes some grain of rice in a bell metal plate and after uttering some magical word and counting the rice he traces particular reason of illness. After knowing the actual reason he prescribes to *Chinta* ceremony from the influence of *Aathane/Charrane* etc. (the spirit who stolen the soul of the patient). As per suggestion of *Jhakri* the *Chinta* ceremony is held on an auspicious day and some of the performed rituals is as follows–

In this ceremony the patient's family clean their courtyard (if it is not available then the nearest plain space from their house is cleared & cleaned) and a room of the house at early morning and mopped with fresh cow dung paste. The actual ceremony would start after 9 p.m. Two banana plants are planted in the middle of the mopped area. At the base of banana plants two rings are drawn, which indicates the mother earth. A long thread is tied up in the middle of banana plants. Egg, rice, banana, *phapar, jar* (local drinks), *Kuvindo* (a variety of pumpkin), leafs of few trees, sugar, *dal,* honey, a piece of iron rod, holy water, *nong pani* (the water in which the nail were washed), etc. are needed for offering to worship the spirit.

The patient sits at the front of banana plants and *Jhakri* sits her/his left side. The assistant of Jhakri starts beating *Dhangro* (a type of drum) and bell metals plate. Patient's husband/ father greet patient by waving a lamp, *Kuvindo* and a hen. Then *Jhakri* starts exorcising the evil spirit from patient's body by reciting incantations (spiritual word) and beating the patient by leaves. Later on one of the participants unfasten the thread on the banana plants and the *Jhakri* beating the *Dhangro* and round the banana plants and patient with singing and uncontrolled dancing . After few minutes he being senseless falls in the ground and as soon as patient party cut the neck of hen and another man cut *Cuvindo* . Few minutes later the *Jhakri* became normal. The next part of the *puja* is held on inside the room. Here 16 crosses were driven into the bark of banana plant. Few horns with skull, few specific stones, two strings (one is made by snake's bone and another is made by *rudraksha*), few animal bones (including human bones), fired coal, holy water, rice, *Barsha* (weapon), *Channe* (weapon) , egg, oil, a plate, lamp, leafs etc. are needed to offering the spirit. When the *puja* started in the room then all the windows and doors are closed and exclusively the adult member of the patient's *Bansha* (dispersed lineage) and *Jhakri* only present there. The *Jhankri* uttering a few magical words, and beating the *Dhangro* and tries to satisfy the soul. It is a long-term process-near about 2-3 hours is needed to complete of it. The patient sits at the right side of the *Jhakri*. Patient's husband/ father collects a pail of water from 7 water sources and boiled it inside this room. As a result whole room is covered with smoke. After completion of *puja* the patient is sitted nearer the boiling pot (She/he sited half nakedly; i.e. the upper portion of her/his body remain uncovered). And the *Jhakri* puts some leaves inside the boiling water and immediately he is powerfully beating patient's body (both in front and back) with these leaves. Then he takes plate and oil, and rubs it on the patient's brest, back, and hands with uttering the *montros* and exorsing the evil spirit from the patient's body.

Significantly the *chinta* ceremony is divided into two phases- first one is to find out lost soul of the patient and second one is for the re-establishment of that soul on the patients body The drawing ring at the base of banana plants is regarded as mother earth and the banana plant is the benevolent power. The tied thread at the middle portion of banana trees is regarded as the evil power tied the benevolent power. After doing some magical activity of the *Jhankri*, a man unfasten the tie, it means that the strength of the malevolent power gradually decreased. After the completion of unfastens process the *Jhankri* become senseless i.e. he sends his soul to find out the stolen soul of the patient and the soul of hen and *kuvindo* will help him in this process. Few minutes later when *Jhakri* becomes normal it seems that he finds out the patient's stolen soul and the remaining work is the reestablishment of the soul in the patient's body. This process is as follows-

Inside the room the *Jhakri* at first calls the deity and tries to please him. He shoots away the malevolent effects from stolen soul by the *mala* (string which is made by snake's bone), fired coal, *Chhane, Barsha, Khukuri,* animal bones, and the *montros*. After completion of this process he purifies the stolen soul by the *Rudraksha mala,* holy water, milk, fired coal, and *montros*. Then he expels the bad effects from patient's body with the help of incantations and *rudraksha mala*. Later on he reestablishes the soul in the patient's body.

DISCUSSION AND CONCLUSION

The *Jhakri* has a great influence in this society. The members of this society revere him as the representative of the deities and thus they show respect to his words as Devine order. If we look deeply into this structure, we find that, *Jhankris* are the 'observer participant researchers' of this society, thus they successfully trace out the patient's psychology, and this experience would help them in their treatment process. Thus, when the patients consult their illness with *Jhankri,* he minutely observes the patient and diagnoses the cause of illness- spirit caused or natural one. He knows in which way it deals successfully- only ethno medicinally or psychologically or in both way, and treats them in appropriate way.

Physiotherapy is, of course, not the only scientific significance of the shamanic healing procedures among the Tamangs; massage, ethnomedicine, musical therapy etc. are in the quest for restoring health. Massage and blown into and onto the body are the very popular methods of shamanic treatment process. Aromatic medicinal substances in oils or butter are applied in conjunction with massage. The blown into and onto the body help to stimulate the partly damaged nerves of the patient and help her/him to came in normal position. The ethnomedicine or herbal medicine appears to be quite popular in shamanic healing process. These people (*Jhankri*) are aware about the several herbs which have medicinal property and available in their villages. Due to great influence of *Jhankri* his fellow villagers have a limited chance to access the modern medicinal facilities. Again, these people want result and if they get well, they do not ponder the problem of formalities of modern health care system. However, they (*Jhankris*) try to cure the diseases from their traditional experiences and his fellow villagers accept these fully. There is no doubt of potency of the ethnomedicine prescribed by the *Jhankris*.

Silverman (1967) and Wallace (1970) consider the shamanic experience to be pathological, but they also point out that cultural acceptance and validating labels for the experience distinguish it from other pathological experience. Nevertheless, the questions of whether or not the shaman is pathological, is not a simple one. Some researchers have administered Rorschach tests (Boyer et al. 1964; Lantis 1960), Holtzman inkblot techniques (Fabrega and Silver 1970) and other type of psychiatric examinations (Sasaki 1969), all with equivocal results. It may well be that the particular experiences a shaman undergoes include some that, by Western standards, are associated with neurosis or psychosis. However, interpretations differ. There are many reports of shamans with strong stable personalities who manifest no evidence of distorted episodes or deviance (Handleman 1967; Nadel 1965, Opler 1959). There is also evidence suggesting the opposite. For example, Firth (1967) reports that the medium for the Principal Tikopian god had "periodic fits of craziness" and would at times "rush shrieking into the lake." But "even when mad he would, on the appropriate ritual occasions, enter into trance and behave in an organized manner. His psychic controls were evidently strong enough so that the social call of duty restored him to some equilibrium, form which he relapsed gain after the rite was over." In the issue of shamanic experience is pathological or not; there is no univocal answer among the scholars (Peters,1998), rather we call it psychopathological one. To supporting this Peters, 1998 wrote that, loss of memory for trance stated is generally considered to be a "dissociative reaction" and therefore psychopathological one and the shamanic spirit procession has viewed as mental pathological context because it is too close to the classic hysteria. Prince (1973) is an estimation that, in Tamang healing rituals, many psychotherapeutic effects seem to result from the personal influence of the shaman over patient. However, the involvement of him and influence the cultural expectations for disease, and the belief of the patient is the efficacy of the *Puja* (Frank, 1973).

Psychotherapeutically the Tamang shamanic healing process has a great significance. The noise of *Dhangro* and the rhythm of *mantro* act as musical therapy for the patient. Again, the loss of sense of *Jhankri* comprehends strongly in patient's mind that, *jhankri* sends his soul to find out the stolen soul of him/her. Very low light and smoky environment of the *puja* room make a situation that patient is compelled to believe his/ her soul is extricated form the evil spirit and it is purified in *puja* place and is restored into his/her body. So, it is a renewal process and in their own words it is one kind of rebirth of the patient. Kiev (1972) argues in this context, emotional catharsis by allowing the patient to ventilate aggression of frustration, provides a sense of renewal of an improved capacity for healing with reality. During the crisis, patient's feelings are expressed through the spirit and the *chinta* ceremony is enabling to break patients' confusion, frustration and anxiety. Just after knowing the disease, patient's anxiety deducted immediately and when he/ she enters the *puja* room, this environment gives him/her mental strength that the divine power protects her soul and restores it on his/her body- this event helps him/her to overcome the state of confusion and frustration. So, in *chinta* ceremony firstly diagnosis finds out the cause of the diseases, and then the treatment process proceeds on as per ideology of the patient and that is the real therapeutic effectiveness of this shamanic healing process. So, if we look upon the psychological structure of the patient then it would be found that, a person converted as patient due to loss of his/her soul and after renewal of soul or rebirth the patient returns to the normal position. So, this ceremony helps the patient to restore his/her mental stability.

A Sketch of the Changing Status of the Patient

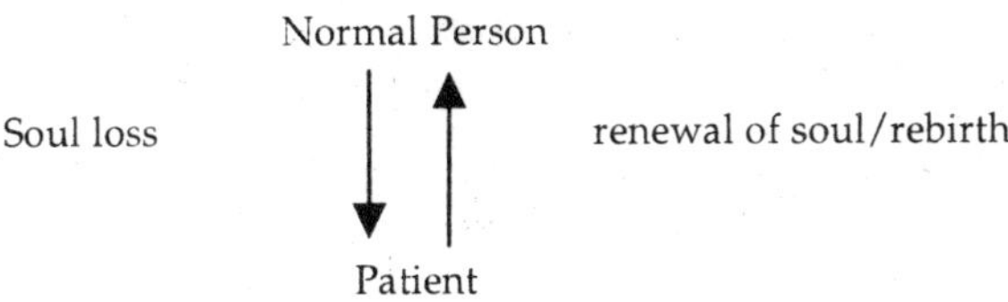

A question may be raised after going through the discussion, done above, why do such treatments continue to be practiced, since it is clear that the whole procedure based on supernatural ideas? One reason for their persistence lies, no doubt, in the very fact that the treatment procedure basically lying upon the mystical belief pattern which itself constitutes an explanation; and this helps them to acknowledge their norms, values, sanctions which finally help them to maintain their social structure.

REFERENCES

Boyer, L., B. Klopfer, F.B. Brawer and H. Kawai (1964), Comparison of the Shamans and Pseudo–Shamanic of the Apaches of the Mescalero Indian Reservation: A Research study. *Journal of Projective Techniques and Personality Development*. 28:446-456

Bhasin, V. (1997), *The Human Settlements and Heath Status in Sikkim.* New Delhi. Kamala Raj Enterprise.

Chaudhari, B. (1986), *Medical Anthropology in India With Special Reference to Tribal Population* in B. Chaudhari ed. *Tribal Health: Socio cultural dimensions.* New Delhi Inter India Publication.

Fabrega, H. and D. Silver (1970), Some Social and Psychological Properties of Zinacenteco Shamans. *Behavioral Science.* 15: 471-486.

Firth, R. (1967), *Individual Fantasy and Social Norms: Séances with Spirit Mediums* in R. Firth ed. *Tikopia Ritual and Belief.* Boston. Beacon Press.

Frank, J. (1973), *Persuasion and Healing: Revised Edition*. Baltimore. Johns Hopkins University Press.

Fox, R.C. (1976), *The Sociology of Modern Medical Research* in Leslie Charles ed. *Asian Medical System*. pp. 102.

Gillian, J. (1948), Magical Fright. *Psychiatry*. 11:387-400.

Grossinger, R. (1982), *Plant Medicine- From Stone Age: Shamanism to Post Industrial Healing*. London. Shambhala Publications.

Handleman, D. (1967), The Development of the Washo Shaman. *Ethnology*. 6:444-464.

Kiev, A. (1972), Trans Cultural Psychiatry. New York. The Free Press.

Lewis, Oscar (1958), *Village Life in Northern India*. Ilionois.

Lowie, R.H. (1940) *An Introduction to Cultural Anthropology*. New York. Harper & Row.

Mayer, J.R. (2002), *Body, Psyche and Society: Conception of Illness in Ommura, eastern Highlands, Pupua New guinea* in S.M. Channa ed. *Health and The Supernatural: Diseases and Curve in Tribal Societies*. New Delhi. Cosmo Publication.

Nadel, S. (1965), *A Study of Shamanism in the Nuba Hills* in W. A. Lessa and E. Z. Vogt eds. *Reader in Comparative Religion*. New York. Harper & Row.

Opler, M. K. (1959), *Dream Analysis in Ute Indian Therapy* in M.K. Opler ed. *Culture and Mental Health*. New York, Macmillan.

Penderson, D. and V. Barruffati (1989), Healers, Deities, Saints and Doctors: Elements for the Analysis of Medical System. *Soc.Sic.Med*. 29:4

Peters, L. (1998), *Tamang Shamans: An Ethno Psychiatric Study of Ecstasy of Healing in Nepal*, New Delhi. Nirala Publication.

Prince, R. (1973), *Mystical Experience and the Certainty of Belonging: An Alternative to Inside and Suggestion in Psychotherapy* in R.H .Cox ed. *Religious Systems and Psychotherapy*. Springfield III. Charles C. Thomas.

Roy Burman, J.J. (2003), *Tribal Medicine*. New Delhi. Mittal Publication.

Sarkar, R.M. (2001), *Applied Anthropology*, Kolkota, Maity Press.

__________(1993), Dimension of Folk Medicine Traditions in Human Society, *Man in India*. 73:328.

__________(1986), *Regional Clubs and Rural Traditions*. New Delhi. Inter India Publications.

Sasaki, Y. (1969), *Psychiatric Study of the Shaman in Japan* in W.Caudill and T.Lin eds. *Mental Health Research in Asia and Pacific*. Honolulu, East-West Center Press.

Silverman, A. (1967), Shamans and Acute Schizophrenia. *American Anthropologist*. 69:21-31.

Singh, I.P. (1991), Some Front Areas of Anthropology, *Man in India*. 71(1): 96

Swain, S. (1994), *Health, Diseases and Health Seeking Behaviors of Tribal People of India* in S. Basu ed. *Tribal Health*. New Delhi, National Institute of Health and Family Welfare.

25 Interwoven Pattern of Indigenous Healing in Folk Life– Rural Indian Perspective

R.M. Sarkar

Diseases bring catastrophic situation everywhere and in all cultural levels. Since prehistoric times man had been fighting unabated to resist the demon of disease and thereby to save the ailing persons from hazards and anxieties. It is to be noted that this pattern of activities is still continuing, of course, in the following of different methodological principles. The story of emergence of medicinal system is specifically characterized by a long and continuous history. On tracing back to that path it would be understood that the knowledge on medicine is the outcome of gradual awareness gained through intuitive and observational experience. It has, no doubt, resulted into the development of indigenous pattern of medicine which is regarded as the vast reservoir of empirical knowledge. The indigenous pattern of therapy is patterned by the cultural traditions of the people concerned which provided an integrated perspective of human sentiments characterized by the interactions of thoughts, beliefs, conceptual ideas as well as psychological principles of the group concerned.

In primitive and rural societies an indigenous pattern of medicine has been developed which tries to resist the "Troubles" arising out of the evil influence of diseases. It is to be noted that this indigenous pattern of medicine is characterized by the age-old experience on human body in relation to the surroundings, both natural and supernatural, traditional knowledge on observations of varied phenomena of human life situation together with the close understanding of the association of factors like customs, habits, charms and incantations as well as continuous process of trial and error that is influenced by experience stepping down through generations. The indigenous patterns of recipes are the result of the close set process of orientation of cultural traditions with the religious sentiments, psychological perspectives, economy, moral ideas, social values as well as therapeutic process. This indigenous pattern of therapy is specifically characterized by the impact of age-old cultural traditions and value orientations which ultimately has based its foundation on the life - philosophy of the people concerned. The socio-ritualistic perspective and the supernatural belief patterns round which this particular therapeutic process has become expressive is understood by the term "Folk medicine".[1]

Folk medicine is governed by a tradition - that has been developed through time in the perspective of age-long experience of the people. Folk medicine system has its very root in the cultural settings and thus the whole workings and the behaviour-patterns relating to the healing practices are inter-woven in the cultural matrix of the people. The systematic and integrated study of the system of medicine pledges to unfold the basic nature and extent of the social mind and intrinsic philosophy of the people. In the total understanding of the socio-psycho-cultural interactions in the sphere of public health and hygiene this particular situation based on folk medicine is of specific importance. The medico-socio-ritualistic analysis of the integrated perspectives of folk medicine would explore a scientific horizon which helps a lot in the evaluation of the integrated pattern of the folk medicine system with folk life.

It has been understood from many - sided discussions that "medicine is the institution through which societies deal with mind/body relationship and their ramifications" (Grossinger, 1982: 27). It is through the medical process and performance that birth, disease and death meet a collective cultural security.

The history of medicine depicts two conspicuous parallel traditions - the folk tradition or magico-religious tradition and the secular scientific tradition. The former is influenced by the activities of magic, charms, amulets, exorcism, and in addition to these there are some herbal preparations. The latter system is based on research-oriented biochemical as well as physio-psychical interactional patterns. Among advanced groups of people the latter tradition of healing practices is highly practised but still, in some specific situations, the folk medicine system is also functioning among them.

There should not be any reason for believing that there exists a conspicuous clash between the folk and scientific traditions. On getting into the proper working pattern and their relative trends of approach to meet the problematic situation it is seen that there is a close link between these two traditions. It is true that the ways adopted by them strikingly differ from each other. The folk practitioner comes forward to treat the disease through the medium of magic and supernatural activities whereas his scientific counterpart tries to ward off the diseased condition through the adoption of scientific procedures based on the principles of anatomy, physiology, pathology etc. Still there is an intimate coherence between the folk and scientific medicines. This particular attitude would be cleared if the observations made by different authorities in the line are analysed. Fejos has shown that there is practically no difference between the modes of approach of the folk healers and the scientific medical practitioners. During his work on the comparison of these two systems he categorically observes that "both the Physician and the Shaman[2] are learned men. Both of them are subject to rigid discipline and a prodigious amount of education for many years. Both are under rules of professional ethics. Both are usually respected members or leaders of their communities (1959 : 22)". But what is different amongst them is the adoption of the process for treatment as has been discussed elsewhere in the paper. It cannot be denied that the existence of some queer practices in the field of folk medicine have caused the repel of the scientific practitioners from the sphere of the former. But it is difficult to draw a clear-cut boundary line between these two and there are many medications that are being used by the modern medical practitioners, have been originated from the tradition of folk medicine.

From his extensive study on the Malayesian therapeutic practices Dodds has shown that the principle of modern physiotherapy has been rooted to the ideas of massage frequently practised by the primitive people which is based on the intention to drive away the evil spirits from the body of the ailing persons. Thus from the different observations it can be concluded "that no conflict exists between the folk and scientific tradition, a practical collaboration conditioned by unbiased mind between these would very naturally unfold a new horizon of human welfare" (Sarkar, 1986 : 216). This view can also be supported by the study of Louis Golomb on multiethnic Thailand communities, as regards anthropology of curing, who has emphasized that the therapy of many traditional healers practically indicates reverse procedural activities in so far as it ignores biological process. But it does much to evaluate the patient's expectancy of cure and help him in concording his mental disturbance caused by conflicting attitudes.

II

A worldwide interest regarding folk medicine developed during the 1970s. A conference on "Traditional Medicine" was held in 1978 under the auspices of the World Health Organisation. The intention of that conference was to bring the traditional healing practice from disreputed condition and thereby to acknowledge its appeal to save the ailing humanity. It has been accepted through different discussions that traditional medicine is highly effective in curing the culturally linked diseases and allied problematic issues. As an integral part of the people's culture folk medicine achieves spectacular success and the peoples' confidence on it is deep-rooted. In 1972, another conference was held at the University of Kent, Canterbury, under the auspices of the Association of Social Anthropologists in which anthropological interpretations of the traditional medicines were taken up with due seriousness.

There is no universal methodology of recipe. The treatment of disease in any particular society depends on the world view of the people concerned – it is directly related to the attitude of the general public in respect of looking at the universe. Different cultures put forward varied aspects of human condition. The concept and treatment of disease both touch the core of human sentiments. The efforts of man in pinpointing the cause of disorder and suggest remedy for it is directly related to the ways and means of imagination of human existence of body and mind.

Medicine is both a craft and a philosophy (Grossinger, 1982), and it is designed to explore meaning and nature of illness and with this it provides means to cure the ailments. Thus the study on medicine demands an integrated knowledge on the life and culture of the people first and secondly on the interactional patterns of diverse beliefs and thoughts that have been developed round the society through generations.

In the world perspective of primitive communities it is seen that there is a remote history of magic-animistic curing ceremonies[3], these are perfectly attuned to the life- philosophy of the people. In these communities scances play a great role in the etiology of diseases and with these spiritual media and variegated performing arts have been combined to make the total system of magical medicine an integrated whole. From the study of the different communities; in relation to their effort to combat the diseases it is seen that "the magical transference of disease is one of the most engaging subjects in the whole field of folk medicine (Hand, 1980; 17)". It is a kind of spiritual medicine which attaches prime importance to the spiritual origin of the diseases and thus, according to this principle, these should be cured through spiritual plane. It has got a broad-based spread throughout the world.

The study of folk medicine has a conspicuous background throughout the different countries of the world. In Europe the study on the interrelationship of magic and medicine was initiated by Frazer. He collected diversified data from the different countries of the world and showed that magical procedures had great role on the life of the primitive people trying incessantly to ward off the evil influence of diseases. Following his lead a good many scholars worked on this particular subject matter and as a result of which there developed broad-based literatures on the primitive medicine system. In this connection, mention may be made of the two edited books[4] on the theory pattern and practice of folk medicine which were the results of group discussions and symposium analysis. The editor of the first book was Cart-Herman. Tillhagan and Elfriede Grabner were the editors of the second book. In these two books there are large mass of data which have been synthesized to explore the broad horizon of folk-medical understanding.

In the United States of America the folk medicine tradition was successfully explored through the effective roles played by the Journal of American Folklore. From the very beginning successful attempts were made to highlight the neglected tradition of human communities. W. M. Hudson edited a book centering round the healers of Los Olmos in 1951 and W. D. Hand presented his celebrated works, in two volumes during 1961-64, where there was an attempt of focusing diversified ethnic and regional treatments. Pennsylvania Research Society took a lead in the earlier period to encourage some scholars for exploring the multifarious dimension of folk-medical treatment. It resulted in a very good response from the scholars. American folk medical tradition and its understandings were carefully highlighted by the works on the "Dictionary of American popular beliefs and superstitions" edited by W.D. Hand. It was a kind of national project on folk-medical research emphasizing the gradual development of the interests of the scholars of the United States in this particular line. During recent years W.D. Hand's book entitled *Magical Medicine* (1980) presents a broad-based synthesis of magical elements in the concept and treatment of disease.

Russian folk medicine tradition has also a glorious background and while commenting on the situation of folk healing practices Konrennoff has said "that religious faith healers have largely disappeared underground, but not the dedicated and knowledgeable folk medicine practitioners. And even though the Soviet union has more doctors per capita than any other country, folk medicine has not lost its popularity and prestige particularly among older citizens" (1970 : 6). He also emphasized that the recent attempts made by some medical institutions towards the scientific evaluation of the tradition bound folk medicine in Siberia and allied region are very much encouraging. Attempts have been and are being made by a good number of well-trained scientific medical personnel to visit different remote corners of the country to collect the vast amount of materials relating to the native healing practices which range from the forwarding of herbal medicines up to the adoption of the practices of the queer customs. It has been felt by the workers in this line that these have got specific values in the life of the people though it is now on the verge of extinction. In Russia, there is always an attempt to "rediscover" these healing traits and to evaluate these in the background of the scientific reality. The research activities of Dr. Alexander Dogel in this sphere have put forward many new thinking patterns which deserve serious consideration. His specific findings in relation to the "Sonic therapy"[5] or the utilisation of sound in the treatment of different diseases leads us to support the view that certain types of human voices, produced in a rhythmic manner, exert physiological influence on human bodily organisation. The "witchcraft medicine" of the Shamans, which is a popular practice in Siberia, specifies a pattern of sonic treatment. The Shamans use tambourine which produces melodious tune and with this the rhythmic voice developed through the singing of devotional songs joins collectively to bring forth effective change on the physiological function of the body. This sort of sound therapy is performed in many countries through various incantations and prayers that are produced in a rhythmic tune which ultimately go deep into the physiological organisation of the body. Mention may be made that the production of a particular pattern of rhythmic sound can be made effectively only by the trained healers which carry the traditions through generations.

African tradition of folk medicine is very naturally conspicuous in diversified view points. Kitiman has conducted an inquiry into the African traditional system of healing practices and has indicated that the traditional healers "are Psychiatrists and Psychotherapists. They have immense wisdom, sagaciousness, expertise and knowledge regarding the African Psyche, mentality, society, tradition, and social problems" (1976 : 414). The specialists in the field of folk medicine "treats illness, injury and disease and quite frequently the person corresponds to the leader of religious practice, whatever he or she may be called" (Grollig, 1976 : 5). These features have developed immensely around medicine and anthropology giving rise to a state of collaborative atmosphere formed by medical and social scientists. From this Nigerian data, Onoge has said that the collaboration between these two domains of treatment "has placed a heavy premium on the conclusions and directives preferred by social scientists" (1977: 220). During recent time specific attempts have been made by the administration to recognise these folk healers and thereby help them processing their modes of treatment in a more refined and realistic way. In an edited volume entitled "The Professionalization of African Medicine" Murray List and G.L. Chavunduka have presented the varied trends of utilisation of native African medicines in the spheres of modern life situation. In Africa, the traditional medicine plays a dominant role in social control in the indigenous social system. It is indispensable to the social stability of the tradition-bound communities because of the fact that it is integrated into the prevailing religious and moral beliefs and ideas.

Coming to India, it is seen that from time immemorial folk medicine traditions has not only been integrated with the societal patterns but also it has been penetrated into the value attitude system of the people. According to the renowned medical-historian Ackerknecht (1942), medicine should be studied as a form of institution; the different concepts relating to disease and health of the folk contribute basic materials to the core of folk culture. The cultural aspect of health and hygiene is highly conspicuous in Indian traditional medicine but no exhaustive study analysing the whole situation of events has yet been conducted on all India basis. Indian folk medicine is highly conditioned by spiritualism and this state of affair has given rise to many cure deities which are of specific importance in the psycho-philosophical settings of the peoples' life and culture. The socio-cultural aspects of medicine deserves proper explanation in the line of individual and group sentiments for the overall development of public health in this country where the life of the people is highly governed by multifarious beliefs and superstitions. McKim Marriott's fascinating study in a North Indian village has highlighted the fact that medicine in rural society is highly controlled by the factors like kinship, caste and outside world. While studying deep into the pattern of indigenous medicine he has indicated how the diverse roots of it is pierced through the socio-cultural matrix of the people. The rest of the works done on the Indian society depict the parallel findings though there are some basic variations according to the norms of the society concerned. All the works here could trace a direct relationship pattern between health and cultural traditions comprised of customs, beliefs, and superstitions as well as moral values and religious taboos.

III

The perspective of the indigenous medicine is conspicuous by the origin and development of multiple cure deities which are known by different names. The etiology of diseases in the traditional Indian society is governed by the belief that the diseases are caused due to supernatural influence. The society of man is surrounded by diversified supernatural powers and their influence is far reaching. Multifarious caste groups, heterogeneous classes and diversified religious groups approach the village deities in order to get recipe for the cure of the diseases. It is to be seen that a well-knit social fabric is functionable round such deities who are regarded as the controller of human sufferings that reach through disease. The rigidity of the caste system, the utter differences in class categories and religious diversities cut across the age-old rural tradition to search out a concerted socio-ritual understanding.

Diseases are as old as human social system - the origin and development of village deities are rooted to the remote past period. In course of time the reliance of human beings on these deities became indispensable because of utter helplessness of the people at the face of specific calamities caused by diseases, and this dependence on the folk deities gave rise to a complicated pattern of medico-ritual understanding in the total cultural setting of man.

Rural folk believe that diseases are caused by supernatural wrath. It is a wide spread idea that the deities who are residing in and outside the village bring calamities to the life of man through the imposition of diseases if they are neglected or tortured. The diseases caused by such angry attitudes are many-sided. The roles of these deities in the causation and cure of the diseases are broad-based and very old as well as tradition- bound. The diseases that are caused by the deities may he individual or village-based. The rural folk having such an idea regarding the development and treatment of diseases very naturally approach these deities. They believe that these supernatural agencies having gradation in potentiality and power exert a good control over the human activities.

In Bengal villages there are a large number of folk deities, these are seen in the vast open field, under the shade of trees, within a dilapidated temple and sometimes under a knee-deep water of the tank. They are Chandi, Manasa, Sitala, Dharmaraj, Mahadana, Panchanand, Bipadtarini etc. who have been looking over the human life and activities, and are pledged to help ailing persons if they are properly approached. It is for this reason they as known as cure deities.

The specific feature of these cure deities is that they are not worshipped by the Brahmin priests through the Sanskritic procedures. The folk deities are propitiated by the non-Brahmin priests who come from the lower caste communities. Sometimes these priests are represented by the untouchable section of the people who are considered impure in the perspective of purity and pollution concept. These lowly caste priests of the folk deities perform double functions - they worship the deities as well as they prescribe spiritual medicines to the patients. It is for this reason they are known as priest-cum-medicine men or locally known as *Deyashis*.[6]

The Deyashis of the folk deities enjoy respectful position in the folk society despite their low social status in the Hindu caste system. They may come from the different caste groups but they are allowed to propitiate the village deities, and not only so, they offer blessings of the deities even to the higher caste people who are ritually pure. The conflict between ritually pure and ritually impure cuts across at the shrine of the folk deities and there develops a close-set ritualistic link between the two communities characterized by opposite features of activities.

The Deyashis are to follow restricted way of life and they must go through certain ordeals at the time of taking initiation. The Deyashis have got many specific features of their own. They believe that their activities are governed by some sort of diverse influence. They are the persons who have been appointed by the God in order to help the people in distressed condition specially who have been suffering from different diseases. The rural folk whole-heartedly believe that the Deyashis are the parts of divine embodiment and their activities in different phases of life cycle of the people are indispensable. Their specific ways of life, activity patterns and modes of resistance against diseases are all-oriented with supernatural power. It is so deep-rooted that the Deyashis and their allied deities have been identified as integrated whole round which the life-philosophy of the Deyashis is expressed which can be assessed through their modes of behaviour. A similar phenomenon has been identified by Yoder during his work among the American folk healers. He reported that "they were, if we may be permitted the term, a kind of folk-clergy, recognized as 'God-given' powers of healing" (1977 : 205).

The Deyashis are regarded as all rounders. They look into the different affairs of human activities all through the time. So far as the healing art is concerned they are the possessors of age-long experience on diversified nature. The Deyashis are exorcists, snake-bite doctors, bone-setters, skin disease specialists, magician and even skilful herbalists having a good knowledge over the medicinal effects of hundreds and thousands of plants, roots and tubers that grow wild in the jungle. The patients are treated in front of the deities, prescriptions are made before them and the medicines are handed over as well as the requisite instructions are given in direct association with the deities. This procedure is provided with double headed advantages. The Deyashis who regard themselves as parts of the deities do not like to dissociate from them at the time of their healing practice as it is conditioned by the mercy of the deities concerned. On the other hand, the patients who are at the bottom of mental disturbance due to diseased condition get mental strength owing to the fact that the medicines and allied instructions are given to them as if by the deities through the medium of the Deyashis concerned.

The folk deities are worshipped on the fixed days of the week. During this time the patients visit the shrines at the different villages for having requisite treatment by the Deyashis of the concerned deities. First of all, the Deyashis propitiate the deities according to his own procedures and then the patients are called, one by one, to communicate their troubles. On hearing all these the Deyashis try to find out the cause of disease through the adoption of various means which include the methods like exorcism, magical performance, message, study of human anatomy and physiology. At times, the Deyashis become 'possessed' before the deities and in that abnormal condition they analyse the exact cause of the disease of the individual patient. Then the Deyashis offer medicines to the patients in front of the deities. The patient receives it with due respect and afterwards he bows down before the deities with some votive offerings. For this service, which is of a very complicated nature, the Deyashis get nominal fees, and, mention may be made, that the whole activities of the Deyashis are directed by philanthropic attitude and thought pattern.

IV

The Shrines of the folk deities specially those which are directly associated with the treatment of disease are regularly visited by the people of both rural and urban settings. In Bengal villages the deities of such nature largely include Chandi, Manasa, Dharmaraj, Sitala, Mahadana and Kali. These deities have got regular features of worship by their non-Brahmin priests who conduct the whole affairs of worship through the following of non-sanskritic procedures. An exhaustive study on a number of folk deities of such kind has been made which depict the integrated relation between the deities and ailments. These deities are of very remote origin and each of them has an illustrated background of folklore and mythology so far as their appearance in human society is concerned. The following table provides an overall idea regarding this particular feature.

Table 1
Various Village Deities and their Concerned Treatment

Name of Deities	*Name of Villages*	*Diseases/Abnormalities that are cured here*
Chandi	Metala	1. All types of female diseases especially the problems relating to abortion
		2. Measles, Small-pox and Cholera cases
		3. Cases of witchcraft and other evil influences
-do-	Lauberia	1. Female disease
		2. Measles, Small-pox and Cholera cases
		3. Supernatural influence
-do-	Parsundi	1. Prevention against epidemics
		2. Female disease
		3. Eye troubles
Mangal Chandi	Khairadihi	1. Skin disease of all types
		2. Abscess and curbuncles
Dharmaraj	Lakshindarpur	1. Bone fracture and all kinds of osteological troubles
-do-	Tentutbandh	1. Female disease
		2. Ophthalmic disease
		3. Rheumatism
-do-	Sijekaddang	1. Serious types of asthma
		2. Hysteria
		3. Eye troubles
-do-	Bele	1. All types of rheumatism
		2. Skin disease
Dharmaraj	Sira	1. Female disease
		2. Cases of Witchcraft
		3. Attack by evil spirits
-do-	Bhadulia	1. Skin disease
		2. Hysteria
Manasa	Tantipara	1. Snake bite
		2. Preventory measure against snakes
-do-	Bhanra	1. Snake bite
		2. Cases of Small-pox and Cholera

Contd.

Name of Deities	*Name of Villages*	*Diseases/Abnormalities that are cured here*
		3. Attack of malevolent spirits
-do-	Metela	1. Snake bite
		2. Body binding against the influence of snakes
-do-	Joydev Kenduli	1. Snake bite
		2. Case of Small-pox and Cholera
		3. Controlling of epidemics
		4. Female disease
-do-	Koridhya	1. Snake bite
		2. Prevention against spread of epidemics
Mahadana	Metela	1. Attack of evil spirits
		2. Witchcrafts
		3. General village problems
-do-	Shibpur	1. Diseases through supernatural wrath
		2. Evil influences by malevolent spirits
Kali	Shibpur	1. Diseases caused through malevolent spirits
		2. Hysteria and mental troubles
		3. Female disease

The folk deities have got their own priest-cum-medicine men. It has already been pointed out that most of the time they belong to the lower caste groups. Also they are regarded as untouchables by the people belonging to the higher castes. But these priest-cum-medicine men or the *Deyashis* enjoy great respect in the life of the whole region despite their very low social rank. The following Table would furnish the names, caste affiliations of the different *Deyashis* and the respective deities they serve :

Table 2
Particulars about the Deyashis

Name of Deyashis	*Caste*	*Village*	*Deity or Deities they Serve*
Sanatan Bauri	Bauri	Metela	Chandi/Mahadana/ Kali/Manasa
Abadhut Bagdi	Bagdi	Bhanra	Manasa/Kali
Rampada Bauri	Bauri	Lauberia	Chandi
Balaram Das	Tantubaya/ Weaver	Khairadihi	Mangol Chandi
Nityananda Dhibar	Jele/Fisherman	Tantipara	Manasa
Madan Bagdi	Bagdi	Joydev-Kenduli	Manasa
Nepal Bagdi	Bagdi	Shibpur	Mahadana/Kali
Rasamoy Mondal	Sadgop	Tentulbandh	Dharmaraj
Narayan Mondal	Sadgop	Lakshindarpur	Dharmaraj

The integrated relation that has been developed between the deities and various ailments forms the basic cultural traits in the everyday life of the rural society. These folk deities are regarded as the guardian of the people and in no circumstances these create a specific divine world as is seen in non-folk religious beliefs and practices. Thus the people from all levels of culture and economic status get an easy access to these deities to forward their earnest prayer for relief from the evil hands of the diseases. These prayers are made directly through the Deyashis. The patients those who approach the folk deities with their earnest appeal for treatment are known by the term Faridi.[7] In the background of the folk medicinal system there develop an intimate relation between the Deyashi and the Faridi which is based on mutual collaboration and reciprocal understanding. The Faridi is easily accessible to the Deyashi. The communication is direct and the Deyashi is always ready to receive his patients with due sympathy, and also he can readily come down to the level of the Faridi. The Faridi looks at the Deyashi as his well-wisher and saviour during the most critical phase of life. The Deyashi regards himself as a mediator between the human and the divine world and therefore he believes that his diagnosis is always oriented with the divine sponsorship. This particular sentiment has prevented the Deyashis from becoming business minded, most of the time they do not receive any cash payment from the patients. This philanthropic attitude of the Deyashis has raised them to such a level that they have been able to create a halo of reverence around them.

V

In an all India enquiry into the nature and extent of folk medicine and the cure deities in the background of the traditional folk healers and their clients i.e. persons inflicted with disease it will be seen that the whole situation is based on the same philosophical principles. There may be some sort of differences in belief-pattern and mode of behaviour of the people as well as the procedures of performances but there is always an all-India linkage conditioned by parallel thinking and psycho-philosophical settings. Therefore, a variety of comparison can be attempted, region by region, which should be processed through intraculturally and interculturally. In the domain of diagnosis, explanation patterns of the disease and modes of treatment, cross-cultural comparisons may provide a good indication in the evaluation of the total perspective of the Indian folk medicine system and its socio-cultural and medico-legal horizons.

The rural folk whose life-philosophy is highly characterized by the ritualistic performance would very naturally seek the solution of the problems relating to disease and medicine through ritualistic procedures. From the works that have so far been done in India on the medicine and faith in rural setting it has been found out that the people have got depth-oriented appeal to this folk medicinal system and the situation is highly governed by the cultural traditions. The folk healers and the patients understand each other in the background of a common cultural setting. The folk healers are easily accessible by the patients and the latters are received by the former with profound sympathy and with brotherly affection which are highly valued by the folk patients. The folk healers by virtue of their traditional philosophy feel for the suffering humanity and ultimately it becomes their vow to give relief to the endangered people through supernatural assistance. This very state of affairs provides the rural folk a mental relief which do a great deal in minimizing the bodily sufferings. The folk healers do not demand anything from the patients and they may offer cash and/or kinds to the deities if they so desire. If in case there is any demand from the folk healers it is very insignificant, and at the same time it is easy for these economically depressed people to pay it right away. Above all, the patients consider the folk healers as their own men and this perception ties these two ends in a well-knit pattern of relationship.

Medicine is regarded as an institution which means an organised system of relationship embodying collective mode of response or behaviour and binding the members of the group together into an association. Thus in the medial perspective there should be such interrelationship conditioned by mutual understandings and friendly sentiments amongst the doctors, patients and other related personalities. During recent time the social and cultural factors have been accepted by all concerned as of specific importance in the field of medicine and public health programme. In the implementation of the present day programme of public health and hygiene special stress are being laid in this country to consider the socio-cultural traditions of the people for whom the programme has been framed up. Mention may be made that in the western or scientific medical system there is a great psychological distance between the doctor and the patients. In rural setting this gap becomes more prominent. Cultural heterogeneity also plays a great role in the enhancement of this distance which becomes a conspicuous obstacle in the formation of an integrated relationship between the doctors and the patients. It has been argued that successful practices of medicine is dependent not only on the therapeutic skill and diagnostic ability of the physicians but also on the understandings of the socio-psychological and cultural factors related to health and hygiene. Of late, there has been a great demand in the reorientation of the medical education to foster social concepts in the minds of the students to understand the socio-cultural matrix of health and disease. In order to maintain the institutional perspective in relation to medicine there is an urgent need to develop and foster the atmosphere of interrelatedness of activities and interpersonal perceptibility in the society concerned.

It is our great concern in this domain of discussion that folk medicine is traditionally oriented with such qualities of human behaviour. The integral part of the peoples' culture is directly linked with the workings of the diverse factors of the folk medicine system. This is why the pattern of indigenous medical procedures is attuned with the human cultural sentiments - a particular situation which becomes more effective and more illustrative in the effort of exploring the domain of disease perception and healing, in locating the bodily disorder and remedying it. Medicine is a comparatively unexplored territory and because of the fact that it is the general inquiry into the disease there is a specific need to highlight the interacting forces of biological, psychological and socio-cultural processes and sentiments as well as man-nature-environment relationship patterns. In order to have a full view of this particular territory of man and medicine there is a special requirement of interdisciplinary understandings of facts and features of action. Anthropological interpretation of medicine provides specific ideas on the process of cultural relativism in the attempt of exploration of the absolutist models of disease etiology and cure. The native medicines and their application principles should be taken up as the substratum of variegated medico-social traits in an attempt to explore the totalistic medicinal system developed through the interchanging ideas and intermingling processes of different patterns and principles, both primitive and modern, healing procedures.

REFERENCES

Ackerknecht, E.H. (1945), "On the Collection of Data Concerning Primitive Medicine". American Anthropologist, Vol. 47.

Biswas P.C. (1934), Concepts of Disease Among the Primitive People of India, Journal of the Dept. of Letters, Vol. XXV, Calcutta University Press.

Dodds, J.W. (1959), "The Humanist Looks at the Doctor", in Medicine and Anthropology, ed. by Iago Gladston, New York, International University Press.

Dorson, R.M. (Ed.) (1972), Folklore and Folk Life: An Introduction, Chicago, University of Chicago Press.

Fejos, Paul (1959), "Man, Magic and Medicine", in Medicine and Anthropology, ed. by Iago Gladston.

Grollig, Francis & H.B. Haley (1976), Medical Anthropology, The Hague, Paris, Moutan Publishers.

Grossinger, Richard (1982), Plant Medicine, From Stone Age Shamanism to Post Industrial Healing, London, Shambhala Publications, Inc.

Golomb, Louia (1985), An Anthropology of Curing in Multiethnic Thailand, Chicago, University of Illinois Press.

Hand, W.D. (1961-64), Popular Beliefs and Superstitions from North Carolina Folklore- The Frank C. Prown Collection of North Carolina Folklore, Durham, Duke University Press.

__________(1980), Magical Medicine, California, University of Cailifornia Press.

Harley, G.W. (1970), Native African Medicine, London Frank Cass and Co. Ltd.

Hasan, K.A. (1967), The Cultural Frontier of Health in Village India- A Case Study of a North Indian Village, Bombay, Manaktalas.

Kitima, Kamuti (1976), "Traditional African Medicine" in Medical Anthropology, ed. by E.X. Grollig & H. B. Haley, The Hague, Paris, Moutan Publishers.

Kourennoff, P.M. (1970), Russian Folk Medicine, Translated by George St. George, New York, W.H. Allen.

List, Murray & G. L. Chavunduka (ed.) (1986), The Professionalizadon of African Medicine, Manchester, Manchester University Press.

Loudon, J. B. (Ed.) (1976), Social Anthropology and Medicine, London, Academic Press.

Marriott, McKim (1955), "Little Communities in an Indigenous Civilization", in village India, ed. by McKim Marriott, Chicago, Chicago University Press.

Parson, Clairem D.F. (1985), Healing Practices in the South Pacffic, Hawaii, The Institute of Polynesian Studies.

Paul, B.D. & W.D. Miller (1955), Health, Culture and Community- Case Studies of Public Relations to Health Programme, New York, Russel Sage Foundation.

Sarkar, R.M. (1976), "Folk Medicine in relation to Folk life", in Indian Folklife, Vol.1, Calcutta.

__________(1986), Regional Cults and Rural Traditions, New Delhi, Inter-India Publications.

Yoder, D, 1977. "Folk Medicine", in Folklore and Folk life ed. by R. M. Dorson, Chicago, University of Chicago Press.

NOTES

1. A kind of indigenous medicine conditioned by age-old customs and traditions and processed through time-long experience of the people. The principle of folk medicine is based on the solution of problems in

the perspective of the interactions of man, nature and environment. Folk medicine has a long and honourable history and it is characterized by the multi-dimensional interactional patterns of thoughts and ideas developed through close-set observations of the surroundings.

2. Shaman is a kind of medicine man who holds a fairly high status in his community. The term shaman is of Siberian origin. The shaman works through the adoption of variegated traditional magico-religious practices to ward off diseases and evil effects in man and society. The native healers in Indian villages, popularly known as Ojha, show proficiency in healing arts.
3. It is a kind of recipe where spiritual origins of the disease are detected and attempts are then made to cure these through the adoption of various spiritual procedures. This process of treatment is processed through magico-animistic curing ceremonies, exorcism and scances with spirit media.
4. These two books on folk medicine have got specific importance. "Symposium on Folk medicine", the first book, is the result of an International Symposium at Stockholm, 1961. It is the best example of multidisciplinary discussions on the relation between scientific and folk-medical traditions. The second book is entitied "Folk Medical Research", 1967, embraces multitude of data on the indigenous medicinal practices.
5. It is a novel method of therapy in which sound constitutes the basic trarit. Dr. Alexander Dogel has conducted a broad-based experiments on the therapeutic procedures followed by the folk healers when sound treatment forms the basic part. He has shown through experiment that certain types of human voices that are used in a particular way produce important physiological changes. The nervous system is very much responsive to the sonic treatment. The sound produced by the Shamans through the recitation of incantations and the playing of the tambourine in front of the patient brings physiological effects in his body. It has been proved by experiment.
6. The priest-cum-medicine man. Generally they come from the low caste groups. The Deyashis perform varied types of ritualistic activities in front of the village deities and they believe that their activities are processed through divine sanction. In Bengal villages the Deyashis have got a very respectable position and they are regarded as the saviours in various troublesome situations specially caused by disease and epidemics. The Deyashis wear copper rings on their fingers or copper fillets round the upper arm as sacred symbols.
7. The literal meaning of this word is complainant. The patients suffering from varied diseases lodge complaint before the village deities in the hope of curing the ailments. Their complaints are ceremonially received by the Deyashis who ultimately forward these to the deities concerned. The patients or the faridis then wait for receiving the medicines or instructions which, they believe, come through divine assistance.

Index

N